Establishing Security Operations Center

Cyber incident detection analysis and
threat hunting for robust security operations

Sameer Vasant Kulkarni

bpb

www.bpbonline.com

First Edition 2025

Copyright © BPB Publications, India

ISBN: 978-93-65896-060

LIMITS OF LIABILITY AND DISCLAIMER OF WARRANTY

To View Complete
BPB Publications Catalogue
Scan the QR Code:

www.bpbonline.com

Dedicated to

My parents, wife, children and family

Foreword

In an era of relentless cyber threats and technological disruptions, the establishment of a **security operations center** (**SOC**) is no longer an option, it is a fundamental necessity for organizations striving to protect their digital assets and ensure operational resilience. From military institutions to financial enterprises, the ability to detect, analyze, and respond to security incidents in real time has become paramount.

Having spent decades leading cybersecurity initiatives within defense establishments, I have witnessed firsthand how SOCs evolve from reactive entities into predictive and adaptive intelligence hubs. The transformation requires meticulous planning, the right set of tools, a structured approach to incident detection and response, and, most importantly, a culture of continuous improvement. Organizations embarking on this journey must integrate strategic frameworks, automation tools, and compliance standards to ensure their SOCs operate at peak efficiency.

The journey of SOC evolution, as discussed in *Section 1: Understanding Security Operations Center* covering evolution and modern developments in SOC, reflects the shift from traditional perimeter-based security to intelligence-driven operations. Modern SOCs are no longer confined to passive monitoring; they are dynamic, leveraging automation, threat intelligence, and advanced analytics to stay ahead of adversaries. This transformation requires a meticulous understanding of its foundational elements, a topic comprehensively covered in *Section 2: SOC Components*, which outlines the strategic role of threat intelligence in proactive detection and response.

Implementing a SOC successfully demands a balance between people, processes, technology, and infrastructure, a principle central to *Section 3: Implementing SOC*. The human aspect, analysts, engineers, and leaders, remains the bedrock of effective security operations, complemented by well-defined workflows and the right technological enablers. Organizations must structure their SOCs around these pillars to ensure both efficiency and adaptability.

While security operations primarily focus on immediate threat detection and mitigation, their relevance extends beyond incident response. *Section 4: Practical Implementation Aspects* reinforce the need for SOCs to align with global standards such as NIST SP 800-53, ISO/ IEC 27001, CIS Controls, and industry-specific mandates. By integrating compliance into SOC operations, organizations not only safeguard their ecosystems but also reinforce trust with stakeholders and regulators.

Emerging technologies are reshaping cybersecurity landscapes at an unprecedented pace. *Section 5: Changing Dynamics of SOC with Evolving Threats Fueled by Emerging Technologies* explores how artificial intelligence, machine learning-driven threat detection, cloud-native SOC architectures, and quantum computing advancements are redefining security operations. The convergence of these technologies presents both opportunities and challenges, making it imperative for security teams to adopt forward-thinking approaches.

Finally, achieving cyber resilience requires a strategic and structured approach, which is the cornerstone of the concluding chapters. From effective incident containment strategies to leveraging automation for response orchestration, this book provides invaluable insights into strengthening security postures. It highlights key methodologies for mitigating ransomware, phishing, insider threats, and ensuring rapid recovery from security incidents.

Cybersecurity is a domain that thrives on collaboration, knowledge-sharing, and continuous innovation. As enterprises and governments worldwide race to fortify their cybersecurity posture, SOCs play a crucial role in ensuring proactive defenses and swift incident response. Establishing SOC offers readers a robust foundation to build upon, equipping them with the knowledge necessary to create efficient and resilient security operations that stand the test of time.

I commend the author for his dedication to advancing cybersecurity education and fostering a robust SOC mindset among professionals. Whether you are embarking on your SOC journey or refining existing operations, *Establishing Security Operations Center* offers an indispensable blueprint to navigate modern cybersecurity challenges with confidence.

Air Vice Marshal (Dr.) Devesh Vatsa, VSM
Cybersecurity and Critical Technologies Advisor
Data Security Council of India, NASSCOM

About the Author

Sameer Vasant Kulkarni is currently working as senior vice president, IT infrastructure, cloud, cybersecurity at Decimal Point Analytics. He received his BE degree in electronics and telecommunications from Amravati University in 1996, higher diploma in software engineering from Aptech, Amravati in 1996, **master of science** (**MS**) in software systems from BITS Pilani in 2012, post graduate diploma in satellite communication from Space Application Centre, ISRO, Ahmedabad in 2012 and M.Tech in technology management from DIAT, Pune in 2022.

In 1997, he joined the Indian Air Force as an aeronautical engineer (electronics). He was instrumental in project management and maintenance management of various communication (wired/wireless) and IT infrastructure and simulators in IAF. He has also managed the navigational and recovery aids for a typical airport. He has managed enterprise-level data centers (private cloud) and network operations center efficiently. His focus areas include security in enterprise networks, governance, risk and compliance management, digital transformation, and effective use of technology for humanity. He was instrumental in the publication of the bi-annual magazine communication mirror in IAF. His areas of interest include emerging technologies like quantum computing, cloud computing, cybersecurity, artificial intelligence and machine learning, IoT, big data analytics, their exploitation in automation, and ease of life. He is an ISO 27001 lead auditor, senior member of IEEE, and fellow member of IETE. Sameer Kulkarni is an esteemed member of various associations and has contributed extensively to the ICT and cybersecurity field through his research papers published in reputed journals and conferences. In addition to his roles and achievements, he is a certified career counsellor.

About the Reviewers

❖ **SuryaPrakash Nalluri** is a senior vice president and executive cybersecurity leader at Citigroup, with over 20 years of experience in information technology, including more than a decade in cybersecurity. He is a recognized subject matter expert in application security and has led global vulnerability management, penetration testing, and secure software development initiatives. SuryaPrakash is known for driving innovation in DevSecOps, secure by design practices, and cybersecurity automation. A frequent speaker and mentor in the cybersecurity community, he actively contributes to industry thought leadership, serves on award juries, and has authored influential research in secure system design and blockchain security. His passion for advancing cyber defense has influenced both enterprise strategies and academic discourse. As a fellow of BCS, IE, and IETE, he bridges industry expertise with academia, focusing on AI-driven security and governance.

❖ **Rahul Anand** is a passionate cyber resiliency and risk management leader with over 15 years of experience in cybersecurity, digital forensics, disaster recovery, IT governance, and offshore delivery strategy. He has successfully led global programs across industries, delivering measurable improvements in cyber posture, compliance, and operational resilience.

Rahul holds multiple industry certifications including CISM (ISACA), certified in cybersecurity (ISC2), and certified disaster recovery professional. He earned his MBA from XLRI, Jamshedpur, and a bachelor's in engineering from Shivaji University.

He specializes in building and scaling cyber resiliency frameworks aligned with NIST, PCI DSS, and ISO 27001, and has consistently delivered high-impact results, like:

- Achieved 100% compliance in cyber resiliency assessments across multiple frameworks.

- Led implementation of NIST controls, reducing vulnerabilities by 40%.

- Directed PCI DSS audits with a 98% compliance score and ISO 27001 certification with zero non-conformities.

- Reduced audit preparation time by 30% through automation and continuous monitoring.

- Managed a team of 70+ cybersecurity engineers, achieving a 95% team satisfaction rate.

- Delivered 24x7 incident management with a 95% resolution rate within SLA.

- Improved system uptime by 20% and reduced incident response time by 30% through automation and observability enhancements.

- Spearheaded a **disaster recovery as a service** (**DRaaS**) initiative, enabling cost-effective cloud-based failover solutions.

He is currently working at BDO RISE as director–cyber resiliency, risk and resiliency, where he leads global cybersecurity initiatives and is part of the leadership team driving innovation, compliance, and resilience across critical systems and services.

Acknowledgement

I would like to acknowledge my sincere gratitude to all those who played an important role in the completion of this book. I express my warm appreciation to my father Vasant Kulkarni, mother Kumudini Kulkarni, my beloved wife Ashwini Kulkarni, my daughter Aditi Kulkarni, my son Amogh Kulkarni, my sister Dr Samidha Chendke and friends for their unwavering support and encouragement throughout this journey. Without their unconditional love and continuous support, this dream would not have come true.

I would like to extend my special thanks to AVM (Dr) Devesh Vatsa (Retd) for his valuable input and guidance to this project. Your trust in me, insights and feedback have been instrumental in shaping the content and improving the quality of this book. Thank you for your invaluable support.

I am immensely grateful to BPB Publications for their guidance and expertise in bringing this book to fruition. Their support and assistance were invaluable in navigating the complexities of the publishing process.

I would also like to acknowledge the technical reviewers, and editors who provided valuable feedback and contributed to the refinement of this manuscript. Their insights and suggestions have significantly enhanced the quality of the book.

Last but not least, I want to express my gratitude to the readers who have shown interest in my book. Your support and encouragement have been deeply appreciated.

Thank you to everyone who has played a part in making this book a reality.

Preface

In today's fast-paced, digital landscape, cybersecurity has evolved from a specialized discipline to a must-needed pillar of organizational resilience. With cyber threats growing in complexity and sophistication, organizations worldwide recognize the necessity of **security operations center (SOC)** to safeguard their digital assets and maintain trust.

This book, *Establishing Security Operations Center*, is designed to provide a comprehensive roadmap for building and optimizing SOC operations. Whether you are launching a SOC from the ground up or refining an existing structure, this guide offers practical insights into key components, from governance frameworks and compliance considerations to advanced threat detection methodologies and automation strategies.

Comprising eighteen insightful chapters in five sections, this book covers a wide range of topics essential for understanding the intricacies of SOCs. We start with Section 1, covering the background of SOCs, providing a solid grounding in the evolution, basics, and modern developments in SOC. From there, we go into Section 2, covering SOC components like incident management, threat intelligence/hunting, and creating a solid base for security operations.

Section 3 focuses on implementing SOC, highlighting the key aspects of people, process and technology in building the SOC. It also explores the infrastructure requirements in establishing SOC. Section 4 discusses practical implementation aspects aimed at ensuring business continuity. It also explores regulatory frameworks and their relevance to compliance management in SOCs. This section also covers the best practices.

In the realm of security operations, Section 5 discusses changing dynamics of SOC with evolving threats, fueled by emerging technologies, offering insights into the latest advancements shaping our digital future.

Through practical examples, best practices, comprehensive real-world examples, and a structured approach, this book aims to equip readers with a solid understanding of security operations center. Whether you are a novice or an experienced learner, I hope this book will serve as a valuable resource in your journey of exploring the cyber threat landscape and mitigation measures to stay safe.

Section 1: Understanding Security Operations Center

Chapter 1: Cybersecurity Basics - This chapter will provide the background of cybersecurity, threat landscape to create a base for security operations. The application of cybersecurity to end points, networks, and cloud scenarios is critical to understand the attack surface. This chapter also covers layers of Security to understand complex web of security configurations.

Chapter 2: Cybersecurity Ramifications and Implications - This chapter will explore the domains of security operations. It covers how the security incidents impact the ecosystem. Businesses, and individuals alike face disparate threats, bringing out the need for increased security. You will understand the short and long-term ramifications of cyberattacks across verticals.

Chapter 3: Evolution of Security Operations Centers - This chapter starts with the history of SOC and how it has evolved till now. The ever-changing attack surface with Industry 4.0/5.0, 5/6G, needs dedicated security monitoring. However, the evolution of SOC will give a clear understanding of the incident reporting, handling, and mitigation.

Chapter 4: Domains of Security Operations Centers - This chapter covers the exact domains of Security operations. A clear understanding of these domains is essential to help prevent, respond or recover from any cyberattacks. This chapter also covers compliance management with various regulatory requirements.

Chapter 5: Modern Developments in Security Operations Centers - This chapter covers the modern developments in handling security incidents. The understanding of Cyber Kill Chain or MITRE frameworks is essential to understand the intricacies of cyberattacks. You will understand these processes in order to defend against these complex attacks.

Chapter 6: Incident Response - This chapter exactly covers the basic SOC operations. The logs are collated from disparate sources, from endpoints, network devices, IPS/IDS, etc. It is important to know the log management and how they are co-related, leading to SIEM use cases.

Section 2: SOC Components

Chapter 7: Analysis - This chapter covers the analysis part of operations at level 2. After the incidents are monitored, there is a need to correlate them with different incidents for inter-relation. The analysis forms the basis of eliminating time and energy resources on dependent incident mitigation.

Chapter 8: Threat Intelligence and Hunting - This chapter covers the details of threats, corelating the incidents, and going forward towards threat hunting. This domain deals with the emerging threat landscape and dealing with them upfront before they turn into attacks. This leads to taking the SOC operations to next level in mitigation.

Chapter 9: People - This chapter covers the staffing requirements for the security operations. The human element is at the core of SOC operations. The incident monitoring tasks, subsequent analysis by skilled professionals can make a huge difference in keeping the breach under checks. It is important to know the roles and responsibilities at multiple levels in the SOC.

Section 3: Implementing SOC

Chapter 10: Process - This chapter explores the processes involved in carrying out security operations. It covers in detail the current security capabilities of any organization against cyber risks and takes it further to identify measures to reduce the time to detect and respond with standard frameworks. These processes lead to more cyber resilience.

Chapter 11: Technology - This chapter covers the technologies involved in implementing security operations center. Technology is the key element on which the defenses are built. The tools and technologies used for collecting logs, correlating and analyzing them to facilitate real-time threat detection will make the organizations vigilant and well-prepared to tackle the cyberattacks.

Chapter 12: Building Security Operations Centers Infrastructure - The exact facilities required to establish the SOC are covered in this chapter. SOC services must be accessed securely and reliably. The CIA triad needs to be ensured at all times through effective measures in physical infrastructure. The cloud hosting adds complexity to managing the security.

Chapter 13: Business Continuity - This chapter explores the business continuity aspects. SOCs play a vital role in ensuring business continuity. In the ever-evolving cyberattacks, SOC can identify key threats, analyze them in real-time, and ensure measures are taken to mitigate the threats to ensure seamless business operations. This chapter also covers key aspects of ESG concerns.

Section 4: Practical Implementation Aspects

Chapter 14: Frameworks - This chapter covers the frameworks and regulations involved in SOC operations. The SOC framework is a structured approach to manage SOC operations, be it people, process, or technology. Compliance management is also a key component of SOC operations. This chapter covers all associated regulations.

Chapter 15: Best Practices - This chapter covers the best practices followed for SOC operations. These can be great resource to build, operate and manage the SOC. The standard operating procedures being followed worldwide to ensure a cyber-safe environment and the associated tools used are covered.

Section 5: Changing Dynamics of SOC with Evolving Threats Fueled by Emerging Technologies

Chapter 16: Impact of Emerging Technologies - This chapter dives into emerging technologies impacting the security operations and how they will shape the future. The emerging technologies are changing the threat landscape significantly. These technologies are also empowering better situational awareness and predicting threats in real time.

Chapter 17: Cyber Resilient Systems - This chapter will cover the aspects of building cyber resilient systems. After understanding the various facets of SOC operations, the impact of emerging technologies on the ever-evolving threat landscape, and the availability of those very emerging technologies can build a cyber resilient system. This chapter explores how to building those resilient systems.

Chapter 18: Future Directions - SOCs are evolving every day. As the threat actors are deploying advanced techniques, there is a need to constantly evolve and mitigate those threats. Continual improvement is the key. The future roadmap for SOC will be the mainstay of this chapter.

Coloured Images

Please follow the link to download the
Coloured Images of the book:

https://rebrand.ly/sc07rwj

We have code bundles from our rich catalogue of books and videos available at https://github.com/bpbpublications. Check them out!

Errata

We take immense pride in our work at BPB Publications and follow best practices to ensure the accuracy of our content to provide with an indulging reading experience to our subscribers. Our readers are our mirrors, and we use their inputs to reflect and improve upon human errors, if any, that may have occurred during the publishing processes involved. To let us maintain the quality and help us reach out to any readers who might be having difficulties due to any unforeseen errors, please write to us at :

errata@bpbonline.com

Your support, suggestions and feedbacks are highly appreciated by the BPB Publications' Family.

Did you know that BPB offers eBook versions of every book published, with PDF and ePub files available? You can upgrade to the eBook version at www.bpbonline. com and as a print book customer, you are entitled to a discount on the eBook copy. Get in touch with us at :

business@bpbonline.com for more details.

At www.bpbonline.com, you can also read a collection of free technical articles, sign up for a range of free newsletters, and receive exclusive discounts and offers on BPB books and eBooks.

Piracy

If you come across any illegal copies of our works in any form on the internet, we would be grateful if you would provide us with the location address or website name. Please contact us at business@bpbonline.com with a link to the material.

If you are interested in becoming an author

If there is a topic that you have expertise in, and you are interested in either writing or contributing to a book, please visit www.bpbonline.com. We have worked with thousands of developers and tech professionals, just like you, to help them share their insights with the global tech community. You can make a general application, apply for a specific hot topic that we are recruiting an author for, or submit your own idea.

Reviews

Please leave a review. Once you have read and used this book, why not leave a review on the site that you purchased it from? Potential readers can then see and use your unbiased opinion to make purchase decisions. We at BPB can understand what you think about our products, and our authors can see your feedback on their book. Thank you!

For more information about BPB, please visit www.bpbonline.com.

Join our Discord space

Join our Discord workspace for latest updates, offers, tech happenings around the world, new releases, and sessions with the authors:

https://discord.bpbonline.com

Table of Contents

Section 1
Understanding Security
Operations Center

CHAPTER 1
Cybersecurity Basics

Introduction

With advances in technology and the convergence of data handling technologies, information has attained new dimensions. This information explosion is not only impacting organizations, but also individuals. The ease of operations to attack the information resources, and the potential to alter the national ambitions is making this cyber domain critical. In this era, following quote from the *The Art of War* by *Sun Tzu* is worth noting.

If you know your enemy and yourself, you need not fear the result of a hundred battles.

-Sun Tzu

This quote amply applies to the cyber domain as well. Knowing the potential of adversaries and one's own defenses is paramount for effective defenses. States are waging silent wars through the cyber domain with all the resources at their disposal, making defenses even more complex. In this situation, it is important to understand the evolving threat landscape and the solutions to mitigate any attacks.

The explosion of public internet, e-commerce platforms, personal computers, mobiles or wired/wireless networks substantially increases the attack surface. However, when these assets are not secured properly, they become vulnerable to damaging cyberattack. Apart from hackers, malware, or viruses, disgruntled employees (insider threat) and human errors in configuration can also emerge as potential threats. Be it a casual internet user with a smartphone or an employee of a multinational company, cyberattacks impact privacy equally for all parties. Both government sectors and large technical behemoths are affected by security breaches. These cyberattack or breaches can easily be avoided through proactive preventive measures.

Data is exponentially exploding at an unprecedented rate, even surpassing *Moore's* law. Technologies like **artificial intelligence (AI)**, **machine learning (ML)**, and big data analytics heavily depend on data. With 5G coming and 6G on the horizon, data will become even more pervasive and ubiquitous. Commercial transactions are increasing every day. Though this information explosion has improved living standards, it has also led to vulnerabilities and cyber threats.

The **Information and Communication Technologies (ICT)** have brought in a paradigm shift in terms of how data is consumed. In the dynamic data management perspective, this chapter will explore the fundamentals of cybersecurity, examine the latest trends and challenges in the evolving threat landscape.

Structure

In this chapter, we will discuss the following topics:

- Cybersecurity principles
- Individuals, endpoints, network security
- Cloud security
- Threat landscape
- Industry-wise use cases
- Challenges of cybersecurity
- Layers of security

Objectives

By the end of this chapter, you will gain an understanding of the diverse realm of cybersecurity, emerging threat landscape and its impact of individuals, society or organizations.

Cybersecurity principles

In today's rapidly evolving digital age, sensitive information needs to be protected with utmost sincerity. Though the targets, be they individuals, systems, or processes, need to be protected through different methods, information is at the core of all this. All the cyber attacks in digital domains are aimed at gaining access to sensitive information, amending the information, destroying that information, or extorting money.

The key principles required to ensure effective and efficient cyber defense are at the core of the thinking of world-leading organizations like **National Institute of Standards and Technology (NIST)**. These principles form the basis for **security operations centers (SOC)**. Let us explore these core principles.

Knowing the adversary

There is a need to comprehensively understand who they are and what their **tools, tactics, and procedures (TTP)** are. If we analyze some historical attacks, identifying the threats and attack vectors in advance will bolster cyber defense capabilities. With access to information becoming easily available in today's pervasive environment, the motives and intentions of attackers are crucial for building defenses in the cyber world. Cyberattacks on organizations are damaging as they impact the larger population, but when such attacks are inflicted upon the privacy of individuals, their medical records, and **personally identifiable information (PII)**, the implications are more damaging. Privacy, time, and data are all at stake. In order to take adequate precautions to mitigate these threats, it is extremely important to understand threat actors and possible attacks.

Threats to the privacy and integrity of data come from a small hacker community. If we compare the hacker community with thieves, there is an easily observable distinction. Thieves steal an asset one at a time. Hackers, on the other hand, can damage larger information assets with a basic computer, sitting anywhere, and causing damage worldwide.

Potential threat actors can be identified as hackers. Though in general, hackers are termed adversaries, they are experts who can gain access to devices or networks using programming skill s. There is a term called ethical hacking as well, which is required to identify vulnerabilities. Hacking in itself is not unauthorized, although who is doing it and the intent behind it matter. The types of hackers can be from one of the following:

- **Script kiddies**: Script kiddies are novices exploiting already created scripts, password crackers and software tools to cause substantial damage. These can be identified from the signatures of the malicious contents. These kinds of hackers do not have the wherewithal to wage cyberattack on a large scale. However, the instinct to prove themselves can lead them to explore unchartered territories, causing larger damage to information assets. These hackers can cause website defacement, **denial of service (DoS)** attacks, or social engineering attacks. The response to possible attacks can then be decided accordingly. Some attacks inflicted by script kiddies include the *HBGary Federal* hack and the *TalkTalk* cyberattack.

- **Hackers**: These are programming experts capable of gaining access to other people's computers or networks. Many hackers remain content with simple footprints, whereas other hackers are more malicious, causing widespread disruption in businesses. The basic difference between different types of hackers can be identified based on their motivation and intent to break into the systems:

o **White hat**: These are ethical hackers. Their primary aim is to find and fix the vulnerabilities in the system. White hat hackers take requisite permission from organizations and uncover weaknesses in their systems. They may have access to all the information needed to carry out vulnerability assessment and penetration testing. Organizations employ these tools with complete awareness, making it a transparent process. Considering the expertise levels, these hackers are best suited to identify the cyber issues in the systems and find potential measures to safeguard the information assets. With these efforts, organizations can improve their cyber defenses with strong security measures.

o **Black hat**: These are cybercriminals. The intent of black hat hackers is malicious, and they illegally break into the systems by exploiting known vulnerabilities. They are also capable of finding unknown vulnerabilities through various measures like social engineering and backdoors. They mostly deploy viruses, malware, and Trojans to take control of the asset or disrupt the services, causing significant damage to information resources in any organization. Their competence and wherewithal available with them can cause substantial damage even to individuals, adversely impacting their privacy.

o **Gray hat**: These are neither ethical nor malicious. The intent, skills, and expertise levels of gray hat hackers may not be to destroy or disrupt. However, they do not have legal permission from individuals or organizations to use their information assets. Gray hat hackers can unearth zero-day vulnerabilities that are not known in the environment. In order to ensure that those vulnerabilities are not exploited, they report these vulnerabilities to the respective organizations. They have the necessary tools and resources to break into any information system. They may demand payment to disclose all the discoveries or vulnerabilities.

• **Hacktivists**: Hacktivists are purpose-driven hackers motivated by a political or social cause. They are mostly ethical, using their skills and resources to uncover the vulnerabilities. However, it is important to identify the motivation and intent against a specific organization or government agency. The cyber defenses can then be worked out accordingly. Although they can be categorized under any of the hacker types, they primarily exploit the vulnerabilities in specific government agencies or organizations illegally. The outcome of their hacking can uncover secrets that are not intended for general public disclosure. However, they are driven by what they feel is a just cause. If the agency or organization does not fall into its scheme of things, hacktivists may inflict damages on the information resources, adversely affecting its functioning and reputation. While deciding on cyber defenses, varying intents must be examined to pinpoint the attempts and mitigate them in time to avoid embarrassment at later stages.

Securing the CIA triad

The idea of cybersecurity is to ensure that the CIA triad is secure:

- **Confidentiality**: Ensuring that information is accessible only to those authorized to have access. This requires protecting data at rest, in transit, or in use through encryption technologies. The use of encryption in messaging apps like *WhatsApp* ensures that only the intended recipient can read the messages. This prevents unauthorized access to sensitive information.

- **Integrity**: Maintaining the accuracy and completeness of data. This ensures the protection of data from unauthorized modifications. This can be ensured through procedures like digital signatures. Blockchain technology in cryptocurrencies like Bitcoin ensures data integrity. Transactions are recorded in a way that makes them tamper-proof, as altering one block would require changing all subsequent blocks.

- **Availability**: Ensuring that authorized users have access to information and resources when needed. This ensures protection from **DoS/distributed denial of service (DDoS)** attacks or natural calamities. This can be ensured through load balancing and disaster recovery plans. Cloud service providers like AWS or Google Cloud implement redundancy and failover mechanisms to ensure their services remain available even during hardware failures or cyberattacks.

Apart from the CIA triad, two more principles are often required in the cybersecurity domain:

- **Authentication**: Ensuring that information and communication come from trusted sources. This is required to stop impersonation, spoofing, or identity theft fraud. This can be ensured through digital certificates and multi-factor authentication. **Multi-factor authentication (MFA)** used by platforms like *Gmail* or online banking services ensures that only authorized users can access accounts by requiring multiple forms of verification.

- **Nonrepudiation**: Ensuring that a party cannot deny having sent or received a message or transaction. This is primarily aimed at avoiding replay attacks. Digital signatures can be effectively used to ensure non-repudiation. Digital signatures in email communication or contracts ensure that the sender cannot deny sending the message or signing the document, as the signature is uniquely tied to the sender.

Security awareness

Human errors constitute the weakest link in cybersecurity and several studies and statistics highlight its impact:

- *Cybersecurity Intelligence Index Report* of *IBM* in 2014 claimed human error contributed to over 95% of breaches. More recent reports focus on other human aspects as well.

- According to the 2023 *Verizon* **Data Breach Investigations Report** (**DBIR**), approximately 74% of all breaches involved the human element, including errors, social engineering, misuse, or stolen credentials.

- IBM's cost of a data breach report in 2023 found that human error was responsible for 21% of data breaches, with an average cost of $4.35 million per breach.

- *Stanford University* research indicates that 88% of all data breaches are caused by employee mistakes rather than by direct attacks.

- Proofpoint's human factor report of 2023 revealed that 82% of breaches involved the human element, with phishing remaining the most common attack vector. According to SANS institute research, 95% of all successful cyberattacks begin with a phishing attempt.

- Microsoft security research shows that 99.9% of compromised accounts did not use MFA.

- A Stanford study found a 238% increase in cybersecurity incidents related to remote work environments and 30% of remote workers admit to allowing other household members to use their work devices.

NIST studies show that proper security awareness training can reduce security incidents by up to 70%. It is crucial to spread awareness among maximum potential individuals to recognize potential threats, understand safe online practices, and adhere to security policies. There is a need for continuous, periodic awareness programs for all stakeholders.

Individuals, endpoints and networks

In the realm of cybersecurity, protecting individuals, endpoints, and networks is fundamental to ensuring cyber-safe functioning. Let us look at each of these components in detail.

Individuals

Individuals are often the first layer of defense against cyber threats. Educating users about safe online practices, recognizing phishing attempts, and maintaining strong, unique passwords are crucial steps in safeguarding personal and organizational data. Individuals can be outsiders, hackers, or disgruntled insiders. Individual users are the ones who lose privacy/information resources and prevent the same from happening. Security event monitoring, response, and analysis are all done by individuals. Making these very individuals aware of their vulnerabilities and protecting them is paramount. Behavioral analysis of individuals is the key to identifying the anomalies in security incident and event management.

Endpoints

Endpoints refer to devices like computers, smartphones, and servers that connect to a network. They have software, hardware, and firmware, all of which are subject to cyberattacks. Be it an operating system, antivirus, or other application software, if these are not adequately configured and updated periodically, they can form the basis of vulnerabilities that attackers can thrive on. The firmware and hardware are strictly controlled in a manufacturing environment. Unless the state actors utilize these manufacturing agencies to install malicious content, it is difficult to target hardware/firmware. Nevertheless, even these are targeted by preying adversaries. Endpoint security involves protecting these devices from malicious threats and cyberattacks. This includes using physical access control measures, antivirus software, firewalls, and advanced **endpoint detection and response (EDR)** solutions to monitor and mitigate potential risks. Nowadays, **Internet of Things (IoT)** or **Internet of Everything (IoE)** sensors are the latest endpoints, increasing the attack surface beyond imagination. If these are not properly configured/secured, they can form the media for most of the cyberattacks.

Networks

Network security encompasses the TTP designed to protect an organization's network and critical infrastructure from unauthorized access, cyberattacks, and data breaches. In the ever-increasing internet domain, network devices, whether wired or wireless, are crucial to individuals worldwide carrying out their business. However, these communication devices are the source of distance attacks by hackers with basic tools and resources by the hackers. These networking devices, if not properly configured, patch-updated, or secured, can become the victims of the malicious intent of hackers. The hackers can then gain access through the network, being all pervasive, to exploit the vulnerabilities in individuals and endpoints. This involves implementing firewalls, intrusion detection systems, redundant paths, and secure access protocols to ensure the confidentiality, integrity, and availability of data transmitted across the network.

Together, these elements form a comprehensive cybersecurity strategy that helps protect against a wide range of cyber threats. All these aspects become complex with the introduction of cloud computing.

Cloud security

With the advent of cloud technologies, the realm of individuals, endpoints, and network security has transformed into a sophisticated and complex web of information assets. Be it private clouds (organizations owning the data centers), public clouds (sharing of data centers resources over the internet), or hybrid clouds (combination of private / public), the information assets have been centralized. This adds to the challenges for cybersecurity professionals. Also, it provides a set of trained cyber professionals to secure the centralized resources better. Cloud security models are essential frameworks that help protect data, applications, and infrastructure in cloud environments. The three primary models are:

- **Infrastructure as a service (IaaS)**: This model provides virtualized computing resources, i.e. endpoints over the shared internet infrastructure. Individuals or organizations can manage their own applications, data, and operating systems while the cloud provider handles the underlying infrastructure, including servers, storage, and networking. Users have significant control over the virtualized environment, which increases the risk of misconfigurations, such as open ports or weak access controls, and limited visibility into the underlying infrastructure managed by the cloud provider can also pose challenges. To overcome these, there is a need to implement strict access controls, regular monitoring and patching systems, and use encryption for data at rest and in transit. Adopting a shared responsibility model is crucial to ensure both the provider and user fulfill their security roles.

- **Platform as a service (PaaS)**: PaaS offers a platform allowing customers to develop, run, and manage applications without dealing with the underlying infrastructure. This model includes endpoints from servers and storage to networking and databases. This facilitates the developers' focus on coding and deploying applications. Some of the challenges in PaaS are vulnerabilities in the platform or applications developed on it can be exploited and limited visibility into the platform's infrastructure and potential mismanagement of sensitive data. The best practice is to secure development workflows, encrypt data at rest and in transit, and use identity as the primary security perimeter. Also, regularly audit and monitor the platform to detect and mitigate threats.

- **Software as a service (SaaS)**: SaaS delivers software applications over the internet on a subscription basis. The cloud provider manages everything, including the infrastructure, middleware, application software, and data. Users can access the software from any device with an internet connection. SaaS applications often store sensitive data, making them attractive targets for cyberattacks. Misconfigurations, unauthorized access, and compliance with data protection regulations are key challenges. The best practices to overcome these are implement MFA, enforce strict access controls, and regularly review security configurations. Use **SaaS security posture management** (**SSPM**) tools to monitor and manage risks effectively.

These models provide flexibility, scalability, and cost-efficiency. Each model has its own security considerations and best practices to ensure data protection and compliance. The need for trained cybersecurity professionals to deal with security incidents in these cloud domains is growing exponentially. Though centralized cloud resources provide a better management perspective for handling security incidents, they also pave the way for strictly guarding the information assets to the hilt.

Security event generation and collection

Having gone through the cybersecurity principles, threat actors, and actual threats, it is now time to understand how to protect against such threats. Security event generation and collection are critical components of a robust cybersecurity strategy. They form the basis of responses to cyberattacks. It involves capturing a vast array of data points from disparate sources. These may be individual user actions happening on endpoints or network devices, network traffic, and cloud environments. Vast amounts of data that get generated are often referred to as logs or events. They provide valuable insights into vulnerabilities and potential threats leading to cyberattacks. By aggregating and analyzing these logs and events, organizations can identify suspicious activities and detect security incidents in real-time. This further leads to planning the response for mitigating the threats.

The endpoints, network devices, or cloud resources generate logs of every instance, which are normally stored on them only. Logs like individual logging in/out with timestamps, equipment switching on/off, any addition/alteration/amendments to the software, installation/deletion of applications, media flaps, etc., get recorded. Security events are generated by devices like firewalls, intrusion detection systems, servers, or applications whenever they detect a change or anomaly. These logs will be collected and sent over a network to a centralized management tool, typically **Security Information and Event Management (SIEM)** systems. SIEM can collect data in a variety of ways. Specialized agents are installed on endpoints/network devices to exfiltrate the logs. The logs/events can be captured directly through network protocols. The logs from a variety of devices can be sent/logged/stored on central storage. SIEM can then get these from centralized storage. SIEM systems are able to gather data from multiple sources, standardize it, and store it in central repositories. The collected data, through continuous monitoring, is then analyzed to identify patterns, anomalies, and potential security instances. Here are some examples of common security events and how they are managed in a SIEM system:

- Unauthorised access attempts due to typical pattern of multiple failed login attempts on a server or application gets detected by the SIEM system, which generates an alert. Security teams investigate the source of the attempts and may block the IP address or enforce additional authentication measures.

- A file flagged as malicious by the endpoint detection system can be seen in SIEM as it aggregates logs from the endpoint system, correlates them with other network activity, and triggers an alert. The security team isolates the affected system and initiates malware removal procedures.

- In phishing attempts scenario like employees receiving emails with suspicious links or attachments, SIEM collects and analyzes email logs, identifying patterns of phishing attempts. It alerts the security team, which can then block the sender and educate employees about the threat.

SIEM systems help organizations detect threats, respond to incidents, and comply with regulatory requirements. This proactive approach toward security event management is essential for maintaining the integrity and security of an organization's IT infrastructure.

Threat landscape

The cyber threat landscape encompasses the entire scope of potential and recognized cybersecurity threats that can affect individuals or organizations alike. This landscape is constantly evolving due to advancements in technology and ease of communication. The attacks are getting more complex and sophisticated due to the emergence of new attack surfaces. Key contributing factors in this dynamic environment include the proliferation of digital technologies, the rise of the IoT, the emergence of 5G/FTTH, and the growing reliance on cloud services.

The COVID-19 pandemic has created an increasing reliance on online systems, be it economic activities, online education, or business processes, and all these factors have significantly increased the attack surface. Further, geopolitical conflicts like the *Russia-Ukraine war and the Israel- Palestine war have significantly expanded the threat landscape*. These events have expanded the attack surfaces and introduced new vulnerabilities, particularly with the shift to remote work and the adoption of **bring-your-own-device** (**BYOD**) policies. Organizations are increasingly becoming dependent on third-party agencies to manage specific services. This has further led to a rise in supply chain attacks, where cybercriminals target multiple providers to gain unauthorized access to sensitive data.

The threat landscape includes a wide range of cyber threats, not just the threats covered. Let us look at them in detail:

- **Viruses**: Viruses are the most common security threat. They get maximum attention due to extensive press coverage. Viruses are computer programs that are written with specific signatures by devious programmers and are designed to replicate themselves and infect computers when triggered by a specific event.

- **Malware**: Cyber attackers employ malware, ransomware, spyware, or worms to gain access to the system. When the malicious links are clicked by individuals, these codes get activated, triggering an incident. If this goes undetected, it can significantly damage the information resources.

- **Phishing**: These are typically employed to lure unsuspecting individuals to open a message, follow instructions, and click on the links. If the individual falls prey to these tactics, the attackers can gain access to your system, malware can be deployed, or personally identifiable information can be compromised.

- **Spoofing**: These techniques are mostly deployed to trick an individual or organization into giving the required information to the adversary. A fake caller ID, fake IP Address, fake domain name, and fake website are common examples of ways of tricking people into submitting their critical information.

- **Denial of service attacks**: These are deliberate attempts by the attackers to disrupt the services by flooding the server with redundant traffic. This overwhelming traffic can cause system crashes also, thereby impacting the availability.

- **Ransomware**: Cyber attackers encrypt an organization's data and demand a ransom for its release. These ransomware attacks have become more frequent and damaging. These attacks can disrupt operations and lead to significant financial losses. There is a need for backups and disaster recovery plans to ensure business continuity.

- **Social engineering attacks**: Social engineering is the most prevalent technique of obtaining confidential security information through non-technical means. For example, a social engineer might pose as a technical support representative and make calls to employees to gather password information. Other examples of social engineering include bribing an associate to gain access to a server or searching a colleague's office to find a password that has been written in a hidden spot.

- **Advanced persistent threats (APT)**: APT involves sophisticated and stealthy cyberattacks. They are often state-sponsored, gain access to a network, and remain undetected for an extended period. Unlike other hackers, APTs have the skills, resources, and willpower of the corresponding state to persistently carry out cyberattacks on stated adversaries, be it organizations or government agencies. They employ advanced techniques using social engineering and spear phishing. They are skilled in exploiting zero-day vulnerabilities. The primary goal of an APT is to steal sensitive data, conduct espionage, or sabotage critical systems without being noticed. These attacks are meticulously planned and executed, allowing attackers to move laterally within the network, establish multiple backdoors, and maintain long-term access. The prolonged presence of APTs enables attackers to gather intelligence, exfiltrate data, and potentially cause significant damage to the targeted organization. These are the most dreaded attacks that any cybersecurity professional must guard against by employing effective countermeasures.

As technologies continue to advance, so do the tactics, techniques, and procedures used by threat actors, making it essential for organizations to stay vigilant and continuously update their security measures to protect against these evolving threats.

Industry-wise use cases

In today's fast-changing digital era, cyberattacks are experienced by almost every individual or organization. However, considering the statistical aspect, some industries are more prone to cyberattack owing to their importance to public life. Cyberattacks not only disrupt operations but also lead to substantial financial losses and damage reputations. If we concentrate on major industries affected by understanding the modus operandi of such cyberattacks and their TTPs, it can result in the development of better security measures and policies across the board. Now, we will be looking at some of the industry use cases impacted by cyberattacks.

- **Manufacturing industry**: Cyberattacks mostly target manufacturing industries. This is primarily due to the rapid digitization of the industry through the adoption of **Industrial Internet of Things (IIoT)** devices, which often lack robust security measures. These IoT devices are highly vulnerable. The hackers know that if these processes are disrupted, it will lead to significant operational and financial losses. **operational technology (OT)** security is gaining significant attention. OT involves the hardware and software to be monitored and controls physical processes or devices in the manufacturing infrastructure. Securing the OT becomes a prime role for cyber professionals. OT devices are mostly from disparate vendors, making it more complex to manage the security. Third-party involvement creates additional attack surfaces, which need to be protected. Cyberattacks have had a profound impact on the manufacturing industry, as illustrated by several notable examples as follows:

- o **JBS ransomware attack:** In 2021, JBS, a global meat processing company, faced a ransomware attack that disrupted operations for five days. This attack affected the global food supply chain and resulted in an $11 million ransom payment.

- o **Toyota supply chain attack:** In 2022, Toyota experienced a cyberattack targeting its supply chain, forcing the temporary shutdown of 14 production plants. This led to the loss of approximately 13,000 vehicles in output.

- o **Applied materials supply chain breach:** In 2023, Applied Materials, a major player in the manufacturing sector, suffered a supply chain attack that caused significant production delays. The financial impact was estimated at $250 million.

- **Banking, financial services and insurance (BFSI) sector:** The BFSI sector is another prime target for cybercriminals. This sector works on vast amounts of sensitive financial information, be it PII like credit card details, security numbers, etc. Hence, it is a lucrative target for all cybercriminals. Cyberattacks in this sector can lead to direct financial theft, fraud, and severe breaches of customer trust. This sector also deals with different stakeholders, from individuals, organizations, internet and cloud service providers, and security agencies, making them complex systems to manage. Further, the operations across the world make it even more complex from a compliance management perspective. PII in one country may not be so sensitive in another country. Similarly, some regions may deal with privacy more stringently than others. This compliance management makes the job of cybersecurity professionals more complex. To deal with compliance in the BFSI sector, the **Payment Card Industry (PCI) Data Security Standards (DSS)** have been established to protect payment card data and transactions better. Cyberattacks have significantly impacted the BFSI sector. Here are some notable examples:

- o **Cosmos Bank cyber heist (India):** In 2018, hackers infiltrated Cosmos Bank's systems and siphoned off ₹94 crore (approximately $13.5 million) through fraudulent transactions. The attackers used malware to compromise the bank's ATM switch server and conducted unauthorized withdrawals across 28 countries.

- o **Bangladesh bank heist**: In 2016, cybercriminals exploited vulnerabilities in the SWIFT payment system to steal $81 million from the Bangladesh Bank's account at the *Federal Reserve Bank* of *New York*. The attack highlighted the risks associated with interbank payment systems.

- o **Capital One data breach**: In 2019, a misconfigured firewall allowed a hacker to access the personal data of over 100 million Capital One customers. The breach exposed sensitive information, including Social Security numbers and bank account details.

- **Healthcare**: The healthcare sector is the most susceptible to cyberattacks. This is primarily due to the sensitive nature of the data they manage, including patient records and medical histories. The average cost of a data breach in healthcare is also the highest among all industries, making it a lucrative target for cybercriminals. As with the manufacturing industry, the healthcare industry also relies heavily on IoT devices. Integrating these devices into the scheme of things to extract critical medical records reliably is a complex process. Stringent compliance with guidelines like the **Health Insurance Portability and Accountability Act (HIPPA)** makes the data cyber-safe. Cyberattacks have had a significant impact on the healthcare sector, with several notable examples as follows:

  - o **MedSecure health systems**: MedSecure, a leading healthcare provider, faced ransomware attacks targeting patient data and hospital operations. The organization responded by overhauling its cybersecurity measures, including deploying advanced machine learning algorithms for threat detection and implementing biometric authentication systems.

  - o **Change Healthcare cyberattack**: In February 2024, Change Healthcare experienced a cyberattack that disrupted crucial payment systems, impacting 100 million Americans. The attack highlighted vulnerabilities in centralized platforms and prompted federal regulators to investigate the company's security measures.

  - o **Ascension ransomware attack**: Ascension, one of the largest nonprofit health systems, suffered a ransomware attack that took its electronic health records offline, diverted ambulances, and impacted clinical operations across 11 states. The attack contributed to a $1.1 billion net loss during its fiscal year.

- **Fast-moving consumer goods (FMCG) and services sector:** The FMCG and services sector accounts for significant cyberattacks. The diversity and volume of data handled by this sector make it an attractive target. Most services like **customer relationship management (CRM)**, **enterprise resource planning (ERP)**, **project management planning (PMP)**, and **point of sale (POS)** are widely exploited as the handling of these services is done through a diverse group of individuals. The operators can become the weakest links in the exfiltration of sensitive data they collect, including payment information. The shift toward online shopping has further exposed these businesses to cyber threats. Guarding these systems, therefore, becomes of paramount importance to cyber professionals. Here are some notable examples of cyberattacks in the FMCG and services sectors:

- o **Mondelez International—NotPetya attack**: In 2017, Mondelez International, a global FMCG giant, was hit by the NotPetya ransomware attack. The incident disrupted production and logistics, leading to an estimated $140 million in losses. This attack highlighted vulnerabilities in supply chain operations and the importance of securing interconnected systems.

- o **JBS ransomware attack**: In 2021, a ransomware attack forced the company to shut down operations temporarily, impacting global food supply chains. JBS paid an $11 million ransom to regain control of its systems.

- o **Marriott International data breach**: In 2018, Marriott International revealed that hackers had accessed the personal data of approximately 500 million guests over four years. The breach involved unauthorized access to the Starwood guest reservation database, highlighting the importance of securing customer data in the hospitality industry.

- **Energy sector**: The energy sector is critical for maintaining national security and economic stability. Cyberattacks in this sector can have far-reaching consequences and significant economic impacts. It can be devastating owing to the impact on routine operations. The disruption in any of these services will not only affect the masses, but their restoration will involve significant financial burdens. The cyberattacks on **supervisory control and data acquisition** (**SCADA**) systems or **programmable logic controllers** (**PLC**) can greatly impact the functioning of the energy sector. These SCADA / PLC systems are legacy systems, often not updated, providing a host of vulnerabilities. Even patching them or updating these systems to the latest hardware and software will cause significant delays in the provisioning of services. Therefore, protecting these vulnerable but critical legacy assets has to be the topmost priority for cybersecurity professionals. Cyberattacks have had a significant impact on the energy sector, with several notable examples as follows:

- o **Colonial Pipeline ransomware attack**: In 2021, the Colonial Pipeline, a major fuel pipeline in the *United States*, was targeted by a ransomware attack. The attack disrupted fuel supplies across the East Coast, leading to panic buying and fuel shortages. The company paid a $4.4 million ransom to regain control of its systems.

- o **Ukraine power grid attack**: In 2015, a cyberattack on Ukraine's power grid caused widespread outages, leaving over 230,000 people without electricity. The attackers used malware called BlackEnergy to compromise the grid's systems, marking one of the first known instances of a cyberattack causing a power outage.

- **Saudi Aramco Shamoon attack**: In 2012, Saudi Aramco, one of the world's largest oil companies, was hit by the Shamoon malware. The attack wiped data from approximately 30,000 computers, severely disrupting operations and highlighting the vulnerabilities in the energy sector.

- **Government and military**: Cyberattacks on government and military entities have been on the rise due to the sensitive and classified information they handle. Attacks on government systems can lead to national security threats and significant disruptions in public services. APT actors, which are often backed by states, indulge in sabotage, phishing, and other tactics to infiltrate these agencies to extract secrets and strategies. Here are some notable examples of cyber attacks in the government and military sectors:

  - **AIIMS ransomware attack (India)**: In November 2022, the **All India Institute of Medical Sciences** (**AIIMS**) in *New Delhi* faced a ransomware attack that crippled its servers and disrupted critical healthcare services. The attack forced the hospital to revert to manual operations, causing delays in patient care. Investigations suggested potential state-sponsored involvement.

  - *US* **office of personnel management data breach**: In 2015, a cyberattack on the OPM exposed sensitive personal information of over 21 million federal employees, including social security numbers and security clearance details. The breach highlighted vulnerabilities in government data storage and led to significant reforms in cybersecurity practices.

  - **Lockheed Martin F-35 data breach**: In 2007, Chinese hackers reportedly accessed sensitive data related to the F-35 fighter jet program. The breach involved spear-phishing techniques and resulted in the theft of terabytes of classified information, potentially aiding the development of *China's* J-20 and J-31 fighter jets.

  - **Viasat satellite network attack**: On February 24, 2022, during *Russia's* invasion of Ukraine, a cyberattack disrupted Viasat's KA-SAT satellite network. The attack impacted military communications and civilian internet access across Europe, showcasing the risks to critical infrastructure during conflicts.

The ever-expanding attack surfaces, frequent cyberattacks in these sectors, and digitization resulting in the rise of sophisticated cyberattacks highlight the urgent need for robust cybersecurity measures. Organizations or government agencies must invest in advanced security technologies, training and awareness, and comprehensive response plans to mitigate the risks associated with cyber threats. Organizations and relevant stakeholders can be better prepared to protect themselves by understanding the specific vulnerabilities and threats faced by those sectors from the devastating impacts of cyberattacks.

Statistical analysis of 2023 from *Statista* clearly shows the cyberattack worldwide in industries in 2023. Refer to the following figure:

Distribution of cyberattacks across worldwide industries in 2023

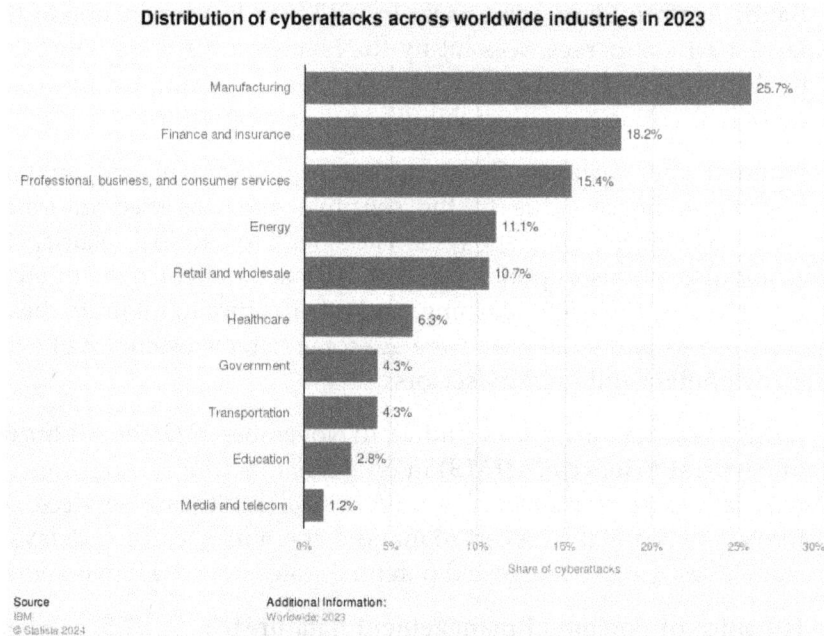

Source
IBM
© Statista 2024

Additional Information:
Worldwide; 2023

Figure 1.1: *Industry-wide distribution of cyberattacks*

Challenges of cybersecurity

Cybersecurity is of concern to individuals or organizations. Everyone needs to be responsive and sensitive to cyberattacks. However, cyberattacks are still taking place due to some of the key challenges.

Let us look at them in detail:

- **Evolving threat landscape**: Cyber threats are constantly evolving, with cybercriminals developing new TTPs to exploit vulnerabilities. This makes it difficult for cybersecurity professionals to employ security measures to protect against all potential attacks efficiently. The 2021 Colonial Pipeline ransomware attack disrupted fuel supplies across the U.S., showcasing the growing risks to critical infrastructure.

- **Sophistication of attacks**: Modern cyberattacks are exploiting advanced artificial intelligence and machine learning, making them increasingly sophisticated. The time involved in generating malicious codes with such advanced, sophisticated tools has been reduced considerably. Also, variants of these malicious contents can be staggering, making detection and prevention more challenging. Often, the traditional security measures get bypassed due to a signature mismatch or unknown vulnerabilities, making these ineffective. Cybercrime costs are projected to reach $10.5 trillion annually by 2025, driven by advanced tactics like AI-powered phishing.

- **Shortage of skilled professionals**: The ever-increasing threats are adding significant stress to the available manpower. There is a significant shortage of skilled cybersecurity professionals. This makes it difficult for organizations to implement robust security measures and ensure cyber-safe operations. The global cybersecurity workforce gap reached 4 million professionals in 2024, highlighting the urgent need for talent.

- **Human error**: Human errors are arguably the weakest links, creating the biggest vulnerabilities in cybersecurity. Individuals may inadvertently click on phishing links, use weak passwords, or fail to follow security protocols, leading to breaches. Security training and awareness remain the most required measures to ensure human errors do not contribute to exploiting vulnerabilities. IBM reports that human error accounts for 95% of cybersecurity breaches, emphasizing the need for better training.

- **Converged systems**: The ICT are converging rapidly. The jobs done by multiple systems like calculators, personal computers, cameras, clocks, and mobile phones are being increasingly converged into single devices, making them crucial from a cyber perspective. Increasing interconnectivity of systems and devices, especially with the rise of the IoT, expands the attack surface. Each connected device can potentially be a point of entry for cybercriminals. Nearly 90% of organizations with connected OT infrastructures experienced security breaches in their SCADA/ICS systems.

- **Regulatory compliance**: The world is still divided in responses to cyber incidences. Organizations must navigate a complex landscape of regulatory requirements related to data protection and privacy. Cybersecurity professionals face tremendous challenges in ensuring compliance with these regulations. Often, the measures are so resource and time-intensive that minor vulnerabilities in their implementation can lead to major security breaches, resulting in loss of reputation. The complexity of adhering to frameworks like GDPR and CCPA has led to increased scrutiny and fines for non-compliance.

The challenges covered above are not exhaustive. A holistic approach is required to address these challenges, involving, but not limited to, advanced security technologies, continuous monitoring, training and awareness, and a proactive incident response plan. Organizations must share intelligence and stay prepared to better protect themselves against the ever-evolving cyber threats.

Layers of security

The cyber threat landscape is vast. Covering all the tracks or attack surfaces is complex. Therefore, addressing cyber threats must be incorporated at different layers, making it a complex web of security measures for cyber attackers to tackle defense in depth or using a multi-layered approach to protect digital information assets, which is paramount for cyber-safe operations. The **Open Systems Interconnection (OSI)** models were devised to provide a proper understanding of communication practices in the digital domain. Security measures at each OSI model can create layers of security that are difficult for hackers to breach.

Multiple layers can include the following:

- **Physical layer**: Protection of the endpoints, hardware, physical infrastructure and communication infrastructure from unauthorized access, theft, or damage can be very effective in limiting cyberattack These can include measures like security guards, surveillance cameras, and access control systems apart from EDR tools.

- **Network layer**: Protection at this layer ensures the integrity and usability of the network and data. It can include firewalls, **intrusion detection/prevention systems (IDS/IPS)**, and VPNs.

- **Data layer**: Protection at this layer ensured confidentiality by protecting the data from unauthorized access and corruption. The measures involved can be encryption of data at rest, in transit, or in use.

- **Application layer**: Protection at this layer ensures that software applications are safe from threats. It may involve secure coding practices, application firewalls, and regular security testing.

- **Identity and access management**: This protection controls who has access to information assets. It can involve **single sign-on (SSO)**, MFA, and **role/rule based access control (RBAC)**.

- **Training and awareness**: This is the most important proactive measure to educate users to follow best secure practices, know about vulnerabilities, and prepare effectively for defenses.

Conclusion

Cybersecurity is a critical concern in today's digital world, with numerous challenges that organizations must address to protect their data and systems. It is important to know the threat actors to understand their intent, motives, and prospective tools, techniques, and procedures. This awareness will help us be better prepared for the reliable defenses required for business continuity.

In the next chapter, we will explore the ramifications of cyberattacks and their impacts on various stakeholders in more detail.

Points to remember

Here are some key takeaways from this chapter:

- Knowing the adversary and their TTPs is a primary concern.

- Preparing against these threats has to be followed up to ensure effective responses.

Multiple choice questions

1. **Cybersecurity principle includes protection of:**
   a. Confidentiality
   b. Availability
   c. Integrity
   d. All of these

2. **Cybersecurity principle includes protection of:**
   a. Confidentiality
   b. Availability
   c. Integrity
   d. All of these

3. **Which cybersecurity layer focuses on ensuring only authorized users have access to information assets?**
   a. Physical layer
   b. Network layer
   c. Identity and access management
   d. Application layer

Answers

1	b
2	d
3	c

Questions

1. What are threat actors? Explain different types of threat actors.

2. Explain the threat landscape and how industries are impacted by cyberattacks.

Key terms

Some key terms used in this chapter are:

- **Threat landscape**: It covers the broad contours of cyberattacks.
- **Threat actors**: Hackers contribute to vulnerability assessment or illegal breaching.

Join our Discord space

Join our Discord workspace for latest updates, offers, tech happenings around the world, new releases, and sessions with the authors:

https://discord.bpbonline.com

CHAPTER 2
Cybersecurity Ramifications and Implications

Introduction

This chapter will explore the domains of security operations. It covers how security incidents impact the ecosystem. Businesses and individuals alike face disparate threats, bringing out the need for increased security. This chapter will examine cyberattacks' short and long-term ramifications across verticals. It also covers the implications of future cybersecurity measures and investments required to manage the threats. Collaboration in information sharing and focus on cyber resilience can significantly counter the implications of cyberattacks.

The ramifications and implications of cybersecurity are far-reaching. They affect not only the attacked entity but also the larger information ecosystem. Digital systems need to be guarded, and the responsibility needs to be shared amongst all stakeholders.

These cyberattacks will result in financial losses, reputation damage, and business disruptions. Apart from these issues, there is a more significant issue of regulatory compliance. Data privacy is gaining increasing attention. Every stakeholder needs to ensure compliance with regulatory requirements across different domains. There is a need for larger sensitization and ownership when it comes to handling cybersecurity issues. Understanding broader domains, how they affect people, processes, and technology, and the consequences of neglecting cybersecurity needs to be clear. This will lead to robust strategies to protect against the ever-growing threat landscape. This is the second most crucial step for a digitally safe future.

Structure

In this chapter, we will discuss the following topics:

- Cybersecurity for enterprises and individuals
- Cybersecurity broad domains
- Cybersecurity affecting people, processes, and technology
- Types of attacks
- Consequences of neglecting cybersecurity
- Impact on economy

Objectives

By the end of this chapter, you will be able to understand the impacts of cybersecurity on individuals and enterprises. This chapter will explore various domains, such as identity and access management, asset security, information security, etc. After reading this chapter, readers will gain a clear understanding of the types of cyberattacks along with their effects on people, processes, and technology. The chapter will highlight the potential repercussions of failing to implement adequate cybersecurity measures, analyzing the economic implications of cybersecurity, including financial losses and regulatory compliance costs.

Cybersecurity for enterprises and individuals

In today's fast-evolving digital age, cybersecurity is a critical concern for enterprises and individuals. There is an increasing reliance on digital technology, be it for personal requirements, collaborations, or mission-critical requirements. However, the underlying infrastructure, technologies involved, and compliance requirements are too exhaustive and diverse and the scale and complexities involved are too dynamic. Having said that, the fundamental principles involved are the same from a cybersecurity perspective.

Enterprises

Enterprises across the world face a complex threat landscape. There are multiple dimensions in protecting sensitive organizational data, ensuring business continuity while safeguarding the reputation. The key focus areas for enterprises are:

- **Data protection**: It is crucial for enterprises to protect sensitive information such as:
  - o **Encryption**: Encrypting the data at rest, in transit, or in use ensures confidentiality. Even if the data is lost, unless the decryption keys are

compromised, the attacker will not gain anything. Enterprises can rebuild lost data from backups.

- o **Backups**: Backups at periodic intervals are key to mitigating the impact of data loss. The backups need to be at different locations and multiple media types to have effective resilience.

- o **Disaster recovery and business continuity plans**: Extracting backed-up data and integrating it into business processes is crucial to ensuring that operations are not affected.

- **Infrastructure protection**: Protecting enterprise infrastructure is essential to ensure the confidentiality, integrity, and availability of critical systems and data. Infrastructure protection involves:

  - o **Access control**: Embracing the Zero Trust model can be the best technical access control to avoid insider or outsider threats with equal impunity.

  - o **Physical security**: This includes measures like access control, CCTV surveillance, security guards, and environmental controls to ensure that there is no impact on the critical infrastructure assets. The threats can be from natural disasters, manmade situations, theft, fraud, or negligence. Guarding against all these threats will enhance the security posture.

- **Network security**: The dependence of enterprises on communication devices requires adequate network security measures to avoid breaches. Whether it is network devices themselves or the media connecting them across multiple locations, securing the network infrastructure will ensure the first line of defense for any cyberattacks.

- **Threat detection and response**: The key idea is to identify and address potential threats to enterprises' digital information assets. This will require continuous monitoring, behavioral analysis, and on-the-go analysis of threat intelligence. Considering the speed of cyberattacks, setting up a **security operations center** (**SOC**), is of paramount importance. SOC can be dedicated on premises, or it can be offered as a service.

- **Human factor**: It is always perceived that humans are the weakest link, and security is as strong as the weakest link. It is important to assign equal importance to the human element. There is a need to safeguard intellectual property, and this can be ensured through proper cybersecurity measures. Potential human factors can be:

  - o **Insider threat**: To obviate potential insider threats, a Zero Trust model needs to be adopted. Measures like RBAC and multi-factor authentication play a key role in avoiding the loss of individual assets.

  - o **Training and awareness**: To ensure that the larger employees of the enterprise are aware of the potential dangers of phishing, social engineering, and possible attack vectors, there is a continual need for training and awareness. Skilled manpower is needed to tackle the actual attacks, semi-skilled manpower is needed to assist in stopping the impact of cyberattacks, and every individual needs to be vigilant and contribute by not falling prey to malicious campaigns by hackers.

- **Compliance overheads**: Over the years, government agencies have increasingly implemented regulatory requirements to protect enterprises and individuals from dangerous cyberattacks. Enterprises need to ensure compliance with all these regulatory requirements.

Individuals

The probability of individuals getting targeted is limited. However, as part of social engineering attacks, if an individual is subjected to a cyberattack, the consequences can be severe. Therefore, Individuals need to protect their privacy and PII to stay safe. The focus areas for individuals are:

- **Personal device security**: In today's digital environment, every individual is part of the digital ecosystem. It can be personal computers, laptops, mobile phones, or the latest AI and ML buzzwords like *Alexa* or *Siri*. Individuals need to be vigilant to ensure that privacy is not compromised. Here are some measures for ensuring device safety:

  o **Patch updates**: To ensure the safety of individual digital assets, patch updates, be they operating systems or anti-virus software, are continually required. Even the applications on PCs/laptops/mobiles need to be updated periodically so that vulnerabilities are not exploited.

  o **Password management**: This is by far the most neglected area. Even after considerable efforts by different agencies, individuals keep their default or easy passwords for easy remembering. Hackers pounce on such instances to exfiltrate PII as well as other information, which, after correlation, can be used for other nefarious activities.

- **Online safety**: After password management, this is the second most neglected area but needs equal importance in dealing with cyberattacks.

  o **Public network or Wi-Fi**: Various agencies such as airports or the governments provide free internet agencies. However, these are the most vulnerable places as everyone's security-handling responsibility becomes nobody's. There is a need for individuals not to use public networks unless they are sure about the security measures.

  o **Phishing**: This is the technique hackers most often try. Most of the victims fall for unsolicited information or unwanted benefits. There is a strong need for individuals to realize that nothing comes for free. Individuals must guard against any such attempts by hackers.

- o **Suspicious links, fake websites**: On lines of phishing, suspicious links and fake websites are prepared to lure individuals, providing them with unsolicited adult content. This leads to the exfiltration of the PII, which can subsequently be used as ransomware or to extract other sensitive information.

- o **Privacy settings**: Even on mobile phones or PCs/laptops, the applications are installed, and all permissions are given to access location as well as other personal information. There is no need for a camera app to investigate contacts. However, these are not reviewed periodically. Individuals must be vigilant for their privacy and allow only the piece of information that is required by the applications.

- **Data protection**: Data protection needs to be at the top of every individual's agenda. If the sensitive data is lost, it may lead to other complex and dangerous repercussions. Measures to safeguard data can be:

- o **Encryption**: To ensure that the data is safe, even if it gets into the wrong hands, encryption is the only solution. All individuals must store their sensitive data in an encrypted drive with proper authentication.

- o **Backups**: Backups are another way to improve resilience from encrypted data thefts. If backups are kept at regular intervals and their veracity is periodically checked, Individuals can be safe despite the breaches.

- **Awareness**: Being vigilant is the key to staying safe. To be vigilant, individuals must be aware of what's happening around them, the modus operandi of different cyberattacks, and ways to protect themselves.

By understanding specific challenges, enterprises and individuals can adopt precautionary measures and implement security protocols to enhance their cybersecurity posture. They also reduce the risk of falling victim to any kind of threat. By taking adequate backups, enterprises and individuals can also become resilient to any type of attack. The key to staying safe is to be aware, share intelligence, and stay vigilant, in addition to taking the necessary precautions.

Cybersecurity broad domains

In cybersecurity, a wide range of domains interplay in a complex web of privacy and security. The important domains are covered in this section. Let us look at some important domains of cybersecurity:

- **Identity and access management**: The first line of defense, be it for enterprises or individuals alike, starts with **identity and access management (IAM)**. This is the crucial aspect of controlling user access to digital resources. It involves processes and technology in managing the digital identity of individuals and controlling their access to data content. IAM ensures that role/rule-based processes are in place to leverage the technology to control access, whether insider or third party. Unauthorized access can be restricted with a multi-factor authentication mechanism or Zero Trust Network Access frameworks. This is the key element in regulatory requirements. Compliance with these regulatory requirements confirms that the enterprise is geared up to handle any cyber challenges.

- **Asset security**: The second line of defense for any organization is asset security, which is securing the physical infrastructure for digital assets. Security measures are implemented to avoid unauthorized access, disruption/destruction of services, and theft of valuable digital assets. It involves processes and technology for safeguarding digital assets. Asset security ensures that ownership and responsibilities are fixed and that adequate protection measures are instituted to protect assets and meet regulatory requirements. It is an essential element in maintaining the CIA triad. Measures like surveillance systems and environmental monitoring can significantly reduce the associated risks. In a cloud environment, the security aspects of digital assets can be entrusted to third parties.

- **Information security**: The ultimate goal of cybersecurity professionals is to protect the CIA triad. This involves protecting information systems and data from unauthorized access or breaches. Information security primarily involves processes and technology protecting data. Various measures like encryption of data at rest, in transit, and in use, secure backup and retrieval processes, risk identification and mitigation measures, etc. Information security also plays an important role in incident responses and regulatory requirements. Protecting sensitive organizational data ensures trust in the information systems.

- **Governance, risk, and compliance (GRC) management**: GRC provide a comprehensive framework to ensure that organizations can effectively manage their Information system's security. Governance entails setting up standard policies and processes to streamline activities in the cyber domain. Risk management can be crucial to increasing the organization's cybersecurity posture. Compliance incorporates adhering to stringent regulatory requirements. GRC, as a unified approach, can effectively reduce risk, leading to better decision-making. ISO 27001, NIST cybersecurity Framework, COBIT5, and ITIL are standards accepted worldwide to project security posturing through compliance. Regular auditing for GRC compliance can effectively ensure a continued safe environment.

- **Communication and network security**: One of the vital functions in the cybersecurity domain is protecting the communication media and associated networking infrastructure. Communication and network security ensure CIA triad for data in transit. Networks are to be protected by segmenting, reducing the attack surface considerably by routing traffic through intrusion detection and prevention systems. Encryption at the block/stream layer, network layer, and session layer can be effective in data protection. Encrypting wireless networks needs to be considered as part of the overall strategy. Network monitoring and logging can provide meaningful insights into potential cyberattacks.

- **Cloud security**: Cloud computing has brought a paradigm shift in the way digital assets are managed. Cloud computing, encompassing compute, memory, and storage resources along with associated network infrastructure, has created distinct shared resources. This has created a unique attack surface with shared responsibilities. Cloud infrastructure security is typically handled by the service provider, whereas protection of data, applications, access control, threat detection, and response remain with the organization. Creating a robust cloud security strategy must be the focus area for cyber professionals.

- **Operations technology security**: Like cloud computing, industry 4.0 and the integration of legacy information systems have brought in different cybersecurity challenges. OT security constitutes industrial information systems and associated critical infrastructure. The software and hardware typically control the industrial activities through SCADA or PLC systems. The industrial sectors typically affected are manufacturing, energy, and transportation. Cyberattacks impact the processes and technology of OT systems. Apart from financial and economic impacts, the attacks can adversely impact the safety of individuals and the environment. Securing these systems needs to be on the top agenda of cyber professionals.

- **Security operations**: Security operations are the most critical functions in cybersecurity. It involves continuous monitoring, detecting cyber incidents, analyzing them, and responding to mitigate malicious attempts on an organization's digital assets, including data, information, people, and technology. All instances of unauthorized access, inadvertent behaviors, abnormal network activity, and disruption in services are detected in real time. The threat intelligence leading to threat hunting can then be used to react to the potential threats proactively. **Security Incident and Event Monitoring (SIEM)** and **Security Orchestration Automation and Response (SOAR)** take security operations forward to mitigate threats efficiently and secure organizations from unwanted cyberattacks.

- **Training and awareness**: One of the most important domains in cybersecurity is training and awareness to overcome shortfalls in measures commensurate with threats. It ensures that the people understand the potential threats and vulnerabilities and act based on their level of cybersecurity handling. Significant cyber breaches are attributed to a lack of awareness among individuals and their attitudes towards cybersecurity measures. If the impact of the cyberattacks is appropriately communicated and the measures to mitigate them are clearly described, the risks can be completely mitigated or reduced to a large extent. Training during onboarding, periodic training, and continuous assessment can be effective in addressing all the cyber challenges.

- **Application security**: A critical cybersecurity domain is application security. Most cyberattacks are directed through the application's vulnerabilities. Security cannot be considered an afterthought in software application development. Secure coding practices are the cornerstone of safe software applications. Quality testing and assessment throughout the software development lifecycle can effectively create safe applications. Further, as the hackers uncover vulnerabilities, the software applications also need to be patched periodically. Cross-site scripting, SQL injection, and Buffer overflows are typical issues in software applications. Making the application secure with strict access control can significantly reduce the risk element.

Cybersecurity affecting people, processes, and technology

Cyberattacks adversely impact different facets of an organization. In the present modern ICT environment, the implications and ramifications of cyberattacks are not restricted to the technical domain. They affect people, processes, and technology to varying degrees. Understanding the impact of these factors is worthwhile in assessing the shortfall critically and addressing it holistically.

People

The first notable impact is on people. Cyberattacks affect people's way of working and their personal lives alike. Let us look at some aspects in detail:

- **Roles and responsibilities**: The people are the first responders to any cyberattack. Though lots of automation has been achieved in responding to threats, clear roles need to be assigned to handle cyber incidents. Every responsibility must be clearly understood by the respective people, especially in the cloud era, where security is often managed by a third party. However, governance, incident response, and appropriate controls need to be implemented by the people in the organization.

- **Training and awareness**: This is a continuous process. The training of people directly involved in responding to threats, the training of others in containing the threats, and finally, the awareness of all the individuals in the digital domain in the organization to avoid phishing attacks must be instituted. New threats require new skill sets to handle them. People associated with threat handling need to upgrade themselves constantly.

- **Psychological impacts**: Cyberattacks can impact people to differing degrees, inducing stress and anxiety and affecting their productivity. Organizations need to be aware of these and take precautionary measures so that people are motivated and prepared to handle and respond to any cyberattacks or recover from them.

Process

Processes are the next, where the maximum impact of the cyberattacks can be experienced. Let us look at processes such as incident response, regulatory compliance, and security controls, which are highly impacted by cyberattacks. Let us read about them:

- **Incident responses**: A response mechanism needs to be instituted to address cyber threats immediately. Organizations need to implement strict policies and measures to protect their assets. The processes of inventory management and data protection play crucial roles in mitigating the attacks.

- **Business continuity and disaster recovery**: Business continuity planning is extremely crucial from an availability perspective. The processes set up to take regular backups, check their recovery, encryption/decryption processes and periodic auditing of the processes is important to ensure that the data remains safe.

- **Compliance management**: The regulatory compliances are the most stringent processes any organization encounters. These are essential to meet any contingency with tried and tested security controls.

- **Security measures**: Various security measures for IAM, asset security, and GRC compliance must be instituted with well-planned processes to ensure that these best practices are followed in letter and spirit. At times, hackers find loopholes in these processes to lure their potential targets.

Technology

Technology is at the core of cyberattacks and their mitigation. The impacts of technology can be felt in the following ways:

- **Convergence**: Information and communication technologies have already converged, providing seamless services across multiple devices. Identifying cyberattacks impacting specific devices is a challenge. With well-defined processes, this aspect can be tackled. The adoption of cloud computing, IoT, and 6G has further complicated the reach of technology, increasing the attack surface manifold.

- **Encryption**: Encryption technologies have been evolving at a rapid pace. Cryptography has been the most complex yet undervalued aspect of data protection. Traditional brute force attacks can be devastating with AI and ML boosts. Implementing strong encryption for data at rest, in transit, or in use is key to protecting sensitive data. Quantum technologies are expected to enhance the cryptography domain significantly. However, till such time, periodic key changeovers and the use of digital signatures can be effectively used to counter attacks.

- **Auditing**: Continuous logging, monitoring of the cyber incidences through technology is of paramount importance for effective analysis and responses. The periodic auditing can help detect the vulnerabilities in technology so that adequate controls can be implemented in time.

The impact on all people, processes, and technology can be far-reaching. With increased awareness, improved security measures, and technological advances, organizations can protect their assets from threats and stay safe.

Types of attacks

Cyberattacks are aimed at different facets of an organization. Targets on individuals have different connotations, which can be mitigated with people-centric IAM measures. It is important to know the targets which can potentially affect the digital assets.

Host

The attacks on hosts, i.e., endpoints, are primarily aimed at gaining unauthorized access and exploiting its compute, memory, and storage resources for further attacks. Various host-based attacks can be as follows:

- **Keyloggers**: Keyloggers are malicious programs that record every keystroke made on a computer. They are often used to steal sensitive information such as passwords and credit card numbers. These can be hardware or software, as shown in the following figure:

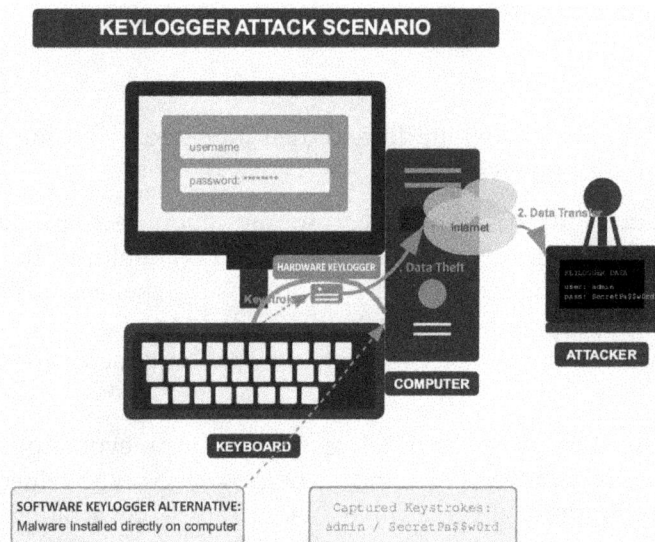

Figure 2.1: Keylogger in action

For example, a keylogger installed on an employee's computer captures their login credentials for the company's sensitive financial system. Such unauthorized access may lead to potential financial loss and data breaches.

- **Rootkits**: Rootkits are designed to gain unauthorized root or administrative access to a computer. This enables the attackers to gain complete control of the endpoint for their unauthorized activities. They hide their presence and activities from users and security software. For example, a rootkit installed on a server allows attackers to control the server remotely without detection. Complete control over the compromised system enables data theft, manipulation, and further attacks.

- Malware, spyware, Trojans, ransomware, and viruses are various types of malicious codes designed to harm, exploit, damage, or infiltrate other systems or encrypt data. For example, ransomware encrypts a user's files and demands payment for the decryption key. This results in data loss, financial extortion, and operational disruption.

- **Phishing**: Phishing involves tricking individuals into clicking malicious links to reveal sensitive information by pretending to be a trustworthy entity. For example, an email that appears to be from a bank asks the recipient to click a link and enter their account details. It results in identity theft, financial loss, and unauthorized access to personal or corporate accounts.

- **DoS attacks**: These are aimed at overwhelming the host to make it inaccessible. For example, an attacker floods a website with traffic, causing it to crash. It results in service disruption, loss of revenue, and damage to reputation.

Network

Network-based attacks target the networking infrastructure and service providers. This can be dangerous as the entire information system opens as an attack surface. Some of the common network-based attacks are as follows:

- **Man in the middle (MITM) attack**: MITM attacks involve intercepting and altering communication between two parties without their knowledge through spoofing. For example, an attacker intercepts communication between a user and a banking website, capturing login credentials. It results in data theft, unauthorized transactions, and compromised communication. A typical MITM attack is shown in the following figure:

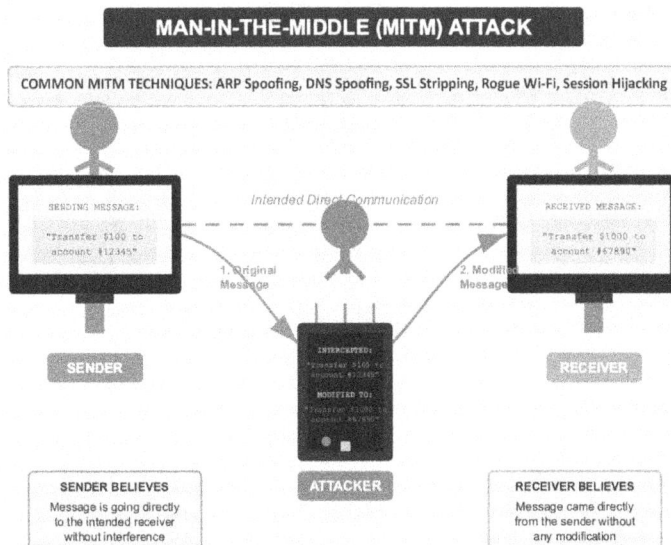

Figure 2.2: MITM attack in action

- **Sniffing attacks**: Sniffing involves capturing and analyzing network traffic to extract sensitive information. For example, an attacker uses a packet sniffer to capture unencrypted data transmitted over a network. It provides unauthorized access to sensitive information, such as passwords and personal data.

- **Eavesdropping**: Eavesdropping is a passive attack where the attacker listens to private communications aimed at getting sensitive information from the network. For example, an attacker intercepts VoIP calls to gather confidential information. It results in loss of privacy, exposure of sensitive information, and potential blackmail.

- **DDoS attack**: This involves overwhelming network devices to target hosts from multiple sources, making stopping difficult. For example, A botnet of compromised devices floods a website with traffic, causing it to go offline. It results in extended service outages, significant financial losses, and damage to brand reputation.

Application

The attackers target the software applications to disrupt the operations/services. This, again, has wider ramifications for information systems. Some of the application-based attacks can be as follows:

- **Buffer overflow**: These are the most common attacks exploiting the memory buffer to execute malicious codes. Buffer overflow attacks exploit vulnerabilities in software to execute arbitrary code. For example, an attacker sends a specially crafted input to a vulnerable application, causing it to execute malicious code. This results in unauthorized access, data corruption, and system crashes.

- **SQL injection**: SQL injection involves inserting malicious SQL code into a query in web applications to manipulate data in a database. For example, an attacker inputs a malicious SQL statement into a web form, gaining access to the database. It results in data theft, unauthorized data manipulation, and potential data loss.

- **Cross-site scripting (XSS)**: XSS attacks inject malicious scripts into web pages viewed by other users to compromise their sessions. For example, an attacker injects a script into a comment section, which executes when other users view the page. It leads to session hijacking, data theft, and unauthorized actions on behalf of the user.

- **API attacks**: API attacks exploit vulnerabilities in application programming interfaces to gain unauthorized access. For example, an attacker exploits a poorly secured API to access and manipulate data in a web application. It results in data breaches, unauthorized transactions, and service disruption.

Understanding these attack vectors can help implement corresponding security measures. These categories are not sacrosanct. Oftentimes, attackers combine different types of attacks to target individuals or organizations. The mitigation can be regular patch management, reducing the attack surface as much as possible, segmenting the network, encrypting the data, and implementing firewalls, intrusion detection/prevention systems, secure coding practices, regular security testing, and user awareness.

Consequences of neglecting cybersecurity

Cyberattacks cannot be seen in isolation. It has larger connotations in terms of exposing the vulnerabilities for a larger hacker community to exploit. The hackers have already found vulnerabilities, which are attacked to impact routine functioning. After the attacks, a larger hacker community started phishing campaigns to further increase their attack surface under the disguise of providing a resolution to the threats. There are instances of impersonation, trying to trick enterprises and individuals into finding solutions. With such a diverse aftermath, the consequences are phenomenal.

Impact on economy

The impact of cybersecurity on economy is reflection on business stability, viability and continued business operations. As per estimates, the total impact of cyber-crimes in 2023 is estimated to be a staggering $8 trillion, much higher than some of the largest national economies. The average cost of a data breach in 2024 was $4.88 million. Business email compromises alone accounted for over $2.9 billion in losses in 2023.

In a recent incident in 2024, there was a simple security incident involving a CrowdStrike. It claimed not to be a cyberattack but only a simple update issue. However, it resulted in **blue screen of death (BSOD)**, affecting almost 8 million Windows devices and causing considerable disruption in the aviation, healthcare, public transit, financial services, and broadcasting industries. The economic impact of these disruptions is estimated to be approximately $6 billion in direct financial losses.

The financial industry faces exceptional exposure to cyber threats, with almost 20% of all cyber incidents targeting financial institutions. For instance, in 2023, a ransomware attack on a cloud-based IT service provider resulted in outages across 60 credit unions in the United States.

With these ever-increasing, dynamic, and sophisticated challenges, even government authorities are putting stringent compliance requirements in place. Some stringent data privacy regulations enacted by governments include the **Health Insurance Portability and Accountability Act (HIPPA)** United States and the **General Data Protection Regulation (GDPR)** Europe. Be it HIPPA or GDPR, compliance requirements put a substantial burden on the economic front for enterprises and individuals alike. Cyberattacks disrupting essential services like payment networks can have a profound impact on economic activities. A notable example is the December 2024 attack on the *Central Bank of Lesotho*, which halted the national payment system and impeded transactions for domestic banks.

There are solutions that can be integrated into business operations or personal computers. Though it is difficult to assess the exact economic impact, the broad factors contributing to the financial impacts of cyberattacks can be as follows (Not limited to):

- Having backups and disaster recovery plans for business continuity.

- Implementing Security measures to stop or prevent cyberattacks, be it endpoint, network devices, access control measures, or encryption costs.

- Training and awareness costs.

- Regulatory compliance costs involving periodic audits by third parties or periodic audits of service providers

- Employment of skilled cybersecurity professionals

As can be seen, cybersecurity is no longer a technical issue. It has a larger economic angle. The positive and negative impacts of cybersecurity on the economy are covered in the following table:

Positive impacts	Negative impacts
With strong posturing, economic growth is achieved to extract the benefits of digital transformation.	Financial losses, as covered previously, are significant economic burdens.
The cybersecurity industry itself contributes to job growth.	Critical infrastructure operations are impacted, resulting in issues in production and supply chain.
Strong security measures increase Consumer confidence, resulting in increased business.	Cyberattacks reduce investor confidence, resulting in a loss in business.
Ensures data protection from intentional or malicious threats/breaches.	Insurance costs can be higher, owing to the associated risks involved.
Ensure resilience through cyber measures for business continuity and disaster recovery plans.	It can give a false sense of security through adopted measures overlooking other risk management parameters.
Facilitates remote work and innovative workflows to improve business.	Integration of disparate security solutions with existing systems, with skilled manpower, is a big economic burden

Table 2.1: Impacts of cybersecurity on the economy

Conclusion

Cybersecurity has a profound economic impact, be it positive or negative. Cyberattacks do not distinguish between an individual and an enterprise. In fact, through the weakest human link, enterprises can become vulnerable. Knowing the implications and ramifications can substantially enhance overall awareness. This will foster collective willpower to strengthen the cyber posture to negate the adverse impacts of cyberattacks and, at the same time, be resilient enough to rise if attacked.

In the upcoming chapter, we delve into the fascinating history and evolution of SOCs, exploring their transformative journey in safeguarding organizations. As cyber threats have grown in complexity, SOCs have become the nerve center of cybersecurity, adapting to an ever-changing landscape of vulnerabilities and attack techniques. Understanding how security operations have evolved from addressing isolated incidents to managing sophisticated, multi-vector attacks provides valuable insights into the capabilities and strategies that SOCs employ today.

Points to remember

- Knowing the ramifications and implications of potential or impending cyberattacks is primary to building defenses. Thereafter, creating a safe strategy to avoid the threats must be followed up to ensure effective responses.

- Cybersecurity impacts individuals and enterprises alike. varying degrees, the underlying issues are similar. Cyberattacks impact people, processes, and technology.

- The targets of the cyberattacks can be host, network or application based. It is important for all to understand the economic impacts of these kinds of cyberattacks.

Multiple choice questions

1. **Cybersecurity domains involve protecting the intellectual property rights of an organization.**

    a. True

    b. False

2. **DoS attacks are aimed at:**

    a. Applications

    b. Network

    c. Host

    d. None of the above

3. **Application-based attacks do not include:**

    a. CSS

    b. DoS/DDoS

    c. SQL injection

    d. API attacks

4. **IAM is part of asset security:**

    a. True

    b. False

Answers

1	a
2	c
3	b
4	b

Questions

1. What are the impacts of cybersecurity on individuals and enterprises?

2. Explain different cybersecurity domains in brief.

3. Explain the economic fallout of cyberattacks.

Key terms

- **Data privacy and protection**: Applicable for individuals and enterprises.

- **Identity and access management**: Important for Zero Trust network access.

- **GRC management**: Key to compliance management.

Join our Discord space

Join our Discord workspace for latest updates, offers, tech happenings around the world, new releases, and sessions with the authors:

https://discord.bpbonline.com

CHAPTER 3
Evolution of Security Operations Centers

Introduction

It is worthwhile to know the evolution of security operations as it will give the right perspective in handling cyberattacks. This chapter starts with the history of security operations and how the **security operations center** (**SOC**) has evolved till now. Initially, the network was evolving, and security was considered as an afterthought. The primary aim was to get connected over larger distances and collaborate. However, when information and communication technologies evolved and converged, the explosion of data and its potential misuse became easy. Initially, the attack surface was limited to wired networks / simple wireless networks. Monitoring cyberattacks and mitigating them was relatively easy.

However, with optical technology maturing, the evolution of wireless technologies like Bluetooth and 5/6G has brought in a paradigm shift in the IoE/IoT, leading to Industry 4.0/5.0. Advanced technologies like AI and big data analytics, along with their reach to the masses, have made data handling ubiquitous. This ever-changing attack surface needed dedicated security monitoring. Accordingly, methods of cyberattacks evolved, and the need to detect and protect from these cyberattacks also evolved. This chapter dwells on the historical perspectives and evolution of SOC. There have been challenges in the SOC due to the ever-evolving threat landscape. SOCs evolved with these dynamic requirements and the adoption of concepts like the zero-trust philosophy. The efforts were bolstered with automation in the incident reporting, handling, and mitigation processes.

Structure

In this chapter, we will discuss the following topics:

- Historical perspectives
- Evolution of SOC
- SOC challenges
- Threat landscape
- Zero Trust philosophy
- Automation journey

Objectives

By the end of this chapter, you will know the historical perspectives and evolution of security operations. This chapter will give a clear understanding of various challenges encountered in security incidents handling, the evolving practical threat landscape, and how the SOCs have transformed to be modern proactive defense mechanisms against ever-evolving cyber threats.

Historical perspectives

In the early days of computing, security was primarily focused on physical access controls to computer systems. The initial computers were large mainframes housed in secure rooms with limited access for academic research or sharing. The threat landscape was simplistic, often limited to insider threats such as unauthorized access by employees or physical theft of storage devices.

As organizations began to network their computer systems, the threat landscape expanded. The advent of the internet in the late 20th century brought new challenges, such as remote unauthorized access, viruses, and worms. This period saw the emergence of more formalized security practices. Firewalls, **intrusion detection systems (IDS)**, and antivirus programs became essential tools. During this time, the concept of a SOC began to take shape, albeit in a rudimentary form. Organizations started to realize the need for a centralized location to monitor and respond to security incidents.

Let us look at some practical instances from the early days of handling cybersecurity incidents. The *Morris Worm*, launched on November 2, 1988, marked a turning point in cybersecurity history. Created by *Robert Tappan Morris*, this worm exploited vulnerabilities in Unix systems and disrupted early internet networks. It emphasized the fragility of interconnected digital systems and spurred significant advancements in cybersecurity. In response to this, the U.S. government established the **Computer Emergency Response Team (CERT)** to address cybersecurity threats and foster coordinated responses. Organizations began adopting firewalls, strengthening password policies, and ensuring regular software updates to prevent similar issues. This incident was the first case prosecuted under the *Computer Fraud and Abuse Act*, reinforcing the need for legal frameworks to address cybercrimes.

It became clear that identifying and addressing vulnerabilities in advance is crucial. The event demonstrated the importance of organizations working together and sharing knowledge to counteract cyber threats. It also underscored the need to educate users and system administrators about best practices in cybersecurity. The *Morris Worm* was not only a disruptive event but also a catalyst for improving how cybersecurity is approached. It set the stage for developing modern practices and raised awareness about the evolving nature of digital threats.

The ILOVEYOU virus, also referred to as the *Love Bug*, surfaced on May 4, 2000, and is regarded as one of the most damaging malware outbreaks in history. Masquerading as a romantic email attachment, it spread at an alarming rate by exploiting weaknesses in Microsoft Outlook and Windows operating systems. Within a matter of days, millions of computers around the globe were compromised, with financial damages estimated at $10 billion. The virus infiltrated systems in various sectors, including government institutions such as the Pentagon and the UK Parliament, prompting temporary shutdowns of email systems. The costs of removing the virus, recovering corrupted data, and restoring systems were substantial, affecting operations and labor productivity. Files were overwritten and corrupted, leading to significant data loss for users and organizations alike.

In response to this, organizations adopted advanced filtering mechanisms to block harmful email attachments. The need to educate people about the risks of opening unknown email attachments became evident. Companies emphasized the importance of timely software updates to address system vulnerabilities. The virus, which originated in the *Philippines*, spurred the introduction of new legal measures to address and penalize cybercrimes. The ILOVEYOU virus served as a critical lesson in cybersecurity, underscoring the necessity of proactive measures and user awareness in countering digital threats. Its impact reshaped the global approach to securing networks and systems against evolving cyber risks.

Network operations center

Network professionals play a crucial role in maintaining the security of evolving computer networks. The foundation laid by these network technicians in handling security incidents paved the way for the modern SOC.

Physical security and access control

In the initial stages of computing, security operations were heavily focused on physical security. Computer systems were large, expensive, and often housed in dedicated rooms with restricted access. Network professionals were responsible for ensuring that only authorized personnel could access these systems. The measures included are as follows:

- **Secure facilities**: Computers were kept in locked rooms with limited access, often requiring physical keys or combinations to enter.

- **Personnel controls**: Strict protocols were in place to vet individuals who could access the computer systems, including background checks and role-based access.

- **Basic network security measures**: As networks began to form, albeit in very basic and isolated forms, the need for protecting data and communication channels became evident. Network professionals implemented rudimentary security measures such as:

- **Password protection**: Simple password schemes were used to control access to computer systems and sensitive data.

- **User authentication**: Basic authentication mechanisms ensure that users are who they claim to be before granting access to the network.

Early threat detection and response

During this period, the concept of real-time threat detection and response was still in its infancy. However, network professionals employ several strategies to identify and mitigate threats, such as:

- **Manual monitoring**: In the early days of SOC evolution, network professionals manually reviewed system logs to detect unusual activities by collecting and aggregating logs from various sources, searching for keywords or patterns with basic tools like grep, analyzing timelines, filtering routine entries, and documenting findings in notes or spreadsheets. However, they faced significant challenges: overwhelming data volumes, lack of contextual insights, time-intensive correlation across unsynchronized systems, reliance on individual expertise, reactive responses due to delayed detection, and difficulty identifying evolving threats that left subtle traces. These labor-intensive efforts highlighted the limitations of manual processes, paving the way for the automated, centralized systems that later defined modern SOC operations.

- **Incident response**: In the early days of SOCs, network professionals relied heavily on manual processes and technical expertise to investigate incidents, lacking today's advanced tools. For example, when a network faced a DDoS attack, analysts used raw packet captures from tools like tcpdump to identify floods of ICMP or SYN packets overwhelming servers. With no SIEM or automated correlation, they manually inspected router logs and traffic patterns to pinpoint spoofed IP sources, then applied basic firewall rules or coordinated with ISPs to block the traffic, remedying the issue through hands-on configuration. Similarly, during a suspected data breach, professionals manually reviewed server access logs and used command-line tools to trace unusual outbound connections, identifying a compromised account leaking data via FTP. Their deep understanding of TCP/IP and protocol behavior helped them isolate the affected system, terminate the connection, and update passwords or patch vulnerabilities like outdated software. In this nascent SOC phase, before integrated systems like IDS or EDR, investigations hinged on analysts' ability to dissect packets and logs, driving remedies through direct network adjustments and laying the groundwork for the evolution toward automated, intelligence-driven SOCs.

- **Security policies and procedures**: As SOCs evolved, the establishment of formal security policies and procedures became pivotal in safeguarding computing resources. Network professionals played a key role in defining these policies, such as implementing access control measures, password policies, and guidelines for handling sensitive data. They enforced compliance through regular audits and monitoring tools, ensuring adherence to standards like ISO 27001 or NIST frameworks. For example, they developed incident response protocols to address cyberattacks swiftly, including steps for detecting, reporting, and mitigating threats. Practical initiatives like restricting access to critical systems via role-based permissions and instituting mandatory security training for employees demonstrated their proactive approach to fortifying organizational security. These efforts laid the foundation for robust and scalable SOC operations.

- **Operational guidelines**: To ensure the efficient operation and maintenance of computer systems, clear guidelines were established that encompassed both technical and security protocols. These guidelines included comprehensive documentation on system configurations, software updates, and routine maintenance schedules to prevent system vulnerabilities. Security protocols outlined processes, such as regular patch management, endpoint protection measures, and backup strategies to safeguard critical data. For instance, administrators were instructed to follow **standard operating procedures** (**SOPs**) for applying security updates, conducting vulnerability assessments, and monitoring for unauthorized access. Training materials were developed to educate staff on adhering to these protocols and recognizing potential threats. Such structured practices not only streamlined system operations but also reinforced the organization's ability to detect and respond to emerging cybersecurity challenges effectively.

- **Training and awareness**: Significant efforts were directed toward educating users about fundamental security practices to build a robust defense against threats. Training programs emphasized the importance of not sharing passwords, creating strong, unique credentials, and regularly updating them to prevent unauthorized access. Awareness campaigns focused on teaching users to identify potential security threats, such as phishing emails, unfamiliar links, and suspicious attachments. Organizations distributed brochures, guidelines, and checklists to provide users with practical tips for safeguarding their accounts and devices. Additionally, in-person sessions and early forms of simulated exercises, like mock phishing attempts, were conducted to test users' understanding and vigilance. These proactive measures laid the groundwork for fostering a security-conscious culture, even when the cybersecurity landscape was in its infancy.

Evolution of network security tools

The development and deployment of network security tools started during this era. While primitive compared to today's standards, the following tools were essential in protecting early networks:

- **Access control lists (ACLs)**: Basic ACLs were used to control which users could access specific resources on the network.

- **Firewalls**: Early firewalls, both hardware and software, began to be used to filter traffic and protect networks from unauthorized access.

The early days of computing laid the groundwork for modern security operations. Network professionals during this time were tasked with protecting valuable and often experimental computing resources in a rapidly evolving technological landscape. Their focus on physical security, basic network protections, and the development of security policies established the foundations upon which today's sophisticated cybersecurity strategies are built. Despite the relatively primitive tools and techniques available to them, these pioneers played a crucial role in shaping the future of network security.

Security operations center

The modern SOC began to emerge in the early 2000s, driven by several key factors, such as the following:

- **Increasing cyber threats**: The frequency, sophistication, and impact of cyberattacks grew exponentially. High-profile incidents, such as the *Morris Worm* in 1988 and the ILOVEYOU virus in 2000, highlighted the need for robust cybersecurity measures.

- **Regulatory requirements**: Regulations such as the **Sarbanes-Oxley Act (SOX)**, **Health Insurance Portability and Accountability Act (HIPAA)**, and later the **General Data Protection Regulation (GDPR)** mandated stringent security controls and incident response capabilities.

- **Technological advancements**: The development of advanced SIEM systems enabled better collection, correlation, and analysis of security data, making it possible to detect and respond to incidents in real time.

Evolution of security operations center

In the realm of cybersecurity, security operations have evolved over a period of time. Security was an afterthought in the network implementation. The whole idea of networking was to collaborate and share resources, especially among academic and research institutes. Since DARPA was involved in the network design, some security was envisioned. Initially, these security operations were basic and reactive only. With the changing technology landscape, SOCs have also transformed into proactive defense mechanisms. Now, these SOC have emerged as a centralized facility for monitoring, detecting, and responding to enormous cyber threats.

Focusing on confidentiality

In earlier days, managing security was a relatively simple affair. The interconnection between the two locations was through physical cables. These cables also evolved from coaxial to underground copper cables to unshielded/shielded twisted pairs to optical fibers. These networks were terminated in a networking device, typically a switch or firewall. With satellite communication and radio communication, wireless communication started evolving as an overlay network for backup communication.

However, these were also terminated over the same networking devices. In this scenario, the information technology staff, often not trained in security, handled security incidents as they happened. The focus was reactive only and never aimed at preventing them. A sample computing environment is shown in the following figure:

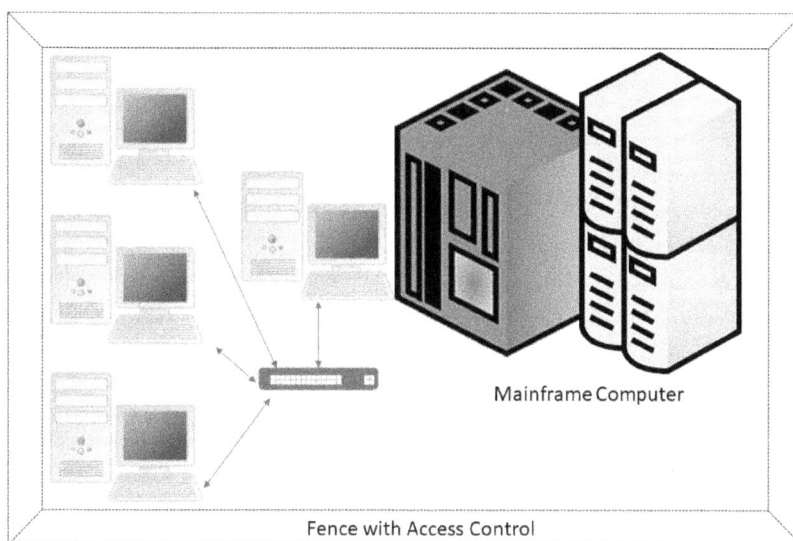

Mainframe Computer

Fence with Access Control

Figure 3.1: *Early computing environment*

Focusing on integrity

Organizations often employ physical security measures to prevent physical access to networking devices. As the threats of viruses and malware dawned, basic anti-virus software was deployed to protect their information systems. Then, the networking domain brought in a paradigm shift in interconnection, and the networks started converging. Mobile technology, Bluetooth, and enhancements in radio and satellite communication have made the networks complex. The convergence of networks into the World Wide Web paved the way for an increased threat landscape with a much larger attack surface. A typical networked environment with wired and wireless networks converging is shown in the following figure. The attack surface has increased manifold, and the possibility of hackers attacking from anywhere on the internet has become possible.

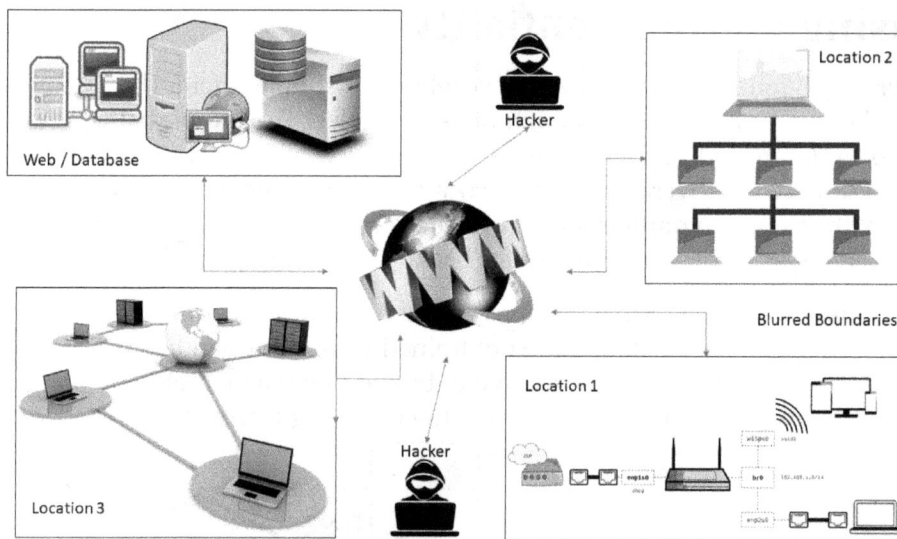

Figure 3.2: Networked computing environment

Cybercriminals started exploiting the vulnerabilities in software and associated networking systems. Targeted attacks were possible given the interconnectivity of organizations over the internet. Threats like MITM attacks and impersonation resulted in integrity issues. To counter these threats, organizations started deploying their specialized teams to monitor their networking infrastructure and respond to the incidents to maintain data integrity. These teams laid the foundation for modern-day security operations.

The focus shifted from organizations and personal computing to social media. People started sharing their personal information, including their passwords and other sensitive personal information. It was then easy for cyber hackers to exploit this easily available information to target individuals and their organizations through social engineering attacks.

Establishing SIEM systems was felt to be necessary. These centralized platforms provided a much-needed view of the organization's assets, enabling teams to monitor security events and respond to them in real time. With improvements in SIEM, SOCs evolved, becoming capable of detecting and responding to a wider range of cyberattacks.

Cloud or IoT

Thereafter, another paradigm shift happened with the emergence of cloud computing. The local information systems infrastructure shifted to the cloud, be it networking devices, computing, or storage. This cloud adoption introduced new vulnerabilities and attack surfaces. The onset of the IoT with connection-oriented sensors added another level of complexity to the attack surface. SOCs evolved to mitigate the threats from such diverse attack surfaces by adopting their capabilities to protect against emerging threats.

The convergence of information and communication technologies, increased bandwidth handling capabilities, and the emergence of 5G/6G and IoT/IoE facilitated data generation and storage. This also facilitated mobile applications for easy data access. The complex-converged network is shown in the following figure:

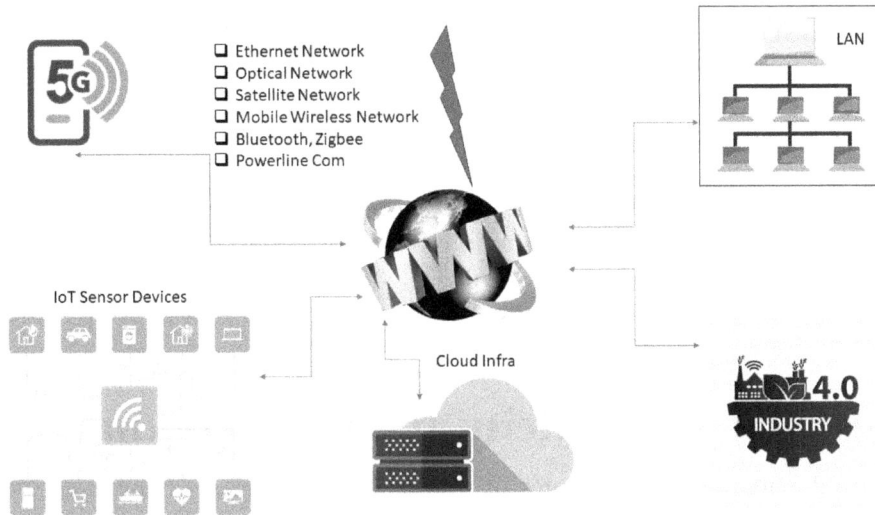

Figure 3.3: Converged computing environment

In this converged network, the integration of disparate technologies like ethernet, optical, satellite communication networks, mobile wireless networks, Bluetooth, IoT, Industry4.0, etc., has increased the attack surface manifold. At the same time, hacking from a simple device anywhere on the internet became possible. Sensitive personal information and organizational confidential information started flowing as data through this complex web of networks. The ease of access to these sensitive data made it vulnerable for cyber attackers to exploit the weak areas. This necessitated the development of advanced analytics and automation tools to help SOC analysts make sense of the events and identify potential threats to build effective defenses.

Emerging technologies

Cyber threats continue to evolve, and SOC has to adapt to remain effective. In the future, greater emphasis will be on proactive threat hunting, automation, and providing an integrated, holistic security handling capability to organizations or individuals. SOCs will have to handle emerging technologies like AI and ML, blockchain, and quantum computing, introducing new vulnerabilities and attack vectors.

With the rise of **advanced persistent threats** (**APT**) and more sophisticated cyberattack, the need for more robust security frameworks became evident. SOCs started integrating intrusion detection/prevention systems with advanced threat intelligence gathering/ analysis tools.

Focus on availability

SOC has undergone a remarkable transformation over the years. It has changed from a simple reactive mechanism to a sophisticated and proactive defensive mechanism. Adapting to the ever-changing threat landscape is essential in protecting organizations from cyberattacks. As the technologies are evolving, so are the cyberattacks. Business continuity is paramount in such a dynamic, complex threat environment. Even a slight disruption in the availability of services has a huge impact on the financial viability of the business. Accordingly, the focus was also required on availability, apart from confidentiality and integrity. Having multiple backups and redundancy in every computing domain, networking has brought in additional attack surfaces to defend. The syncing requirements amongst multiple disaster recovery options added to the complexities of managing security for data at rest and data in transit. The monitoring of all redundancy/recovery options and ensuring their security through SOCs will remain a critical component in any cybersecurity strategy.

Focusing on authenticity and non-repudiation

The CIA triad remained at the center of cybersecurity measures. However, with ever-changing TTPs by cyber attackers, ensuring the legitimacy and integrity of data transmission became essential for maintaining robust cybersecurity.

Authenticity involves verifying the source or origin of data to ensure that it has not been tampered with during transmission. Various authentication mechanisms like login credentials, biometric data, digital signatures, and multi-factor authentication are employed to improve security operations. Continuously monitoring these aspects through SOC became inescapable.

Non-repudiation ensures that once an entity sends a message or completes a transaction, it cannot deny having done so. This is ensured through digital signatures, timestamping, and secure audit trails. As SOCs have evolved, the focus on authenticity and non-repudiation has become more pronounced. With this additional focus, SOCs can significantly improve their ability to detect, prevent, and respond to cyber threats, ensuring the security and integrity of data. As SOCs have evolved, modern security operations leverage advanced technologies such as AI and ML. SOCs started using AI to detect anomalies and enhance authentication processes, implement automated systems to ensure that all transactions are logged and verified, and utilize sophisticated tools to identify and respond to threats in real time. The overall evolution of SOCs is depicted in the following figure:

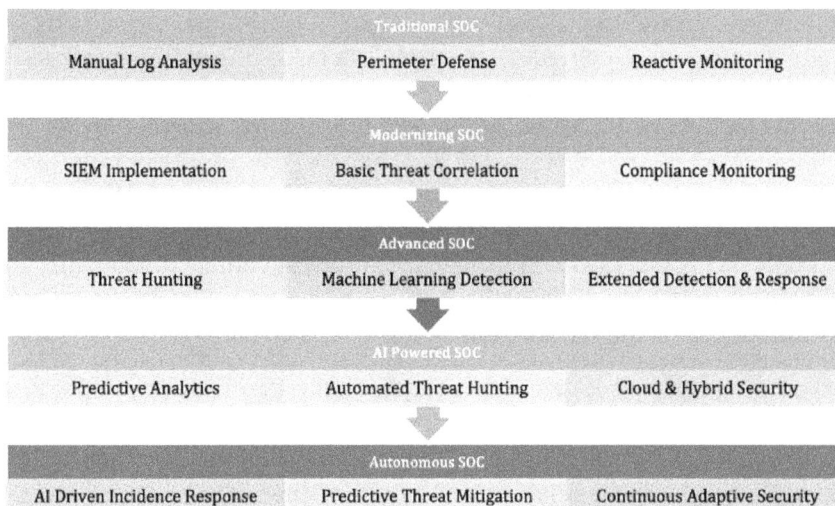

Figure 3.4: *Evolution of SOC*

The preceding figure illustrates how SOCs have transformed from reactive, manual security monitoring to proactive, intelligent, and autonomous defense systems. Progression highlights the increasing complexity, technological sophistication, and strategic importance of security operations in protecting modern digital infrastructures. Let us understand the SOC implementations in various industries to better understand its impacts and relevance.

In the high-stakes world of **finance**, cyber threats are not just an inconvenience; they are a constant danger that can erode trust and jeopardize livelihoods. One prominent example is a major bank that faced an increasing number of phishing attacks and attempts at unauthorized access by cybercriminals eager to exploit sensitive financial data. To safeguard its operations, the bank established a cutting-edge SOC. Equipped with advanced threat detection capabilities, the SOC acted as the bank's vigilant guardian, analyzing millions of data points daily for suspicious activity. When a coordinated phishing campaign targeted the bank's employees, the SOC swiftly identified the threat, isolated affected systems, and launched a comprehensive response plan. The attackers' attempt was thwarted, protecting customer accounts and the bank's reputation from potential disaster.

The impact of this SOC implementation was transformative. Threats that once loomed large were now caught in the early stages, reducing the chances of any escalation. Faster response times meant potential breaches were mitigated before they could wreak havoc, ensuring seamless business continuity. Moreover, the SOC's meticulous documentation of incidents and proactive compliance measures helped the bank meet stringent regulatory standards effortlessly. With its newfound resilience, the institution not only safeguarded its digital fortress but also won back the trust of its customers in an era of mounting cyber risks. This illustrates why a robust SOC is not just an operational enhancement, it is an essential pillar for building confidence in the financial industry.

In an era where **healthcare** increasingly relies on digital systems, the security of sensitive patient data is paramount. One notable example is a large hospital network that grappled with escalating cyber threats, including ransomware attacks targeting **electronic health records** (**EHR**). Determined to shield its operations and protect patient privacy, the network implemented a state-of-the-art SOC. The SOC continuously monitored network activity, leveraging AI-driven tools to identify and neutralize threats. When a ransomware attack attempted to lock down the EHR system, the SOC's swift action contained the breach, restored encrypted files using backups, and prevented further disruption. This proactive approach not only thwarted attackers but also maintained critical access to patient information, ensuring timely medical care.

The impact of the SOC was transformative. According to industry reports, healthcare data breaches cost organizations an average of $10.1 million annually, highlighting the importance of robust defences. The SOC reduced the hospital network's vulnerability, ensuring compliance with regulatory frameworks like HIPAA. Moreover, its rapid response capabilities minimized downtime, enabling uninterrupted patient services, a vital consideration in life-and-death scenarios. By securing patient data and fortifying its digital infrastructure, the organization reaffirmed trust among patients, demonstrating that privacy and continuity in care go hand in hand in today's interconnected world. This underscores the indispensable role of SOCs in safeguarding the heart of healthcare.

In the **manufacturing** sector, where precision and efficiency are paramount, the rise of connected devices has brought both opportunities and risks. A prominent example is a global manufacturing company that faced challenges in securing its IoT devices and **industrial control systems** (**ICS**), which manage everything from robotic assembly lines to energy consumption. With vulnerabilities like outdated firmware and insecure network configurations exposing critical systems, the company established a dedicated SOC. The SOC continuously monitored these devices, identifying anomalies like unauthorized access attempts or unusual network traffic. When a vulnerability in an IoT sensor allowed hackers to attempt remote control of a production line, the SOC promptly detected the breach, isolated the compromised devices, and applied patches to prevent future attacks, avoiding what could have been a major disruption to production schedules.

The value of this SOC implementation was evident in its ability to prevent costly downtime and protect vital infrastructure. According to research, unplanned downtime can cost manufacturers up to $260,000 per hour, underscoring the importance of proactive security measures. The SOC's real-time monitoring reduced the likelihood of disruptions and increased operational resilience, ensuring smooth production processes. Additionally, by securing sensitive ICS, the company met global compliance standards like ISO/IEC 27001, enhancing trust among partners and customers. This success highlights the crucial role SOCs play in defending the backbone of modern manufacturing against evolving cyber threats, enabling companies to thrive in an increasingly interconnected industry.

In the rapidly growing **e-commerce** landscape, a major retail company faced mounting cyber threats targeting its online platform, including payment fraud and attempts to steal customer data. To combat these challenges, the company implemented a sophisticated SOC to monitor and protect its digital infrastructure around the clock. The SOC utilized machine learning algorithms to analyze transaction patterns, quickly identifying anomalies such as fraudulent purchases and unauthorized account access. When a coordinated attempt was made to exploit a vulnerability in the payment gateway, the SOC's immediate response neutralized the threat, safeguarding not only the company's financial assets but also sensitive customer information. This vigilance not only averted potential monetary losses but also upheld the retailer's promise of secure shopping.

The implementation of the SOC delivered tangible benefits to the company's operations and reputation. Statistics reveal that the global cost of online payment fraud is expected to exceed $40 billion by 2027, demonstrating the critical need for robust cybersecurity measures in retail. By preventing breaches and securing online transactions, the SOC helped maintain customer trust, a cornerstone of e-commerce success. Moreover, the streamlined threat response minimized disruptions, allowing the business to operate without interruption during peak shopping seasons. This example highlights the indispensable role of SOCs in securing the retail industry, ensuring that customers can shop with confidence while businesses thrive in an increasingly digital marketplace.

SOC challenges

It is evident from the evolution of SOC that the threat landscape is evolving at a much faster pace than envisaged. The complex web of information and communication technologies poses significant challenges for SOC analysts to sift through the incidents and prepare defenses in real-time. It is important to understand the challenges for developing strategies for protection against evolving cyberattacks and enhancing the cyber posture. The challenges being encountered by SOCs are as follows:

- **The increasing complexity of the IT environment**: The modern IT infrastructure is highly complex and dynamic in nature. On-premises infrastructure may include servers, desktops/laptops, storage, networking devices, firewalls, intrusion detection/prevention systems, biometric access control systems, and CCTV surveillance systems. Application-level security monitoring, DLP, backup, and encryption add an additional level of complexity. The inclusion of cloud computing adds another level of complexity to security operations monitoring.

- The diverse digital resources belong to one enterprise/entity. However, in this hyper-connected world, supply chain management risk handling entails monitoring the IT environments of third parties as well, adding to the complexities of cyber incident handling.

- **Increasing volume, velocity**: The sheer volume of data, logs, and alerts generated by diverse IT environments can overwhelm any SOC analyst. The alert fatigue can overpower real threats. Also, the velocity with which these alerts are generated is very high, making it complex for timely responses, especially in handling zero day attacks.

- **Increasing complexity of threats**: SOCs must deal with sophisticated and evolving threats such as zero-day vulnerabilities, APTs and social engineering attacks. These threats are often difficult to detect and mitigate due to their complexity and the lack of known solutions at the time of discovery.

- **Cybersecurity skill shortage**: There is an acute shortage of qualified cybersecurity professionals. It is extremely difficult to find and retain experienced analysts, incident responders, and threat hunters. This shortage adversely impacts the effectiveness of a SOC.

- **Integration issues**: Many organizations use a variety of security tools, and these tools often do not communicate well with each other. This lack of integration can make it difficult to correlate information and respond to threats effectively. Considering the diverse threat sources, SOCs may lack comprehensive threat intelligence, including **indicators of compromise (IOCs)**, which can make it difficult to detect and respond to threats in a timely manner.

- **Insufficient authority**: There is always a dichotomy in operations and security. Oftentimes, operations toward business continuance take precedence over security measures. SOCs may lack the authority to implement necessary changes or enforce security policies, which can hinder their ability to respond effectively to threats. SOCs can only monitor and respond; the actual mitigation measures in networking devices, servers, and endpoints need to be ensured by separate IT staff, which may delay the response mechanism.

- **Privacy issues**: Balancing the need for security with privacy concerns is another challenge, especially when organizations rely on data and collect and analyze more user data to detect threats.

Addressing these challenges requires a combination of advanced technologies, skilled personnel, and strategic planning. By focusing on these areas, SOCs can enhance their ability to detect, prevent, and respond to cyber threats, ensuring the security and integrity of organizational data.

Threat landscape

In *Chapter 1, Cybersecurity Basics* and *Chapter 2, Cybersecurity Ramifications and Implications*, we have briefly discussed the threat landscape and various cyber threats encountered by people, processes, and technology. The threat landscape is constantly evolving. Every day, new challenges are presented to cybersecurity professionals, requiring them to adapt continuously. The evolution of the threat landscape has significantly impacted the operations of SOCs. Here are some practical use cases that illustrate how SOCs have adapted to these changes:

- **APTs**: A large financial institution detected unusual network traffic indicating a potential APT. The SOC team used advanced threat intelligence and behavioral analytics to identify the source and nature of the attack. By correlating this information with known APT patterns, they could isolate the compromised systems, prevent data exfiltration, and initiate a thorough investigation to remove the threat.

- **Ransomware attacks**: A healthcare organization faced a ransomware attack that encrypted critical patient data. The SOC team quickly activated their incident response plan, isolating affected systems to prevent the spread of the ransomware. They used backup data to restore services and implemented additional security measures to prevent future attacks. The team also conducted a forensic analysis to understand the attack vectors and improve their defenses.

- **Phishing and social engineering**: An e-commerce company experienced a phishing attack targeting employees. The SOC team conducted a security awareness training session to educate employees on recognizing phishing attempts. They also implemented email filtering solutions to detect and block phishing emails, reducing the risk of successful attacks.

- **IoT vulnerabilities**: A manufacturing company discovered vulnerabilities in their IoT devices. The SOC team conducted a vulnerability assessment and implemented security patches to address the issues. They also established continuous monitoring of IoT devices to detect and respond to any suspicious activities promptly.

- **Cloud security**: A software development company migrated its infrastructure to the cloud. The SOC team implemented cloud security best practices, such as configuring access controls, enabling encryption, and monitoring cloud environments for unusual activities. They also integrated cloud security tools with their existing SOC infrastructure to ensure comprehensive coverage.

- **Zero-day exploits**: A technology firm identified a zero-day exploit in one of its applications. The SOC team worked closely with the software vendor to develop and deploy a patch. In the meantime, they implemented additional security controls to mitigate the risk and monitored the network for any signs of exploitation.

- **Supply chain attacks**: A retail company discovered that one of its third-party vendors was compromised in a supply chain attack. The SOC team conducted a thorough review of all vendor connections and implemented stricter security controls for third-party integrations. They also established a continuous monitoring process to detect any future supply chain vulnerabilities.

- **Insider threats**: An organization detected suspicious behavior from an employee accessing sensitive data. The SOC team conducted an investigation, which revealed that the employee was attempting to exfiltrate data. They immediately revoked the employee's access, secured the affected systems, and implemented stricter access controls to prevent similar incidents in the future.

The evolving threat landscape has necessitated continuous adaptation and improvement in SOC operations. By leveraging advanced technologies, threat intelligence, and proactive security measures, SOCs can effectively anticipate threats based on global threat data and trends and detect, respond to, and mitigate a wide range of cyber threats, ensuring the protection of organizational assets and maintaining business continuity.

Zero Trust philosophy

The Zero Trust philosophy fundamentally changed the approach to cybersecurity. The core principle of Zero Trust is *Never trust, always verify*. This means that no user or device, whether inside or outside the network, is automatically trusted. Instead, every access request must be authenticated, authorized, and encrypted. Some of the key milestones in the evolution of Zero Trust philosophy are as follows:

- **BeyondCorp Initiative (2010)**: Google's BeyondCorp initiative was one of the first implementations of Zero Trust principles. It aimed to secure access to resources based on identity and context, moving away from the traditional perimeter-based security model.

- **Adoption by Industry (2010s)**: Over the years, the Zero Trust model gained traction across various industries as organizations recognized its effectiveness in protecting against both internal and external threats.

- **Zero Trust eXtended (ZTX) framework**: This framework expanded the principles of Zero Trust to include data, workloads, and identity, providing a more comprehensive approach to security.

The adoption of Zero Trust has had a profound impact on the operations of SOCs. Here are some key ways in which Zero Trust has influenced SOC practices:

- It provides enhanced security posture through the following means:
  - **Continuous verification**: SOCs now implement continuous verification processes, ensuring that every access request is authenticated and authorized in real-time.
  - **Micro-segmentation**: By segmenting networks into smaller, isolated segments, SOCs can limit the spread of threats and reduce the attack surface.
- It aids in improved threat detection and response due to the following factors:
  - **Visibility and monitoring**: Zero Trust requires comprehensive visibility into network activities, allowing SOCs to detect anomalies and respond to threats more quickly.
  - **Automated security controls**: Integrating automated security controls helps SOCs respond to incidents faster and more effectively.
- It enhances user and device security through the following measures:
  - **Least privilege access**: Implementing the principle of least privilege ensures that users and devices have only the access necessary to perform their tasks, reducing the risk of unauthorized access.

   o **Identity-based security**: Emphasizing identity-based security measures helps SOCs to verify the identity of users and devices before granting access.

- It ensures compliance to regulatory requirements through following means:

   o **Data protection**: Zero Trust helps organizations meet regulatory requirements by protecting sensitive data through encryption and access controls.

   o **Audit and reporting**: Enhanced audit and reporting capabilities allow SOCs to demonstrate compliance with regulatory standards and provide transparency into security practices.

The adoption of Zero Trust principles will require SOCs to continuously verify all access requests, regardless of their origin, leading to more stringent and comprehensive monitoring. The evolution of the Zero Trust philosophy has significantly enhanced SOCs' security operations by promoting a proactive, adaptive, and comprehensive approach to cybersecurity. By continuously verifying access, segmenting networks, and implementing robust security controls, SOCs can better protect their organizations from a wide range of cyber threats.

Automation journey

The automation journey in SOCs has been transformative, significantly enhancing their efficiency and effectiveness in combating cyber threats. Here is an overview of how automation has evolved within SOCs:

- **Early days**: In the early days, SOCs relied heavily on manual processes. Security analysts manually monitored logs, detected anomalies, and responded to incidents. This approach was labor-intensive and often delayed threat detection and response.

- **Introduction of SIEM**: The implementation of security incident and event monitoring correlated multiple logs, identifying root causes, reduced the time to respond to incidents, and improved efficiency by automating routine monitoring tasks.

- **Introduction of SOAR**: The introduction of SOAR tools marked a significant milestone in SOC automation. SOAR platforms enabled security teams to automate repetitive tasks, orchestrate workflows, and respond to incidents more efficiently. This reduced the burden on analysts and allowed them to focus on more complex tasks. While SOAR brought many benefits, it had its limitations, particularly in handling the increasing volume and complexity of threats. This led to the adoption of hyper-automation, which integrates multiple automation tools and technologies to cover a broader range of security operations. Hyper-automation allows for seamless integration of various security tools and provides a more comprehensive approach to threat detection and response.

- **Integration of AI and ML**: The incorporation of AI and ML into SOC operations has been a game-changer. AI and ML algorithms can analyze vast amounts of security data, identify patterns, and detect threats with unprecedented speed and accuracy. This has significantly improved threat detection and response times, allowing SOCs to stay ahead of cybercriminals.

- **Integration of extended detection and response (XDR)**: The integration of XDR revolutionizes the automation journey of a SOC by unifying security tools, streamlining data analysis, and enabling faster threat detection and response. This holistic approach enhances efficiency, minimizes manual intervention, and strengthens an organization's security posture.

- **Integration of robotic process automation (RPA)**: The integration of RPA in a SOC's automation journey streamlines repetitive tasks such as alert triaging and incident reporting, allowing analysts to focus on higher-value activities. This approach enhances operational efficiency and accelerates threat response capabilities.

A comparison of these automation tools is as follows:

Automation tools	Prospective solutions	Benefits	Challenges
SIEM	Splunk, IBM QRadar, Wajuh.	Real-time threat detection, log correlation, and comprehensive visibility into network activities.	Managing false positives and integrating with other security tools.
SOAR	Palo Alto Networks Cortex XSOAR and Splunk Phantom.	Automated incident response, playbook execution, and streamlined workflows.	Complexity in setup and integration with existing SOC infrastructure.
XDR	CrowdStrike Falcon and Microsoft Defender	Unified threat detection across endpoints, networks, and cloud environments.	Ensuring comprehensive coverage and managing data from multiple sources.
RPA	UiPath and Automation Anywhere.	Automating repetitive tasks, reducing human error, and improving operational efficiency.	Limited applicability to complex security tasks and potential for automation errors.

Table 3.1: Automation tools in SOC

As in any other domain, automation in SOCs has brought significant improvements in handling threats and mitigating them. Some of the benefits are as follows:

- **Enhanced threat detection**: Automation enables continuous monitoring and real-time threat detection, reducing the time to identify and respond to incidents.

- **Efficiency and productivity**: By automating routine tasks, SOCs can operate more efficiently, allowing analysts to focus on strategic initiatives and complex investigations.

- **Reduction of alert fatigue**: Automation helps filter out false positives and prioritize genuine threats, reducing alert fatigue among security analysts.

- **Scalability**: Automated processes can be scaled to handle large volumes of data and a growing number of security events, ensuring that SOCs can keep pace with evolving threats.

The cybersecurity landscape has undergone a remarkable transformation, with automation playing a crucial role in enhancing the efficiency of SOCs. Picture a busy SOC where analysts face an overwhelming influx of alerts every day, each requiring immediate attention. This is where automation tools step in, turning disarray into streamlined processes as brought out as follows:

- **Real-time threat detection**: It is a cornerstone of effective SOC operations, with tools like XDR and **intrusion detection systems (IDS)** excelling in identifying threats swiftly. XDR integrates data from multiple sources, enabling faster detection and response, while IDS focuses on monitoring network traffic for anomalies. For instance, organizations leveraging XDR have reported a 40% reduction in detection times, allowing them to neutralize threats before escalation. These tools utilize AI-driven analytics to process vast amounts of data in milliseconds, ensuring that SOCs can stay ahead of increasingly sophisticated cyberattacks. The speed and precision of such technologies are vital in minimizing potential damage and maintaining operational continuity.

- **Automated incident response**: Incident response playbooks significantly enhance the speed and efficiency of managing security incidents by standardizing containment and remediation processes. These playbooks leverage predefined workflows to ensure swift action during events like ransomware attacks or data breaches. For instance, organizations using automated playbooks have reported a reduction in containment time by up to 90%, minimizing the impact on operations. By eliminating manual delays and enabling rapid decision-making, these tools help SOCs mitigate threats effectively, preserve business continuity, and uphold customer trust in an era of rising cyber risks.

- **Integration**: Effective SOC operations rely heavily on the seamless integration of automation tools with existing infrastructure, such as SIEM systems and other security solutions. Well-integrated tools streamline workflows, reduce complexity, and ensure a cohesive threat management approach. For example, companies adopting integrated frameworks have reported a 250% improvement in incident resolution efficiency. Equally critical is scalability, as automation tools must handle escalating data volumes and alert traffic without compromising performance. Studies indicate that scalable platforms enable organizations to process a 300% increase in alerts while maintaining accuracy and efficiency. Together, integration and scalability ensure that SOCs remain agile and resilient in an increasingly complex threat landscape.

- **User experience**: This is pivotal in optimizing SOC operations, as tools with intuitive interfaces and customizable dashboards enable analysts to perform their tasks with greater ease and efficiency. Simplified workflows and reduced learning curves help analysts adapt quickly, while vendor-provided support and training ensure sustained proficiency. Studies indicate that user-friendly tools can boost SOC analyst productivity by up to 30%, as they spend less time navigating complex systems and more time on critical threat analysis and response. A well-designed user experience not only enhances operational effectiveness but also reduces burnout, ensuring a more engaged and efficient SOC team.

The future of SOC automation lies in the continued integration of advanced technologies such as AI, ML, and hyper-automation. By leveraging automation, AI, and ML, SOCs can enhance their threat detection and response capabilities, improve efficiency, and better protect organizations from cyber threats. These technologies will enable SOCs to achieve machine-speed response times, enhance threat intelligence, and provide more proactive security measures. The automation journey in SOC evolution has been instrumental in transforming how security operations are conducted.

Conclusion

In the 21st century, the SOC evolved from a reactive to a proactive function. The evolution of SOC reflects the dynamic nature of the cybersecurity landscape. From the early days of basic physical security to today's sophisticated, proactive approaches, SOCs have continuously adapted to meet emerging threats and technological advancements. As organizations face new challenges, SOCs will remain critical in safeguarding digital assets and ensuring the resilience of business operations.

In the next chapter, we will start exploring the domains of SOCs. These specific domains, like asset management, continuous monitoring, and compliance management will give you a sense of SOC operations after going through the evolution.

Points to remember

Here are some key takeaways from this chapter:

- Knowing the evolution of security operations can significantly improve defense mechanisms.

- The pillars of confidentiality, integrity, availability, authenticity, and non-repudiation play a key role in SOC planning, operations, and defense mechanisms toward improving the security posture.

- Automation and orchestration of the workflows is the future of SOCs, along with AI and ML.

Multiple choice questions

1. **What was the primary focus of security operations in the early days of computing?**
   a. Network segmentation
   b. Physical security
   c. Cloud security
   d. Zero Trust architecture

2. **Which of the following significantly influenced the development of modern SOCs?**
   a. Rise of social media
   b. Increasing complexity and frequency of cyber threats
   c. Development of mobile applications
   d. Advent of computing

3. **What does the Zero Trust model emphasize?**
   a. Continuous verification of all access requests
   b. Trusting all internal network traffic
   c. Limiting access based on physical location
   d. Relying on traditional perimeter defenses

Answers

1	b
2	b
3	a

Questions

1. Explain how automation impacted SOC operations.
2. How does the Zero Trust philosophy impact the SOCs?
3. Explain the evolution of SOCs from the CIA perspective.

Key terms

Here are some key terms used in the chapter:

- **Zero Trust philosophy**: Applicable for ensuring security by not trusting and verifying always.

- **Automation**: Automating, hyper-automating the routine tasks to improve security incident responses.

Join our Discord space

Join our Discord workspace for latest updates, offers, tech happenings around the world, new releases, and sessions with the authors:

https://discord.bpbonline.com

CHAPTER 4
Domains of Security Operations Centers

Introduction

This chapter covers the domains of security operations. A clear understanding of these domains is essential to help prevent, respond, or recover from any cyberattacks. Each domain is critical for maintaining robust cybersecurity and ensuring effective incident response. This chapter also explores compliance management with various regulatory requirements. The effectiveness of security operations depends on many factors, which are evolving day by day. A preliminary understanding of some of the critical aspects of establishing a security operations center can be a great starting point in the mitigation journey.

Structure

In this chapter, we will discuss the following topics:

- Asset management
- Continuous monitoring
- Coordination amongst systems
- Recovery and remediation
- Root cause analysis
- Compliance management

Objectives

By the end of this chapter, you will be able to know the domains of the security operations center. The idea is to understand the nuances of these domains in establishing SOC practical aspects in integrating various systems in SOC and deriving meaningful insights into creating a robust cyber-safe environment.

Asset management

In today's converged digital landscape, organizations or individuals face disparate cyber threats that can compromise their sensitive data. To combat these threats effectively, a robust SOC is essential. At the heart of an efficient SOC lies a crucial domain: asset management.

Asset management involves the identification, classification, and continuous monitoring of all **Information and Communication Technology (ICT)** assets, including hardware, software, and networking devices. A comprehensive understanding of these ICT assets leads organizations/individuals to identify and mitigate potential vulnerabilities proactively. The asset visibility results in not only responding effectively to security incidents but also ensuring compliance with relevant regulations.

Asset management strategy offers significant benefits to organizations such as:

- It provides enhanced visibility into the ICT environment. The SOC teams can gain a clear picture of the organization's attack surface by knowing what assets exist, where they are located, and how they are configured. This visibility of all devices, systems, and applications enables SOC teams to prioritize security efforts, allocate resources effectively, and make informed decisions in threat mitigation.

- Asset management facilitates proactive threat detection. SOC teams can identify potential entry points for attackers before they are exploited by regularly scanning assets for vulnerabilities and misconfigurations. This allows for early detection and response to incidents. Such a proactive approach significantly reduces the risk of successful cyberattacks.

- Asset management is crucial for incident response and recovery. In the event of a security breach, having a comprehensive inventory of assets allows SOC teams to quickly identify compromised systems, contain the damage, and restore normal operations. This rapid response can minimize the impact of an incident and reduce financial losses.

- Asset management plays a vital role in regulatory compliance. In the present times of stringent regulations and privacy concerns, organizations can demonstrate compliance with these regulations and avoid costly penalties by maintaining accurate, up-to-date records of ICT assets and implementing appropriate security controls.

To effectively implement asset management, a comprehensive asset inventory must be created and maintained. This inventory must include detailed information about each asset, such as its location, owner, criticality, and vulnerabilities. There is a need to conduct regular reviews of the asset inventory to ensure accuracy and identify new assets. The asset management must be a centralized system wherein automation tools can be used for asset discovery, vulnerability scanning, and patch management. Regular vulnerability assessments must be conducted to identify and address security weaknesses and monitor assets for signs of compromise or unauthorized access. Assets must be classified based on their sensitivity and value to the organization. This classification with respect to confidentiality, integrity, and availability, helps prioritize security efforts and allocate resources accordingly. Based on these CIA aspects, the risk status of the assets can be deduced to measure the urgency of mitigation measures. From a compliance perspective, a robust change management process must be in place to ensure that changes to ICT assets are properly authorized and documented.

Asset management in action

Asset management involves inventory management, lifecycle management of ICT assets, and documentation for compliance requirements. The inventories of hardware, software and cloud resources must be maintained for any organization. The hardware inventory includes but is not limited to desktops, laptops, and major ICT accessories like HDD, keyboard, mouse, etc. switches, firewalls, racks, UPS, batteries, Biometric devices, CCTV and NVR/DVR, etc.

The software inventory includes but is not limited to operating systems, anti-virus, **endpoint detection and response (EDR)**/XDR solutions, office applications, productivity applications, Adobe, Visual Studio, Copilot Studio, etc. Cloud inventory includes, but is not limited to, vCPU, vRAM, vStorage, networking and cloud security solutions, load balancers, etc.

The asset inventory can be considered as model inventory for maintaining the asset information, be it hardware, software or cloud. The application can then be developed with this basic information. The significance covered in the tables clearly brings out the importance of the information required of the assets. This is crucial from SOC standpoint as this knowledge will substantially improve the awareness of SOC analysts to plan and implement measures to thwart any cyberattacks. This information must be maintained with granular details covered in the table, as it will serve various compliance and regulatory requirements.

A sample inventory list can include the following details as covered in *Table 4.1*:

Sl. No.	Column	Details covered	SOC and compliance significance
1	Name	Unique name	To identify the asset
2	Assignee	Who owns the asset	To know the responsibility
3	Asset type	Hardware, software, or cloud	To understand the potential threat
4	State	Whether the asset is running, stopped, active, terminated state or end of life/end of support/end of sale	To know the attack surface
5	Reference	Unique code	To identify with QR codes
6	Asset status	Whether in use, under repair, spare or retired	To know the present holding from attack surface perspective
7	Serial number	Unique number of OEM	To know the origin of the equipment OEM
8	Location	Where available, region in case of cloud	To ascertain impact on business operations
9	Hardware details	Processor, generation, RAM, HDD/SDD, GPU, etc.	To know the currency in market
10	Software details	Operating system, anti virus, other software applications installed	To know the vulnerabilities
11	Software versions	Unique number of OEM, for software whitelisting	To know the currency of the software asset from threat perspective
12	Network details	MAC address, IP address	To know the reachability
13	Previous assignee	Assignment trail	To track the responsibility
14	Purchased date	When procured	To manage the lifecycle of the asset
15	Due date	For renewal/upgrade/shutdown	To keep hardware/software up to date
16	Warranty	Whether on warranty or repair	To know third party involvement
17	Confidentiality rating	Rated 1,2,3 based on sensitivity of the assets	To monitor confidentiality of asset

Sl. No.	Column	Details covered	SOC and compliance significance
18	Integrity rating	Rated 1,2,3 based on possibility of disruptions in communication between the systems	To monitor integrity of asset
19	Availability rating	Rated 1,2,3 based on business continuity, disaster recovery options	To know the availability aspect of asset
20	Risk status	Low, medium, high	To plan for incident response based on CIA ratings

Table 4.1: *Asset inventory*

Having seen the inventory management aspects, let us see how these assets management impacts the security posture in some domains:

- **Automated asset discovery in financial services**: A financial institution implemented automated asset discovery tools to identify all hardware and software assets across its network. This approach replaced manual inventory processes, which were prone to errors and outdated information. The automated system provided real-time visibility into assets, including shadow IT and unauthorized devices, enabling the institution to address vulnerabilities proactively. Patch management compliance soared by 35%, and vulnerabilities were reduced by 40% in the first six months. This resulted in reduced risk of data breaches by identifying and securing unpatched systems, improved compliance with regulatory requirements, such as GDPR, PCI DSS and enhanced incident response capabilities by ensuring accurate asset information during investigations.

- **IoT asset management in healthcare**: A hospital deployed an IoT asset management solution to monitor connected medical devices, such as infusion pumps and patient monitors. The system tracked device usage, firmware versions, and network connectivity, ensuring that all devices were accounted for and operating securely. Firmware updates increased by 70%, and vulnerabilities associated with IoT devices dropped by 50%. This resulted in minimized risks associated with outdated firmware and unpatched vulnerabilities, strengthened defenses against cyberattacks targeting IoT devices and improved patient safety by ensuring reliable operation of critical medical equipment. As the healthcare sector faced a 123% increase in cyberattacks over the past five years, the hospital became a shining example of resilience and responsibility.

- **Cloud asset management in retail**: A retail company adopted a cloud-based asset management platform to oversee its digital assets, including e-commerce applications, customer databases, and marketing tools. The platform provided centralized control and automated updates for cloud resources. Unauthorized access attempts were reduced by 25%, and downtime caused by security incidents plummeted by 40%. This resulted in reduced exposure to threats by ensuring consistent security configurations across cloud environments, enhanced scalability and flexibility to adapt to evolving security needs and improved detection and mitigation of unauthorized access attempts. In an era where 43% of cyberattacks target small and medium businesses, this retailer proved that investing in asset management is investing in customer trust.

Asset management is a fundamental component of a robust SOC. Companies that implement robust asset management see a 29% reduction in security incidents and are 40% more likely to maintain regulatory compliance, according to industry studies. Organizations or individuals alike can significantly enhance their security posture, reduce the risks of cyberattacks, and protect valuable data and intellectual property by effectively managing ICT assets. As the threat landscape continues to evolve, investing in a strong asset management program is essential for organizations. You cannot secure what you don't know you have. Asset management illuminates the blind spots, empowering organizations to face the evolving threat landscape with confidence.

Continuous monitoring

In the ever-evolving field of cybersecurity, continuous monitoring is a cornerstone of effective SOCs. As organizations face an increasing number of sophisticated cyber threats, the ability to detect, analyze, and respond to security incidents in real-time is of paramount importance. Continuous monitoring not only enhances the security posture of an organization but also ensures that threats are identified and mitigated promptly.

Continuous monitoring within SOCs has a significant impact on overall cybersecurity strategy. The key benefits of continuous monitoring are as follows:

- **Early threat detection**: Continuous monitoring allows SOCs to identify potential security incidents as they occur rather than after the fact. This real-time detection is crucial for minimizing the impact of threats such as malware, ransomware, and unauthorized access. By identifying and addressing threats early, SOCs can prevent them from escalating into major security breaches.

- **Proactive security posture**: Rather than relying solely on reactive measures, continuous monitoring enables a proactive approach to cybersecurity. By continuously analyzing network traffic, user behavior, and system activities, SOCs can anticipate potential threats and take pre-emptive actions to mitigate risks. This proactive stance helps organizations stay ahead of cyber adversaries and reduce their attack surface.

- **Compliance and regulatory requirements**: Many regulatory frameworks and industry standards, such as the GDPR and the **Payment Card Industry Data Security Standard (PCI DSS)**, mandate continuous monitoring as part of their compliance requirements. By implementing continuous monitoring, organizations can ensure they meet these regulatory obligations and avoid potential fines and reputational damage.

- **Improved incident response**: Continuous monitoring provides SOCs with the visibility and contextual information needed to respond effectively to security incidents. By having access to real-time data and comprehensive logs, security analysts can quickly investigate incidents, understand their scope and impact, and initiate appropriate response actions. This capability is vital for minimizing downtime and mitigating the damage caused by security breaches.

Continuous monitoring provides SOCs with enhanced visibility into an organization's security posture. By having a comprehensive view of network activities, user behavior, and system events, SOCs can identify potential threats and vulnerabilities that may otherwise go unnoticed. The insights gained from continuous monitoring enable SOCs to make informed decisions about security measures and resource allocation. By understanding the nature and frequency of threats, SOCs can prioritize their efforts and invest in the most effective security solutions. Continuous monitoring allows SOCs to adapt their security measures in response to emerging threats. By staying informed about the latest threat trends and attack vectors, SOCs can update their defenses and strategies to address new challenges. This adaptability is crucial for maintaining a robust cybersecurity posture in an ever-changing threat landscape.

Key components of continuous monitoring

To ensure continuous monitoring within SOCs, key essential technologies are as follows:

- **SIEM**: SIEM systems are the backbone of continuous monitoring, collecting, and analyzing security data from various sources across the organization. By correlating events and identifying patterns, SIEM systems provide valuable insights into potential threats and anomalies. Advanced SIEM solutions also integrate with threat intelligence feeds to enhance detection capabilities.

- **Network monitoring**: Continuous monitoring involves the constant surveillance of network traffic to identify suspicious activities. Tools such as IDS and **intrusion prevention systems (IPS)** play a critical role in detecting malicious traffic and preventing unauthorized access. Network monitoring ensures that SOCs have a comprehensive view of network activities and can detect threats as they emerge.

- **Endpoint monitoring**: Monitoring endpoints, such as workstations, servers, and mobile devices, is essential for detecting threats that may bypass network defenses. EDR solutions provide continuous visibility into endpoint activities, enabling SOCs to detect and respond to threats at the endpoint level. EDR solutions also help in identifying IOC and facilitating forensic investigations.

- **User behavior analytics (UBA)**: Continuous monitoring includes analyzing user behavior to detect anomalies that may indicate insider threats or compromised accounts. UBA leverages machine learning algorithms to establish baselines for normal user behavior and identify deviations that could signal malicious activities. By monitoring user behavior, SOCs can detect threats that may not be apparent through traditional security measures.

Continuous monitoring is a critical domain within SOCs, providing the real-time visibility and insights needed to detect, respond to, and mitigate cyber threats. By leveraging advanced technologies such as SIEM, network monitoring, endpoint monitoring, and user behavior analytics, SOCs can enhance their security posture, meet regulatory requirements, and ensure the resilience of their organizations. As the threat landscape continues to evolve, the importance of continuous monitoring in maintaining effective cybersecurity cannot be overstated.

Coordination amongst systems

In the present interconnected and converged landscape of cybersecurity, the coordination among various systems, network, application, **operational technology (OT)**, and **information technology (IT)** is crucial for the effective functioning of a SOC. This integrated approach enhances the ability to detect, respond to, and mitigate security threats across the entire organizational infrastructure.

By integrating network, application, OT, and IT systems, SOCs can achieve a holistic view of the security landscape. Threats can originate from multiple vectors, and the ability to monitor all these systems ensures that no potential attack surface is left unprotected. For example, a threat detected on the network level can be correlated with activities at the application level, providing a more comprehensive understanding of the threat.

Coordination amongst different systems allows for a unified incident response strategy. When a security incident occurs, having synchronized data and processes across network, application, OT, and IT systems enables SOC teams to respond more effectively and efficiently. This unified approach ensures that all aspects of the incident are addressed, reducing the potential impact.

Integrating various systems helps streamline SOC operations. Unified platforms and centralized dashboards provide security analysts with consolidated information, reducing the complexity of managing disparate tools and systems. This streamlined approach improves operational efficiency and allows analysts to focus on more critical tasks.

Coordination among systems ensures that resources are utilized optimally. For instance, automated workflows can be established to prioritize and escalate incidents based on their impact and severity. This ensures that critical incidents are addressed promptly while routine tasks are handled efficiently. Coordination allows for the consistent application of security policies across all systems. This uniformity is crucial for maintaining a robust security posture, as inconsistencies can lead to vulnerabilities.

For example, access control policies applied at the network level should align with those enforced at the application and IT levels. Coordinated systems provide enhanced visibility into all activities across the organization. This visibility is essential for monitoring and detecting anomalies that may indicate security threats. For example, unusual network traffic patterns can be investigated in conjunction with application logs to identify potential breaches.

The integration of all systems allows SOCs to adopt a proactive approach to threat management. By analyzing data from multiple systems, SOCs can identify emerging threats and implement preventive measures before they can cause significant damage. For instance, threat intelligence gathered from network activities can inform the configuration of application firewalls to block potential attacks. In the event of a security breach, coordinated systems enable effective containment and recovery. SOCs can quickly isolate affected systems and implement remediation measures across the network, application, OT, and IT environments. This coordinated response minimizes the impact of the incident and ensures a swift recovery.

Coordination amongst network, application, OT, and IT systems is vital for the effective operation of a SOC. This integrated approach provides a comprehensive security posture, enhances efficiency, ensures consistent security controls, and improves adaptability and resilience. As the cybersecurity landscape continues to evolve, the significance of such coordination will only increase, making it a cornerstone of modern SOC strategies.

A standard framework involving practical steps in the integration of any system in SOC is covered in *Figure 4.1*:

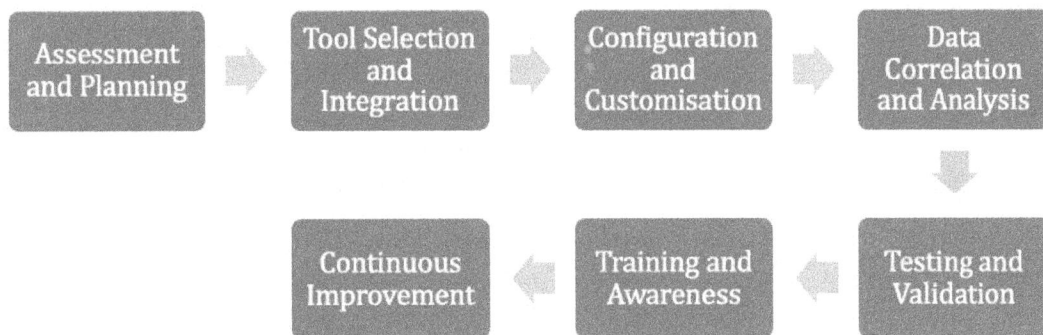

Figure 4.1: *Standard framework for system integration with SOC*

Assessment and planning

The assessment and planning phase includes:

- Determine which network systems need to be integrated, including firewalls, IDS, IPS, network monitoring tools, and SIEM or SOAR systems.

- Establish clear goals for integration, such as improving threat detection, enhancing incident response, and ensuring compliance with regulatory requirements.

Tool selection and integration

An important aspect of integrating any system with SOC is to:

- Select tools that can be integrated seamlessly. Ensure they support standard protocols and APIs for data sharing and communication.

- Implement a centralized dashboard that provides a unified view of all integrated systems. This helps SOC analysts monitor and manage security events more effectively.

Configuration and customization

The systems getting integrated with SOC must ensure the following:

- Configure alerts and thresholds for each system to ensure timely detection of anomalies and potential threats.

- Tailor workflows to match the organization's specific security policies and procedures. This includes defining incident response processes and escalation paths.

Data correlation and analysis

The next step in integration is data correlation and analysis, which can be ensured through:

- Use SIEM/SOAR systems to correlate data from different network systems. This helps in identifying patterns and detecting sophisticated threats that might be missed by individual systems.

- Implement automation tools to analyze large volumes of data quickly. This reduces the manual effort required and speeds up the detection process.

Testing and validation

The next critical step in the integration is to test and validate periodically with the following measures:

- Regularly test the integrated system through simulations and drills. This helps identify any gaps or weaknesses in the setup.

- Ensure that all configurations are validated and working as intended. Regularly review and update configurations to adapt to new threats and changes in the network environment.

Training and awareness

Training and awareness are important aspects of ensuring continuity and maintaining currency. The efforts required are as follows:

- Provide training to SOC analysts on how to use the integrated systems effectively. This includes understanding the data flow, interpreting alerts, and responding to incidents.

- Raise awareness among all employees about the importance of network security and the role of the SOC in protecting the organization.

Continuous improvement

The last critical step is to strive for continuous improvement in response to the evolving threat landscape through the following means:

- Continuously monitor the performance of the integrated systems. Use metrics and KPIs to measure effectiveness and identify areas for improvement.

- Regularly update and upgrade the systems and tools to keep up with evolving threats and technological advancements.

Organizations can effectively implement network systems integration in their SOC by following these steps, leading to improved threat detection, faster incident response, and overall enhanced security posture.

Practical systems integration with SOC

Following the same approach as covered in *Figure 4.1*, any system integration with SOC can give first-hand information about threats and intrusion attempts in an organization's information systems and gain insights into potential vulnerabilities to address them. Let us take an example of integrating a router (network system), a web application (application), a **supervisory control and data acquisition** (**SCADA**) system (operations technology), and a DBMS (information technology) in a SOC. The steps will be as follows:

Assessment and planning

Determine which systems need to be integrated, including network, application, OT, and IT systems. Establish clear goals for the integration, such as improving threat detection, enhancing incident response, and ensuring compliance with regulatory requirements. Assessment and planning include the following points:

- The objective of network systems integration is to monitor traffic for anomalies and detect potential intrusions. Assess the router's compatibility with existing SIEM/SOAR and IDS tools.

- Identify the web application to be integrated and define security objectives, such as preventing SQL injection attacks and monitoring user activities.

- The objective of integrating the OT system is to monitor and secure SCADA systems controlling critical infrastructure, such as a power grid or water treatment plant.

Assess the existing SCADA system, including all sensors, PLC, and communication protocols.

- The objective of specific IT system integration is to monitor and secure the **database management system (DBMS)** to protect sensitive data and ensure compliance with regulations. Assess the current DBMS, including database servers, configurations, and access controls.

Tool selection and integration

Select tools that can be integrated seamlessly and support standard protocols and APIs for data sharing and communication. Tool selection and integration involve the following points:

- Choose an SIEM / SOAR system like Splunk and an IDS like Snort. Configure the router to send Syslog data to Splunk and SNMP traps to Snort.

- Choose a **web application firewall (WAF)** that supports API integration with the SOC's SIEM/SOAR system.

- Choose a specialized OT monitoring solution, such as Nozomi Networks or Claroty, and ensure it can integrate with the SOC's SIEM, like Splunk or QRadar. Configure the SCADA system to send logs and telemetry data to the chosen monitoring tools and the SIEM.

- Choose an SIEM system like Splunk and a **database activity monitoring (DAM)** tool such as IBM Guardium or Imperva. Configure the DBMS to send audit logs and activity data to the DAM tool and the SIEM.

- Implement a centralized dashboard that provides a unified view of all integrated systems.

Configuration and customization

Configure alerts and thresholds for each system to ensure timely detection of anomalies and potential threats. Tailor workflows to match the organization's specific security policies and procedures. While performing configuration and customization, keep these points in mind:

- Set up alerts in Splunk for unusual traffic patterns and failed login attempts. Customize Splunk dashboards to display real-time data from the router.

- Set up the WAF to detect and block common web application attacks. Configure the SIEM to receive logs from the WAF and create custom alerts for unusual activities.

- Set up alerts for operational anomalies, such as unexpected changes in process variables or unauthorized access attempts. Customize SOC dashboards to display real-time SCADA data, including trends and potential security events.

- Set up alerts for unauthorized access attempts, significant changes to database configurations, and unusual data access patterns. Customize SOC dashboards to display real-time DBMS data, including audit trails and potential security events.

Data correlation and analysis

SIEM or SOAR systems are used to correlate data from different systems and identify patterns and sophisticated threats. Implement automation tools to analyze large volumes of data quickly. While performing data correlation and analysis, keep the following points in mind:

- Collect logs from the router and correlate with data from other network devices in Splunk. Use Splunk's automated analysis features to detect anomalies and generate alerts.

- Aggregate logs from the web application and correlate them with network and endpoint data to identify potential threats.

- Collect and correlate SCADA logs with data from IT and network systems in the SIEM to provide comprehensive threat analysis. Use automated analysis tools to detect patterns and anomalies indicative of potential threats or operational issues.

- Collect and correlate DBMS logs with data from other IT systems in the SIEM to provide comprehensive threat analysis. Use automated analysis tools to detect patterns and anomalies indicative of potential threats or policy violations.

Testing and validation

Regularly evaluate the integrated system through simulations and drills to identify gaps or weaknesses. Ensure that all configurations are validated and working as intended. While performing testing and validation, keep these points in mind:

- Conduct penetration testing to ensure the router's configurations are secure. Regularly review and validate the router's integration settings.

- Conduct penetration testing on the web application to identify vulnerabilities and ensure the WAF is effectively blocking attacks.

- Conduct regular penetration testing on the SCADA system to identify vulnerabilities. Continuously review and validate the SCADA system configurations and integration settings.

- Conduct regular penetration testing on the DBMS to identify vulnerabilities. Continuously review and validate DBMS configurations and integration settings.

Training and awareness

Provide training to SOC analysts on how to use the integrated systems effectively. Raise awareness among all employees about the importance of security and the role of the SOC. For training and awareness, keep these points in mind:

- Train SOC analysts on interpreting router logs and responding to incidents. Educate staff on router security best practices.

- Train SOC analysts on interpreting WAF logs and responding to web application security incidents. Educate developers on secure coding practices to prevent vulnerabilities.

- Train SOC analysts on interpreting SCADA logs and responding to OT-specific incidents. Educate OT staff on cybersecurity best practices and the importance of collaboration with the SOC.

- Train SOC analysts on interpreting DBMS logs and responding to database-related incidents. Educate IT staff on database security best practices and the importance of collaboration with the SOC.

Continuous improvement

For continuous improvement, keep these points in mind:

- Continuously monitor the performance of the router and the integration with the SOC tools. Regularly update the router's firmware and the SOC's monitoring tools.

- Regularly review the performance of the WAF and update configurations based on the latest threat intelligence.

- Continuously monitor the effectiveness of the integrated SCADA security measures. Regularly update SCADA systems and SOC monitoring tools.

- Continuously monitor the effectiveness of the integrated DBMS security measures. Regularly update the DBMS and SOC monitoring tools.

By following these steps, organizations can enhance their network security, improve threat detection, improve incident response capabilities for their applications, enhance their OT/ IT security, ensure robust protection of sensitive data, and ensure robust protection of critical infrastructure.

As covered in the next section, some of the successful integrations will provide practical insights into the coordinated aspects of integrating systems, networks, and OT and IT systems for better security posture management.

Manufacturing industry

In 2022, a large automotive manufacturing firm faced a critical challenge. Their production downtime had skyrocketed by 25% over the past year, costing them nearly $10 million annually. The root cause was hidden within their OT systems, specifically their SCADA infrastructure, which operated in isolation from their IT network. This siloed approach left them blind to inefficiencies and vulnerabilities. Determined to turn things around, the company embarked on an ambitious integration project, bridging the gap between OT and IT. By enabling real-time monitoring of production processes and equipment health, the company gained unprecedented visibility. SCADA data was correlated with IT network logs, revealing anomalies that could signal equipment failure or cyber threats.

The transformation was extraordinary. Within six months, they experienced a 40% reduction in unplanned downtime, saving an estimated $4 million in operational costs. Efficiency surged; production output increased by 15%. Additionally, proactive maintenance based on predictive analytics from integrated systems reduced equipment failure rates by 30%. On the security front, the company uncovered potential threats that had gone unnoticed for years, including malicious attempts to exploit outdated firmware in robotic assembly arms. With integrated data streams, their SOC swiftly neutralized these risks, reinforcing their defense against the rising tide of ransomware attacks on OT systems, which increased by 87% industry-wide in the previous year.

A similar success story can be found in Toyota's manufacturing plants. In recent years, Toyota adopted IT-OT integration to streamline operations and improve cybersecurity. By harmonizing their production line's SCADA data with IT analytics, they not only achieved significant operational gains but also enhanced their security posture, safeguarding proprietary designs and customer data against evolving cyber threats.

Healthcare industry

In 2023, a large healthcare network managing over 20 hospitals and 50 clinics faced a pressing challenge. They handled tens of millions of EHRs, yet incidents of unauthorized access to patient data had surged by 30% compared to the previous year. With healthcare breaches costing an average of $10.93 million per incident, according to IBM's 2022 report, the organization knew it was time for a major overhaul. They implemented a sophisticated integration between their EHR systems, IT infrastructure, and network security tools. This wasn't just about connecting systems—it was about creating a seamless ecosystem for real-time data monitoring. By correlating EHR logs with network traffic, they uncovered patterns of suspicious activity that had previously gone unnoticed.

The results were remarkable. Within the first year, attempted unauthorized access was reduced by 40%, and potential breaches were halted before any patient data was compromised. Compliance with HIPAA regulations was no longer just a box to check; it became a pillar of their operational excellence. Incident response times improved by an astounding 50%, enabling swift containment of threats.

The *University of Vermont Health Network's* journey mirrors this success. After a ransomware attack disrupted operations in 2020, the network prioritized integrating its EHR systems with advanced cybersecurity tools. This proactive investment not only improved patient data security but also safeguarded critical operations, such as scheduling and diagnostics, ensuring uninterrupted care for patients.

Energy sector

In 2024, a major energy company supplying electricity to over 10 million households faced a growing threat. The company's aging OT systems, including power grid management and monitoring networks, were increasingly targeted by cyberattacks. With the energy sector seeing a 74% year-over-year increase in ransomware incidents, the stakes were higher than ever. A successful attack on their systems could cause widespread blackouts and endanger critical infrastructure. Recognizing this vulnerability, the company embarked on an ambitious integration project to bridge its OT systems with its IT network and security tools. The goal was to create a centralized, unified view of their entire infrastructure, enabling real-time monitoring and threat detection. This included correlating data streams from power grid management systems with IT network logs to detect anomalies and potential threats proactively.

The impact was groundbreaking. Within a year of the integration, the company achieved a 60% improvement in identifying and mitigating cyber threats, reducing response times to incidents by an impressive 50%. This proactive approach thwarted an attempted malware attack on their power grid system, potentially saving millions of dollars in damages and preventing significant disruptions. Operational safety also reached new heights. The unified infrastructure allowed for advanced analytics, which helped predict equipment failures, reducing downtime by 25% and boosting energy distribution reliability. Customers experienced fewer outages, and trust in the company's ability to deliver uninterrupted power grew stronger.

The 2015 Ukrainian power grid cyberattack served as a wake-up call for the energy industry. Hackers infiltrated OT systems, cutting off power to nearly 230,000 citizens. Learning from this, many energy companies worldwide, including utilities in the U.S., began integrating OT and IT systems. For instance, **Pacific Gas and Electric Company (PG&E)** adopted such integration, strengthening grid resilience against increasingly sophisticated attacks.

Retail industry

In the cutthroat world of retail, where every second counts, a leading global retailer discovered a troubling trend: a spike in fraudulent transactions, amounting to $2.5 million in potential losses annually. With the added pressure of safeguarding millions of customer card details and adhering to PCI DSS compliance, the company knew their legacy systems were not enough to tackle modern threats. Taking action, the retailer launched an ambitious initiative to integrate its POS systems with its IT network and advanced security tools. This integration enabled real-time monitoring of every transaction alongside continuous surveillance of network activities. By correlating POS logs with network traffic data, the company uncovered patterns that signaled unauthorized access attempts and fraudulent activities.

The results spoke volumes. Within the first six months, fraud detection efficiency soared by 45%, allowing them to block fraudulent transactions worth over $1 million. Additionally, compliance audits became significantly streamlined, and they avoided hefty PCI DSS fines, which can exceed $500,000 per incident. Beyond compliance, customer trust surged, and data breaches plummeted by 60%, reassuring millions of shoppers worldwide.

A similar success story unfolded at target after their infamous 2013 data breach that compromised 40 million credit card records. In its aftermath, the company invested heavily in integrating POS systems with next-generation IT and security tools. Today, Target boasts a far more robust cybersecurity framework, preventing large-scale breaches and cementing its reputation as a responsible retailer.

Recovery and remediation

In the realm of cybersecurity, the domains of recovery and remediation are critical components of an effective SOC. These domains focus on restoring normal operations after a security incident and implementing measures to prevent recurrence. Recovery ensures that business operations are quickly restored after a security incident, minimizing downtime and disruption. The remediation process involves identifying and addressing vulnerabilities that led to the incident and strengthening the overall security posture. xSwift remediation helps reduce the financial impact of security breaches, including costs associated with data loss, system repairs, and potential fines for regulatory non-compliance.

Effective recovery and remediation restore customer confidence by demonstrating that the organization can handle and recover from security incidents. A quick and efficient response reassures stakeholders, including partners, investors, and regulators, that the organization is resilient against cyber threats. Recovery and remediation also provide valuable lessons that inform future security strategies, policies, and procedures.

Key components of recovery and remediation

The key components of recovery and remediation, which should be adopted in security operations, are as follows:

- **Incident response planning**: Develop and regularly update an incident response plan that outlines steps for recovery and remediation. This includes defining roles, responsibilities, and communication strategies. Conduct regular training and simulation exercises to ensure that the SOC team is prepared to handle real incidents efficiently.

- **Data backup and restoration**: Implement regular data backups to ensure that critical information can be restored in the event of data loss or corruption. Establish clear procedures for restoring data from backups, including verification of data integrity and security.

- **Patch management**: Apply patches and updates to address vulnerabilities that were exploited during the incident. This includes both software and firmware updates. Implement a regular patch management schedule to ensure that systems are consistently updated with the latest security patches.

- **System hardening**: Make necessary configuration changes to harden systems against future attacks. This may include adjusting firewall rules, changing access controls, and improving authentication mechanisms. Adopt security best practices such as the principle of least privilege, multi-factor authentication, and network segmentation to enhance system security.

- **Communication and coordination**: Ensure clear and timely communication within the organization during and after the incident. This includes informing relevant teams and stakeholders about the incident and recovery progress. Communicate with external parties, such as customers, partners, and regulators, as required. Transparency and timely updates are crucial for maintaining trust.

- **Continuous improvement**: Conduct a post-incident review to identify lessons learned and areas for improvement. This review should involve all relevant stakeholders and result in actionable recommendations. Update security policies and procedures based on insights gained from the incident and the remediation process. Implement enhanced monitoring and detection mechanisms to identify potential threats early and prevent future incidents. Leverage threat intelligence to stay informed about emerging threats and adjust security measures accordingly.

Recovery and remediation are crucial domains within a SOC, playing a vital role in restoring operations, mitigating damage, and strengthening the organization's security posture. By having well-defined processes for incident response, data backup, root cause analysis, patch management, system hardening, and communication, SOCs can effectively manage and recover from security incidents. Continuous improvement through post-incident reviews and enhanced monitoring ensures that the organization is resilient against future threats.

Root cause analysis

Root cause analysis (RCA) is a crucial domain within SOC that involves identifying the underlying causes of security incidents to prevent their recurrence. By understanding the root cause of an incident, SOCs can implement effective remediation measures, improve security posture, and enhance overall resilience against future attacks. Here is an in-depth look at the significance of RCA and how it can be effectively executed within a SOC.

RCA helps in identifying the fundamental weaknesses or vulnerabilities that were exploited during a security incident and refining incident response strategies by identifying gaps and areas for improvement in existing processes and protocols. By addressing these root causes, organizations can prevent similar incidents from occurring in the future. Rather than applying temporary fixes, RCA allows SOCs to implement long-term solutions that enhance the overall security architecture of the organization.

Understanding the root cause of an incident provides valuable insights that inform decision-making during incident response. This leads to more effective and targeted remediation efforts. RCA uncovers systemic issues that may be affecting the organization's security posture. Addressing these issues leads to a more robust and resilient security environment.

RCA is an integral part of the continuous improvement process within SOC. By learning from past incidents, SOCs can continuously enhance their security measures and practices.

Key components of root cause analysis

To ensure effective security operations, critical root cause analysis is essential. The steps involved in crafting an effective RCA are as follows:

- **Data collection**: Ensure that all relevant data is collected from various sources, including logs from network devices, endpoints, applications, and security tools. This data serves as the foundation for RCA. Maintain detailed documentation of the security incident, including timelines, actions taken, and initial observations.

- **Investigation and analysis**: Begin by identifying the symptoms of the incident, such as unusual network traffic, system crashes, or unauthorized access attempts. Trace the path of the attack to understand how the threat actor gained access, moved laterally, and achieved their objectives. This involves analyzing logs, network traffic, and system behaviors. Use techniques such as the 5 Whys or fishbone diagrams to drill down to the underlying cause of the incident. This may involve identifying vulnerabilities, misconfigurations, or human errors.

- **Validation and confirmation**: Validate findings by cross-verifying with multiple sources of data and collaborating with other teams, such as IT, network, and application teams. Seek input from subject matter experts to ensure that the identified root cause is accurate and comprehensive.

- **Remediation and mitigation**: Address the root cause by implementing necessary fixes, such as applying patches, reconfiguring systems, or enhancing access controls. Implement additional mitigation measures to strengthen security and prevent similar incidents. This may include deploying new security tools, enhancing monitoring, or updating policies.

- **Communication and documentation**: Prepare a detailed incident report that outlines the root cause, investigation findings, remediation actions, and lessons learned. Communicate findings and remediation efforts to relevant stakeholders, including management, IT teams, and affected users.

- **Post-incident review and continuous improvement**: Conduct a post-incident review to identify lessons learned and areas for improvement. Use these insights to enhance security policies, procedures, and incident response plans. Continuously update security measures based on the findings from RCA to ensure that the organization remains resilient against evolving threats.

RCA is a vital domain within a SOC that focuses on identifying and addressing the underlying causes of security incidents. By conducting thorough RCA, SOCs can prevent the recurrence of incidents, improve incident response, and strengthen the overall security posture of the organization. Through effective data collection, investigation, validation, remediation, communication, and continuous improvement, SOCs can ensure that they are well-prepared to handle future threats and maintain a robust security environment.

Compliance management

Compliance management is a critical domain within a SOC that ensures an organization adheres to relevant laws, regulations, and standards. Effective compliance management helps protect sensitive data, avoid legal penalties, and build trust with customers and stakeholders. In this section, we will take an in-depth look at why compliance management is vital and how it can be effectively implemented within a SOC.

Organizations must comply with various legal requirements, such as the GDPR, the HIPAA, and the PCI DSS. Compliance management ensures these regulations are met to avoid legal penalties and fines. Adhering to industry standards like ISO/IEC 27001 helps demonstrate that an organization follows best practices in information security, enhancing its reputation and trustworthiness.

Compliance management helps identify and address security vulnerabilities, reducing the risk of data breaches and other security incidents. Ensuring compliance with incident response requirements ensures that organizations are prepared to handle security incidents efficiently and effectively. Compliance with regulations and standards builds confidence among customers, partners, and stakeholders, enhancing the organization's reputation. Demonstrating compliance through regular audits and reporting fosters transparency and trust. Compliance management helps standardize and streamline security processes, leading to more efficient operations within the SOC. Regular compliance assessments drive continuous improvement in security practices and policies.

Key components of compliance management

Compliance management involves intricate coordination between all stakeholders. The key elements in ensuring that all regulatory requirements are met within the ambit of SOC are as follows:

- **Regulatory frameworks**: Determine which regulations and standards apply to the organization based on its industry, location, and operations. Map regulatory requirements to specific security controls and measures within the SOC.

- **Policies and procedures**: Create and maintain comprehensive security policies that address regulatory requirements and industry standards. Establish SOP for implementing and enforcing security policies, including incident response, data protection, and access control.

- **Audits and assessments**: Conduct regular internal and external audits to assess compliance with regulations and standards. Use the findings to address gaps and improve security practices. Implement continuous monitoring to ensure ongoing compliance and detect deviations from established policies.

- **Training and awareness**: Provide regular training to employees on compliance requirements, security policies, and best practices. Ensure that employees understand their roles and responsibilities in maintaining compliance. Implement awareness programs to keep employees informed about the latest regulatory changes and security threats.

- **Documentation and reporting**: Keep detailed records of compliance activities, including audit results, training sessions, and incident response actions. Generate regular compliance reports for management, stakeholders, and regulatory authorities. Ensure that reports are accurate, transparent, and timely.

- **Incident management**: Ensure that incident response procedures comply with regulatory reporting requirements. This includes timely notification of data breaches to relevant authorities and affected individuals. Conduct post-incident reviews to assess the effectiveness of compliance measures and identify areas for improvement.

- **Continuous improvement**: Establish a feedback loop to continuously improve compliance management practices based on audit findings, incident reviews, and changes in regulations. Regularly update policies and procedures to adapt to evolving regulatory requirements and emerging security threats.

Compliance management is a crucial domain within a SOC, ensuring that an organization adheres to relevant laws, regulations, and standards. By implementing effective compliance management practices, organizations can mitigate risks, build trust, enhance operational efficiency, and maintain a robust security posture. Key components of compliance management include regulatory frameworks, policies and procedures, audits and assessments, training and awareness, documentation and reporting, incident management, and continuous improvement. By focusing on these areas, SOCs can ensure ongoing compliance and resilience against evolving cyber threats.

Conclusion

The assets inventory knowledge will be crucial to know the attack surface and be prepared to mitigate any threats. Continuous monitoring will further enhance the awareness of the evolving threat landscape. The interplay between various systems and their integration into SOC is critical to effectively neutralize the attacks.

Each of these domains plays a crucial role in the overall effectiveness of a SOC. These domains may not be comprehensive. With the ever-evolving threat landscape, domains are getting more specific. However, the basic domains covered in this chapter will create a base for establishing a robust security operations center. By covering these areas comprehensively, organizations can enhance their security posture, ensure compliance, and be better prepared to handle and recover from security incidents.

In the next chapter, we will explore the SOC models and different Cyber Kill Chain frameworks. These are important from knowing the attacker perspectives in order to improve preparedness.

Points to remember

Here are some key takeaways from this chapter:

- Knowing the SOC domains will help in knowing the assets, in turn the attack surface.

- Understanding other domains like continuous monitoring, coordination amongst integrated systems, recovery and remediation, and root cause analysis will enhance the effectiveness of security operations.

- Compliance management as an important SOC domain will ensure trustworthiness and project safe cyber posture.

Multiple choice questions

1. **Asset risk status cannot be decided based on which of the following?**

    a. Confidentiality

    b. Non-repudiation

    c. Integrity

    d. Availability

2. **Which SOC domain ensures the organization adheres to relevant laws, regulations, and industry standards?**

    a. Compliance management

    b. Root cause analysis

    c. Recovery and remediation

    d. Asset management

3. **What does the RCA domain aim to achieve in SOC?**

    a. To automate security processes

    a. To identify the underlying causes of security incidents

    b. To manage encryption keys

    c. To design network architecture

Answers

1	b
2	a
3	b

Questions

1. Explain how asset management is important for SOC operations.

2. How can root cause analysis improve security posture?

3. Explain how recovery and remediation are critical for security operations.

Key terms

Here are some key terms used in the chapter:

*   **CIA rating and risk status**: Applicable for tagging assets to plan appropriate security measures.

*   **OT and IT**: The systems integration is critical in the SOC domain.

*   **RCA**: This is crucial to analyze the events and take corrective actions.

Join our Discord space

Join our Discord workspace for latest updates, offers, tech happenings around the world, new releases, and sessions with the authors:

https://discord.bpbonline.com

CHAPTER 5
Modern Developments in Security Operations Centers

Introduction

This chapter covers the modern developments in handling security incidents. Initially, when network technicians handled security incidents, it was restricted to in-house expertise. However, with the ever-evolving threat landscape, SOCs have also evolved from being reactive to proactive. Cyber incidents need to be managed by trained professionals. Some organizations can afford skilled professionals, whereas some cannot. Also, the **tools, techniques and procedures** (**TTP**) in the cyber domain is overwhelming. Accordingly, there is a need to adopt appropriate strategies to manage the shortage of skilled resources and ever-evolving tools to monitor and respond.

Understanding the Cyber Kill Chain or MITRE frameworks is essential to understanding the intricacies of cyberattacks. This chapter dwells on these processes in order to defend against these complex attacks.

Structure

In this chapter, we will discuss the following topics:

- SOC models
- Cyber Kill Chain
- MITRE ATT&CK and D3FEND frameworks

- Evolving threat landscape
- SOC function optimization

Objectives

By the end of this chapter, you will be able to understand how SOCs are managed and evolved over a period of time. You will gain insights into various SOC implementation models, clarifying which SOC model suits which kind of organization. The chapter also covers Cyber Kill Chain frameworks and mitigation measures to thwart cyberattacks.

Security operations centers models

A SOC is a centralized unit responsible for monitoring and managing an organization's security posture. Typically, SOCs started evolving from reactive to proactive incident response mechanisms. The dynamic and complex nature of cybersecurity has driven the evolution of various SOC operating models. Each model is tailored to different organizational needs, technological advancements, and threat landscapes. Some SOC models are traditional SOCs, virtual SOCs, and meta morphing into a SOC as a service. Let us see the nuances of how these SOC models function.

Traditional SOC

Traditional SOCs are centralized, physical locations where security analysts monitor, detect, and respond to security incidents. They are fully in-house SOCs, typically staffed 24/7 by dedicated security personnel. They encompass direct control over security operations, quick decision-making, and strong team collaboration. Being internal to the organization and having complete visibility of the ICT infrastructure, traditional SOCs deeply understand internal systems and processes.

They have direct access to decision-makers. The attack surface is increasing day-by-day, and the threat landscape is evolving rapidly. Keeping pace with this dynamic nature of threats, with available staffing, is difficult. Often, more manpower is required, and more tools are required to monitor and manage. This involves high upfront and ongoing operational costs. There is potential for staff burnout. If the business is growing, so is the threat landscape. Scaling up the operations to handle increased cyberattacks may be difficult.

Virtual SOC

With the dynamic nature of cyberattacks, specialized manpower is required to manage such risks. Every organization cannot afford these skilled professionals. Virtual SOC leverages remote skilled security analysts and cloud-based tools to perform SOC functions without a dedicated physical location. It is highly cost-effective, flexible, and scalable. It allows for a distributed workforce, which can benefit global organizations. However, coordination and communication among remote team members can be challenging. Further, complexities are added to the overdependence on internet connectivity and cloud services. Also, there are potential security risks associated with remote access.

Hybrid SOC

Hybrid SOCs combine elements of both traditional and virtual SOCs. It uses a mix of on-premises and remote security personnel and resources. It is primarily aimed at balancing control and flexibility. Hybrid SOCs can optimize resource utilization by leveraging both internal and external expertise. In such an implementation, a major challenge is the complexity of managing and integrating different components. This entails robust coordination and communication strategies amongst local and remote teams. Integrating disparate tools and meeting the requirements of diverse teams into seamless incident monitoring is another challenge.

Co-managed SOC

In co-managed SOC implementation, the organization partners with an external **managed security service provider** (**MSSP**) to share responsibilities between in-house and outsourced teams for security operations. Akin to hybrid SOC implementation, co-managed SOCs can access specialized expertise and resources. Instead of relying on remote security personnel and resources, co-managed SOCs rely on MSSPs owing to their knowledge and focus. MSSPs are offering SOC as a service, providing a range of services in security incident handling and remediation. Such MSSPs can alleviate the burden on internal teams and provide around-the-clock coverage. This is a cost-effective solution because of optimized resource allocation. It is scalable and flexible. However, this may create dependency on the third-party provider for critical security functions, which can sometimes be counter-productive. It also requires clear communication and coordination to avoid overlaps or gaps.

Next-Generation SOC

Next-Generation SOC (**NG-SOC**) employs advanced technologies like AI, ML, and automation to enhance threat detection, analysis, and response capabilities. Advanced technologies bring improved efficiency and effectiveness in handling sophisticated threats. It enables proactive threat hunting and predictive analytics. However, NG-SOC entails a significant investment in advanced technologies and skilled personnel. Continuous learning and adaptation are necessary to keep up with evolving threats.

Global SOC

Global SOCs operate on a worldwide scale with multiple, geographically dispersed SOCs working in coordination. It ensures 24/7 coverage by leveraging different time zones, providing comprehensive coverage and redundancy. It can quickly respond to incidents affecting multiple regions. Global SOCs facilitate knowledge sharing across locations, as the repository of incidences is ever-increasing. However, coordination and management amongst regional SOCs are highly complex. It requires standardized processes and robust communication channels to function effectively.

Federated SOC

The threat landscapes are increasingly focusing on specific sectors. Accordingly, expertise levels are being generated for sector-specific requirements. Multiple sector-specific SOCs within an organization (such as different business units or subsidiaries) operate independently but share threat intelligence and best practices. Such federated SOCs provide autonomy for individual units while benefiting from shared insights. It can quickly adapt to the specific needs of different units. However, it has the potential for inconsistencies in security posture across the organization. It requires strong governance and oversight to ensure alignment and collaboration.

Key considerations for choosing a SOC model

Having seen different SOC models, deciding which model suits a specific organizational need is worthwhile. Some of the critical factors that can assist in adopting a particular SOC model are as follows:

- **Organizational size and complexity**: Larger organizations may benefit from an entirely in-house or hybrid model, while smaller organizations might opt for an MSSP or co-managed model.

- **Security maturity**: Organizations with a higher security maturity level may prefer an entirely in-house model, while those with lower maturity may benefit from an MSSP or co-managed model.

- **Budget**: The budget available for security operations will significantly impact the choice of model.

- **Skillset**: The availability of in-house security talent will influence the decision to build an in-house SOC or outsource to an MSSP.

- **Compliance requirements**: Certain industries have specific requirements that may necessitate a particular SOC model.

By carefully considering these factors, organizations can select the most suitable SOC model to protect their valuable assets and mitigate security risks. Each SOC model offers unique advantages and challenges, and the choice of model depends on factors such as the organization's size, industry, budget, and specific security needs. Modern advancements in technology, such as AI and cloud computing, have significantly influenced the development and capabilities of these SOC models. Organizations must carefully evaluate their requirements and resources to select the SOC model that best fits their cybersecurity strategy.

Cyber Kill Chain

Cyber Kill Chain is a framework developed by *Lockheed Martin* to describe the stages of a typical cyberattack, from initial reconnaissance to achieving the attacker's objectives. This framework provides a comprehensive understanding of the stages followed by cyber attackers. The degrees of involvement in specific stages may vary. However, the steps involved are wide-ranging. Security teams can proactively identify and respond to threats by understanding these stages. A SOC is key in defending against these attacks, using the Cyber Kill Chain as a framework for its operations. A typical Cyber Kill Chain is depicted in *Figure 5.1*:

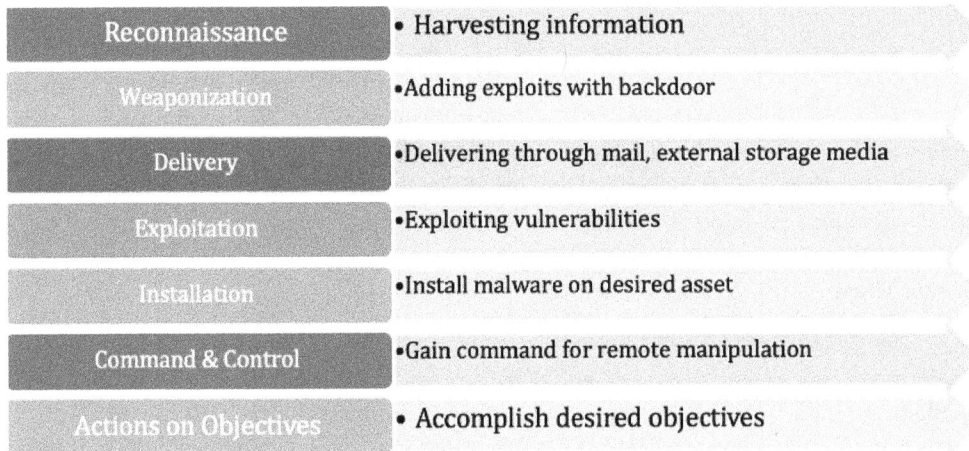

Reconnaissance	• Harvesting information
Weaponization	•Adding exploits with backdoor
Delivery	•Delivering through mail, external storage media
Exploitation	•Exploiting vulnerabilities
Installation	•Install malware on desired asset
Command & Control	•Gain command for remote manipulation
Actions on Objectives	• Accomplish desired objectives

Figure 5.1: *Cyber Kill Chain framework*

Understanding Cyber Kill Chain is crucial for SOCs as it helps identify, prevent, and mitigate cyber threats. The seven stages of the Cyber Kill Chain and their relevance to SOCs are covered in *Table 5.1*:

Stage details	Relevance to SOC	SOC roles	SOC tools envisaged
Reconnaissance			
The attacker gathers information about the target to identify vulnerabilities and plan the attack, through harvesting emails, web or USBs.	SOCs can monitor for signs of reconnaissance, such as unusual network traffic or probing attempts, to detect potential threats early.	Threat intelligence teams monitor for IOC and suspicious activity, such as scanning or probing.	Threat intelligence platforms, network traffic analysis tools, deep/dark web monitoring tools and vulnerability scanners.

Stage details	Relevance to SOC	SOC roles	SOC tools envisaged
Weaponization			
The attacker creates or modifies malware with backdoors to exploit the identified vulnerabilities.	SOCs can use threat intelligence to identify new malware variants and update their detection mechanisms accordingly.	Security analysts monitor for the creation or distribution of malicious code, such as malware or exploit kits.	Malware analysis tools, sandboxing environments, and threat intelligence platforms.
Delivery			
The attacker delivers the malware to the target system, often through phishing emails, infected websites, USBs, network access.	SOCs can implement email filtering, web filtering, and intrusion detection systems to block malicious payloads.	Security analysts monitor for phishing attacks, malicious emails, and other delivery methods.	Email security gateways, web application firewalls, and intrusion detection systems.
Exploitation			
The attacker exploits the vulnerabilities to gain unauthorized access to the target systems.	SOCs can use vulnerability management tools to patch known vulnerabilities and reduce the attack surface.	Security analysts monitor for successful exploitation attempts, such as system compromises or data breaches.	Intrusion detection systems, SIEM systems, and EDR solutions.
Installation			
The attacker installs additional tools or malware to maintain access and control over the compromised system.	SOCs can monitor for unusual system behaviour and unauthorized software installations to detect and respond to intrusions.	Security analysts monitor for the installation of malicious software or backdoors.	EDR solutions, FIM tools, and behavioural analysis tools.

Stage details	Relevance to SOC	SOC roles	SOC tools envisaged
Command and control (C2)			
The attacker establishes a command and control channel to remotely control the compromised system.	SOCs can monitor network traffic for signs of C2 communication and block malicious IP addresses or domains.	Security analysts monitor for communication between compromised systems and attacker-controlled servers.	Network traffic analysis tools, firewall logs, and DNS traffic analysis.
Actions on objectives			
The attacker achieves their goals, such as data exfiltration, encryption for ransomware, or disruption of services.	SOCs can implement DLP measures, encryption, and backup solutions to protect critical data and ensure business continuity.	Security analysts monitor for data exfiltration, system damage, or other malicious activities.	DLP solutions, SIEM systems, and **user behaviour analytics (UBA)** tools.

Table 5.1: Cyber Kill Chain

By understanding and applying the Cyber Kill Chain framework, SOCs can better detect, prevent, and respond to cyber threats. Each stage of the Kill Chain provides opportunities for SOCs to implement defensive measures and mitigate the impact of potential attacks.

By aligning the operations with the Cyber Kill Chain, a SOC can effectively do the following:

- Actively search for threats and vulnerabilities before they can be exploited.

- Quickly detect and respond to security incidents.

- Analyse security incidents to determine the root cause and prevent future attacks.

- Continuously monitor networks, systems, and applications for signs of compromise.

SOCs have used the Cyber Kill Chain to thwart specific cyberattacks. Some real-world scenarios using the Cyber Kill Chain are covered here:

- **The WannaCry ransomware attack**:

    o **Reconnaissance**: Attackers identified systems primarily running Microsoft's Windows 7 and Windows Server 2008 as their targets. They gathered information about these systems' vulnerabilities, particularly focusing on the **server message block (SMB)** protocol.

o **Weaponization**: The attackers leveraged the EternalBlue exploit, which took advantage of a vulnerability in Microsoft's SMB protocol (CVE-2017-0144), to create the WannaCry ransomware.

o **Delivery**: The ransomware was propagated via phishing emails and malicious downloads. Users inadvertently downloaded the malware, which then began its attack.

o **Exploitation**: Upon gaining access to a system, the EternalBlue exploit was used to compromise the target. The ransomware exploited the SMB vulnerability to spread across networks.

o **Installation**: The ransomware encrypted user files, effectively locking them and displaying a ransom note demanding payment for decryption.

o **Command and control (C2)**: The ransomware connected to an external server operated by the attackers to report new infections and update its encryption algorithms.

o **Actions on objectives**: The attackers achieved their goal of encrypting files and demanding ransom payments. Many organizations faced significant disruptions and financial losses.

- **SOC response using the Cyber Kill Chain**:

o **Reconnaissance**: SOCs monitored for signs of reconnaissance, such as unusual network traffic or probing attempts, to detect potential threats early.

o **Weaponization**: SOCs used threat intelligence to identify new malware variants and updated their detection mechanisms accordingly.

o **Delivery**: SOCs implemented email filtering, web filtering, and intrusion detection systems to block malicious payloads.

o **Exploitation**: SOCs used vulnerability management tools to patch known vulnerabilities and reduce the attack surface.

o **Installation**: SOCs monitored for unusual system behavior and unauthorized software installations to detect and respond to intrusions.

o **C2**: SOCs monitored network traffic for signs of C2 communication and blocked malicious IP addresses or domains.

o **Actions on objectives**: SOCs implemented **data loss prevention (DLP)** measures, encryption, and backup solutions to protect critical data and ensure business continuity.

- **The DNC phishing incident**:
  - **Reconnaissance**: Attackers gathered information about key personnel within the **Democratic National Committee (DNC)** and identified potential targets for phishing attacks.
  - **Weaponization**: The attackers created spear-phishing emails with weaponized attachments designed to exploit vulnerabilities in the recipients' systems.
  - **Delivery**: The phishing emails were sent to targeted individuals within the DNC, prompting them to open the malicious attachments.
  - **Exploitation**: Upon opening the attachments, the malware exploited vulnerabilities in the recipients' systems, gaining unauthorized access.
  - **Installation**: The malware installed additional tools to maintain access and control over the compromised systems.
  - **C2**: The attackers established a command and control channel to remotely control the compromised systems and exfiltrate sensitive data.
  - **Actions on objectives**: The attackers achieved their goal of exfiltrating sensitive information, which was later leaked to the public.

- **SOC response using the Cyber Kill Chain**:
  - **Reconnaissance**: SOCs monitored for signs of reconnaissance, such as unusual unauthorized access attempts or information gathering on public-facing platforms, to detect potential phishing campaigns targeting the organization.
  - **Weaponization**: SOCs used email filtering and sandboxing to detect and block malicious attachments and updated their security awareness training to help employees recognize spear-phishing attempts.
  - **Delivery**: SOCs implemented advanced email security solutions to identify email traffic for suspicious patterns, such as emails with unusual attachments/ links and quarantine phishing emails.
  - **Exploitation**: SOCs used EDR tools to identify and block malware execution and patched systems.
  - **Installation**: SOCs monitored for unauthorized software installations or changes to system configurations to detect and respond to intrusions. SOCs also used application whitelisting to prevent unauthorized programs from running.
  - **C2**: SOCs monitored network traffic for signs of C2 communication and blocked malicious IP addresses or domains.
  - **Actions on objectives**: SOCs implemented DLP measures to monitor and block unauthorized data exfiltration to protect critical data and ensure business continuity.

Cyber COBRA

Cyber COBRA is an emerging cybersecurity awareness framework. It is designed to enhance the Cyber Kill Chain by providing contextual details about the threats. This can be integrated into the Cyber Kill Chain, providing more contextual information about the environment and circumstances around the vulnerabilities. These granular details can be helpful in understanding the true impact. SOCs can become more specific in their response strategy. Consider a specific vulnerability in a web server. Cyber COBRA can provide SOC teams with more specific context about the potential attacks on web servers, such as SQL injection/cross-site scripting. This information is crucial to have effective mitigation measures.

Splunk's Cyber Kill Chain

Splunk's version of the Cyber Kill Chain includes similar stages to Lockheed Martin's model but emphasizes the integration of SOAR tools. Splunk enhances incident response and threat detection by leveraging automation and orchestration. This is essential to identify and stop sophisticated attacks. With automation, this model helps SOC teams prevent cyberattacks before they impact any organization. As covered in *Table 5.1*, Splunk provides tools to monitor, detect, and mitigate threats at every stage of the Cyber Kill Chain.

Microsoft's Cyber Kill Chain

Microsoft's framework includes an additional stage called Monetization, which focuses on the attacker's goal of profiting from the attack. This is an essential factor in understanding the motive behind the potential attacks. It provides a more comprehensive view of the attacker's objectives and helps organizations prepare for and respond to advanced threats. This information can be extremely helpful in threat hunting to target potential attackers and be safe proactively.

Diamond model of intrusion analysis

The diamond model is another framework for SOC analysts to understand and analyze cyber threats and intrusions. The key components of the diamond model include adversary, infrastructure used to attack, capability, and victim, as shown in *Figure 5.2*:

Figure 5.2: Diamond model

This diamond model of instruction analysis uses a structured approach. If the security incidents are mapped to these four components, SOC analysts can completely understand the impending attack. Such an approach helps SOC identify the adversary behind the attack, the resources used by the attackers, the TTPs employed, and the target that needs to be protected clearly. This information is crucial to developing effective responses by the SOC teams. This also helps identify vulnerabilities and mitigate them. Some of the real-world examples of exploiting the diamond model are covered here:

- **The Target Data Breach (2013)**:

    o **Adversary**: The attackers were a group of cybercriminals who targeted Target Corporation to steal credit card and personal information.

    o **Infrastructure**: The attackers used a compromised third-party vendor's credentials to gain access to Target's network. They set up malware on Target's POS systems to capture payment card data.

    o **Capability**: The attackers used sophisticated malware known as **BlackPOS** to infiltrate the POS systems and exfiltrate data. They employed techniques such as memory scraping to collect payment card information.

    o **Victim**: The victims were Target Corporation and its customers, whose payment card information was stolen.

- **SOC response using the diamond model**:

    o **Adversary**: SOCs identified the cybercriminal group behind the attack and monitored their activities to gather intelligence.

    o **Infrastructure**: SOCs analyzed the compromised vendor's credentials and the malware used to infiltrate target's network. They implemented stronger access controls and vendor management practices.

    o **Capability**: SOCs studied the BlackPOS malware and developed detection mechanisms to identify similar threats. They used sandboxing environments to analyze the malware's behavior.

    o **Victim**: SOCs focused on protecting Target's customers by implementing DLP measures and enhancing encryption protocols for payment card data.

- **The SolarWinds Supply Chain Attack (2020)**:

    o **Adversary**: The attackers were believed to be a state-sponsored group known as **UNC2452** or **Dark Halo**, targeting SolarWinds and its customers.

    o **Infrastructure**: The attackers compromised SolarWinds' Orion software update mechanism, inserting a backdoor known as **Sunburst** into the software updates.

    o **Capability**: The attackers used advanced techniques to infiltrate the Orion software and distribute the backdoor to SolarWinds' customers. They employed stealthy methods to avoid detection and maintain persistence.

- o **Victim**: The victims were SolarWinds and its customers, including government agencies and large corporations, who installed the compromised software updates.

- • **SOC response using the diamond model**:

  - o **Adversary**: SOCs identified the state-sponsored group behind the attack and monitored their activities to gather intelligence.

  - o **Infrastructure**: SOCs analyzed the compromised software update mechanism and the Sunburst backdoor. They implemented stronger software supply chain security measures.

  - o **Capability**: SOCs studied the Sunburst backdoor and developed detection mechanisms to identify similar threats. They used advanced threat intelligence platforms to track the attacker's techniques.

  - o **Victim**: SOCs focused on protecting SolarWinds' customers by implementing incident response plans and enhancing network segmentation to limit the impact of the attack.

- • **The Equifax Data Breach (2017)**:

  - o **Adversary**: The attackers were a group of cybercriminals who exploited a vulnerability in Equifax's web application to steal sensitive information.

  - o **Infrastructure**: The attackers used a known vulnerability in the Apache Struts framework to gain access to Equifax's network. They set up malware to exfiltrate data from the compromised systems.

  - o **Capability**: The attackers used techniques such as SQL injection to exploit the vulnerability and gain unauthorized access. They employed data exfiltration methods to steal sensitive information.

  - o **Victim**: The victims were Equifax and its customers, whose personal information, including Social Security numbers and credit card details, was stolen.

- • **SOC response using the diamond model**:

  - o **Adversary**: SOCs identified the cybercriminal group behind the attack and monitored their activities to gather intelligence.

  - o **Infrastructure**: SOCs analyzed the compromised web application and the vulnerability in the Apache Struts framework. They implemented stronger web application security.

  - o **Capability**: SOCs studied the Apache Struts and implemented **web application firewalls (WAF)** to detect and block SQL injection attempts. They conducted frequent security scans to identify exploitable weaknesses in web applications and enhanced log monitoring to identify abnormal database queries indicative of data exfiltration.

o **Victim**: SOCs focused on isolating compromised systems and revoking unauthorized access. They conducted thorough investigations to determine the scope of the breach and the affected customers. They also notified impacted users, provided identity theft protection, and enforced additional security measures.

By understanding the Cyber Kill Chain, SOC teams can better anticipate threats, improve response times, and protect their organizations from cyberattacks. Security teams can develop effective defense strategies by understanding these frameworks and their interconnections. Organizations can identify and mitigate potential vulnerabilities and threats by focusing on each stage of the Cyber Kill Chain.

These frameworks and variations of the Cyber Kill Chain help organizations understand the stages of a cyberattack and develop effective defense strategies. By leveraging these models, SOCs can better detect, prevent, and respond to cyber threats.

MITRE ATT&CK framework

The MITRE ATT&CK framework, developed by MITRE Corporation, provides a detailed knowledge base of adversary TTPs. It covers the full spectrum of attacker behaviors, from initial access to impact, and includes specific strategies and methods used at each stage. It covers enterprise networks, including cloud technologies, mobile devices, and industrial control systems, as depicted in the following figure:

Figure 5.3: *MITRE ATT&CK Framework*

The MITRE ATT&CK framework provides detailed adversary tactics and techniques used in cyberattacks, which is a valuable resource for SOCs as it allows for a comprehensive knowledge base of adversary TTPs. This knowledge is relevant for SOC as it helps in the following:

- **Threat handling**: This framework covers specific techniques and procedures used by attackers. Based on this, SOCs can better understand attack patterns and trends.

- **Incident response**: Knowing the detailed TTPs, SOC can develop effective response strategies.

- **Vulnerability management**: The MITRE knowledge base provides SOC analysts deep understanding of the potential vulnerabilities in assets so that mitigation measures can be implemented in time.

The MITRE ATT&CK framework and the Cyber Kill Chain are widely used in cybersecurity to understand and prevent cyberattacks, but they serve different purposes and offer different perspectives. The Cyber Kill Chain helps identify potential attack stages to monitor, while MITRE ATT&CK provides specific **indicators of compromise** (**IOCs**) and mitigation strategies. Many organizations use both frameworks together. The Cyber Kill Chain provides a high-level roadmap of an attack, while MITRE ATT&CK offers detailed, granular information on the techniques and procedures used at each stage. By combining the two, organizations can better understand the attacker's process and develop more comprehensive defense strategies.

Some real-world scenarios exploiting the MITRE ATT&CK framework are:

- **Financial institution enhances threat detection**:

    o **Challenge**: A large financial institution faced frequent phishing attacks and needed to improve its threat detection capabilities.

    o **Solution**: The SOC team mapped the phishing attack techniques to the MITRE ATT&CK framework. They identified specific tactics and techniques used by attackers, such as Spearphishing Attachment (T1566.001) and Spearphishing Link (T1566.002).

    o **Implementation**: The SOC team used the ATT&CK framework to develop detection rules and signatures for their SIEM system. They also implemented email filtering and web filtering solutions to block malicious payloads.

    o **Outcome**: By leveraging the MITRE ATT&CK framework, the institution improved its ability to detect and respond to phishing attacks. The SOC team reduced the number of successful phishing attempts and minimized the impact of such attacks on the organization.

- **Healthcare organization improves incident response**:

    o **Challenge**: A large healthcare organization needed to enhance its incident response capabilities to protect sensitive patient data from cyber threats.

    o **Solution**: The SOC team mapped recent cyber incidents to the MITRE ATT&CK framework. They identified techniques such as Credential Dumping (T1003) and Data Encrypted for Impact (T1486).

- o **Implementation**: The SOC team used the ATT&CK framework to develop playbooks for incident response. They implemented **endpoint detection and response (EDR)** solutions to monitor for suspicious activities and automate response actions.

- o **Outcome**: By using the MITRE ATT&CK framework, the healthcare organization improved its incident response capabilities. The SOC team was able to quickly detect and contain cyber threats, protecting sensitive patient data and ensuring compliance with healthcare regulations.

- **Retail company enhances threat hunting**:

  - o **Challenge**: A global retail company needed to enhance its threat hunting capabilities to proactively identify and mitigate cyber threats.

  - o **Solution**: The SOC team mapped threat hunting activities to the MITRE ATT&CK framework. They focused on techniques such as Lateral Movement (T1078) and Command and Control (T1071).

  - o **Implementation**: The SOC team used the ATT&CK framework to develop threat hunting hypotheses and search queries. They implemented advanced threat intelligence platforms to gather and analyze data from various sources.

  - o **Outcome**: By leveraging the MITRE ATT&CK framework, the retail company enhanced its threat hunting capabilities. The SOC team was able to proactively identify and mitigate cyber threats, reducing the risk of data breaches and improving the overall security posture.

D3FEND frameworks

The MITRE D3FEND framework is a standardized counterpart of MITRE Attack framework. It covers defensive cybersecurity techniques. The key components of the D3FEND framework are as depicted in the following figure:

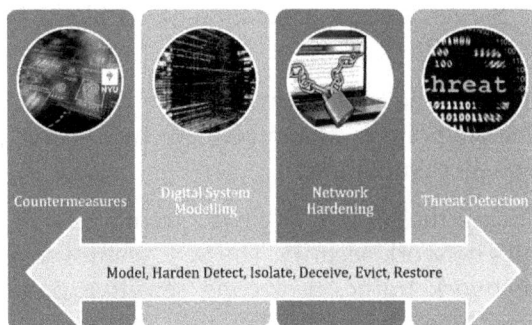

Figure 5.4: *MITRE D3FEND framework*

MITRE D3FEND framework provides techniques and strategies to detect, isolate, deceive, and evict attackers. It further helps create security baselining through modeling digital systems to enhance security. The D3FEND framework provides strategies to strengthen network defenses and reduce vulnerabilities. After providing all these countermeasures, digital system modeling, network hardening, and threat detection functionalities, it further looks into effective incident response strategies for SOC analysts. With these standardized countermeasures, SOC teams can build a robust cyber-safe environment. D3FEND framework helps SOCs implement proactive measures to prevent cyberattacks.

Some real-world scenarios exploiting the MITRE D3FEND framework are covered here:

- **Financial institution enhances endpoint security**:
  - **Challenge**: A large financial institution faced frequent malware attacks targeting its endpoints.
  - **Solution**: The SOC team mapped the malware attack techniques to the MITRE D3FEND framework. They identified defensive techniques such as Endpoint-based Web Server Access Mediation (D3-EBWSAM) and Per Host Download-Upload Ratio Analysis (D3-PHDURA).
  - **Implementation**: The SOC team used the D3FEND framework to develop endpoint security policies and implement tools for web server access mediation and download-upload ratio analysis.
  - **Outcome**: By leveraging the MITRE D3FEND framework, the institution improved its endpoint security. The SOC team reduced the number of successful malware attacks and minimized the impact on the organization.

- **Healthcare organization strengthens network security**:
  - **Challenge**: A large healthcare organization needed to enhance its network security to protect sensitive patient data from cyber threats.
  - **Solution**: The SOC team mapped network attack techniques to the MITRE D3FEND framework. They identified defensive techniques such as Proxy-based Web Server Access Mediation (D3-PBWSAM) and Byte Sequence Emulation (D3-BSE).
  - **Implementation**: The SOC team used the D3FEND framework to develop network security policies and implement web server access mediation tools and byte sequence emulation.
  - **Outcome**: Using the MITRE D3FEND framework improved the healthcare organization's network security. The SOC team was able to detect and block malicious network traffic, protecting sensitive patient data and ensuring compliance with healthcare regulations.

- **Retail company enhances threat detection**:
  - **Challenge**: A global retail company needed to enhance its threat detection capabilities to proactively identify and mitigate cyber threats.

- o **Solution**: The SOC team mapped threat detection techniques to the MITRE D3FEND framework. They focused on techniques such as File Content Analysis (D3-FCA) and Identifier Reputation Analysis (D3-IRA).

- o **Implementation**: The SOC team used the D3FEND framework to develop threat detection policies and implement tools for file content analysis and identifier reputation analysis.

- o **Outcome**: By leveraging the MITRE D3FEND framework, the retail company enhanced its threat detection capabilities. The SOC team was able to proactively identify and mitigate cyber threats, reducing the risk of data breaches and improving the overall security posture.

- **Government agency strengthens defensive measures**:
  - o **Challenge**: A government agency needed to strengthen its defensive measures against sophisticated cyber threats.

  - o **Solution**: The SOC team mapped known adversary techniques to the MITRE D3FEND framework. They identified defensive techniques such as Disk Encryption (D3-DE) and Driver Load Integrity Checking (D3-DLIC).

  - o **Implementation**: The SOC team used the D3FEND framework to develop defensive measures and implement tools for disk encryption and driver load integrity checking.

  - o **Outcome**: By using the MITRE D3FEND framework, the government agency strengthened its defensive measures. The SOC team was able to protect critical infrastructure and sensitive data from cyber threats.

Evolving threat landscape

The cyber threat landscape is continuously evolving, driven by increasingly sophisticated techniques, advanced AI, and the rise of new attack vectors. To effectively combat these threats, SOCs must adapt and develop accordingly. The threat landscape constantly evolves, with cybercriminals becoming more sophisticated and leveraging new technologies to launch attacks. SOCs must adapt to these changes to effectively protect organizations. The threat landscape was covered in *Chapter 1, Cybersecurity Basics* earlier. However, the threat landscape is evolving with changing times and advanced technologies. Some of the key threats observed in this era are covered in the upcoming subsections.

AI-powered attacks

AI has brought a paradigm shift in how operations are carried out. Even in cybersecurity, AI is revolutionizing attack and defense mechanisms. AI can automate attacks beyond human thinking, making them more lethal and difficult to detect. Cybercriminals use AI and machine learning to automate attacks and create more sophisticated malware and exploits. SOCs must also leverage AI to counter such AI-powered threats and enhance threat detection and response.

SOCs can employ AI and machine learning to detect anomalies and predict attacks. SOCs can leverage AI to analyze vast amounts of threat intelligence data in real-time and build automated responses.

Supply chain attacks

Given the present volatile geo-political scenario, supply chains are getting the worst impact. Third-party vendors, suppliers, and their interaction with the target organization enhance the attack surface manifold. The number of data leaks discovered nowadays provides a typical modus operandi for planning cyberattacks. Getting potential target information through open-source intelligence and monitoring the diverse attack surface can help cyber attackers employ the right TTPs to target third-party vendors and suppliers to compromise the entire supply chain. Attackers target the supply chain to compromise multiple organizations through a single attack vector.

SOCs need to implement rigorous vendor security assessments and monitoring. SOCs must gain visibility into the entire supply chain to identify potential vulnerabilities.

Ransomware and extortion

Cyber attackers are gaining unauthorized access to information systems. They are thereafter encrypting critical systems and demanding ransom payments. Ransomware attacks are becoming more frequent and complex. Attackers are also targeting essential infrastructure and using double extortion tactics.

SOCs need to be ever-vigilant in identifying such ransomware attacks. SOCs can help implement strong backup and recovery strategies to counter such ransomware attacks and ensure business continuity. SOCs can also develop detailed incident response plans to minimize downtime.

IoT and OT security

With Industry 4.0 and 5G technologies, IoT is getting integrated into OT and IT environments. The legacy nature of these sensors brings in additional vulnerabilities. Exploiting these vulnerabilities in IoT devices and industrial control systems becomes an easy target for attackers.

SOC teams need to be sensitized toward this critical integration aspect. SOCs can deploy security solutions specifically designed for IoT devices. To counter such threats, they need to integrate OT security into the overall security strategy.

Cloud security challenges

Cloud adoptions are increasing daily, providing disparate attack surfaces for attackers to exploit. Misconfigurations, data breaches, and unauthorized access to cloud environments are the most common attack vectors.

SOCs need to monitor cloud environments for misconfigurations and vulnerabilities. SOCs can significantly improve security posture by controlling access to cloud applications and data.

By staying informed and vigilant about the latest threats, leveraging advanced technologies, and fostering a culture of innovation and collaboration, SOCs can protect organizations from the ever-evolving cyber threat landscape. Here is how organizations have adapted to evolving threats through real-world scenarios and strategic security measures:

- **AI-powered attacks**:
  - **Organization**: A large technology company
  - **Challenge**: Attackers leveraged AI-powered techniques to evade traditional security defenses, dynamically adjusting their tactics to bypass detection.
  - **Solution**: The SOC team deployed AI-driven threat detection systems capable of identifying abnormal behaviors and predicting attack patterns. They integrated machine learning models to analyze vast amounts of real-time security intelligence, improving proactive defense mechanisms.
  - **Outcome**: By embracing AI-embraced cybersecurity, the company strengthened its ability to counter sophisticated threats, reducing false positives and detecting attacks earlier in the intrusion cycle.

- **Supply chain security strengthening**:
  - **Organization**: A multinational retail corporation
  - **Challenge**: Attackers exploited vulnerabilities in third-party software used by the company, leading to a supply chain compromise.
  - **Solution**: The organization enforced vendor risk management protocols, including continuous monitoring of external dependencies, strict access controls, and vulnerability assessments of third-party integrations.
  - **Outcome**: Strengthened security across the supply chain, reducing exposure to indirect cyber threats while ensuring safe collaboration with external vendors.

- **Ransomware defense strategy**:
  - **Organization**: A healthcare provider
  - **Challenge**: The organization was targeted by ransomware, threatening critical patient data and operational systems.
  - **Solution**: The SOC implemented network segmentation, behavioral analytics, and endpoint protection platforms to detect and block ransomware before encryption occurred. They also established secure backup protocols and incident response frameworks to recover operations swiftly.

- o   **Outcome**: The proactive approach helped minimize downtime, prevent significant data loss, and strengthen resilience against future ransomware attacks.

- **Industrial control system (ICS) protection against cyberattacks**:

  - o   **Organization**: A global manufacturing company

  - o   **Challenge**: The company experienced cyber threats targeting its SCADA systems, potentially disrupting industrial operations.

  - o   **Solution**: The SOC implemented network segmentation, strict access controls, and IDS for ICS networks. They also enforced behavioral anomaly detection to monitor deviations from normal industrial processes.

  - o   **Outcome**: The enhanced security measures prevented unauthorized access to industrial control systems, safeguarding critical manufacturing operations.

- **OT security in energy sector—defending against supply chain attacks**:

  - o   **Organization**: A national power grid operator

  - o   **Challenge**: Attackers attempted to compromise power distribution systems by exploiting vulnerabilities in third-party OT vendors supplying hardware and software solutions.

  - o   **Solution**: The organization adopted supply chain security protocols, including vendor risk assessments, secure software development practices, and real-time threat intelligence integration for industrial networks.

  - o   **Outcome**: By tightening security controls on OT assets, the operator minimized cyber risks, ensuring uninterrupted energy distribution while preventing adversarial sabotage.

- **Cloud-based security enhancements**:

  - o   **Organization**: A global financial institution

  - o   **Challenge**: The adoption of cloud computing introduced risks such as unauthorized access, misconfigurations, and data breaches.

  - o   **Solution**: The SOC established a zero-trust architecture, implementing identity-based authentication, continuous monitoring, and **cloud security posture management (CSPM)** tools. They also leveraged cloud-native SIEM solutions to detect anomalies in cloud environments.

  - o   **Outcome**: By reinforcing cloud security measures, the institution improved its ability to prevent unauthorized access, mitigate insider threats, and ensure regulatory compliance.

Security operations centers function optimization

Optimizing a SOC involves a multi-faceted approach to enhance efficiency, effectiveness, and security posture. People, processes, and technology can be optimized effectively to harness defense mechanisms against complex cyber threats. The optimization will be covered in detail in *Section 3* of this book. Monitoring some **key performance indicators (KPI)** for SOC Optimization is worthwhile. These can be as follows:

- **Mean time to detect (MTTD)**: It is the time taken to identify a security incident, which is crucial for effective response and containment of the damage.

- **Mean time to respond (MTTR)**: The time taken to respond to a security incident is crucial for mitigation measures.

- **False positive rate**: It is the percentage of alerts that are not security incidents. This needs to be minimized to the greatest possible extent.

By focusing on these areas and continuously monitoring performance metrics, organizations can optimize their SOC functions, improve overall security posture, and mitigate risks effectively.

Conclusion

Modern SOC's development has significantly transformed how organizations protect themselves against the evolving threat landscape. By integrating advanced frameworks and models, SOCs are more equipped to detect, respond to, and mitigate cyber threats efficiently. Modern SOCs leverage various models to enhance their operations, including centralized, distributed, and virtual SOCs.

To combat the evolving threats, SOCs must adopt proactive defense strategies, leverage threat intelligence, and continuously update their knowledge and tools. By employing various attack and defense frameworks, SOCs can provide robust defenses against cyber threats, ensuring the security and resilience of their organizations.

In the next chapter, we will discuss incident response. The key concepts of log management, IOC, IOA, and the incident response lifecycle will improve the incident response strategy and effectively mitigate cyber threats.

Points to remember

Here are some key takeaways from this chapter:

- SOC models provide the flexibility and scalability required to address diverse security needs and ensure robust monitoring and incident response.

- Cyber Kill Chain remains a foundational framework for understanding the stages of a cyberattack.

- MITRE ATT&CK framework provides TTPs, and complimenting it, the MITRE D3FEND framework provides defensive techniques

Multiple choice questions

1. **Which of the following is not a type of SOC model?**
   a. Centralized SOC
   b. Distributed SOC
   c. Virtual SOC
   d. Multi Cloud SOC

2. **At which stage does the attacker transmit the weaponized payload to the target?**
   a. Installation
   b. command and control
   c. Delivery
   d. Actions on objectives

3. **Which domain does the MITRE ATT&CK framework not cover?**
   a. Enterprise
   b. Mobile
   c. Industrial Control System
   d. Automotive

Answers

1	d
2	c
3	d

Questions

1. Describe the key differences between a centralized SOC and a distributed SOC.
2. Explain the significance of the C2 stage in the Cyber Kill Chain and how SOCs can mitigate risks associated with it.
3. Describe how the MITRE ATT&CK and MITRE D3FEND frameworks complement each other in enhancing an organization's cybersecurity posture.

Key terms

Some of the key terms used in this chapter are:

- **MSSP**: These are crucial in providing SOC services for organizations.
- **Cyber Kill Chain**: Critical in identifying the attack methodology.

CHAPTER 6
Incident Response

Introduction

Management of incidents is the basic building block of any SOC. Cybersecurity incidents, whether data breaches, malware attacks, or insider threats, can disrupt an organization's operations, reputation, and financial standing. Therefore, having a robust incident response capability is critical. This chapter exactly covers this essential SOC operation. One of the vital aspects of incident response is log management. The logs are collated from disparate sources, endpoints, network devices, IPS/IDS, etc. It is essential to know the log management and how they are correlated, leading to SIEM use cases.

In today's rapidly evolving threat landscape, organizations must adopt robust incident response capabilities to safeguard their operations. Several high-profile incidents, such as the Equifax data breach, SolarWinds supply chain attack, colonial pipeline ransomware attack, and Microsoft Exchange Server vulnerability, have underscored the critical need for structured response frameworks. These cases highlight how effective incident response measures, such as rapid detection, containment, and recovery, can significantly enhance security posture, minimize downtime, and fortify resilience against future threats. Organizations that have successfully implemented these strategies have demonstrated notable improvements in their security posture, often integrating frameworks like **National Institute of Standards and Technology (NIST)** and **Computer Security Incident Response Team (CSIRT)** best practices to ensure comprehensive coverage. The impact of these incidents has led to widespread adoption of zero-trust architectures, enhanced threat intelligence mechanisms, and continuous monitoring solutions. By analyzing these examples and leveraging AI-powered tools, security teams can refine their incident response strategies to adapt to emerging threats and build a more resilient defense infrastructure.

This chapter examines the core aspects of incident response within a SOC. It outlines the various phases, best practices, and tools for managing security incidents effectively and provides a comprehensive guide on how organizations can establish and maintain a proactive incident response capability, enabling them to counter cyber threats efficiently.

Structure

In this chapter, we will discuss the following topics:

- Log management
- Log monitoring and management with Splunk
- IOC and indicators of attacks
- SOCs using IOC and IOAs
- Incident response lifecycle
- Incident management
- SIEM overview

Objectives

By the end of this chapter, readers will gain a thorough understanding of the incident response lifecycle, the importance of a proactive incident response strategy, and the tools and techniques that can help SOC teams effectively manage and mitigate cyber threats. This knowledge will empower organizations to build a resilient cybersecurity posture, ensuring they are well-prepared to tackle the ever-evolving landscape of cyber risks.

Log management

The effective management of logs is the cornerstone of an effective SOC. Log management refers to handling and maintaining logs generated by various systems, applications, and devices within an organization's ICT infrastructure. These logs contain a wealth of information that can be used to detect, investigate, and respond to security incidents.

In this converged digital landscape, organizations face different kinds of security threats. To effectively combat these threats, SOCs rely on a robust defensive log management strategy. Log management involves systematically collecting, analyzing, and retaining system and application logs to detect anomalies, identify threats, and ensure compliance with regulatory requirements. By effectively managing logs, SOC analysts can gain valuable insights into security incidents, identify potential threats, and respond to attacks promptly. The primary objective of log management in a SOC is to provide actionable intelligence that can help security analysts mitigate risks and enhance the overall security posture. Here are a few reasons why logs are essential:

- **Incident detection and response**: Logs provide a detailed record of events, which can be used to detect suspicious activities and respond to incidents quickly. Log analysis can help identify anomalous behavior or suspicious activity, enabling early detection of security incidents.

- **Compliance and audit**: Many regulatory frameworks require organizations to maintain logs for auditing purposes. Proper log management ensures that organizations can demonstrate compliance. Log data can be crucial evidence in legal proceedings and regulatory compliance efforts.

- **Forensic investigations**: In the aftermath of a security breach, logs are crucial for understanding how the attack occurred and what steps can be taken to prevent future incidents. By examining detailed logs, analysts can reconstruct the timeline of an attack, pinpoint the root cause, and determine the extent of the damage.

- **Operational insights**: Logs can offer insights into the performance and health of systems and applications, allowing for proactive maintenance and optimization. Real-time log monitoring allows SOC analysts to keep track of system and application activity, identifying potential vulnerabilities and misconfigurations. Analysts can detect deviations that indicate security incidents by establishing baseline behavior and using statistical analysis.

- **Threat hunting**: By searching for specific patterns in log data, analysts can identify signs of compromise, such as unauthorized access or data exfiltration. Advanced log analysis techniques, such as behavioral analytics and machine learning, can uncover hidden threats and potential attacks before they materialize.

Log management process

Log management process in a SOC typically involves the following steps, as covered in *Figure 6.1*:

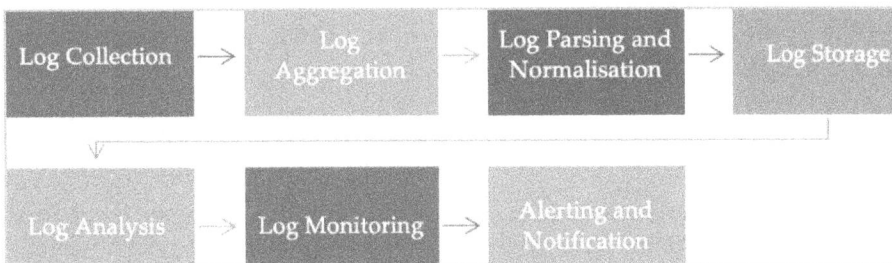

Figure 6.1: *Log management process*

The log management process, as depicted in the preceding figure, has several inter-dependent steps. Let us look at them in detail:

1. **Log collection**: Logs are collated from various sources, such as firewalls, IDS/IPS, endpoint devices, **operating system (OS)**, **Active Directory (AD)**, and applications.

2. **Log aggregation**: Log data gets stored in a single centralized repository to facilitate easy access and analysis.

3. **Log parsing and normalization**: Log data is converted into a standardized format to ensure consistency and enable practical analysis. Standardization entails converting logs from different sources into a consistent format for more straightforward analysis. Relevant information is extracted from log messages, such as timestamps, source IP addresses, and error codes.

4. **Log storage**: Log data is stored securely, ensuring it is protected from tampering and can be retained for the required retention period to meet compliance and forensic requirements. Scalable storage is essential for ensuring the ability to handle increasing volumes of log data.

5. **Log analysis**: Various tools and techniques, such as powerful search queries, are used to filter and analyze log data, identify patterns, and detect anomalies. These tools also identify relationships between log events to uncover complex attack patterns.

6. **Log monitoring**: Logs are continuously monitored in real time to detect and respond to security events as they occur.

7. **Alerting and notification**: Alerts are generated for critical security events, such as unauthorized access or system failures. This also involves triggering automated responses, such as blocking IP addresses or sending notifications to security teams.

Tools for log management

Several tools and solutions are available to assist with log management in a SOC. Some of the popular ones are listed here:

-   **SIEM systems**: These platforms collect, aggregate, and analyze log data from multiple sources to comprehensively view an organization's security posture.

-   **Log management solutions**: Tools specifically designed for collecting, storing, and analyzing log data, such as **Elastic Stack (ELK Stack)**, Splunk, and Graylog.

-   **Cloud-based solutions**: Many organizations are adopting cloud-based log management solutions for scalability and ease of use, such as AWS CloudTrail and Microsoft Azure Sentinel.

- **SOAR systems**: It involves integrating diverse security tools and technologies to streamline security operations and enhance response efforts against cyber threats. By automating repetitive and manual tasks, SOAR allows security teams to focus on more critical activities and respond to incidents with increased speed and accuracy.

Best practices for effective log management

To ensure effective log management, organizations should adhere to the following best practices:

- **Define clear objectives**: Establish clear goals for log management based on the organization's security requirements and compliance obligations.

- **Develop a log management policy**: Create a comprehensive policy that outlines the procedures for log collection, storage, analysis, and retention. Establish a clear policy for log retention, balancing security needs with storage costs.

- **Ensure log integrity**: Implement measures to protect the integrity of log data, such as encryption and access controls. Protect sensitive information within logs by encrypting them at rest and in transit.

- **Automate log analysis**: Use automation tools and techniques to streamline the log analysis process and reduce the workload on security analysts. Implement a SIEM/SOAR solution to correlate log data from multiple sources and generate actionable insights. Utilize UBA to detect unusual user behavior that may indicate malicious activity.

- **Regularly review and update**: Periodically review and update log management practices to ensure they remain effective and aligned with the evolving threat landscape. Regular reviews of log data should be conducted to identify potential threats and anomalies.

It is essential to conduct regular tests to ensure the effectiveness of log management processes and fine-tune alert thresholds. Log management is a fundamental aspect of a robust cybersecurity strategy. By effectively managing logs, organizations can enhance their ability to detect and respond to security incidents, ensure compliance with regulatory requirements, and gain valuable operational insights. In a SOC, where the stakes are high, and the threats are ever-present, mastering log management is essential for maintaining a strong security posture.

Log management tools like Splunk, Elastic Stack, and Graylog have become essential for organizations aiming to strengthen their incident response capabilities. These platforms enable security teams to collect, analyze, and correlate logs from various sources, helping them detect threats faster and respond more effectively.

For instance, *NASA* has leveraged Splunk to enhance its cybersecurity posture, using real-time log analysis to detect anomalies and prevent potential breaches. Similarly, *Netflix* relies on Elastic Stack to monitor its vast infrastructure, ensuring seamless operations while swiftly identifying security incidents. Meanwhile, Graylog has been widely adopted by government agencies and financial institutions, providing them with centralized log management and security analytics to reduce incident response time.

By integrating these tools, organizations can streamline threat detection, improve forensic investigations, and automate response workflows, ultimately minimizing downtime and mitigating risks. Their success stories highlight the growing importance of log management in modern cybersecurity strategies.

Log monitoring and management with Splunk

Splunk is a powerful log monitoring and management tool that offers robust features for collecting, analyzing, and visualizing log data. Here is a practical guide to get you started with Splunk for effective log management:

Follow these steps to set up Splunk:

1. **Installation**: Download and install Splunk on your server or use Splunk Cloud for a cloud-based solution. Follow the on-screen instructions to complete the installation. Note the username and password you set during this process. Once the installation is complete, the application will open in the web browser, as shown in the following figure:

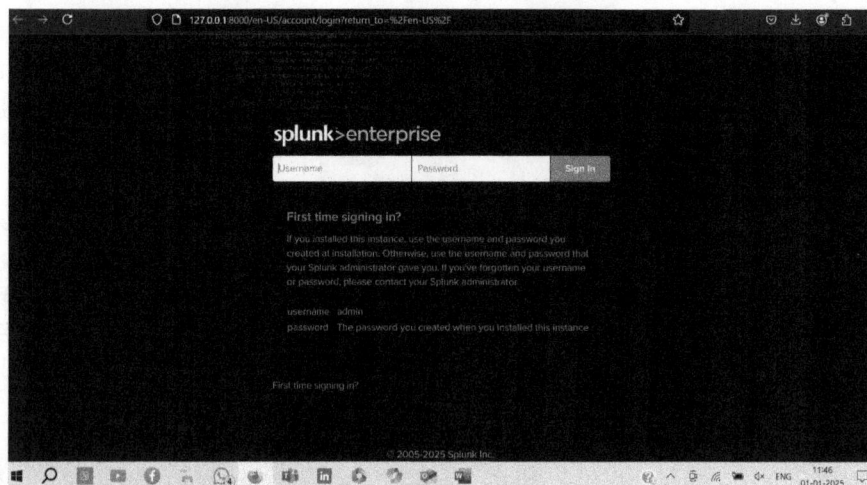

Figure 6.2: Splunk after installation

2. **Configuration**: Configure Splunk to collect log data from various sources such as servers, applications, network devices, and endpoints. This can be found in **Settings | Add Data**, as shown in the following figure:

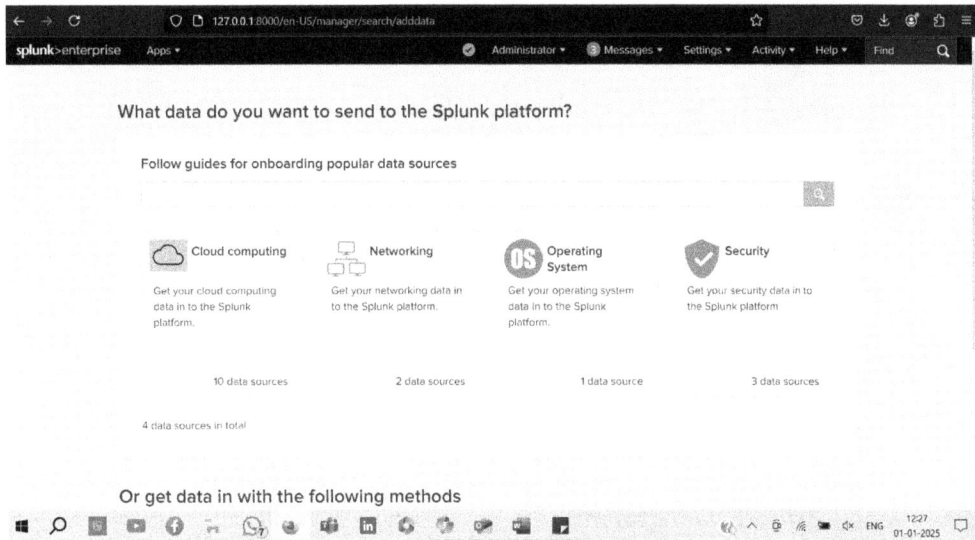

Figure 6.3: Adding Data in Splunk

3. **Log collection**: The logs are to be collected from different sources as follows:

   a. **Data sources**: Identify the sources of log data you want to monitor. This can include web servers, application servers, firewalls, and more. The data can further be extracted with options in Splunk, as shown in the following figure:

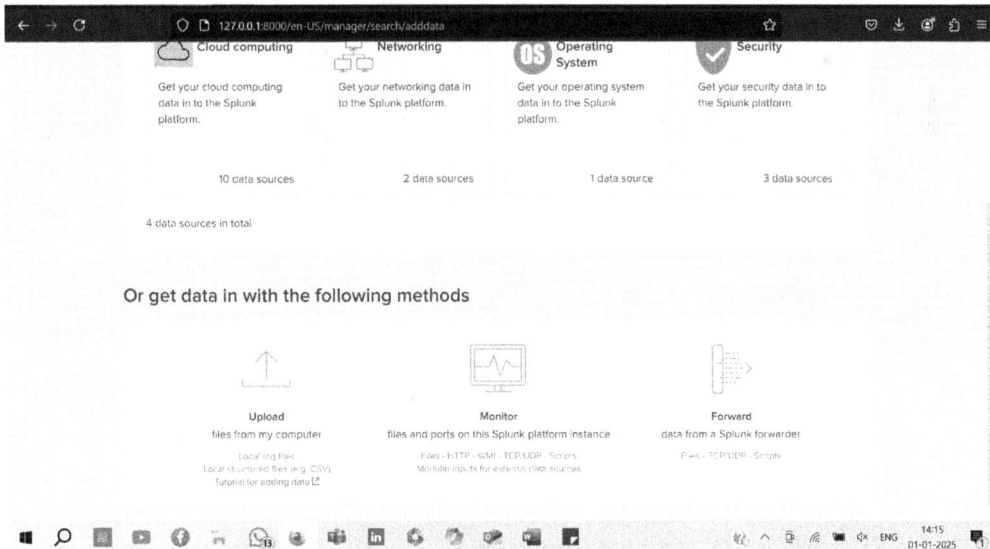

Figure 6.4: Getting data in Splunk

   b. **Forwarders**: Use Splunk forwarders from Settings, Data, Forwarding and Receiving option to collect log data from remote sources and send it to your

Splunk instance. This can be used to forward logs between two or more Splunk instances or receive data from other instances.

   c. **Indexes**: After the data is added, the indexer processes it and stores it in indexes. Index directories, also called buckets, are collections of log files.

4. **Log parsing and normalization:**

   a. **Parsing**: Use Splunk's built-in parsers to extract relevant information from log files.

   b. **Normalization**: Normalize log data to a consistent format for more straightforward analysis.

5. **Log analysis:**

   a. **Search**: Use Splunk's **search and reporting language (SPL)** to query log data and extract meaningful insights, as shown in the following figure:

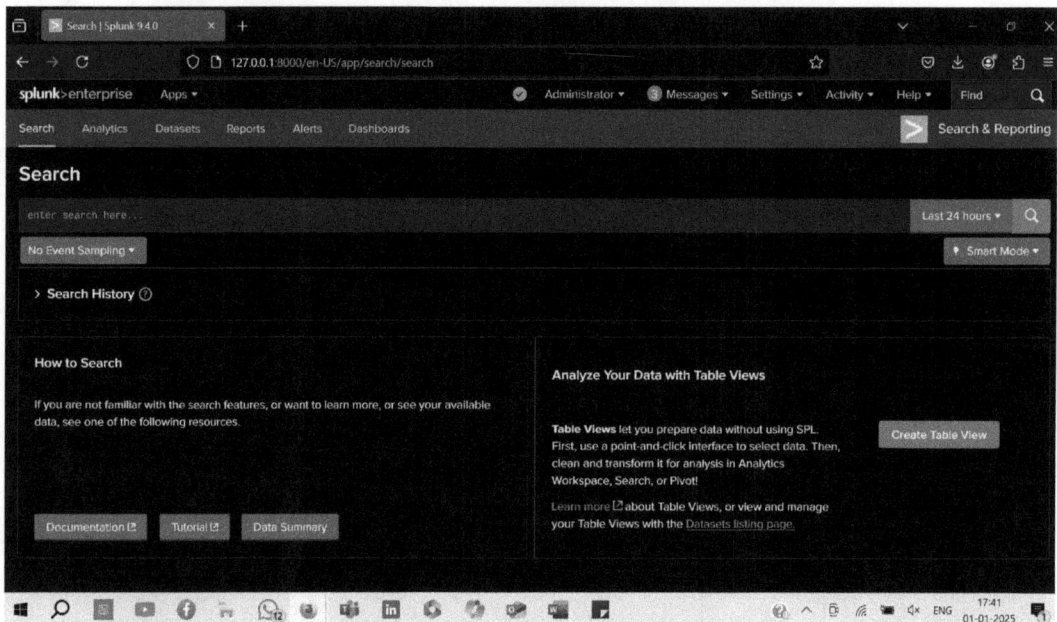

Figure 6.5: Search log data in Splunk

   b. **Dashboards**: Create dashboards to visualize log data and monitor key metrics in real-time as per the key performance indicators set by the organization. Different views can be set to monitor specific instances like abnormal user behavior, the number of incidents discovered, etc.

   c. **Alerts**: Set up alerts to notify you of specific events or anomalies in your log data.

6. **Log monitoring:**

    a. **Real-time monitoring**: Continuously monitor log data in real-time to detect and respond to security incidents promptly.

    b. **Trend analysis**: Analyze log data over time to identify trends and patterns that can help in proactive maintenance and optimization.

Splunk has become a vital tool for organizations looking to strengthen their log management and incident response processes. Its advanced analytics and automation capabilities enable security teams to detect and mitigate threats with greater speed and efficiency.

For example, NASA relies on Splunk to process massive volumes of log data, allowing for quick identification of anomalies and potential security risks. This proactive approach has helped streamline their cybersecurity efforts. Similarly, Check Point, a global leader in cybersecurity, has reported a fivefold acceleration in security investigations since integrating Splunk into its operations. The ability to correlate log data from diverse sources has significantly enhanced their threat detection capabilities.

Retail giant Carrefour has also benefited from Splunk's log management features, leveraging its automation tools to reduce false positives and prioritize alerts based on real risk factors. This has resulted in better resource allocation and a stronger security posture.

Organizations that incorporate Splunk into their security workflows often experience noticeable improvements in key incident response metrics, such as **mean time to detect (MTTD)**, **mean time to acknowledge (MTTA)**, and **mean time to resolution (MTTR)**. By reducing downtime and optimizing threat mitigation strategies, these companies have bolstered their overall cybersecurity resilience.

Once the Splunk is set up and respective logs are configured, the SOC analysts can continuously monitor the dashboards and take appropriate steps to mitigate the cyber threats. The response to such mitigation actions can be automated with tools like SOAR. The SOC analysts can then concentrate on threat hunting by monitoring ever-evolving IOC and **indicators of attacks (IOA)**.

IOC and indicators of attacks

IOC and IOAs are crucial concepts in cybersecurity, particularly within SOCs. They help security teams identify potential threats and respond to security incidents more effectively during event monitoring.

Indicators of compromise

IOC are evidence that indicates a system or network has been compromised. They are often used to detect and respond to active attacks.

Common types of IOC include the following:

- **File hashes**: Unique identifiers for files, such as MD5, SHA-1, or SHA-256.

- **IP addresses**: The numerical addresses assigned to devices on a network.

- **Domain names**: Human-readable names for IP addresses.

- **URLs**: Web addresses used to access online resources.

- **Email addresses**: Electronic mail addresses.

- **Malicious code signatures**: Unique identifiers for malicious software.

- **Network traffic patterns**: Unusual network activity, such as excessive data transfer or unusual port usage.

Example of IOC usage: If a SOC analyst detects a malicious file with a specific hash on a system, they can use that hash as an IOC to search for other infected systems or to block the file from being executed.

Indicators of attack

IOAs are early warning signs that a cyberattack is imminent or in progress. They are often used to detect and prevent attacks proactively. Common types of IOAs include the following:

- **Suspicious network traffic**: Unusual network activity, such as scanning or reconnaissance attempts.

- **Phishing emails**: Emails designed to trick users into revealing sensitive information.

- **Watering hole attacks**: Attacks that target specific groups or organizations by compromising websites they frequently visit.

- **Exploit kits**: Automated tools used to exploit vulnerabilities in software.

- **Malicious code delivery methods**: Techniques used to distribute malware, such as drive-by downloads or malicious email attachments.

Example of IOA usage: If a SOC analyst observes a sudden increase in scanning activity from a specific IP address, they can investigate further to determine if it is a legitimate scan or a potential attack.

SOCs using IOC and IOAs

SOCs use IOC and IOAs in a variety of ways, including the following:

- **Threat hunting**: Actively searching for threats by analyzing log data and network traffic for indicators of compromise.

- **Incident response**: Identifying and responding to security incidents by analyzing IOC and IOAs.

- **Vulnerability management**: Identifying and mitigating vulnerabilities that attackers could exploit.

- **Security intelligence**: Gathering and analyzing threat intelligence to stay informed about the latest threats.

By effectively using IOC and IOAs, SOCs can significantly improve their ability to detect, prevent, and respond to cyberattacks.

Significant differences between IOC and IOAs are as follows:

Parameter	IOC	IOAs
Focus	Identify evidence of a past compromise.	Detect ongoing or imminent attacks.
Timeframe	Used post-incident for investigation.	Used proactively to detect threats in real-time
Usage	Valuable for forensic analysis	Help in early threat detection and response

Table 6.1: Difference between IOC and IOAs

Organizations worldwide are leveraging IOC and IOAs to strengthen their threat detection and response strategies, enabling faster identification and mitigation of cyber threats. For instance, Microsoft has integrated IOAs into its Defender for Endpoint solution, allowing security teams to detect malicious behaviors before an attack fully materializes. This proactive approach has significantly reduced the MTTD and MTTR across enterprises using its security suite. Similarly, CrowdStrike employs IOAs within its Falcon platform, focusing on behavioral analytics rather than relying solely on known signatures. This has led to a 40% improvement in threat detection accuracy, helping organizations prevent breaches before they escalate.

Financial institutions such as *JPMorgan Chase* utilize IOC extensively within their SOCs to correlate threat intelligence and identify compromised assets. By integrating IOC into their SIEM systems, they have enhanced their ability to detect anomalies, reducing incident response times by 30%. Meanwhile, government agencies and critical infrastructure providers have adopted IOA-driven threat hunting methodologies to proactively identify adversarial **tactics, techniques, and procedures** (**TTPs**), strengthening their cyber resilience.

These real-world implementations highlight the growing importance of IOC and IOAs in modern cybersecurity frameworks. By combining historical compromise indicators with real-time attack detection, organizations can fortify their defenses, minimize downtime, and improve overall security posture.

Incident response lifecycle

Incident response is critical in any SOC that identifies, manages, and mitigates security incidents. This structured approach encompasses a series of sequential steps, from the initial detection and identification of a security incident to its complete resolution and recovery. The incident response lifecycle has several phases that guide the response team in effectively handling security breaches. The phases are as shown in the following figure:

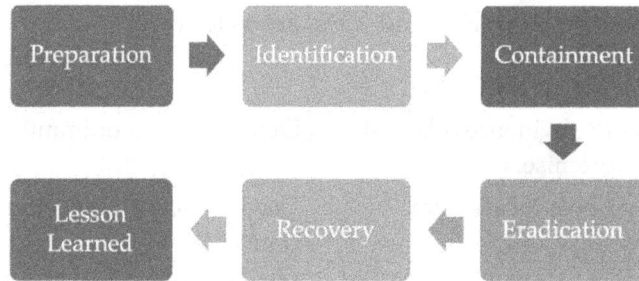

Figure 6.6: Incident response lifecycle

Let us understand the phases in detail:

- **Preparation**: This phase involves establishing and maintaining an incident response capability. Some of the key activities include the following:

  o **Developing an incident response plan**: It involves documenting the procedures and processes for incident response. This includes defining roles and responsibilities, establishing communication channels, and outlining procedures for each phase.

  o **Setting up tools and resources**: This entails ensuring that necessary tools (like SIEM, EDR, and SOAR platforms, antivirus software) and resources (trained personnel) are in place.

  o **Training and awareness**: This involves conducting regular training sessions and employee awareness programs. This helps ensure the team is prepared to respond effectively in a real-world scenario.

- **Identification**: This phase focuses on detecting and identifying potential security incidents. Some of the key activities include the following:

  o **Monitoring**: Continuously monitor systems and networks for signs of suspicious activity.

  o **Detection**: Utilize security tools, threat intelligence feeds, and human monitoring to identify anomalies, potential security incidents, and threats.

  o **Initial analysis**: Investigate alerts to confirm whether they are legitimate incidents. Determine the severity and potential impact of the incident to prioritize response efforts.

- **Containment**: Once an incident is identified, the primary goal is to contain the impact. This phase is divided into the following two stages:

  o **Short-term containment**: Taking immediate actions to prevent the incident from spreading further, such as isolating affected systems. Prevent further unauthorized access to critical systems and data.

  o **Long-term containment**: Implementing more stable solutions, such as applying patches and updates, to keep the incident contained while planning eradication.

- **Eradication**: This phase involves removing the incident's root cause and any associated artifacts. Key activities include the following:

  o **Identifying the cause**: Determining the source and nature of the incident.

  o **Removing malicious components**: Eliminate the root cause of the incident, such as malware, unauthorized access points, malicious code, compromised accounts, and other harmful elements. Address any underlying vulnerabilities that may have contributed to the incident.

  o **Validating systems**: Ensure affected systems are clean and secure before proceeding.

- **Recovery**: The goal of the recovery phase is to restore and validate system functionality. The key steps include:

  o **Restoration**: Restore affected systems and data from backups or alternative sources back online in a controlled manner.

  o **Monitoring**: Closely monitor systems for any signs of lingering issues or further attacks.

  o **Validating security**: Thoroughly test systems to ensure they are functioning correctly and securely.

- **Lessons learned**: After resolving the incident, reflecting on the response process to identify improvements is essential. This phase includes:

  o **Post-incident review**: Conduct a detailed review of the incident and the actions taken in response. Determine the underlying causes of the incident to prevent future occurrences.

  o **Documentation**: Document the entire incident response process, including lessons learned and best practices.

  o **Policy and procedure updates**: Update the incident response plan and security controls based on the lessons learned and the insights gained.

By following these phases, organizations can effectively manage security incidents, minimize their impact, and enhance their overall security posture. Each phase is critical for ensuring a structured and efficient response to cybersecurity threats.

Organizations across industries rely on the incident response lifecycle to systematically detect, contain, and mitigate security threats, ensuring minimal disruption and swift recovery. This structured approach, comprising preparation, identification, containment, eradication, recovery, and lessons learned, has proven essential in maintaining cybersecurity resilience.

For instance, Equifax, following its highly publicized data breach, rebuilt its incident response strategy by integrating continuous monitoring, real-time threat detection, and rapid containment mechanisms, significantly reducing future vulnerabilities. Microsoft, during the Exchange Server vulnerability crisis, exemplified the importance of a swift identification and eradication phase, deploying emergency patches that prevented further exploitation across enterprises globally. Similarly, colonial pipeline, after suffering a ransomware attack, leveraged an orchestrated recovery phase, restoring operations while refining its response framework to mitigate future risks.

Financial institutions like *JPMorgan Chase* have optimized their incident response procedures by automating threat identification and containment, reducing their MMTD and MTTR by over 40%. Meanwhile, healthcare organizations, such as the Mayo Clinic, have prioritized early detection and incident preparedness to reduce patient data exposure risks, demonstrating the real-world impact of a proactive response strategy.

Statistically, businesses that embrace a structured incident response lifecycle witness a 30–50% improvement in containment speed, leading to fewer financial losses and significantly lowered downtime. Industry studies reveal that organizations with dedicated incident response teams experience an average of $2.66 million in reduced breach costs, underscoring the value of a well-defined response process.

By adopting these best practices and learning from real-world examples, security teams can enhance detection, streamline mitigation efforts, and establish a robust defense against emerging threats.

Incident management

Incident management is a crucial aspect of SOC's responsibilities. It involves the systematic detection, analysis, containment, eradication, and recovery from security incidents. Some of the tools and technologies used for incident management include SIEM, SOAR, EDR, NTA, and threat intelligence platforms. Practical aspects of incident management in SOC extend beyond the structured phases of the incident response lifecycle. Some of the key considerations are as follows:

- **Prioritization and triage**: Develop a transparent scoring system by assigning points to different factors (e.g., impact, confidentiality, availability) to prioritize incidents objectively. Establish clear escalation paths by defining who to contact and when based on incident severity. Implement automated triage by leveraging AI/ML to automatically categorize and prioritize alerts, freeing up analysts for more critical tasks.

- **Collaboration and communication**: Effective incident management relies heavily on seamless communication within the SOC team and with other departments. Establish clear communication channels by utilizing tools like Slack, Microsoft Teams, or dedicated incident management platforms. Regular briefings, updates, and debriefings ensure everyone is on the same page and can coordinate their efforts efficiently. Foster cross-functional collaboration by encouraging communication and knowledge sharing between SOC analysts, other IT teams, legal, and business stakeholders. Having predefined communication protocols helps to minimize confusion and delays during an incident.

- **Tool integration**: SOC teams typically use various tools for monitoring, detection, analysis, and response. Ensuring these tools are well-integrated to enable seamless data sharing and can communicate with each other can significantly enhance efficiency. Automate repetitive tasks using SOAR platforms to automate tasks like threat hunting, containment actions, and vulnerability remediation. Automated workflows and centralized dashboards can provide a comprehensive view of the incident and streamline the response process.

- **Continuous training and drills**: Incident management requires constant vigilance and preparedness. Regular training sessions and simulated incident response drills help keep the team sharp and ready for real-world scenarios. These exercises also help identify any gaps in the response process and improve overall readiness.

- **Documentation and reporting**: Maintaining detailed documentation of incidents, including steps taken and lessons learned, is crucial. This not only helps in reviewing and improving response strategies but also provides valuable insights for future incidents. Clear and concise reporting ensures stakeholders are informed about the incident's status and potential impacts.

- **Threat intelligence**: Incorporating threat intelligence into incident management allows SOC teams to avoid emerging threats. Leverage threat intelligence feeds about emerging threats and vulnerabilities to proactively identify and mitigate risks. By analyzing threat data and trends, teams can proactively adjust their defences and response strategies to better protect against potential attacks. Conduct regular threat-hunting exercises by proactively searching for and investigating potential threats within the organization's environment. Understand threat actors' TTPs to improve threat detection and response capabilities.

- **Resource management**: Effective incident management requires efficient allocation of resources. This includes managing personnel, ensuring that the right expertise is available when needed, and maintaining an inventory of tools and technologies. Proper resource management provides the SOC can handle multiple incidents simultaneously without being overwhelmed.

- **Post-incident review**: Conducting a thorough review after each incident is essential for continuous improvement. This involves analysing what went well, what could be improved, and how the incident was handled. Incorporating feedback from all involved parties helps to refine processes and enhance the overall incident management strategy. Provide training and development opportunities for SOC analysts to enhance their skills and knowledge.

By focusing on these practical aspects, SOC teams can enhance their incident management capabilities, ensuring a more resilient and effective response to security incidents. Organizations across industries have refined their incident management strategies by integrating structured frameworks. These elements are crucial in ensuring swift detection, containment, and resolution of security threats while minimizing operational disruptions.

For example, JPMorgan Chase has implemented automated risk-based prioritization within its SOC, allowing analysts to focus on high-impact incidents while reducing false positives. This approach has led to a 40% improvement in response efficiency, enabling faster containment of cyber threats. Similarly, *Netflix* leverages machine learning-driven triage within its security infrastructure, automatically classifying incidents based on severity and potential business impact. This has helped the company reduce investigation time by 35%, ensuring that security teams allocate resources effectively.

Microsoft, during the Exchange Server vulnerability crisis, demonstrated the importance of cross-team coordination, rapidly deploying patches and sharing threat intelligence with global enterprises. This proactive communication strategy prevented widespread exploitation and reinforced industry-wide security measures.

In the healthcare sector, the Mayo Clinic has established real-time incident communication protocols, ensuring that security teams, IT staff, and compliance officers work together to mitigate threats. By integrating automated alerts and structured response workflows, the organization has reduced incident resolution time by 30%, safeguarding patient data and critical systems.

Equifax, following its 2017 data breach, revamped its incident review process, incorporating forensic analysis and lessons learned to prevent recurrence. This initiative led to a significant reduction in breach detection time, reinforcing the importance of structured post-incident evaluations.

Meanwhile, *Delta Air Lines*, after experiencing a major operational disruption, refined its post-incident assessment framework, ensuring that IT failures are thoroughly analyzed and mitigation strategies are continuously improved. This approach has enhanced business continuity planning, reducing downtime risks in future incidents.

Organizations that integrate these best practices into their incident response lifecycle experience 30–50% faster containment, leading to fewer financial losses and improved operational resilience. Research indicates that companies with dedicated incident response teams reduce their MTTD and MTTR by up to 40%, reinforcing the value of structured response frameworks. By adopting these industry-specific insights, security teams can enhance prioritization, streamline collaboration, and refine post-incident evaluations, ensuring a more adaptive and resilient cybersecurity posture.

SIEM use cases

SIEM is a powerful tool that can be used to enhance security posture and streamline incident response. Some key use cases of SIEM are as follows:

- **Threat detection and response**: The most prominent SIEM use case is threat detection and response through the following practical scenarios:

  o **Real-time monitoring**: SIEM can monitor network traffic, system logs, and security events in real-time, allowing for immediate detection of threats. SIEM systems aggregate and analyze data from various sources in real time to detect potential security threats and respond quickly.

  o **Anomaly detection**: By analyzing large volumes of data, SIEM can identify unusual patterns and behaviors that may indicate a security breach.

  o **Incident investigation**: SIEM can help security teams investigate security incidents by providing detailed logs and event timelines.

  o **Threat hunting**: SIEM can search for threats that may not have triggered alerts proactively. SIEM enables proactive threat hunting by allowing security teams to search for hidden threats within the network

- **Compliance and regulatory adherence**: A critical use case of SIEM is ensuring compliance and regulatory adherence through the following means:

  o **Policy enforcement**: SIEM can help organizations enforce security policies and procedures. SIEM helps organizations meet regulatory requirements by generating compliance reports and ensuring that security controls are in place.

  o **Audit trail**: SIEM can create a detailed audit trail of system and user activity, which can be used for compliance audits.

  o **Log retention and archiving**: SIEM can help organizations meet regulatory requirements for log retention.

  o **PCI DSS, HIPAA, and GDPR compliance**: SIEM can help organizations meet the stringent requirements of these and other regulations.

- **Security incident management**: A very critical incident management gets significant bolstering with the following practical use cases:

  o **Incident response automation**: SIEM provides detailed information about security incidents, helping incident response teams to identify and mitigate threats quickly. SIEM can automate many incident response tasks, such as isolating compromised systems and blocking malicious IP addresses. SIEM systems can automate responses to certain types of security events, such as isolating compromised systems or blocking malicious IP addresses.

- o **Incident prioritization**: SIEM can prioritize incidents based on severity and potential impact.

- o **Root cause analysis**: SIEM can help identify the root cause of security incidents by analyzing logs and event data.

- **UBA**: Practical use cases of user behavior analytics can be efficient through the following:

   - o **Insider threat detection**: SIEM can detect insider threats by monitoring user behavior and identifying anomalies. SIEM can analyze user behavior to detect anomalies indicating insider threats or compromised accounts.

   - o **Privilege abuse detection**: SIEM can monitor the activities of privileged users to detect unauthorized access or misuse of privileges.

- **Log management and analysis**: SIEM ensures log management and analysis through the following use cases:

   - o **Centralized log management**: SIEM can consolidate logs from various sources, making it easier to search and analyze. SIEM centralizes log data from different systems, making it easier to manage, search, and analyze logs

   - o **Log correlation**: SIEM can correlate logs from different sources to identify relationships between events and gain deeper insights.

- **Network security monitoring**: SIEM can monitor network traffic for signs of malicious activity, such as port scans, DDoS attacks, and data exfiltration. SIEM can monitor network traffic to identify suspicious activities, such as unusual data flows or unauthorized access attempts.

- **Vulnerability management**: SIEM can help identify and prioritize vulnerabilities in systems and applications by correlating security events with known vulnerabilities

- **Cloud security**: SIEM can be used to monitor cloud environments for security threats.

- **Forensic analysis**: SIEM tools can be used to investigate security incidents by providing detailed logs and event data for forensic analysis.

By leveraging SIEM, organizations can improve their security posture, reduce the risk of security breaches, and accelerate incident response times. These use cases demonstrate the flexibility and power of SIEM systems in enhancing an organization's security posture. By leveraging SIEM, organizations can gain better visibility into their IT environment, detect threats more effectively, and respond to incidents more efficiently.

SIEM overview

Imagine a scenario where an SIEM detects a sudden spike in failed login attempts from a specific IP address. The SIEM can be as follows:

- **Generate an alert**: Notify the security team of the suspicious activity.

- **Correlate events**: Analyze the logs to identify any related events, such as unusual file transfers or unusual network traffic.

- **Isolate the threat**: Block the malicious IP address to prevent further attacks.

- **Investigate the incident**: Conduct a thorough investigation to determine the root cause of the attack.

- **Implement countermeasures**: Implement security measures to prevent similar attacks in the future.

Now, let us take another scenario involving a large financial institution with a global presence. In detecting insider threats and preventing data breaches, SIEM can implement **user and entity behavior analytics** (**UEBA**) with the following process:

- The SIEM, using UEBA, flags the anomaly as high-risk, potentially indicating a compromised account or a rogue employee.

- The SIEM, monitoring access control logs, detects this unauthorized access attempt.

- Investigate the login, verify the user's location, and potentially lock the account as a precaution.

- The SIEM, analyzing system event logs, identifies this anomalous activity, potentially indicating malicious intent.

- Investigate the administrator's actions, review system logs for evidence of compromise, and potentially restore system configurations to a previous state.

- By effectively utilizing SIEM, organizations can enhance their security posture, reduce the risk of cyberattacks, and improve their overall security operations.

Organizations across industries have successfully implemented SIEM systems to enhance their security posture and streamline incident response. Let us look at some real-world examples of organizations exploiting SIEM:

- **Financial sector**: JPMorgan Chase has integrated SIEM solutions to monitor billions of security events daily, allowing its SOC to detect anomalies and potential threats in real time. By leveraging automated threat correlation and behavioral analytics, the bank has reduced its MTTD by 40%, ensuring rapid containment of cyber threats.

- **Technology industry**: Microsoft employs SIEM technology within its Defender for Endpoint platform, enabling proactive threat hunting and automated incident response. The company's security teams use machine learning-driven log analysis to identify suspicious activities, leading to a 30% improvement in response efficiency and minimizing the impact of cyber incidents.

- **Retail sector**: Walmart has adopted SIEM systems to secure its vast digital infrastructure, correlating logs from thousands of endpoints and cloud services. By integrating real-time threat intelligence feeds, Walmart has enhanced its ability to detect and mitigate security threats, reducing false positives by 35% and improving overall security operations.

- **Healthcare industry**: Mayo Clinic utilizes SIEM technology to protect patient data and ensure compliance with healthcare regulations. By implementing automated log correlation and anomaly detection, the organization has strengthened its incident response capabilities, reducing breach detection time by 50% and safeguarding sensitive medical records.

- **Government agencies**: U.S. **Department of Defense (DoD)** employs SIEM solutions to monitor national security threats, integrating advanced analytics and threat intelligence to detect cyberattacks targeting critical infrastructure. By leveraging automated response workflows, the agency has improved its incident containment speed by 45%, ensuring rapid mitigation of security risks.

These real-world implementations highlight the transformative impact of SIEM systems in modern cybersecurity frameworks. By adopting these technologies, organizations can enhance threat detection, streamline incident response, and fortify their defenses against evolving cyber threats.

Conclusion

Incident response in SOC highlights the critical components and best practices necessary for effectively managing and mitigating security incidents. From the basic element of log management to the understanding of IOC and IOA, each aspect plays a vital role in building a robust incident response capability.

The incident response lifecycle provides a structured framework for preparing, detecting, analyzing, containing, eradicating, and recovering from incidents. Effective incident management goes beyond these phases, emphasizing the importance of communication, continuous training, tool integration, and thorough documentation. Practical aspects, such as leveraging UEBA within SIEM solutions, showcase real-world applications and demonstrate the value of proactive monitoring and anomaly detection. By integrating these elements, organizations can enhance their resilience against cyber threats, respond swiftly to incidents, and continuously improve their security posture.

In the next chapter, we will analyze part of security operations management. We will understand the nuances of correlation, inter-dependence of incidents, and potential mitigation aspects.

Points to remember

Here are some key takeaways from this chapter:

- IOC and IOA are critical to exfiltrate the threats and vulnerabilities from log management through SIEM tools.

- Incident response lifecycle provides a structured framework in the management of incident responses.

- Some practical aspects like automation, collaboration, communication, and continuous improvement will enhance the incident response in effectively improving security posture.

Multiple choice questions

1. **Which of the following best describes an IOC?**
   a. A user's behavior pattern indicating potential insider threats
   b. A piece of evidence that suggests a system has been breached
   c. A proactive measure to prevent attacks
   d. A network configuration setting to enhance security

2. **What is the primary difference between IOC and IOAs?**
   a. IOC focus on identifying threats after they occur, while IOAs focus on detecting ongoing attacks
   b. IOC are related to network settings, while IOAs are related to user permissions
   c. IOC are proactive measures, while IOAs are reactive measures
   d. IOC and IOAs are the same with different terminologies

3. **Which phase of the incident response lifecycle involves creating and maintaining an incident response plan, tools, and resources?**
   a. Detection and analysis
   b. Containment, eradication, and recovery
   c. Preparation
   d. Post-incident activity

Answers

1	b
2	a
3	c

Questions

1. What is the primary purpose of log management in a SOC?

2. Explain the phases of the incident response lifecycle?

3. What is the primary function of a SIEM system in a SOC?

Key terms

Some key terms used in this chapter are as follows:

- **Log management**: It is key for any SOC implementations.

- **IOC, IOA**: These are crucial in understanding the threat vectors.

- **Incident response lifecycle**: Critical in incident response management.

Join our Discord space

Join our Discord workspace for latest updates, offers, tech happenings around the world, new releases, and sessions with the authors:

https://discord.bpbonline.com

Section 2
SOC Components

CHAPTER 7
Analysis

Introduction

At the core of SOC operations, managing alerts efficiently and events that indicate potential security incidents are important. After the incidents are detected, it is necessary to correlate them with different incidents for inter-relation. The analysis forms the basis of eliminating time and energy resources on dependent incident mitigation. Analyzing enormous amounts of data and identifying potential security threats is crucial in today's rapidly evolving digital landscape. This chapter aims to provide a comprehensive understanding of the analysis processes within a SOC. It will cover methodologies and techniques employed by security analysts to sift through the multitude of data points, identify anomalies, manage alerts, respond to potential threats with precision, conduct post-incident analysis, and perform behavioral and malware analysis.

In 2024, a major healthcare provider experienced a ransomware attack that encrypted patient records and disrupted services. The attackers exploited a vulnerability in the provider's outdated software, leading to significant financial and reputational damage. The attackers used phishing emails to gain initial access to the network. Once inside, they moved laterally across the network, encrypting critical data and demanding a ransom for its release. The breach not only disrupted operations but also eroded patient trust and led to regulatory scrutiny. This incident underscores the importance of robust alert management, thorough post-incident analysis, and effective behavioral and malware analysis. By understanding these processes, organizations can better protect themselves against similar attacks.

Key concepts such as alerts, behavior analysis, malware analysis, and intrusion analysis will be discussed in detail. Understanding these terms is crucial for grasping the subsequent sections. Behavioral analysis is pivotal in detecting anomalies by monitoring and analyzing user and entity behavior. Malware analysis is a cornerstone of incident response, enabling SOCs to dissect and understand malicious software. Threat intelligence integration is a powerful multiplier, enriching the SOC's situational awareness. Machine learning algorithms can detect zero-day attacks, polymorphic malware, and other sophisticated threats by analyzing vast amounts of data and identifying patterns that may elude human analysts. By leveraging behavioral analysis, malware analysis, threat intelligence integration, and machine learning, SOCs can significantly enhance their intrusion detection capabilities and proactively defend against emerging threats. This chapter delves into the best practices for managing and analyzing alerts to maintain robust security defenses.

Structure

In this chapter, we will cover the following topics:

- Dealing with alerts
- Post incident analysis
- Behavior analysis
- Malware analysis
- Intrusion analysis
- Analyzing anomalies with IPS/IDS

Objectives

By the end of this chapter, the readers will identify, categorize, and prioritize alerts to ensure a timely response to potential threats. It will also conduct thorough investigations to understand the root causes and impacts of incidents. Another crucial factor is monitoring and interpreting user and entity behaviors to detect anomalies. This chapter will finally dissect malicious software to understand its behavior, capabilities, and impact and investigate unauthorized access attempts and breaches to strengthen defenses.

Dealing with alerts

In the challenging environment of SOC, alerts are the first line of defense. They warn early that something might be amiss in your information system's environment. Alerts are security tools-generated notifications indicating suspicious activities or potential threats. These could originate from various sources, such as firewalls, intrusion detection systems, antivirus software, or SIEM systems.

In the context of security and monitoring, understanding the diverse types of alerts is crucial for effective threat response.

Distinct types of alerts are shown in following figure:

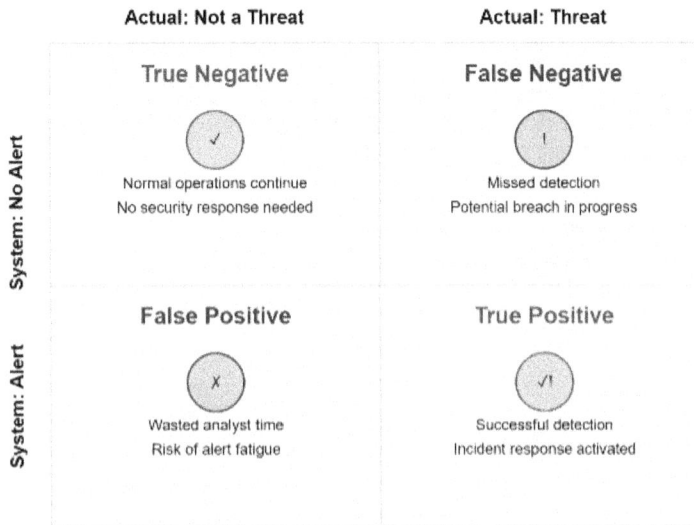

Figure 7.1: *Types of alerts*

These different alerts are important to analyze and respond to cyber incidents. The alerts can be categorized as:

- **False positives**: It is an alert that incorrectly flags a legitimate activity as a threat. False positives occur when a security control incorrectly identifies normal activity as malicious. These create unnecessary work and can lead to alert fatigue. For example, a motion sensor triggers an alarm due to a passing animal, mistakenly identifying it as a human intruder. In technical parlance, a false positive can be identified when a security system flags a legitimate file transfer between two internal servers as a potential data exfiltration attempt when the file transfer is part of a routine data backup process. They might temporarily block the file transfer, disrupting business operations, until they can determine it is safe. The security team investigates the alert, consuming valuable time and resources. Some real-world examples of false positives include:

  o **Network behavior**: A legitimate spike in traffic during a planned software update triggers a DDoS alert.

  o **User authentication**: Multi-factor authentication flags a legitimate login attempt because an employee is accessing from a new location while traveling for business.

  o **Application security**: A web application firewall blocks legitimate API calls containing specific keywords that match its threat signature database.

- o **Behavioral analysis**: An employee downloading multiple files before vacation is flagged as a potential data theft.

- o **Cloud security**: Auto-scaling resources for a planned marketing campaign causes resource utilization alerts.

False positives consume analyst time, create unnecessary incident tickets, and potentially cause business disruption through blocked legitimate activities. Over time, they erode confidence in security tools and can lead teams to ignore certain alert types or sources. The alert needs to be investigated thoroughly to rule out a genuine threat, alert thresholds or rules refined to reduce the likelihood of similar false alarms in the future, and automated response suppression mechanisms implemented for specific low-risk scenarios considered.

- **False negatives**: It is an alert that fails to detect a real threat. False negatives occur when actual security threats go undetected by security controls. These represent the most dangerous failure mode for security monitoring. For example, a virus scanner fails to detect a new, sophisticated malware strain, or when malware disguised as a legitimate software update evades detection by the company's antivirus software. In such a scenario, the malware successfully infiltrates the company's network, potentially stealing sensitive data, disrupting operations, or causing significant financial damage before it is discovered. Some real-world examples of false negatives include:

  - o **Evasion techniques**: Malware that encrypts its payload or uses polymorphic code to avoid signature detection.

  - o **Living-off-the-land**: Attackers using legitimate system tools like PowerShell to execute malicious commands, bypassing application controls.

  - o **Zero-day exploits**: Attackers leveraging previously unknown vulnerabilities that security tools have not been configured to detect.

  - o **Slow-and-low attacks**: Data exfiltration occurring in small increments over extended periods to stay under threshold-based detection.

  - o **Supply chain compromises**: Malicious code embedded in trusted software updates bypassing security controls due to trusted source.

False negatives are the most critical to minimize as they allow real threats to go undetected, causing significant harm. False negatives directly enable security breaches, leading to data theft, system compromise, and potential regulatory violations. The longer these go undetected, the more damage attackers can inflict and the more difficult remediation becomes. To minimize false negatives, security systems (e.g., antivirus, intrusion detection systems) must be regularly reviewed and updated with the latest signatures and threat intelligence, thorough security audits and penetration testing must be conducted to identify vulnerabilities, and SIEM/SOAR systems must be implemented to improve threat detection capabilities.

- **True positives**: An alert correctly identifies a genuine threat. True positives represent the ideal detection scenario—security controls accurately identifying genuine threats. For example, a security system detects a malicious intrusion attempt and triggers an alarm or when a network IDS detects a suspicious pattern of network traffic, indicating a potential hacking attempt and the security team investigates the incident and confirms a malicious attack in progress. Some of the real-world examples of true positives include:

  o **Credential attacks**: Detection of brute force password attempts against a critical system.

  o **Malware C2**: Identification of outbound connections to known malicious domains.

  o **Privilege escalation**: Detection of unexpected user privilege changes or access to restricted resources.

  o **Lateral movement**: Alerts from unusual internal network scanning activity as attackers attempt to map the environment.

  o **Data staging**: Discovery of unexpected compressed archives containing sensitive data before exfiltration.

  Ture positives validate security investments and proper tuning. They enable the SOC to disrupt attack chains before significant damage occurs, though they still require proper prioritization, as not all true detections represent equal risk. These are the most desired outcomes. We want to maximize the number of genuine threats that are correctly identified. We must promptly investigate and respond to these alerts to mitigate the danger.

- **True negatives**: An alert that correctly identifies a legitimate activity as non-threatening. True negatives occur when security controls correctly recognize legitimate activity as non-malicious. These often go unnoticed but represent the normal baseline of security tool operation. For example, a spam filter correctly identifies an email as legitimate and allows it to reach the inbox, or when a fraud detection system analyzes a credit card transaction and determines it to be legitimate, the transaction is approved, and the customer's funds are transferred. Some real-world examples of true negatives include:

  o **Approved software**: Application whitelisting correctly allows authorized applications to execute.

  o **Expected traffic patterns**: Network monitoring correctly classifying normal traffic between business applications.

  o **Legitimate file operations**: Data loss prevention tools correctly allow expected file transfers within policy guidelines.

  o **Authorized access**: Identity and access management systems correctly grant access to users with appropriate permissions.

    o **Normal system changes**: Configuration management systems correctly identify approved system changes during maintenance windows.

True negatives enable business continuity without security friction. While they do not generate alerts, their absence in reporting often indicates well-tuned security controls and appropriate baseline configurations. We want to maximize the number of legitimate activities correctly identified as non-threatening. No further action is typically needed as the system correctly identifies a normal situation.

False positives can lead to wasted resources and unnecessary disruptions, while false negatives can have dire consequences, especially in critical domains like cybersecurity. Regularly updating security systems, employing multiple layers of defense, and conducting thorough security assessments can help minimize false positives and negatives. Striking the right balance between sensitivity (minimizing false negatives) and specificity (minimizing false positives) is crucial for effective cybersecurity. Some of the measures to reduce false positives include:

- **Baseline establishment**: Create behavioral and network traffic baselines during normal business operations to distinguish abnormal from normal activity.

- **Contextual analysis**: Integrate asset inventory, user role information, and business process data to evaluate alerts against expected behavior.

- **Tuning cycle**:
  o Document all false positives with detailed reasoning.
  o Perform periodic rule reviews based on false positive patterns.
  o Implement graduated thresholds based on asset criticality.
  o Use machine learning to identify pattern-based false positives.

- **Whitelisting**: Develop approved exception lists for known benign activities that match detection signatures.

Similarly, measures to reduce false negatives include:

- **Threat intelligence integration**: Continuously update detection systems with the latest threat indicators and attack techniques.

- **Detection diversity**: Implement multiple detection methodologies:
  o Signature-based detection for known threats.
  o Behavioral analytics for anomaly detection.
  o Machine learning for pattern recognition.
  o Heuristic analysis for detecting suspicious activities.

- **Coverage mapping**: Document all attack vectors and ensure detection capabilities exist for each.

- **Adversary emulation**: Conduct red team exercises and purple team activities to identify detection gaps.

- **Threat hunting**: Proactively search for indicators of compromise that may have evaded automated detection.

A comparison of different alert types is covered in following table:

Alert type	Detection impact	Business impact	Optimization focus	Priority
True positive	Successful detection confirms monitoring effectiveness	Enables timely incident response and threat mitigation	Improves response procedures and automation	High
False positive	Wastes analyst time and resources on benign activity	Increases operational costs and creates alert fatigue	Tune detection rules and improve filtering logic	Medium
True negative	Normal system operation without false alerts	Smooth business operations without security friction	Maintain baseline configurations and whitelist accuracy	Low
False negative	Security threat goes undetected by security controls	Increases risk of breaches, data loss, and compliance issues.	Enhance detection capabilities and coverage gaps	Critical

Table 7.1: *Alert type comparison*

By understanding these alert types and their implications, organizations can optimize their alert systems to improve accuracy, reduce false alarms, and ensure timely responses to genuine threats. Organizations need to determine their acceptable level of risk for both false positives and false negatives based on their industry, critical assets, and regulatory requirements.

Lifecycle of an alert

Effective alert management involves four stages, each critical to ensuring accurate detection and response. These stages are depicted in the following figure:

Detection → Triage → Investigation → Response

Figure 7.2: *Alert lifecycle*

- **Detection**: Alerts are detected through various monitoring systems. The SOC must ensure comprehensive coverage to capture all potential threats. Gathering additional data from diverse sources such as network traffic logs, EDR data, and cloud security logs ensures deeper insights into the incident.

- **Triage**: Once an alert is detected, it undergoes triage to determine its severity and priority. This process involves the following:

  o **Classification**: This entails categorizing alerts based on their severity, source, and type, and recognizing distinct types of alerts, such as phishing attempts, malware detections, and suspicious network activity.

  o **Prioritization**: This entails assigning urgency levels to alerts based on potential impact. Use threat intelligence to assess the context of alerts. Focus on high-priority alerts that could indicate significant incidents.

- **Investigation**: Conduct preliminary analysis to understand the nature of the alert. Check logs, correlate with other alerts, and decide the next steps. SOC analysts delve into the details of high-priority alerts to understand the context and potential threat. This process includes the following:

  o **Log analysis**: Review logs to trace the alert's origin and timeline. Employ data visualization techniques to identify trends and patterns within the alert data.

  o **Network traffic analysis**: Examining data flows to detect anomalies.

  o **Threat intelligence**: Leveraging external threat intelligence to contextualize alerts.

- **Response**: Depending on the outcome of the investigation, an appropriate response is formulated. This can involve the following:

  o **Containment**: Implementing measures to isolate affected systems.

  o **Eradication**: Removing the threat from the environment.

  o **Recovery**: Restoring normal operations and verifying system integrity.

Modern SOCs can implement intelligent alert triage frameworks to handle the different alert types more efficiently. A typical alert response decision flow can be as shown in the following figure:

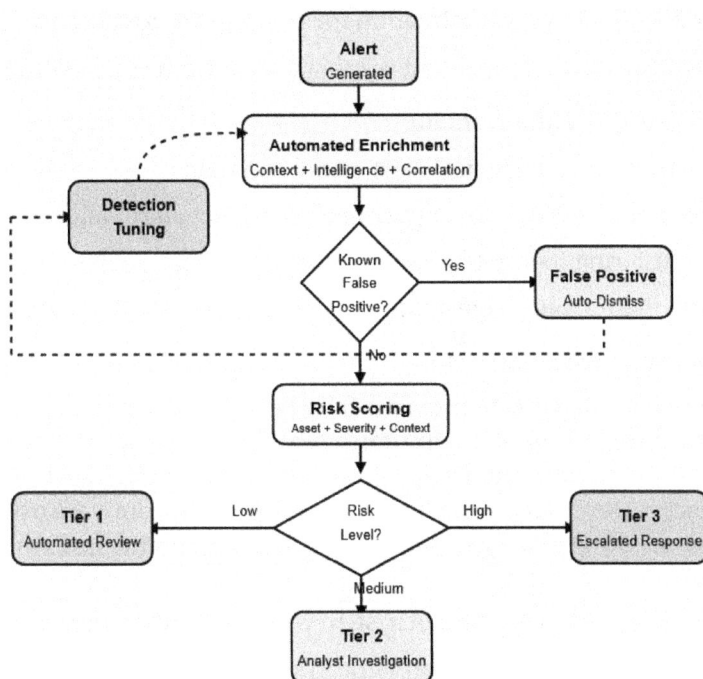

Figure 7.3: Alert lifecycle decision flow

The alert lifecycle decision flow comprises of following measures:

- **Alert scoring system**: Assign dynamic risk scores based on:
  - Asset criticality
  - Threat intelligence correlation
  - Alert fidelity history (previous true/false positive rate)
  - Behavioral deviation severity
  - Alert correlation and clustering

- **SOAR integration**: Automate response actions for common alert scenarios:
  - Automatic enrichment of alerts with contextual data
  - Playbook execution for initial investigation steps
  - Auto-dismissal of known false positive patterns
  - Ticket creation and assignment based on alert category
  - Evidence collection and preservation

- **Response tiering**: Implement a structured response approach:
  - **Tier 0**: Fully automated handling (known false positives or low-risk alerts)
  - **Tier 1**: Semi-automated with analyst verification

- o **Tier 2**: Full analyst investigation for complex or novel alerts
- o **Tier 3**: Escalation to incident response team for confirmed threats

- **Machine learning enhancement**:
  - o Train models on historical alert resolution data
  - o Implement classification algorithms to predict alert validity
  - o Use clustering to identify related alerts for group analysis
  - o Apply natural language processing to extract key information from alerts

Let us look at some real-world case studies involving alert responses:

- **Case study one:** Healthcare provider false negative. A regional healthcare system's SOC missed indicators of compromise for 87 days because its EDR solution was configured to ignore certain system processes commonly used by administrative staff. Attackers leveraged this blind spot to deploy ransomware using these trusted processes, resulting in a major outage. The learning points from this case study are as follows:
  - o Detection gaps in legitimate system processes create significant risk
  - o Regular testing for detection blind spots is essential
  - o Process whitelisting requires continuous review and monitoring

- **Case study two:** Financial institution false positive storm. A major bank implemented a new behavioral analytics system without proper tuning, resulting in over 10,000 false positive alerts during the first week, overwhelming their SOC team. Analysts began ignoring certain alert categories, inadvertently missing several actual intrusion attempts. The learning points from this case study are as follows:
  - o Proper baseline establishment before deployment is critical
  - o Phased implementation with graduated alerting thresholds
  - o Alert fatigue can create critical security gaps
  - o Automation must be applied to manage high alert volumes

- **Case study three:** Technology company true positive success. A technology firm's SOC successfully detected and responded to a sophisticated spear-phishing attack targeting their executive team. Their defense-in-depth approach allowed correlation of seemingly benign individual alerts that, when viewed collectively, revealed the attack chain. The learning points from this case study are as follows:
  - o Correlation across multiple control points increases detection effectiveness
  - o Context enrichment enabled rapid triage and prioritization
  - o Pre-established playbooks accelerated response time
  - o Regular tabletop exercises prepared analysts for the scenario

Post incident analysis

After the incident is contained or remediated, it is crucial to understand what happened and why. A vital element of SOC responsibilities is **post incident analysis (PIA)**, which involves examining incidents to understand their impact, root causes, and preventive measures. PIA is a systematic approach to investigating security incidents. This process helps organizations identify vulnerabilities, understand the breach's scope, improve their defenses, learn from each incident, and develop strategies to prevent future occurrences.

While post-incident analysis is an elaborate process, it can typically involve the following key phases:

- **Incident documentation**: The first step in a PIA is to document the details of the incident. This includes the following:

  o Document all relevant information about the incident, including timelines, affected systems, and the nature of the breach. This includes initial detection, escalation, containment, eradication, and recovery steps. A clear and detailed timeline helps in identifying gaps in the detection and response process. It also serves as a reference for training and future incident handling.

  o Gather logs, network traffic, and other artifacts that can provide insights into the incident. Categorize the incident according to severity, type (e.g., malware, DDoS, insider threat), and any other relevant criteria to ensure consistent future responses.

  o Develop and maintain well-defined incident response playbooks to guide analysts through the investigation and response process. Ensure playbooks are regularly reviewed and updated based on the evolving threat landscape and internal security controls.

  o Generate comprehensive incident reports documenting all investigation and response aspects. Maintain detailed records of all security incidents for future analysis and reporting.

  o Share incident reports with relevant stakeholders, including management, legal, and compliance teams.

- **Root cause analysis (RCA)**: RCA aims to identify why and what happened. Often, incidents occur due to a series of vulnerabilities, misconfigurations, human errors, or lapses in policy enforcement. Investigate the root cause of the incident to identify the vulnerabilities that were exploited. Analyze the collected evidence to identify patterns or anomalies that could indicate the root cause. Analyze the attacker's TTPs to understand their motives and capabilities. Identify and implement appropriate countermeasures to prevent future occurrences. The following techniques can be effective in RCA:

  o **Five whys**: The *five whys* technique is crucial in the RCA of complex, multilayered cybersecurity incidents. By asking why five times, this method helps investigators dig deeper into the underlying reasons behind an incident rather than just addressing the superficial symptoms.

This method promotes a thorough understanding of the incident's context, fosters collaborative problem-solving, and aids in developing more robust security policies and controls. For example, the root cause of a successful phishing attack can be arrived at as shown in the following figure:

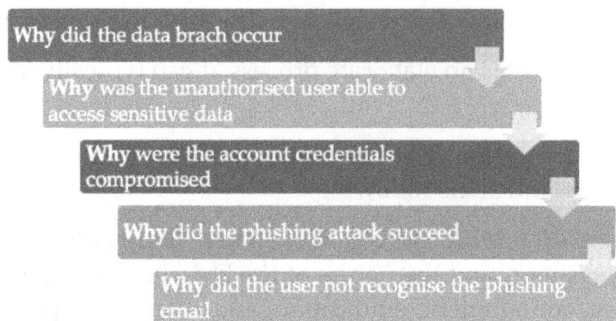

Figure 7.4: Five whys method for RCA

Each answer to the five whys points to a domain that can be addressed holistically. Based on the answers, corrective measures can be taken to avoid recurrence.

o **Fishbone diagrams**: Also known as Ishikawa diagrams, these visual tools help identify the probable causes of an incident by categorizing them into areas like people, processes, technology, and environment.

A sample fishbone diagram for the cyber incident is shown in the following figure:

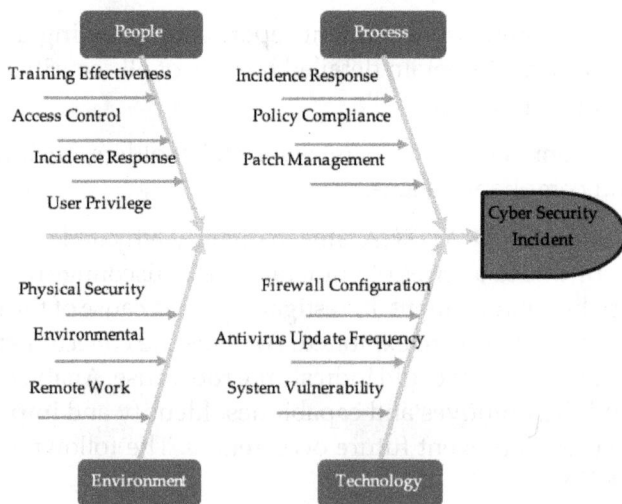

Figure 7.5: Fish bone diagram for RCA

As can be seen from the preceding figure, what is contributing to the cybersecurity incident can be effectively deduced in each of the people, process, technology, and environment domains

Appropriate corrective measures can then be initiated in each domain. Let us look at them in detail:

- **Failure mode and effect analysis (FMEA)**: This systematic, step-by-step methodology allows organizations to identify potential failure points within their systems and assess the impact of these failures. In the context of a cybersecurity incident, FMEA provides a structured approach to analyze how and why the incident occurred, evaluate the effectiveness of existing controls, and develop more robust countermeasures.

The process involved in FMEA is depicted in the following figure:

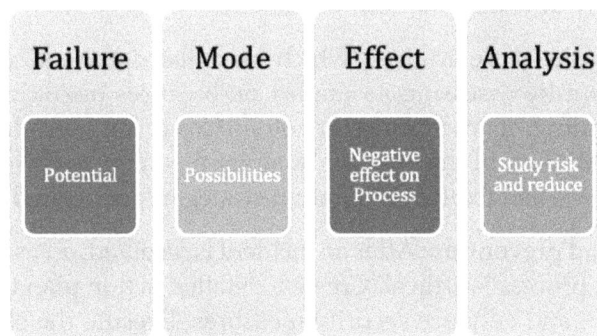

Figure 7.6: FMEA for RCA

As depicted in the preceding figure, failure potential involves identifying all possible ways a cybersecurity system or process can fail. This means scrutinizing every component for vulnerabilities that could be exploited. Mode possibilities refer to the specific ways or mechanisms through which these failures can occur. For example, a failure mode might include a software bug that allows unauthorized access or a misconfiguration in the firewall settings.

The effect on processes evaluates the impact that each failure mode could have on the overall system and operations. This includes assessing the severity of the consequences, such as data breaches, service disruptions, or loss of sensitive information. Analysis systematically prioritizes these risks based on their severity, likelihood of occurrence, and detectability. Ultimately, FMEA enhances an organization's ability to foresee and prevent future cyber threats, ensuring a more assertive, more resilient security posture.

- **Effectiveness of response**: Evaluating how well the incident response process was conducted is crucial for future improvement. Effectiveness can be assessed through the following key areas:

- o **Response speed**: This determines how quickly the incident detection, containment, and remediation phases are executed. Delays in identifying or mitigating an incident can increase the severity of its impact.

- o **Resource allocation**: It is crucial to understand whether the SOC has the right resources, both human and technological, to manage the incident. It is also important to know the training and currency of the trained personnel on call and whether they leverage automated tools like SIEM.

- o **Communication**: It is worthwhile to ensure the response team communicates clearly with internal stakeholders (such as management, IT, legal, and HR) and external parties (e.g., vendors, regulators, and affected customers).

- o **Adherence to protocols**: It is also vital to ensure that the response follows the established incident response protocols. The outcomes need to be analyzed in case of any deviations or improvisations.

- **Impact analysis**: It determines which systems, data, and users were affected by the incident by assessing its impact on business operations, reputation, and financial standing. It involves stakeholders from different departments to get a comprehensive view of the incident. Regular meetings to review findings, discuss potential causes, and explore mitigation strategies are needed.

- **Mitigation and prevention**: After an incident is resolved, assessing the remediation and recovery process is critical. Create a detailed action plan to address identified vulnerabilities and enhance security measures. Execute the changes and monitor their effectiveness over time. Conduct tabletop exercises and simulations to evaluate and refine incident response procedures.

Let us take a real-world scenario involving a ransomware attack and understand the post-incident analysis as per the steps covered previously in post-incident analysis:

- **Incident documentation**: The SOC team documents the ransomware attack that encrypted critical business files. They gather logs and network data from affected systems.

- **Root cause analysis**: Using forensic tools, the team identifies a phishing email as the entry point of the ransomware.

- **Effectiveness of response**: The response speed is checked, and protocol adherence is established.

- **Impact analysis**: They determine the extent of data encryption and assess the potential financial and reputational damage. The team meets with IT, legal, and management departments to discuss the incident's details and initial findings.

- **Mitigation and prevention**: The team develops an action plan to improve email filtering, conduct employee training, and enhance backup strategies.

- Post-incident analysis is a vital part of the SOC's function. It helps understand the cause and impact of incidents and plays a crucial role in strengthening the organization's security posture.

Behavior analysis

Behavior analysis identifies anomalous activities that deviate from established normal system and user behavior baselines. By monitoring behavior patterns, SOC teams can identify anomalies that might indicate potential security threats, such as insider attacks, compromised accounts, or **advanced persistent threats** (**APTs**) attempting to blend in with regular activity.

This involves scrutinizing activities like login times, access requests, data transfers, and other interactions with the system. The behavior analysis techniques are listed here:

- **UEBA**: UEBA monitors both human users and non-human entities for unusual activities that could indicate potential security threats. This is achieved with the following measures:

  o User behavior analytics monitors user activities to establish baselines of normal behavior. Entity behavior analytics focuses on non-human entities like applications, devices, IoT devices, and networks. It entails monitoring user and entity behavior for anomalies such as unusual login times, excessive data transfers, and unauthorized access attempts. It then detects abnormal patterns in entities that could signify an issue.

  o UEBA analyzes patterns over time to detect anomalies. For example, a user logging in from distinct locations within minutes might raise a red flag.

  o UEBA leverages statistical analysis and machine learning to detect subtle indicators of compromise that might otherwise go unnoticed.

  o It identifies deviations that might indicate compromise or malicious intent. It further investigates anomalous behavior to determine if it represents a legitimate activity or a potential threat.

- **Insider threat detection**: It involves identifying malicious or negligent activities conducted by individuals within the organization, such as employees, contractors, or trusted partners. Unlike external threats, insider threats are particularly challenging to detect as insiders leverage their knowledge of internal systems and access privileges. Effective insider threat detection requires a combination of behavioral analytics, monitoring of access patterns, and anomaly detection.

  This involves the following processes:

  o Identify and mitigate the risks posed by malicious or negligent insiders.

  o Monitor activities such as data exfiltration, unauthorized access to sensitive data, and sabotage.

- o Implement appropriate controls to prevent and detect insider threats.

- o **Real-world scenario**: A user account shows multiple failed login attempts followed by a successful login from an unfamiliar location. Behavior analysis helps identify this as a potential brute-force attack.

Malware analysis

In the realm of cyber threats, malware is a constant menace. Malware, short for malicious software, refers to any software intentionally designed to cause damage, disrupt, or gain unauthorized access to computers, networks, or devices.

Malware can take many forms, as covered in the following points:

- **Virus**: A virus attaches itself to a legitimate program or file and spreads from one device to another, often damaging files and software along the way.

- **Worm**: A worm is a standalone malware that replicates itself to spread to other devices, usually exploiting network vulnerabilities.

- **Trojan Horse**: A Trojan masquerades as a legitimate program, but once executed, it can steal data, install other malware, or provide remote access to the attacker.

- **Ransomware**: Ransomware encrypts a user's files or locks them out of their system, demanding a ransom to restore access.

- **Spyware**: Spyware secretly monitors and collects information about a user's activities without their consent.

- **Adware**: Adware displays unwanted advertisements, often redirecting users to malicious websites.

Malware can infiltrate systems through various methods, including phishing emails, malicious downloads, infected websites, and compromised software. To protect against malware threats, robust security measures, such as antivirus software, firewalls, and regular updates, are crucial.

Malware analysis involves examining and understanding the behavior, origins, and impact of malicious software designed to disrupt, damage, or gain unauthorized access to computer systems. Analyzing malware helps us appreciate its capabilities and how to defend against it. By dissecting malware, SOC teams can identify its type, infection vector, and payload.

Here are some techniques employed for gaining comprehensive insights:

- **Malware reverse engineering**: It involves static analysis, examining the malware file without executing it. This means analyzing the binary or source code to understand its structure and behavior. Look at file hashes, strings, headers, and other attributes. Tools like IDA Pro, Ghidra, VirusTotal can help. For advanced analysts, reverse engineering disassembles malware code to understand its inner workings and identify **indicators of compromise (IOC)** through the following:

o   Analyzing malicious software to understand its functionality, behavior, and origins.

o   Identifying malware's techniques to infect systems, steal data, and evade detection.

o   Developing signatures and other detection mechanisms to prevent and mitigate malware infections.

- **Sandboxing and analysis tools**: This entails dynamic analysis, which executes the malware in a controlled environment (sandbox) to observe its behavior. This tool can evaluate any changes malware makes to the system, network connections it attempts, and payloads it drops. This approach can reveal how the malware interacts with the system, network, and other resources, which might not be evident from static analysis alone. Tools for dynamic analysis include OllyDbg, Process Monitor, and x64dbg.

The dynamic analysis involves the following:

o   Utilizing sandboxing environments to execute and analyze suspicious files safely.

o   Employing malware analysis tools to extract information about the malware's behavior and capabilities.

o   Leveraging threat intelligence feeds to identify known malware families and variants.

While malware reverse engineering includes static analysis tools, it often relies on dynamic analysis tools to comprehensively understand the malware's behavior and impact.

Real-world scenario: An email attachment is flagged as suspicious. Through static and dynamic analysis, you discover it is a Trojan designed to steal credentials. Your findings lead to updated antivirus signatures and user alerts.

Intrusion analysis

Intrusions can be sneaky and complex. Analyzing them requires a keen eye and an analytical mindset. Intrusion analysis involves detecting, analyzing, and responding to unauthorized activities within a network or system. The primary goal is to identify potential threats and vulnerabilities before they can cause significant harm. Analysts use various tools and techniques to monitor network traffic, system logs, and user activities for signs of malicious behavior.

Intrusion detection systems and intrusion prevention systems

IDS and IPS are used to monitor and protect information systems from intrusions and malicious activities. Both serve the purpose of detecting potential security threats, but they operate in different ways.

IDS: An IDS is primarily used to detect and alert potential security incidents or suspicious activity within a network or system. It monitors network traffic or system activity and looks for patterns or signatures that match known threats or unusual behavior. When an intrusion is detected, the IDS generates an alert to notify system administrators or security personnel.

Different types of IDS are listed here:

- **Network-based IDS (NIDS)**: It monitors network traffic for malicious activity.
- **Host-based IDS (HIDS)**: It monitors activity on individual hosts or devices, such as servers or endpoints.

IDS could detect a brute force attack attempting to access a server by matching the login attempts against known patterns or thresholds.

IPS: An IPS is designed not only to detect intrusions but also to actively block or prevent them from occurring in real time. Like an IDS, an IPS also monitors network traffic or system activity. However, when an intrusion or suspicious activity is detected, the IPS takes immediate action to block or mitigate the threat. The IPS can stop traffic, block malicious requests, or reconfigure network devices to prevent further attacks.

Different types of IPS are as follows:

- **Network-based IPS (NIPS)**: NIPS protects network traffic by analyzing it for signs of malicious activity and blocking it. This is installed at strategic points within a network to monitor and analyze all incoming and outgoing traffic.
- **Host-based IPS (HIPS)**: Protects specific hosts by monitoring the system for signs of compromise and taking action to stop it. This is installed on individual endpoints and monitors traffic to and from that specific device.

An IPS can block an ongoing DDoS attack by blocking malicious IP addresses or dropping malicious traffic packets.

Some key differences between IDS and IPS are summarized in the following table:

Feature	IDS	IPS
Function	Detects intrusions and generates alerts.	Detects and actively prevents intrusions.
Action taken	**Passive**: generates alerts only.	**Active**: Blocks or prevents attacks in real time.

Feature	IDS	IPS
Deployment position	Often deployed in a monitoring position.	Deployed inline, actively filtering traffic.
Response to threats	Provides alerts but no direct action.	Take immediate action to prevent the threat.
Resource usage	Typically, less resource-intensive than IPS.	More resource-intensive due to real-time action.

Table 7.2: Difference between IDS and IPS

IDS is used when you want to monitor and detect potential threats without actively intervening. It is suitable for environments where administrators want to respond to alerts manually. **IPS** is used when you need a proactive security solution that can block threats automatically, such as in high-risk environments where real-time defense is essential. IDS and IPS can be used together as a layered defense strategy.

During the intrusion analysis, the following processes are executed:

- **Network traffic analysis**: This involves monitoring network traffic for suspicious patterns and anomalies and investigating unusual communication patterns utilizing network flow data.

- **Event correlation**: It then correlates events from diverse sources, such as IDS/IPS, firewalls, and logs, to identify patterns that indicate intrusion.

- **Attack vectors**: The next step is to determine how the intrusion occurred. An intrusion can be through an exploited vulnerability, a brute-force attack, or social engineering. Understanding the vector helps in mitigation.

- **Impact assessment**: Finally, it evaluates the intrusion's impact on your systems and data. It identifies compromised assets and assesses the extent of the damage.

Effective intrusion analysis helps organizations enhance their security posture, mitigate risks, and prevent future breaches by understanding the tactics, techniques, and procedures used by attackers.

Real-world scenario: Multiple failed login attempts across different systems are correlated with firewall logs showing suspicious IP addresses. Intrusion analysis helps you trace the attack back to an external threat actor.

Analyzing anomalies with IPS or IDS

This section will provide practical exercises to enhance the understanding and application of the concepts discussed in this chapter. These are the steps involved in analyzing any cybersecurity incident. Please use the mentioned tools to perform these steps.

Exercise one, analyzing user behavior anomalies

- **Scenario**: A SOC analyst observes a significant increase in login attempts from a specific user account during off-hours.

  Tasks: The task is to mitigate the anomalous behavior with the following steps:

  1. Investigate the user's recent activity, including login locations, file access patterns, and email activity.

  2. Analyze the user's standard behavior patterns to identify any deviations.

  3. Determine if the increased login activity is legitimate or malicious.

  4. Recommend appropriate actions, such as password resets, account lockout, or further investigation.

- **Scenario**: A sudden spike in outbound network traffic from a critical server has triggered an alert.

  Tasks: Carry out the following steps:

  1. **Behavior analysis**: Check if the traffic pattern matches the server's typical behavior. Investigate the destination IPs and the type of data being transferred.

  2. **Malware analysis**: If malware is suspected, collect samples and perform static and dynamic analysis. Look for evidence of data exfiltration or C2 communication.

  3. **Intrusion analysis**: Correlate events with IDS/IPS logs to see if there are signs of intrusion. Identify any unusual login attempts, suspicious connections, or known attack signatures.

By following these steps, you can uncover the root cause of the anomaly, understand the threat, and take appropriate actions to safeguard your systems.

Exercise two, analyzing malware activity

- **Scenario**: A SOC analyst receives an alert from the EDR system indicating the presence of suspicious malware on a workstation.

  Tasks: The task is to mitigate the malware threat with the following steps:

  1. Isolate the infected workstation from the network to prevent further spread.

  2. Collect and analyze malware samples for further investigation.

  3. Utilize sandboxing and malware analysis tools to determine the malware's functionality and behavior.

  4. Develop signatures and other detection mechanisms to prevent future infections.

Exercise three, analyzing intrusion attempts

- **Scenario**: A SOC analyst observes suspicious network traffic patterns, including port scanning and attempted exploitation of known vulnerabilities.

  Tasks: The task is to mitigate the suspicious network traffic with the following steps:

  1. Analyze IDS/IPS logs to identify the source and destination of the attack traffic.

  2. Investigate the attacker's TTPs to understand their objectives.

  3. Implement appropriate countermeasures, such as blocking the attacker's IP addresses, patching vulnerable systems, and strengthening network security controls.

Conclusion

The SOC analysts are critical in detecting, responding, and mitigating security incidents. By effectively analyzing alerts, investigating incidents, and understanding attacker behavior, these analysts can protect organizations from various cyber threats. This chapter has provided an overview of the key concepts and skills required for successful incident analysis and response at the escalation level function within a SOC.

As a SOC analyst, analytical skills are your greatest asset. Dealing with alerts, performing post-incident analysis, understanding behavior, dissecting malware, and investigating intrusions are all critical components of your role. By mastering these areas, you protect your organization and contribute to the broader mission of securing the digital world.

In the next chapter, we will examine threat intelligence and threat hunting and how these techniques help SOCs prepare for any threats in real-time.

Points to remember

Here are some key takeaways from this chapter:

- Alerts provide the first line of defense for any SOC operations. To manage them efficiently, it is important to understand different types of alerts, their significance, and prioritization. It is also worthwhile recognizing the impact of false positives and false negatives on security operations.

- There is a need to conduct a thorough root cause analysis to identify the underlying cause of the incident and ensure proper documentation of the incident, response actions, and outcomes for future reference.

  Monitor and analyze user and entity behavior to detect anomalies and potential insider threats. Establish a baseline of normal behavior to identify deviations. Intrusion analysis is essential for safeguarding sensitive data and maintaining the integrity of critical systems.

Multiple choice questions

1. **What is the primary goal of alert management?**
   a. To generate as many alerts as possible
   b. To prioritize and respond to alerts efficiently
   c. To disable unnecessary alerts
   d. To ignore low-priority alerts

2. **Which of the following is not a type of malware?**
   a. Virus
   b. Worm
   c. Firewall
   d. Trojan

3. **What does static analysis in malware analysis involve?**
   a. Executing the malware to observe its behavior
   b. Determining the file type without execution
   c. Monitoring network traffic
   d. Analyzing the malware in a virtual machine

Answers

1	b
2	c
3	b

Questions

1. Discuss the importance of alert management in a SOC and outline the key strategies for effective alert management.
2. Describe the role of behavior analysis in cybersecurity. Discuss how UBA and EBA can be used to detect anomalies and potential threats.
3. Explain the process of post-incident analysis in detail.
4. **Exercise**: Imagine receiving an alert about unusual outbound traffic from a critical server. Your task is determining whether it is a legitimate activity or a sign of data exfiltration.

Key terms

Some key terms used in this chapter are as follows:

- **False positives and false negatives**: Important alert types for SOC analysts.
- **IDS/IPS**: Critical technologies in intrusion detection and analysis.

CHAPTER 8
Threat Intelligence and Hunting

Introduction

In the ever-evolving cybersecurity domain, staying one step ahead of malicious actors requires a proactive and dynamic approach. Simply responding to alerts after an incident has occurred leaves organizations vulnerable to considerable damage and disruption. The modern **security operations center (SOC)** must adopt a proactive approach, leveraging both threat intelligence and threat hunting to anticipate and neutralize threats before they can materialize.

This chapter explores the critical components of threat intelligence and threat hunting, two pivotal disciplines within a SOC that enable organizations to defend against advanced threats. This domain addresses the emerging threat landscape and mitigates it proactively before it escalates into attacks. This leads to taking the SOC operations to the next level in mitigation.

Threat intelligence is the practice of collecting, analyzing, and disseminating information about current and potential cyber threats. It serves as the foundation for informed decision-making, enabling security teams to understand the TTPs used by adversaries. By leveraging threat intelligence, organizations can anticipate and mitigate risks, enhance their defensive strategies, and respond effectively to incidents.

Threat Hunting, on the other hand, involves the active search for IOC and hidden threats within an organization's environment. Unlike traditional reactive measures, threat hunting is a proactive practice that aims to uncover stealthy attackers who have bypassed automated defenses. It requires skilled analysts who can hypothesize about potential attack vectors, scrutinize data for anomalies, and leverage advanced tools and techniques to uncover malicious activity.

One of the most disruptive ransomware attacks in recent history targeted Colonial Pipeline in May 2021, causing widespread fuel shortages across the U.S. East Coast. A cybercriminal group exploited vulnerabilities in the company's IT systems, deploying ransomware that forced Colonial Pipeline to halt operations, leading to panic buying and economic disruption. The attack resulted in a $4.4 million ransom payment, although law enforcement agencies later recovered a portion of it.

This incident underscores the critical need for threat intelligence and proactive threat hunting in cybersecurity. If Colonial Pipeline had actively monitored its network for early indicators of compromise and utilized intelligence-driven defence strategies, it could have identified potential risks before attackers gained access. Implementing continuous security assessments, detecting anomalies through threat hunting, and maintaining robust access controls are key factors in mitigating such threats. The Colonial Pipeline case serves as a cautionary example of how a proactive cybersecurity posture can significantly reduce the impact of ransomware attacks, protecting vital infrastructure from crippling disruptions.

Together, threat intelligence and threat hunting form a powerful synergy. Threat intelligence informs the hunting process, providing valuable insights into potential threats and the behavior of attackers. Conversely, the findings from threat hunting can enrich threat intelligence, giving real-world observations of adversary activity and validating the relevance of existing intelligence.

Structure

In this chapter, we will discuss the following topics:

- Understanding threat intelligence in SOC
- Relevance of threat intelligence for SOC
- Lifecycle of threat intelligence
- Threat intelligence sharing
- Threat intelligence tools
- Threat hunting
- Threat hunting tools

Objectives

By the end of this chapter, readers will gain valuable insights and practical knowledge to integrate threat intelligence and hunting into their SOC operations effectively. This chapter will examine the methodologies, tools, and best practices in these disciplines, equipping readers with the knowledge and skills necessary to strengthen their organization's security posture.

Understanding threat intelligence in SOC

Threat intelligence is the knowledge derived from data that enables the prevention and mitigation of cyberattacks on digital information systems. It provides informed decision-making capabilities for cybersecurity professionals. Before dwelling further, it is crucial to understand the difference between data, information, and intelligence, which is often used interchangeably.

Here is a detailed distinction for these terms:

- Data refers to raw, unprocessed facts and figures. It can be in the form of numbers, text, images, or any other output from sensors or other devices. Data on its own may not be meaningful until it is processed and organized. Examples of data include IP addresses, URLs, and hashes.

- Information is data that has been processed, organized, or structured in a way that provides context and meaning. Information answers questions like who, what, where, and when. It is more valuable than raw data because it helps us understand and interpret the data. For example, data on social media presence in a month can be processed into information that shows the impact of social media on the organization.

- Intelligence is information that has been analyzed and interpreted to provide insights and support decision-making. It often involves understanding relationships, trends, and patterns within the data. Intelligence extends beyond merely presenting information; it provides actionable insights that can inform strategic planning and guide effective actions. For instance, business intelligence may involve analyzing market trends to inform decisions about product launches or marketing strategies.

Let us look at a real-world phishing attack detection and prevention scenario:

- The raw data could include logs of all incoming and outgoing emails within an organization, logs of all URLs clicked by users, logs of IP addresses accessing the organization's network, or reports submitted by users who suspect they have received phishing emails.

- This raw data is processed and organized to create meaningful information such as:

  o Analyzing email logs, security systems identify patterns such as unusual sender addresses, odd attachments, or common phishing keywords.

- o Reviewing logs of clicked URLs, systems flag links that direct users to known malicious websites or have abnormal characteristics.

- o Analyzing IP addresses, systems identify access attempts from unusual or suspicious locations.

- o Summarizing the frequency and content of user reports to highlight recurring phishing attempts.

- This information is further analyzed to produce actionable intelligence as mentioned:

- o Combining data from suspicious email patterns, URL analysis, and geolocation data to identify and profile potential threat actors.

- o Using machine learning to predict future phishing attempts based on historical data.

- o Implementing measures such as blocking known malicious IP addresses, updating email filters with new phishing keywords, and training employees based on the most common phishing tactics identified.

By transforming raw data into actionable intelligence, organizations can significantly enhance their ability to detect, prevent, and respond to phishing attacks. This proactive approach helps to stay ahead of cyber threats and protect sensitive information.

Cyber professionals are facing increasing challenges from a multitude of threat actors and sources. They handle enormous amounts of data from multiple security systems, facing a significant shortage of skilled professionals. This results in security alerts not being investigated despite an increase in data breaches within organizations.

Digital technologies have permeated into every domain of organizations and societies. With such diverse information, there is a need for practical threat intelligence aiding the automation and mitigation efforts. Threat intelligence provides context, including who is attacking, their motivations and capabilities, and the IOC. This comprehensive knowledge prepares the SOC team to make informed decisions. Threat intelligence enhances the value of security operations, vulnerability management, fraud prevention, and risk analysis teams.

Relevance of threat intelligence for SOC

Cyber threats are becoming increasingly sophisticated and pervasive. To address these ever-evolving threats, SOCs have evolved from mere reactive response units to pro-active defenders of an organization's digital assets. Central to this transformation is the integration of **threat intelligence (TI)** into SOC operations. Traditional security approaches often rely on signature-based detection and reactive incident response. While these methods are essential, they are insufficient against sophisticated and evolving threats.

Threat intelligence provides the crucial context and foresight needed to bridge this gap. It empowers the SOC to perform the following:

- **Proactively identify and mitigate threats**: By understanding adversary TTPs, the SOC can proactively hunt for malicious activity and implement preventive measures. During an incident, threat intelligence plays a vital role in guiding the response and investigation process. For instance, if threat intelligence indicates a surge in phishing emails with a specific attachment type targeting a particular industry, the SOC can proactively create email filtering rules to block such emails before they reach users.

- **Prioritize security efforts**: Threat intelligence helps the SOC focus on the most relevant and impactful threats, optimizing resource allocation and maximizing efficiency. By providing context about the threat actor's TTPs, SOC teams can better understand the attacker's objectives and methods. This information is crucial for containing the threat, eradicating it from the environment, and conducting a thorough forensic analysis to prevent future occurrences. The Reaper botnet attack in 2017 demonstrated the power of threat intelligence in safeguarding networks. This sophisticated malware infected over a million internet-connected devices, exploiting known security flaws in routers and cameras. Early detection by cybersecurity researchers enabled organizations to take preventive action, mitigating potential large-scale damage. By analyzing the attacker's TTPs, SOC teams could understand its objectives, prioritize patching, filter malicious traffic, and reinforce defences. Without proactive monitoring, the botnet might have been used for disruptive cyberattacks. This case highlights how contextual threat intelligence enhances SOC efficiency by focusing on relevant threats and enabling thorough forensic investigations to prevent future incidents.

- **Enhance threat detection and incident response**: Incorporating TI into the SOC improves the ability to detect and respond to threats. With access to up-to-date IOC and threat actor profiles, SOC analysts can quickly identify suspicious activity and correlate it with known threats. This reduces the time it takes to detect and respond to incidents, thereby minimizing the potential impact on the organization. By providing context about the adversary and their motivations, threat intelligence accelerates incident response and enables more effective containment and eradication. A notable example of threat intelligence enhancing incident response is the SolarWinds supply chain attack. In 2020, attackers compromised SolarWinds' software updates, allowing them to infiltrate numerous organizations, including government agencies and Fortune 500 companies. Security teams leveraged threat intelligence to identify IOC, such as unusual network traffic and unauthorized access attempts. By correlating these findings with known threat actor tactics, SOC analysts were able to contain the breach, mitigate further damage, and strengthen defences against similar attacks. This case underscores how timely intelligence accelerates detection and response, minimizing organizational impact.

- **Enhance situational awareness**: TI provides SOC teams with a comprehensive understanding of the threat landscape. By continuously monitoring and analyzing threat data, SOCs can stay informed about emerging threats and vulnerabilities, enabling them to prioritize their defenses and allocate resources effectively. TI can be used to educate employees about current threats and best practices, strengthening the organization's overall security posture. Situational awareness is critical for anticipating and mitigating potential attacks before they materialize. For instance, take a real-world example of the WannaCry ransomware attack in 2017. This global cyberattack exploited a vulnerability in outdated Windows systems, affecting hospitals, businesses, and government agencies. Organizations with strong threat intelligence and proactive monitoring were able to detect early warning signs, patch vulnerable systems, and prevent widespread damage. By continuously analyzing emerging threats and educating employees on security best practices, SOC teams can enhance their ability to anticipate and mitigate cyber risks before they escalate.

- **Validate security controls**: By simulating real-world attacks based on TI, organizations can assess the effectiveness of their security controls and identify vulnerabilities. For instance, consider the Target Data Breach in 2013. Attackers exploited vulnerabilities in Target's network via a third-party vendor, leading to the theft of millions of customer payment details. Had Target conducted red team exercises or penetration testing based on threat intelligence, it could have identified weaknesses in its security controls before attackers did. This case highlights the importance of proactively testing defences to uncover vulnerabilities and strengthen cybersecurity measures before real threats emerge.

Threat intelligence is a broad concept. Considering the sources, impacts and potential decisions, threat intelligence can be categorized based on its focus and application:

- **Strategic intelligence**: It is high-level information that informs decision-makers about the threat landscape, trends, and potential impacts on the organization. It is used for strategic planning and resource allocation.

  For example, strategic intelligence can be a detailed analysis about how nation-state actors/APT groups are targeting the BFSI sector through supply chain attacks, its impact on businesses, and suggested strategic responses. Recent strategic intelligence insights reveal a rise in nation-state cyber operations targeting renewable energy supply chains to compromise critical infrastructure. Attackers infiltrate software providers and hardware manufacturers, embedding malicious code or exploiting **industrial control systems** (**ICS**) before deployment, granting long-term access for espionage or potential disruption. By analyzing geopolitical risks and emerging cyber tactics, organizations can leverage threat intelligence to strengthen defences, mitigate vulnerabilities, and safeguard essential assets against evolving cyber threats.

- **Tactical intelligence**: It is short-term, actionable information about immediate threats, used for incident response and security operations. It entails detailed technical information used by security practitioners to detect and respond to threats.

  This includes IOC such as IP addresses, domain names, and malware hashes. For example, tactical intelligence can be analysis of a phishing campaign targeting employees, their specific social engineering tactics, and recommended security awareness programs. A recent example of tactical intelligence is the emergence of the 8BASE ransomware campaign targeting healthcare organizations in 2024. Cybersecurity researchers analyzed newly identified IOC, including malicious IP addresses, domains, and malware hashes, linked to this ransomware variant. By integrating these threat intelligence feeds into security monitoring systems, SOC teams were able to detect suspicious activity, block malicious infrastructure, and mitigate risks before the attack escalated. This actionable intelligence allowed healthcare providers to fortify their defenses, prevent data breaches, and enhance their response strategies against evolving ransomware threats.

- **Operational intelligence**: It provides details about specific attacks and campaigns, including TTPs and infrastructure, used for proactive threat hunting and mitigation. This information, i.e., threat actor profiles, attack vectors, and campaigns, helps in understanding and mitigating ongoing threats and attacks. For example, operational intelligence can be from dark web forums revealing a ransomware plan to target specific organizations with their specific attack vectors. A recent example of operational intelligence involves the exploitation of a zero-day vulnerability in the Windows **Common Log File System** (**CLFS**) by the Storm-2460 ransomware group. Security analysts uncovered dark web discussions where cybercriminals shared techniques for leveraging this flaw to gain privileged access, enabling them to move laterally within networks. This vulnerability was actively exploited to deploy ransomware, affecting industries such as IT, finance, and retail. By monitoring underground forums and analyzing attacker TTPs, security teams swiftly updated threat intelligence feeds, allowing organizations to patch the weakness and reinforce their defenses. This case underscores the significance of real-time operational intelligence in identifying emerging cyber threats and implementing preemptive security measures.

A comprehensive cybersecurity strategy is a combination of all three types covered previously, each providing unique insights. Strategic intelligence ensures high-level security decision-making along with resource allocations. Tactical intelligence improves threat detection and response abilities. Operational intelligence aids in incident response and proactive threat hunting.

Threat intelligence comes from a variety of sources, each offering unique perspectives and insights. These sources can be broadly categorized as:

- **Open-Source Intelligence (OSINT)**: Freely available information from public sources like blogs, forums, social media, news articles, government advisories, and research publications. While valuable, OSINT often requires careful vetting and analysis due to its potential for inaccuracies. For example, a security researcher's blog post detailing a new vulnerability in a widely used software library.

- **Commercial threat intelligence**: Provided by specialized vendors, these feeds offer curated and analyzed intelligence, often including IOC, TTPs, and threat actor profiles. Commercial intelligence is typically more reliable and actionable than OSINT. It includes technical intelligence like network and systems logs, malware analysis, etc. For example, a threat feed provides up-to-date lists of known command-and-control server IP addresses.

- **Government and industry information sharing**: Organizations like **Information Sharing and Analysis Centers** (ISAC) and **Information Sharing and Analysis Organizations** (ISAO) facilitate the sharing of threat information among members within specific industries. Government agencies also contribute valuable intelligence. For example, the FS-ISAC played a crucial role in mitigating cyber threats during the SWIFT banking attacks by rapidly sharing intelligence, helping financial institutions detect and prevent breaches. This highlights the importance of industry collaboration in strengthening security measures against sophisticated cyber threats.

- **Internal threat intelligence**: Derived from an organization's security logs, incident response data, and vulnerability assessments. This internal intelligence provides valuable insights into the specific threats targeting the organization. A real-world example of internal threat intelligence is how Microsoft detected and mitigated the Nobelium cyberattack in 2021. By analyzing security logs and incident data, Microsoft identified unusual activity linked to the threat actor, enabling swift containment and strengthening defenses against future breaches.

- **Human Intelligence (HUMINT)**: Information gathered through human sources, such as informants or undercover operations, industry conferences and meetups, and community forums. While often highly valuable, HUMINT is typically difficult and expensive to obtain. In 2013, the FBI leveraged HUMINT to dismantle a cyber espionage campaign targeting U.S. government entities. By utilizing informants and undercover operations, authorities uncovered critical details about the attackers, enabling decisive action to neutralize the threat. This demonstrates the importance of human-sourced intelligence in identifying and countering sophisticated cyber adversaries.

- **Dark web intelligence**: The dark web can be a valuable source of threat intelligence for organizations looking to bolster their cybersecurity defenses. This can be achieved through monitoring cybercrime forums, tracking emerging threats and exploits, or following the communications of threat actors. Organizations can gain crucial insights into emerging cyber threats, vulnerabilities, and criminal activities. In 2023, cybersecurity analysts uncovered dark web discussions where threat actors shared exploits for a critical VPN vulnerability, leading to targeted attacks on financial institutions. By monitoring these forums, organizations swiftly patched systems, preventing widespread breaches and reinforcing their defences against emerging cyber threats.

The preceding sources are not the only sources of threat intelligence. Often, threat actors infiltrate or compromise private communication channels and utilize encrypted messaging apps or exclusive forums on the dark web to exfiltrate sensitive data.

Some of the barriers to getting threat intelligence are as follows:

- Most of the communication on the dark web is on private and encrypted channels.

- The languages used for communication can be slang or local languages, making it difficult for analysts to assimilate.

- Threat actors deliberately obfuscate information to avoid detection.

There is a need for investments in tools and infrastructure to monitor such private/ encrypted channels. Some threat intelligence agencies have invested and can share their insights at a cost. The concept of threat intelligence is to enhance decision-making rather than exacerbate confusion when addressing cyber threats.

Integrating threat intelligence into SOC

Incorporating threat intelligence into a SOC is an essential step towards enhancing an organization's cybersecurity posture. By integrating real-time threat data, SOC teams can proactively identify and mitigate potential threats, streamline incident response, and bolster overall network defense strategies. This fusion of intelligence-driven insights and operational processes enables organizations to stay ahead of evolving cyber threats, making their defense mechanisms more resilient and adaptive in an increasingly complex threat landscape.

Effective integration of threat intelligence into SOC operations is crucial for realizing its full potential. This involves the following:

- **Establishing a threat intelligence platform (TIP)**: A TIP aggregates and manages TI from various sources, enabling analysts to correlate information, prioritize threats, and disseminate intelligence to relevant teams. For example, a SOC might use a TIP like ThreatConnect to aggregate threat data from various feeds, automatically score and prioritize it based on relevance to their industry and infrastructure, and then integrate this prioritized intelligence with their SIEM for alerting.

- **Automating threat intelligence workflows**: Integrating threat intelligence with security tools like SIEMs, firewalls, and EDR solutions enables automated threat detection and response. Threat intelligence platforms like MISP can automatically feed IOC into SIEMs, enabling real-time correlation with security logs, while EDR solutions use this data to detect and block malicious activity proactively.

- **Developing threat-hunting programs**: TI informs the development of threat-hunting hypotheses, allowing analysts to search for malicious activity within the network proactively. Threat-hunting platforms like CrowdStrike Falcon use threat intelligence to generate hypotheses based on emerging attack patterns, enabling analysts to proactively search for IOC and detect hidden threats within the network.

- **Training SOC analysts**: SOC analysts require training on how to effectively utilize threat intelligence to enhance their detection, analysis, and response capabilities. SOC analysts receive hands-on training with platforms like SOCRadar, learning how to apply threat intelligence in real-world scenarios. This includes analyzing IOC, profiling threat actors, and integrating intelligence into SIEM systems to improve detection and response capabilities.

By leveraging threat intelligence, SOC teams can proactively identify and mitigate potential threats before they escalate into full-blown incidents. Practical applications include real-time threat detection, where intelligence feeds into monitoring systems to flag suspicious activities, and targeted threat hunting, allowing analysts to search for specific indicators of compromise.

Some practical applications of threat intelligence in the SOC are as follows:

- **Enriching security alerts**: SOC teams must grapple with huge volumes of alerts. Triaging these alerts manually is a humongous task, resulting in low investigations. Alert fatigue sets in the SOC analysts and the response becomes slow. TI adds context to security alerts, helping analysts prioritize and investigate the most critical events. TI also helps in filtering out false alarms and speed up triaging. When a SIEM generates an alert about a suspicious login attempt from an unusual location, integrating threat intelligence might reveal that the originating IP address is associated with a known brute-force attack campaign, automatically increasing the alert's severity.

- **Improving threat detection**: Integrating threat intelligence into a SOC significantly enhances threat detection capabilities. By incorporating TI into security tools, the SOC can detect known malicious activity and identify suspicious patterns. By leveraging real-time threat intelligence, SOC teams gain valuable insights into emerging threats, attack patterns, and indicators of compromise. This proactive approach allows analysts to detect and respond to threats more swiftly and accurately. By continuously updating threat intelligence sources and refining detection rules, organizations can maintain a robust defense against the ever-evolving threat landscape, improving their overall security posture. In 2025, SOC teams leveraged real-time threat intelligence to identify and disrupt stealer malware campaigns that exploited Telegram bots for data exfiltration. This proactive approach enabled organizations to block malicious infrastructure, refine detection rules, and strengthen defences against emerging threats.

- **Enhancing incident response**: Cyber incidents have increased enormously, and threats have become more complex. SOC analysts spend considerable time sifting through data from disparate sources and responding. TI provides valuable information about the adversary and their TTPs, accelerating incident response and enabling more effective containment and eradication. TI can significantly reduce pressure on SOC teams by automatically managing false positive alerts and enriching them with real-time context. In 2025, SOC teams leveraged threat intelligence feeds to swiftly detect and neutralize RedEnergy malware, which exploited cloud misconfigurations to infiltrate enterprise networks, reducing response time and preventing widespread data breaches.

- **Proactive threat hunting**: TI guides threat-hunting activities, allowing analysts to proactively search for malicious actors who may have bypassed traditional security defenses. Threat intelligence supports advanced threat hunting, allowing SOC teams to identify and neutralize hidden threats before they cause harm. In 2025, SOC teams leveraged proactive threat hunting to uncover and neutralize covert malware campaigns that exploited AI-generated phishing tactics, stopping attackers from evading security measures and compromising enterprise networks.

- **Vulnerability management**: Considerable vulnerabilities are disclosed, and some are exploited by threat actors for malicious purposes. There is a need for continuous patching to avoid the exploitation of vulnerabilities. TI can be used to prioritize vulnerability patching based on the likelihood of exploitation. NIST's **National Vulnerability Database (NVD)** serves as the basis for threat intelligence disclosure. However, NVD provides only technical exploitability, and the frequency of updating is not fast enough. TI can bridge this gap and improve the patching cadence to improve security posture. In 2024, Tenable Patch Management incorporated threat intelligence to accelerate vulnerability remediation, significantly reducing exposure time from weeks to days. This approach enabled organizations to swiftly address critical security flaws before they could be exploited by attackers.

Threat intelligence is an indispensable component of a modern SOC. By providing context, foresight, and actionable insights, it empowers security teams to move beyond reactive security and proactively defend against evolving threats. Effective integration of threat intelligence requires a comprehensive approach, encompassing the right tools, processes, and skilled personnel. By embracing threat intelligence, the SOC can significantly enhance its ability to protect critical assets and mitigate the impact of cyberattacks.

To maximize the value of TI, it must be integrated with existing security tools and workflows. Let us look at some strategies for the same:

- **SIEM integration**: Threat intelligence feeds can be integrated with SIEM systems to generate automated alerts for suspicious activities, enabling immediate investigation and enhancing correlation capabilities.

- **Endpoint protection**: Utilizing threat intelligence to update endpoint protection solutions with the latest IOC and threat signatures.

- **Network security**: Enhancing network security devices, such as firewalls and **intrusion detection/prevention systems (IDS/IPS)**, with real-time threat intelligence feeds.

Lifecycle of threat intelligence

By understanding the lifecycle of threat intelligence, SOCs can effectively gather, analyze, and utilize information to anticipate, detect, and respond to threats. The threat intelligence lifecycle is a structured process that ensures the systematic gathering and use of intelligence. It comprises six key stages, as shown in the following figure:

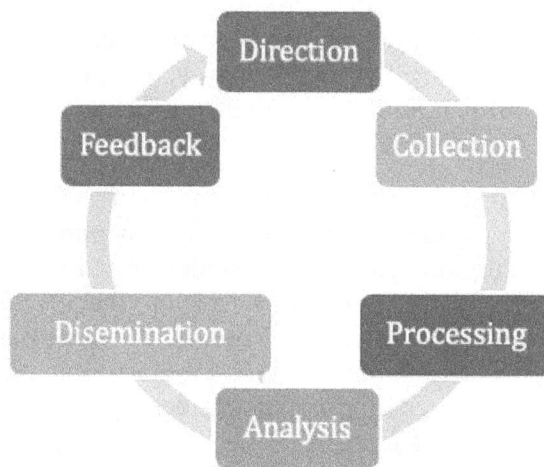

Figure 8.1: Threat intelligence lifecycle

Each phase is interdependent, creating a continuous loop that enhances the organization's security posture. A threat intelligence lifecycle consists of the following stages:

- **Direction**: The direction phase sets the foundation for the threat intelligence lifecycle. During this stage, the objectives and requirements for intelligence gathering are established. This stage involves the following:

   o **Identifying key intelligence needs (KIN)**: This entails determining what information is critical for the organization's security and the potential impacts of losing those assets or interrupting those processes.

   o **Setting priorities**: Allocating resources and focus based on the significance of identified threats.

   o **Developing an intelligence plan**: Outlining the steps and methodologies for gathering and analyzing intelligence.

- **Collection**: In the collection phase, data is gathered from various sources to address the intelligence needs identified in the direction phase. Sources of threat intelligence include:

  o **OSINT**: Publicly available information, such as news articles, blogs, forums, social media, or scraping and harvesting websites/forums.

  o **Technical intelligence**: Data from technical sources like malware analysis reports, network logs, and security feeds from industry organizations and cybersecurity vendors.

  o **Human Intelligence (HUMINT)**: Insights gathered from human sources, including threat actor communications and industry reports, conversations, and targeted interviews with knowledgeable sources.

  o **Internal data**: Information from within the organization, such as metadata, incident reports, and system logs from internal networks and security devices.

  o **Dark web**: Stolen data, exposed credentials, and discussions about software vulnerabilities are commonly found on the dark web.

- **Processing**: The processing phase involves converting raw data into a format suitable for analysis. All data collected needs to be processed, either by humans or by machines. This stage involves the following:

  o **Data cleaning**: Removing irrelevant or duplicate information.

  o **Normalization**: Standardizing data formats for consistency.

  o **Correlation**: Linking related pieces of information to form a comprehensive picture.

  o **Enrichment**: Adding context to raw data to enhance its value.

- **Analysis**: In the analysis phase, the processed data is examined to produce actionable intelligence. The analysis may lead to decisions like investigating the cyber threat or immediately blocking the cyberattack or strengthening the security controls. This stage involves the following:

  o **Contextual analysis**: Understanding the context and relevance of the data.

  o **Pattern recognition**: Identifying trends, anomalies, and patterns in the data.

  o **Attribution**: Determining the threat actor's identity, motives, and capabilities.

  o **Scenario development**: Predicting potential future threats and their impact.

- **Dissemination**: The dissemination phase involves distributing the analyzed intelligence to relevant stakeholders. Key activities include:

  o **Report generation**: Creating comprehensive reports that summarize the findings and recommendations.

- o **Distribution channels**: Sharing reports via appropriate channels, such as emails, dashboards, or meetings.

- o **Timeliness**: Ensuring intelligence is shared in a timely manner to facilitate prompt action.

- **Feedback**: The feedback phase is critical for continuous improvement. It involves:

  - o **Reviewing outcomes**: Assessing the effectiveness of the intelligence and the actions taken based on it.

  - o **Stakeholder feedback**: Gathering feedback from stakeholders to understand their needs and satisfaction.

  - o **Adjusting processes**: Making necessary adjustments to the intelligence process based on feedback and lessons learned.

Incorporating threat intelligence into SOC operations transforms reactive measures into proactive strategies, enabling organizations to stay ahead of adversaries and safeguard their digital assets effectively. As the threat landscape continues to evolve, the importance of a structured and continuous threat intelligence lifecycle cannot be overstated. By continuously cycling through these stages, SOCs can maintain a prominent level of situational awareness. This enables them to anticipate and respond to threats more effectively, minimizing the risk of successful attacks.

Threat intelligence provides valuable context during an incident response. By understanding the threat actor's TTPs, SOC teams can tailor their response strategies and ensure comprehensive mitigation of the threat. The lifecycle of threat intelligence empowers SOCs to adopt a proactive defense posture. Through regular threat hunting and analysis, potential threats can be identified and neutralized before they cause considerable damage.

Let us look into a real-world example of the threat intelligence lifecycle in action, one that unfolded in 2025 with the emergence of ShadowStrike, a sophisticated malware campaign targeting cloud infrastructure. The lifecycle stages in this scenario would be as follows:

- **Direction setting the mission**: Security teams worldwide noticed an uptick in cloud-based attacks, particularly targeting containerized environments. The objective was clear: investigate the ShadowStrike malware, understand its capabilities, and develop countermeasures before it caused widespread damage.

- **Collection gathering the clues**: Threat intelligence analysts scoured dark web forums, malware repositories, and security logs, uncovering discussions among cybercriminals about a zero-day vulnerability in a popular cloud orchestration tool. They collected IOC—malicious IP addresses, file hashes, and behavioral patterns linked to ShadowStrike.

- **Processing, making sense of the data**: Raw intelligence was structured into actionable insights. Analysts reverse-engineered ShadowStrike's payload, revealing its ability to evade traditional defenses, escalate privileges, and deploy ransomware within cloud environments. The malware's attack chain was mapped to the MITRE ATT&CK framework, helping defenders anticipate its next move.

- **Analysis understanding the threat**: Deep analysis uncovered ShadowStrike's unique persistence mechanism—it disguised itself as a legitimate cloud service update, tricking administrators into deploying it unknowingly. Security teams identified its C2 infrastructure, allowing them to predict potential attack vectors.

- **Dissemination sharing the intelligence**: Findings were rapidly shared with cloud service providers, SOC teams, and cybersecurity communities. Security vendors integrated ShadowStrike's IOC into SIEMs, EDR solutions, and firewall rules, enabling organizations to detect and block the malware before it could spread.

- **Feedback refining the defence**: Organizations reported back on detection efficacy, leading to refinements in threat intelligence models. Cloud providers issued emergency patches, and security teams adjusted their hunting techniques to proactively identify similar threats in the future.

Thanks to rapid intelligence sharing, ShadowStrike was neutralized before it could cause widespread disruption. This case underscores the power of proactive threat intelligence, demonstrating how structured intelligence workflows can turn the tide against emerging cyber threats.

The lifecycle of threat intelligence is a critical component of a robust cybersecurity strategy. By systematically gathering, analyzing, and disseminating intelligence, SOCs can enhance their ability to defend against sophisticated cyber threats. Understanding and implementing each phase of the lifecycle ensures that organizations are well-prepared to navigate the ever-evolving landscape of cybersecurity.

Threat intelligence sharing

The ability to preempt, detect, and mitigate cyber threats relies heavily on the seamless exchange of threat intelligence. Collaboration and information sharing are essential components of an effective threat intelligence strategy. SOC teams should actively participate in threat intelligence sharing communities, such as ISACs and industry-specific threat intelligence groups. By sharing insights and collaborating with peers, organizations can gain a broader perspective on the threat landscape and enhance their collective defense capabilities.

Threat intelligence sharing serves as a force multiplier for SOCs. By collaborating and sharing threat data, organizations can achieve a more comprehensive understanding of threats and enhance their defense mechanisms.

Key benefits include the following:

- **Proactive defense**: Access to shared threat intelligence allows SOCs to identify and mitigate threats before they impact the organization.

- **Enhanced detection**: Collaborative TI can reveal patterns and indicators that might be missed when working in isolation.

- **Faster response**: SOCs can leverage shared intelligence to respond swiftly to threats, reducing the potential damage.

- **Resource optimization**: Pooling resources and information reduces redundancy and ensures that efforts are focused on addressing the most critical threats.

While the benefits of threat intelligence sharing are substantial, several challenges and considerations must be addressed. Some such challenges are:

- **Data quality and relevance**: Ensuring the accuracy and relevance of shared data is critical to avoid information overload and false positives.

- **Trust and collaboration**: Building trust among participating organizations is essential for effective sharing. Organizations must establish clear protocols for handling sensitive information.

- **Legal and compliance issues**: Adhering to legal and regulatory requirements related to data privacy and sharing is crucial to avoid potential liabilities.

- **Technical integration**: Seamless integration of shared threat intelligence into existing SOC workflows and tools is necessary to maximize its utility.

To optimize the value of threat intelligence sharing, SOCs should define clear goals and objectives of threat intelligence sharing to align efforts with organizational priorities. SOCs must encourage a culture of openness and collaboration within and outside the organization to facilitate information exchange. Automated tools and platforms must be used to streamline the collection, analysis, and dissemination of threat intelligence. There is a need to regularly assess and refine threat intelligence sharing processes to adapt to evolving threats and organizational needs.

Platforms and frameworks for sharing threat intelligence

Several platforms and frameworks facilitate the sharing of threat intelligence across organizations. Here are some of them:

- **ISAC**: Industry-specific groups that promote the exchange of security information and best practices. Examples include the Financial Services ISAC (FS-ISAC) and the **Healthcare ISAC (H-ISAC)**.

- **Threat intelligence platforms (TIP)**: Software solutions designed to aggregate, analyze, and share threat data. Popular TIPs include ThreatConnect, Anomali, and **Malware Information Sharing Platform (MISP)**.

- **Open-source threat intelligence (OSINT)**: Publicly available sources of threat intelligence, such as blogs, forums, and social media. OSINT can provide valuable insights into emerging threats.

Standards and protocols

In the ever-evolving cyber threat landscape, the ability to quickly, timely, efficiently, and accurately share threat intelligence is critical for organizations to stay ahead of evolving cyber threats. Organizations need to collaborate and share information about emerging threats to strengthen their collective defense. TI standardization and interoperability play a significant role in intelligence sharing, given the rapid and sophisticated nature of cyber threats. The key standards used during sharing are covered here.

TAXII

TAXII addresses the need for a standardized, secure, and automated method of exchanging TI, enabling organizations to stay ahead of adversaries and respond effectively to threats.

The TAXII is a set of protocols and services designed to enable the secure sharing of TI over the internet. TAXII facilitates the exchange of TI in a standardized and automated manner, allowing organizations to efficiently disseminate and consume threat information. Developed by the MITRE Corporation, TAXII complements the STIX framework by providing the necessary transport mechanisms for sharing STIX data.

TAXII was initially introduced in 2012 as a means of automating the exchange of TI. Over the years, TAXII has evolved to become more flexible and scalable, with TAXII 2.0 being a significant milestone. TAXII 2.0, released by the **Open Cybersecurity Alliance** (**OCA**), introduced several enhancements to improve usability, security, and interoperability.

TAXII consists of several key components that work together to enable the secure exchange of threat intelligence. Let us look at them in detail:

- **TAXII servers**: Centralized servers that host TI and provide access to clients.

- **TAXII clients**: Applications or systems that connect to TAXII servers to publish or consume TI.

- **Collections**: Logical groupings of related TI that can be shared and queried.

- **Channels**: Communication pathways that enable the exchange of TI between TAXII servers and clients.

- **APIs**: Application programming interfaces that provide standard methods for interacting with TAXII servers and clients.

These components work in unison to facilitate the sharing of TI in a secure and automated manner. TAXII supports two primary exchange models for sharing TI:

- **Collection model**: In this model, TI is organized into collections, which are logical groupings of related threat data. Clients can subscribe to collections and receive updates as new TI is added.

- **Channel model**: In this model, TI is exchanged through channels, which act as communication pathways between TAXII servers and clients. Channels can be configured to support diverse types of communication, such as one-to-one, one-to-many, or many-to-many exchanges.

The flexibility of these exchange models allows organizations to tailor their TI sharing practices to their specific needs.

Security is a critical aspect of TAXII, ensuring that the exchange of TI is protected from unauthorized access and tampering. TAXII employs several security measures, such as:

- **HTTPS**: Secure communication over HTTPS to protect data in transit.

- **Authentication**: Mechanisms to authenticate clients and servers, ensuring that only authorized entities can access and share TI.

- **Access control**: Granular access control policies to define who can access and modify TI.

These security measures help maintain the integrity and confidentiality of TI during exchange.

TAXII is widely adopted across various industries to enhance cybersecurity through the efficient sharing of threat intelligence. Some everyday use cases include the following:

- **Threat intelligence sharing**: Organizations share TI with industry peers, government agencies, and security vendors to collectively enhance their defense mechanisms.

- **Incident response**: TAXII enables the rapid dissemination of threat intelligence to incident response teams, helping them respond quickly to emerging threats.

- **Threat hunting**: Analysts utilize TAXII to access and analyze TI from multiple sources, facilitating the identification and investigation of potential threats.

While TAXII has significantly improved the sharing of TI, challenges remain. These include ensuring interoperability across different implementations, managing the complexity of large-scale deployments, and maintaining data quality. The TAXII community is actively working on enhancements to address these challenges and further improve the protocol.

By providing standardized protocols and services, TAXII facilitates collaboration and improves the collective ability to defend against cyber threats. As cyber adversaries continue to evolve, TAXII will remain a critical tool in the fight against cybercrime.

STIX

STIX is a comprehensive language and serialization format used to represent structured cyber threat information. Developed by the MITRE Corporation as part of the broader TAXII initiative, STIX is designed to enable the automated sharing, representation, and dissemination of TI.

The development of STIX began in 2012, with the goal of creating a structured and machine-readable format for sharing threat intelligence. Since its inception, STIX has undergone several iterations, with STIX 2.0 representing a significant leap forward in terms of flexibility, scalability, and usability. The OCA now oversees the development and maintenance of STIX.

At the heart of STIX lies its object model, which defines a set of standardized objects representing various aspects of cyber threats. These objects include the following:

- **Indicators**: Patterns identifying suspicious or malicious activities.

- **Observables**: Raw data collected from network traffic, logs, or other sources.

- **Threat actors**: Information about individuals or groups responsible for threats.

- **Courses of action (COA)**: Recommendations for responding to identified threats.

- **Malware**: Detailed descriptions of malicious software, including its characteristics and behavior.

- **Attack patterns: Tactics, techniques, and procedures (TTPs)** used by threat actors.

- **Campaigns and intrusion sets**: High-level information about coordinated attack campaigns.

By leveraging this object model, STIX enables the representation of complex relationships between different elements of a threat, facilitating a comprehensive understanding of the threat landscape.

STIX is designed to be platform-agnostic and can be integrated with various TI platforms, SIEM systems, and security tools. Its flexibility allows organizations to tailor their threat intelligence sharing to specific needs while ensuring compatibility with other systems. Furthermore, STIX supports the exchange of information over TAXII, a transport protocol that facilitates the secure and automated sharing of TI between organizations.

STIX is widely adopted by both the public and private sectors to improve their cybersecurity posture.

Some common use cases include the following:

- **Threat hunting**: Analysts use STIX to identify and investigate potential threats in their networks.

- **Incident response**: STIX provides structured information to guide response actions during and after a cyber incident.

- **Threat intelligence sharing**: Organizations share threat data with peers, industry groups, and government agencies to collectively improve defense mechanisms.

- **Automated detection and mitigation**: Security tools integrate STIX to automate threat detection and response processes.

While STIX has revolutionized the way organizations share and consume threat intelligence, challenges remain. These include ensuring data quality, maintaining interoperability across different implementations, and addressing the complexities of managing large volumes of threat data. As cyber threats continue to evolve, the STIX community is actively working on enhancements to address these challenges and further improve the language.

STIX represents a significant advancement in the realm of TI sharing. By providing a standardized and extensible format, it enables organizations to efficiently exchange and utilize threat information, enhancing their ability to protect against cyber threats. As the cybersecurity landscape continues to evolve, STIX will remain a foundational element in the fight against cyber adversaries.

Common Vulnerabilities and Exposures

CVE is a list of publicly disclosed cybersecurity vulnerabilities and exposures. CVE identifiers provide a standardized way to identify and discuss specific vulnerabilities. This helps organizations and security professionals quickly recognize and communicate about known vulnerabilities. Each CVE entry contains an identification number, a description of the vulnerability, and references to related vulnerability reports and advisories. For example, CVE-2024-1234 is an identifier which refers to a specific vulnerability in a software application that allows an attacker to execute arbitrary code.

CVE entries facilitate information sharing across different platforms, organizations, and industries. This means that threat intelligence gathered by one entity can be easily understood and utilized by others.

Common Vulnerability Scoring System

CVSS is a standardized framework for assessing the severity of security vulnerabilities and prioritizing responses. By integrating CVSS scores into threat intelligence, SOC teams can focus on addressing the most critical vulnerabilities first.

It provides a numerical score ranging from 0 to 10, with higher scores indicating more severe vulnerabilities. CVSS scores enable organizations to prioritize their remediation efforts based on the potential impact of each vulnerability, allowing them to make informed decisions about mitigation strategies. The key components of CVSS are:

- **Base metrics**: This evaluates the intrinsic characteristics of a vulnerability, such as its exploitability and impact on confidentiality, integrity, and availability.

- **Temporal metrics**: This reflects factors that may change over time, such as the availability of exploit code or patches.

- **Environmental metrics**: This adapts the evaluation to specific user contexts, considering the organization's unique environment.

For example, a vulnerability with a CVSS score of 9.0 would be considered critical and require immediate attention, while a vulnerability with a score of 3.0 might be considered minimal risk and addressed later.

Both CVE and CVSS are highly relevant to threat intelligence. By using CVE identifiers and CVSS scores, organizations can effectively manage and prioritize their cybersecurity efforts, ensuring that the most critical vulnerabilities are addressed promptly. Incorporating CVE and CVSS into threat intelligence processes enables organizations to efficiently identify, assess, and respond to vulnerabilities, strengthening their cybersecurity defenses.

Threat intelligence tools

In the dynamic realm of cybersecurity, threat intelligence tools are indispensable for SOCs. Malware, phishing campaigns, and **advanced persistent threats** (**APTs**) continue to target organizations worldwide. Fighting these threats in isolation is never effective. Open-source tools, such as the MISP, can bridge the gaps by facilitating collaborative TI sharing to strengthen cybersecurity defenses.

MISP is an open-source threat intelligence platform that allows organizations to collect, store, analyze, and share structured threat information, enhancing their ability to detect and respond to cyber threats. MISP enables cybersecurity teams to exchange real-time data on cyber threats like **indicators of compromise** (**IOC**) such as malicious IPs, domains, and hashes, TTPs used by attackers, phishing campaigns and malware signatures, threat actor profiles, and behavioral patterns.

MISP operates on a community-driven model. All participating organizations contribute and exploit threat intelligence through:

- **Events**: Collections of threat information related to a specific incident.

- **Attributes**: Individual indicators (IP addresses, hashes, domains, emails, etc.).

- **Tags and taxonomies**: Metadata that helps classify and filter threats.

Relevant case studies

Here are some relevant case studies:

- **Case study one**: A major financial institution integrated threat intelligence into its SOC operations to enhance its threat detection and response capabilities. By leveraging real-time threat intelligence feeds, the SOC team was able to identify and mitigate a sophisticated phishing campaign targeting its customers. The threat intelligence provided valuable context about the threat actor's tactics, enabling the SOC to implement effective countermeasures and prevent further attacks.

- **Case study two**: A healthcare organization utilized threat intelligence to protect its critical infrastructure from ransomware attacks. By analyzing threat intelligence reports, the SOC identified common indicators of compromise associated with ransomware campaigns. This proactive approach allowed the organization to strengthen its defenses and develop incident response playbooks tailored to ransomware threats.

- **Case study three**: A government organization used threat intelligence to identify sophisticated TTPs used by APT groups to detect similar attacks across government sections/industries, helping to pinpoint emerging threats and mitigate risks faster.

Some of the practical use cases are listed here:

- **Threat detection and response**: Threat intelligence tools can be configured to monitor network traffic and identify suspicious activities. For example, tools like Splunk can be used to correlate logs from various sources, detect anomalies, and trigger alerts for further investigation.

- **Incident investigation**: When a security incident occurs, tools like MISP can be used to gather and analyze threat data from multiple sources. This helps SOC analysts understand the scope of the incident and develop effective mitigation strategies.

- **Vulnerability management**: Threat intelligence tools can be integrated with vulnerability management systems to prioritize patching efforts. For instance, Anomali can provide contextual information about vulnerabilities, helping SOC teams focus on the most critical issues.

- **Threat intelligence sharing**: Sharing threat intelligence with other organizations can enhance collective defense. Platforms such as the **Financial Services Information Sharing and Analysis Center (FS-ISAC)** facilitate the exchange of threat data, enabling organizations to benefit from shared knowledge. Joining FS-ISAC involves subscribing to threat intelligence feeds, participating in information sharing events, and contributing to the collective knowledge base. Configuring automated sharing mechanisms and ensuring data privacy are essential for effective collaboration.

Let us try some of these tools for threat intelligence:

- **Splunk configuration**: To configure Splunk for threat detection, SOC teams can set up dashboards to visualize network traffic and create alerts based on predefined criteria. Regularly updating threat intelligence feeds and integrating them with Splunk ensures timely detection of threats. Perform the following steps:

  1. In Splunk ES, navigate to **Configure** and then **Intelligence**.

  2. Within the **Threat intelligence management** section, select **Threat intelligence sources**. Here:

     a. Enable or disable existing sources.

   b. Add new sources by specifying their type and location (URL, TAXII feeds, STIX/OpenIOC files, custom CSV files, Splunk events, Rest API etc.).

   c. Configure settings such as download intervals and data formats.

3. Create **Threat Lists** to refine your threat intelligence. Define the list's name, type, and the sources it should include. Apply filters to include or exclude specific indicators based on scores or types. These enable you to organize and filter threat intelligence data according to your specific needs.

4. Ensure that threat-matching searches are enabled in Splunk ES. This allows Splunk to correlate your security events with the threat intelligence data.

5. Splunk SOAR can be integrated with Splunk ES to automate responses to identified threats. This can include actions such as blocking malicious IPs or isolating affected systems.

• **MISP configuration**: Setting up MISP involves creating and maintaining threat intelligence reports, sharing IOCs, and collaborating with other organizations. Regularly updating the platform with the latest threat data and configuring automated sharing mechanisms enhances its effectiveness.

Here are the specific steps:

1. Follow the official MISP installation documentation, which may involve using virtual machines, Docker, or bare-metal installations.

2. Change the default administrator password immediately. Create your organization within MISP.

3. Add user accounts and assign appropriate roles and permissions.

4. Navigate to the feed management section and add threat intelligence feeds. Enable and synchronize the feeds to populate your MISP instance with data.

5. Ensure that your MISP instance has the latest taxonomies and galaxies. Learn how to apply these classifications to your threat data.

6. Configure sharing settings to control how your organization's threat intelligence is distributed.

7. Explore the MISP API and tools like PyMISP to automate tasks and integrate with other security platforms.

Threat intelligence tools are crucial for SOC operations, enabling organizations to effectively detect, investigate, and respond to cyber threats. By leveraging these tools and adhering to best practices for configuration and use, SOC teams can strengthen their security posture and stay ahead of evolving threats. As the cyber threat landscape continues to grow, the practical application of threat intelligence tools will remain a cornerstone of robust cybersecurity strategies.

Threat hunting

In the constantly evolving cyber threat landscape, reactive measures alone are no longer sufficient to protect organizations from sophisticated attacks. Proactive threat hunting has emerged as a critical component of modern SOCs. Threat hunters are skilled cybersecurity professionals who possess a deep understanding of attacker TTPs. They combine their knowledge with analytical skills to identify potential threats that automated systems might miss.

Threat hunting is the process of actively searching for IOCs, potential threats, and adversary activities within an organization's network. Unlike traditional threat detection, which relies on automated systems and predefined signatures, threat hunting is a proactive and hypothesis-driven approach that leverages human expertise to uncover hidden threats.

Threat hunting is essential due to the following reasons:

- **Early detection**: Threat hunting helps identify threats that may evade traditional detection mechanisms, allowing for early intervention before grave damage occurs.

- **Enhanced security posture**: By uncovering and mitigating advanced threats, threat hunting strengthens an organization's overall security posture.

- **Improved incident response**: Threat hunters provide valuable insights that enhance incident response capabilities, enabling faster and more effective containment and remediation.

- **Knowledge building**: The process of threat hunting generates valuable intelligence about adversary TTPs, contributing to the organization's knowledge base.

The threat hunting process can be broken down into several key phases, let us look at them in detail

- **Hypothesis generation**: The hunt begins with forming a hypothesis about potential threats. This could be based on intelligence reports, known vulnerabilities, or anomalies observed within the network.

- **Data collection and analysis**: Threat hunters gather data from various sources, such as logs, network traffic, and endpoint telemetry. This data is then analyzed to identify patterns and anomalies that may indicate malicious activity.

- **Investigation**: Once potential threats are identified, threat hunters conduct a detailed investigation to determine the nature and scope of the threat. This may involve reverse engineering malware, analyzing communication patterns, and correlating data from multiple sources.

- **Response and mitigation**: After confirming the presence of a threat, the SOC takes appropriate actions to contain and mitigate the threat. This could involve isolating affected systems, applying patches, or updating security configurations.

Tools and technologies for threat hunting

Effective threat hunting relies on a combination of tools and technologies that enable hunters to collect, analyze, and investigate data.

Some key tools include the following:

- SIEM systems aggregate and correlate data from various sources, providing threat hunters with a centralized view of the network. They enable real-time monitoring and alerting suspicious activities.

- EDR solutions provide visibility into endpoint activities, allowing threat hunters to detect and investigate anomalies at the endpoint level. They offer features such as behavioral analysis, threat intelligence integration, and automated response capabilities.

- Threat intelligence platforms collect and disseminate information about known threats, vulnerabilities, and attacker techniques. They help threat hunters stay informed about the latest threats and enhance their ability to detect and respond to emerging threats.

Methodologies and approaches

Effective threat hunting relies on a combination of tools and technologies that enable hunters to collect, analyze, and investigate data.

Some of the methodologies used for threat hunting are listed here:

- **Hypothesis-driven hunting**: This approach involves forming hypotheses about potential threats based on known attack patterns, threat intelligence, and organizational context. Threat hunters then validate these hypotheses through targeted searches and analysis. In 2025, a threat hunter hypothesized that attackers were using living-off-the-land techniques to evade detection. By analyzing PowerShell execution logs, they uncovered unauthorized script executions linked to StealthStrike malware, enabling rapid containment before data exfiltration occurred.

- **IOC hunting**: IOC hunting focuses on identifying and investigating specific indicators, such as malicious IP addresses, domain names, file hashes, and registry keys, which suggest the presence of a threat. Threat hunters use these indicators to identify compromised systems and investigate further. In 2025, a threat hunter identified a suspicious file hash linked to a newly discovered ransomware variant targeting healthcare systems. By correlating this IOC with endpoint telemetry, they uncovered compromised devices and initiated containment measures to prevent further encryption of critical patient data.

- **Behavioral hunting**: Behavioral analysis involves examining the behavior of users, applications, and network traffic to identify deviations from the norm. This can help detect hidden threats that exhibit unusual behavior patterns. Behavioral hunting involves monitoring and analyzing user and network behaviors to detect anomalies that may indicate malicious activities. This approach leverages machine learning and behavioral analytics to identify deviations from normal patterns. For example, a threat hunter might analyze network traffic logs to identify unusual outbound connections from internal workstations to previously uncontacted external IP addresses, which could indicate command-and-control activity.

- **Threat intelligence-driven hunting**: This approach leverages external threat intelligence to guide hunting efforts. Threat hunters use threat intelligence feeds to identify emerging threats and tailor their searches accordingly. In 2025, a threat hunter leveraged threat intelligence feeds to detect a zero-day exploit targeting cloud authentication services. By correlating this intelligence with SIEM logs, they uncovered unauthorized access attempts, enabling swift mitigation before widespread compromise.

- **MITRE ATT&CK framework driven hunting**: The MITRE ATT&CK framework provides a comprehensive knowledge base of attacker tactics and techniques. Threat hunters use this framework to map observed activities to known attacker behaviors, enabling them to identify and investigate potential threats. In 2025, a threat hunter mapped suspicious PowerShell execution patterns to the MITRE ATT&CK framework, identifying a privilege escalation attempt linked to a known APT group. By correlating this activity with endpoint logs, they uncovered lateral movement tactics, enabling rapid containment.

Threat hunting is not without its challenges. Usual challenges include information overload, resource constraints, and the constantly evolving threat landscape.

To overcome these challenges, organizations should adopt best practices, such as the following:

- **Continuous training and skill development**: Threat hunters must continuously update their skills and knowledge to keep pace with evolving threats. Organizations should invest in training programs and certifications to ensure their threat-hunting team is well-equipped.

- **Collaboration and information sharing**: Collaboration and information sharing among different teams and organizations can enhance threat-hunting efforts. Organizations can collectively improve their defenses against cyber threats by sharing threat intelligence and best practices.

- **Automation and integration**: Automating repetitive tasks and integrating threat-hunting tools with existing security infrastructure can improve efficiency and effectiveness. Automation allows threat hunters to focus on more complex and high-value tasks.

Threat hunting is a critical component of a robust cybersecurity strategy. By proactively identifying and mitigating hidden threats, organizations can stay one step ahead of cyber adversaries and safeguard their valuable assets. By adopting a structured approach and leveraging human expertise, SOCs can enhance their ability to detect, respond to, and prevent cyber threats. As the threat landscape continues to evolve, the importance of threat hunting in maintaining a robust security posture cannot be overstated.

Threat hunting tools

Proactive threat hunting involves searching for hidden threats within an organization's network. Tools like ThreatConnect enable SOC teams to create custom queries and search for IOCs across different data sources. To use ThreatConnect for threat hunting, SOC teams can create custom playbooks and workflows. Integrating ThreatConnect with other security tools, such as SIEM systems, allows for seamless data exchange and comprehensive threat analysis. For example, a threat hunter using ThreatConnect might craft a custom query based on a recent intelligence report detailing an APT group leveraging registry keys for persistence. For instance:

```
SELECT endpoints WHERE registry_key ='HKLM\Software\Microsoft\Windows\
CurrentVersion\Run\ShadowStrike' AND last_modified < 30 days
```

This query searches **EDR logs** for endpoints where the **ShadowStrike** malware has modified a registry key within the last 30 days, helping analysts pinpoint compromised systems and initiate containment efforts.

Practical implementation of threat hunting involves the following key steps:

1. **Preparing for threat hunting**: The first step involves:

   a. Clearly outline the goals and objectives of the threat hunting program, aligning them with the organization's security priorities.

   b. Build a team of skilled threat hunters with expertise in various areas, such as malware analysis, network forensics, and endpoint security.

   c. Collect and integrate relevant data sources, such as logs, network traffic, endpoint telemetry, and threat intelligence feeds. Equip the team with the necessary tools, including SIEM, EDR solutions, and network analysis tools.

2. **Conducting threat hunts**: Once all the resources and tools are available, threat hunting can be done as follows:

   a. Develop hypotheses based on known threats, organizational context, and threat intelligence. For example, a hypothesis might be that threat actors are using a specific vulnerability to gain access to the network.

   b. Use tools and techniques to collect and analyze data, search for evidence that supports or refutes the hypotheses. This may involve querying logs, examining network traffic, and conducting endpoint forensics.

c. Investigate any suspicious findings in-depth, correlating data from multiple sources to confirm the presence of a threat. Document findings and assess the potential impact on the organization.

d. If a threat is confirmed, initiate incident response procedures to contain and remediate the threat. Communicate findings to relevant stakeholders and update the threat intelligence database with new insights.

3. **Post-hunt activities**: It is crucial to close the process with documentation and commitment to continual improvement through the following steps:

a. Document the threat hunting process, findings, and lessons learned. Share insights with other teams, such as incident response and threat intelligence, to enhance overall security awareness.

b. Continuously refine threat hunting methodologies and processes based on feedback and evolving threat landscapes. Update tools and techniques to stay ahead of emerging threats.

c. Invest in ongoing training and development for threat hunters to keep their skills up-to-date and ensure they are equipped to handle new challenges.

Let us perform practical, hypothesis-based threat hunting in the upcoming subsections.

Scenario one, insider threat

Hypothesis: An organization suspects that an insider threat is exfiltrating sensitive data to an external server.

The steps to validate this hypothesis using open-source tools are mentioned here:

1. **Gather intelligence**: Use open-source threat intelligence platforms like MISP to collect information about known IOC associated with insider threats. MISP is utilized for validating IOC in insider threat investigations because it enables efficient data correlation from multiple sources. Security teams can leverage MISP to compare suspicious employee activities against historical malicious IPs, file hashes, and behavioral patterns, allowing for precise threat identification while minimizing false positives.

2. **Set up a SIEM**: Deploy an open-source SIEM tool like **Elastic Stack** (**ELK**) or Splunk to aggregate and analyze logs from various sources within the organization. ELK and Splunk are selected for log validation due to their ability to correlate data in real-time and detect anomalies across multiple sources. Security teams utilize ELK's Kibana dashboards to track authentication failures, aiding in the identification of potential brute-force attempts, while Splunk's **Search Processing Language** (**SPL**) enables precise queries to verify suspicious activity patterns.

3. **Network monitoring**: Use Wireshark or tcpdump to capture and analyze network traffic. Look for unusual data transfers or connections to suspicious external IP

addresses. Wireshark and tcpdump are chosen for network traffic validation because they enable deep packet inspection and real-time traffic analysis. For instance, security teams use Wireshark's filtering capabilities to isolate suspicious outbound connections, helping detect potential data exfiltration attempts, while tcpdump's command line efficiency allows rapid capture of malicious packets for forensic investigation.

4. **Endpoint monitoring**: Implement Sysmon on endpoints to monitor and log system activities. Use osquery to query endpoints for suspicious behavior, such as unusual file access patterns or unauthorized software installations. Sysmon is chosen for endpoint activity validation because it provides detailed event logging on process creation, network connections, and registry modifications. Security teams use Sysmon to track unauthorized software installations and detect unusual file access patterns, helping identify potential insider threats or malware persistence mechanisms.

5. **Behavioral analysis**: Utilize YARA to create rules that detect patterns of suspicious behavior, such as large file transfers or access to sensitive files outside of normal working hours. YARA is chosen for behavioral pattern validation because it enables custom rule creation to detect specific threat indicators. Security teams use YARA to flag large file transfers or unauthorized access to sensitive data outside normal hours, helping identify potential insider threats or malware activity before escalation.

6. **Incident response**: If suspicious activity is detected, use Cuckoo Sandbox to analyze any potentially malicious files or payloads. This will help determine the nature of the threat and guide response actions. Cuckoo Sandbox is chosen for malware behavior validation because it provides dynamic analysis in an isolated environment. Security teams use Cuckoo to execute potentially malicious files, observing their runtime behavior, system modifications, and network activity, helping determine the threat's nature and guiding response actions effectively.

7. **Continuous monitoring**: Maintain continuous monitoring and threat hunting to ensure that the organization remains protected against insider threats. Regularly update threat intelligence feeds and refine detection rules based on the latest information.

Outcome: By leveraging open-source tools, the organization can proactively detect and respond to insider threats, minimizing the risk of data exfiltration and enhancing overall cybersecurity posture.

Scenario two, suspicious PowerShell activity

Hypothesis: A threat actor is using PowerShell to execute malicious commands on endpoints within the network. This could involve techniques like downloading malware, establishing persistence, or performing reconnaissance.

Follow these steps to validate this hypothesis using open-source tools:

1. **Data collection**: Deploy Sysmon on critical Windows endpoints to capture detailed PowerShell logs. Configure Sysmon to log events related to command-line arguments, scripts, and process creation.

2. **Log aggregation**: Use Logstash to collect Sysmon logs from endpoints and forward them to Elasticsearch. Normalize and enrich the logs for easier analysis.

3. **Hypothesis testing**: Use Kibana to visualize and query the Sysmon data in Elasticsearch. Look for suspicious PowerShell activity, such as obfuscated commands, downloads of executable files from unusual locations, use of encoded commands, and execution of PowerShell scripts from unusual locations.

4. **Threat intelligence**: Use threat intelligence feeds to identify known malicious PowerShell scripts or techniques. Correlate threat intelligence data with the Sysmon logs to identify potential threats.

5. **YARA rule creation**: Create YARA rules to detect specific PowerShell patterns or techniques associated with malicious activity. Scan endpoints using YARA to identify potential threats.

6. **Investigation and response**: If suspicious PowerShell activity is detected, investigate further to determine the scope and impact of the threat. Take appropriate response actions, such as isolating affected systems, blocking malicious files, and removing persistence mechanisms.

Conclusion

Threat intelligence and threat hunting represent two complementary aspects, working in tandem to enhance an organization's security posture. Threat intelligence provides crucial context, painting a picture of the ever-evolving threat landscape and arming security teams with knowledge of adversary TTPs. It is also the compass guiding the hunt, informing hypotheses, and prioritizing areas of investigation.

Threat intelligence sharing is a cornerstone of modern cybersecurity operations. By fostering collaboration, enhancing detection capabilities, and enabling proactive defense, SOCs can significantly strengthen their security posture. As the cyber threat landscape continues to evolve, the importance of effective threat intelligence sharing will only grow, making it an indispensable component of any robust security strategy.

Threat hunting, on the other hand, is the proactive pursuit of hidden threats within the network. It is envisaged as actively seeking out malicious activity that may have evaded traditional security defenses. By combining the strategic insights of threat intelligence with the proactive approach of threat hunting, organizations can move beyond a reactive security stance and adopt a more proactive and resilient approach.

This powerful combination enables security teams to not only detect and respond to known threats more effectively but also to uncover and neutralize unknown threats before they can inflict severe damage. Ultimately, mastering both threat intelligence and threat hunting is essential for any modern SOC seeking to stay ahead of sophisticated adversaries and protect critical assets. The continuous refinement of both disciplines, driven by lessons learned and evolving attack patterns, is the key to maintaining a robust and adaptive security posture in the face of persistent and evolving cyber threats.

Points to remember

Here are some key takeaways from this chapter:

- Effective threat intelligence enables organizations to understand potential threats, predict attacks, and implement preventative measures. Threat intelligence needs to be timely, clear, and actionable.

- Standards like STIX and TAXII enable the structured sharing of threat data.

- Threat hunting is a vital component of a proactive cybersecurity strategy, enabling organizations to uncover and mitigate advanced threats that may bypass traditional defenses.

Multiple choice questions

1. **What is the primary purpose of threat intelligence?**
   a. To monitor network traffic
   b. To identify vulnerabilities in software
   c. To gather information about potential and existing threats
   d. To manage user permissions

2. **Which of the following is not a typical source of threat intelligence?**
   a. Dark web monitoring
   b. Social media analysis
   c. Employee satisfaction surveys
   d. OSINT

3. **Which protocol is commonly used for sharing TI?**
   a. HTTP
   b. SMTP
   c. FTP
   d. TAXII

4. **What is the common goal of threat hunting?**

    a. To detect and mitigate cyber threats before they cause harm

    b. To decrease server downtime

    c. To increase website traffic

    d. To improve user interface design

5. **Which of the following tools is commonly used in threat hunting?**

    a. Microsoft Word

    b. Wireshark

    c. Adobe Photoshop

    d. QuickBooks

Answers

1	c
2	c
3	d
4	a
5	b

Questions

1. Explain the significance of threat intelligence in modern cybersecurity. Discuss the role of threat intelligence platforms in an organization's security strategy.

2. Why is TI sharing important for organizations? Explain TAXII and STIX.

3. Explain the process of threat hunting and its importance in cybersecurity. Discuss the skills and tools required for effective threat hunting.

Key terms

Some key terms used in this chapter are:

- **Threat intelligence (TI)**: The process of gathering, analyzing, and sharing information about potential and existing cyber threats to help organizations understand and mitigate risks.

- **TAXII**: TAXII is a foundational component in the modern cybersecurity landscape, enabling organizations to securely and efficiently share cyber threat intelligence.

- **STIX**: STIX supports the exchange of TI over TAXII.

- **Threat hunting**: The Proactive practice of searching for cyber threats within an organization's network before they cause harm.

CHAPTER 9
People

Introduction

In the intricate world of cybersecurity, the human element is both a strength and a vulnerability. This chapter looks into the critical role that people play within SOC. From the frontline analysts who monitor and respond to threats to the managers who strategize and coordinate efforts, every individual in a SOC contributes to the overall security posture of an organization. By understanding the human dynamics at play, we can better appreciate the complexities and challenges faced by those who safeguard our digital world.

The human element is at the core of SOC operations. The incident monitoring tasks, subsequent analysis by skilled professionals can make huge difference in keeping the breach under checks. It is important to know the roles and responsibilities at multiple levels in SOC.

Structure

In this chapter, we will discuss the following topics:

- SOC team and staffing
- Roles and responsibilities
- Tiers in SOC operations

- SOC team and CSIRT dilemma
- KPIs for people in SOC
- Best practices for people management

Objectives

By the end of this chapter, we will understand the staffing requirements for security operations. We will further explore the various roles and responsibilities within a SOC, highlighting the skills and expertise required for each position. Additionally, we will discuss the importance of teamwork, communication, and continuous learning in maintaining an effective and resilient SOC.

SOC team and staffing

In today's digital landscape, organizations are increasingly recognizing the critical importance of cybersecurity. At the heart of a robust cybersecurity strategy lies the SOC, a dedicated team of professionals tasked with monitoring, detecting, and responding to cybersecurity incidents. Building and staffing an effective SOC team is a complex endeavor that requires careful consideration of several factors, from defining roles and responsibilities to ensuring continuous professional development. The SOC acts as the central hub for an organization's cybersecurity efforts.

Here are the primary functions:

- Continuously monitoring network traffic, logs, and endpoints for signs of suspicious activity.

- Responding to security incidents swiftly and effectively to mitigate potential damage.

- Gathering and analyzing threat intelligence to stay ahead of emerging threats.

- Ensuring compliance with industry standards and regulatory requirements and generating reports for stakeholders.

Building a capable SOC team to handle these tasks requires a strategic approach to staffing. Some key considerations for staffing are listed here:

- **Recruitment**: Identify candidates with the right mix of technical skills, experience, and certifications. Clearly outline the necessary skills, qualifications, and certifications for each role. This may include knowledge of cybersecurity principles, experience with specific security tools, and relevant certifications (e.g., CISSP, CISM, CEH, SOC analysts). Look for individuals who demonstrate strong analytical thinking, problem-solving abilities, and a passion for cybersecurity.

- **Training and development**: Cybersecurity is an ever-evolving field. Ensure that your SOC team has access to ongoing training and professional development opportunities to stay ahead of emerging threats. Continuous professional development is essential for staying current with evolving threats and technologies. Implement ongoing training programs, certifications, and hands-on exercises to enhance the team's skills. Encourage continuous learning and stay connected with the broader cybersecurity community to keep up with the latest trends and threats.

- **Retention**: Retaining talent is crucial to maintain continuity in the organization's information security journey. Offer competitive salaries, career advancement opportunities, and a positive work environment to keep employees motivated and engaged.

- **Diversity and inclusion**: Foster a diverse and inclusive workforce by promoting equal opportunities and valuing different perspectives. Diversity can lead to innovative solutions and a more resilient SOC team. Foster a team-oriented environment where knowledge sharing and collaboration are encouraged. This helps to build a cohesive and resilient SOC team.

Staffing a SOC comes with its own set of challenges. Here are some common obstacles and best practices to overcome them:

- **Talent shortage**: The cybersecurity talent shortage is a well-documented issue. The SOC talent shortage further presents a significant challenge, particularly in sourcing professionals with specialized expertise in advanced threat detection, incident response, and forensic analysis. One of the most difficult skills to find is threat hunting, which requires deep knowledge of attacker tactics, behavioral analytics, and hypothesis-driven investigations. Additionally, cloud security expertise is in high demand, as securing multi-cloud environments involves complex identity management and real-time threat mitigation. Reverse engineering and malware analysis are also scarce skills, as they require proficiency in dissecting malicious code to uncover adversary techniques. Furthermore, SIEM engineering and automation demand expertise in fine-tuning detection rules, integrating diverse log sources, and optimizing workflows for efficient security operations. Addressing these gaps requires targeted training programs, mentorship initiatives, hiring people from diverse backgrounds and industry-academic collaborations to cultivate the next generation of SOC professionals.

- **Burnout**: The demanding nature of SOC operations often leads to burnout, particularly among professionals with highly specialized skills that are difficult to replace. Threat hunting requires deep analytical expertise and continuous hypothesis-driven investigations, making it one of the most challenging roles to sustain long-term. Similarly, incident response demands rapid decision-making under pressure, requiring mastery of forensic analysis and containment strategies. Cloud security specialists face increasing complexity in securing multi-cloud environments, while malware analysts must reverse-engineer sophisticated threats with precision. Additionally, SIEM engineers play a crucial role in optimizing detection rules and integrating diverse log sources, yet their expertise remains scarce. Addressing burnout in these roles requires structured workload management, promote work-life balance, provide mental health support, and recognition of their contributions, ensuring long-term retention and operational resilience.

Equipping the SOC team with the right tools and technologies is crucial for their success. The key components, which will be covered in subsequent *Chapter 11, Technology* include:

- SIEM
- EDR
- Network security monitoring
- Threat intelligence platforms
- Incident response platforms

An effective SOC team is one that continuously evolves and improves.

Key strategies for continuous improvement include:

- Conduct regular assessments of the SOC's performance, identifying areas for improvement and implementing necessary changes.
- Stay updated on the latest threat trends and adapt the SOC's strategies and processes accordingly.
- Foster collaboration and information sharing with other SOCs, industry peers, and threat intelligence communities to stay ahead of cyber threats.

Roles and responsibilities

The SOC team has a wide range of responsibilities that are crucial for maintaining the security of an organization. Let us look at some of these responsibilities:

- **Incident detection and response**: The primary responsibility of the SOC team is to detect and respond to security incidents. This involves:
    - Continuous monitoring of security systems and networks.
    - Analyzing alerts and identifying potential threats.
    - Coordinating incident response efforts to mitigate the impact of attacks.
- **Vulnerability management**: The SOC team is responsible for identifying and addressing vulnerabilities within the organization's systems. This includes:
    - Conducting regular vulnerability assessments.
    - Applying patches and updates to mitigate vulnerabilities.
    - Collaborating with other teams to ensure secure configurations.

- **Security monitoring and analysis**: Continuous monitoring and analysis of security data are essential for detecting and responding to threats. This involves:

  o Using SIEM tools to collect and analyze data.

  o Identifying patterns and trends in security events.

  o Generating reports and dashboards to provide visibility into the organization's security posture.

- **Incident reporting and documentation**: Proper documentation and reporting of security incidents are crucial for improving the organization's security posture. This includes:

  o Documenting incident details, including the timeline, impact, and resolution.

  o Reporting incidents to senior management and relevant stakeholders.

  o Conducting post-incident reviews to identify lessons learned and areas for improvement.

- **Threat hunting**: Threat hunting involves proactively searching for threats that automated systems may not have detected. This includes the following:

  o Analyzing network traffic and system logs for signs of malicious activity.

  o Identifying and investigating anomalies.

  o Developing and implementing advanced detection techniques.

To meet these SOC responsibilities, the people dimension must be strong enough. A well-structured SOC team comprises various roles, each with distinct responsibilities, as brought out in the following figure:

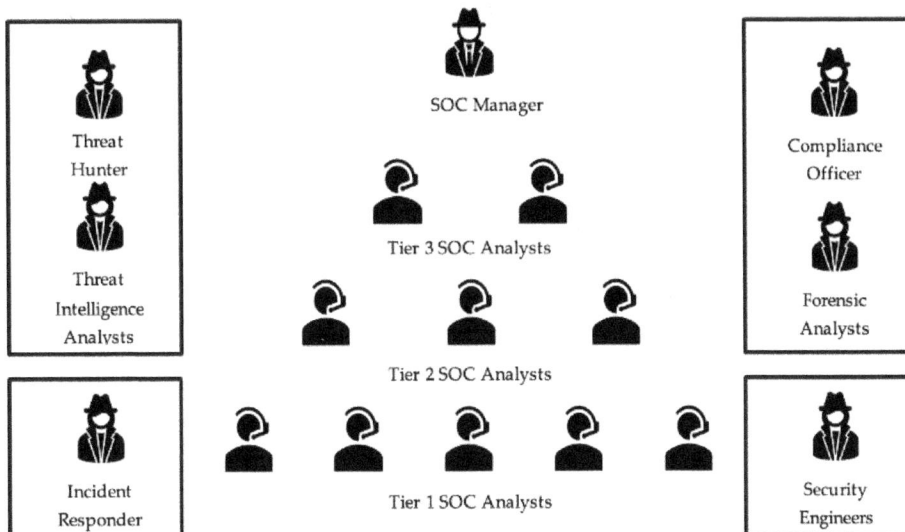

Figure 9.1: SOC roles

The roles in SOC are distinctive with special expertise requirements. Security operations in a SOC require collaborative handling with various stakeholders across the organization. Let us look at some key roles in SOC:

- **SOC manager**: The leader of the SOC team, responsible for overseeing operations, setting priorities, and ensuring alignment with the organization's security objectives. The responsibilities of SOC manager include the following:

  o Developing and implementing security policies and procedures.

  o Managing and mentoring SOC staff.

  o Coordinating incident response efforts.

  o Reporting to senior management on security posture and incidents.

  For example, during a critical cloud breach, the SOC Manager coordinates cross-team communication, ensuring threat intelligence analysts provide real-time IOC while incident responders deploy containment measures to halt lateral movement. Similarly, in response to a zero-day exploit targeting financial systems, the SOC Manager directs rapid patch deployment, collaborates with legal teams for regulatory compliance, and oversees forensic analysis to prevent future attacks.

- **Security analyst**: The frontline defenders who monitor security alerts, investigate incidents, and implement mitigation strategies. These are the frontline defenders who monitor network traffic, investigate alerts, and analyze security incidents. They are categorized into different levels. Let us look at them:

  o **Tier 1 analysts**: These are responsible for the initial triage of alerts and basic investigation. Their responsibilities include:

    ▪ Monitoring security alerts and alarms.

    ▪ Performing initial triage to determine the severity of alerts.

    ▪ Escalating incidents to higher-tier analysts if necessary.

    ▪ Maintaining and configuring monitoring tools.

  For example, a tier 1 analyst receives an alert from the SIEM about unusual login attempts from an external IP address. Following the standard operating procedure, they perform an initial triage and, recognizing the potential severity, escalate the alert to a tier 2 analyst for deeper investigation.

  o **Tier 2 analysts**: These handle in-depth analysis and more complex incidents. Their responsibilities include:

    ▪ Conducting in-depth analysis of security incidents.

    ▪ Utilizing threat intelligence to understand the scope and impact of attacks.

    ▪ Designing and implementing containment and remediation strategies.

- Collaborating with other teams to resolve incidents.

For example, during a cloud-based ransomware attack, tier 2 analysts correlate SIEM alerts with endpoint logs to confirm encryption activity, then escalate findings to incident responders for containment and remediation before further systems are compromised. Similarly, in response to a zero-day exploit targeting financial transactions, tier 2 analysts analyze network traffic anomalies, identifying unauthorized API calls linked to the attack, then collaborate with SOC teams to implement emergency firewall rules to block malicious activity.

- o **Tier 3 analysts**: These are involved in advanced threat detection and response, often using threat intelligence. Their responsibilities include:

  - Proactively searching for threats that may have bypassed initial defenses.

  - Analyzing **advanced persistent threats** (**APTs**) and sophisticated attacks.

  - Developing and implementing advanced detection techniques.

  - Providing guidance and support to lower-tier analysts.

For example, during a nation-state cyberattack, tier 3 analysts conduct deep forensic analysis, reverse-engineering the malware to uncover its command-and-control infrastructure, then collaborate with threat intelligence teams to predict and block future attack vectors. Similarly, in response to a zero-day exploit targeting financial transactions, tier 3 analysts perform advanced memory analysis, identifying hidden payloads and coordinating with SOC managers to implement emergency threat mitigation strategies before widespread impact occurs.

- **Incident responder**: Apart from SOC analysts, incident responders are specialists who handle the containment, eradication, and recovery phases of an incident response. Their responsibilities include the following:

  - o Identify and analyze security incidents to determine their severity and impact.

  - o Implement measures to contain the incident and eliminate the root cause.

  - o Restore affected systems to normal operations and ensure they are secure.

  - o Document the incident response process and report findings to relevant stakeholders.

Following confirmation of a ransomware attack by tier 2 analysts, incident responders are activated to contain the spread of the malware, eradicate the threat from affected systems, and manage the recovery process.

- **Compliance officers**: There are crucial team members who ensure that the SOC adheres to relevant legal and regulatory requirements, conducting regular audits and assessments. Their responsibilities include the following:

  ○ Ensure that the organization's cybersecurity practices align with relevant laws, regulations, and industry standards.

  ○ Develop and enforce security policies and procedures to maintain compliance and mitigate risks.

  ○ Conduct regular audits and assessments to identify compliance gaps and recommend corrective actions.

  ○ Provide training and awareness programs to educate employees about compliance requirements and best practices.

  For example, during a ransomware attack on financial systems, compliance officers ensure regulatory adherence by coordinating with legal teams to assess data breach disclosure requirements, while guiding SOC teams on compliance-driven response protocols. Similarly, in response to a healthcare data breach, compliance officers collaborate with security teams to verify HIPAA compliance, ensuring affected patient records are handled according to legal mandates while overseeing breach notification procedures.

- **Forensic analyst**: There are specialists who conduct post-incident analysis, collecting and preserving digital evidence for legal and investigative purposes. Their responsibilities include the following:

  ○ Gather and preserve digital evidence from various sources following a security incident.

  ○ Analyze collected evidence to understand the scope, impact, and root cause of the incident.

  ○ Document findings and create detailed reports to support incident response and legal proceedings.

  ○ Work closely with incident responders, threat hunters, and law enforcement to ensure a comprehensive investigation.

  For example, during a nation-state cyberattack, Forensic analysts extract volatile memory artifacts, uncovering encryption keys used by the ransomware, then collaborate with Incident Responders to decrypt affected systems and restore operations. Similarly, in response to a financial sector breach, Forensic analysts conduct disk image analysis, identifying hidden malware implants, then work with SOC teams to refine detection rules and prevent future intrusions.

- **Security engineers**: These are inseparable parts of the SOC team entrusted with designing, implementing, and maintaining the technical infrastructure of the SOC.

They also manage security tools and platforms. Security engineers are responsible for maintaining and improving the security infrastructure. Their responsibilities include:

o   Designing and implementing security solutions.

o   Configuring and managing security tools and technologies.

o   Conducting vulnerability assessments and penetration testing.

o   Ensuring compliance with security standards and regulations.

For example, during a cloud service breach, security engineers deploy emergency patches to mitigate exploited vulnerabilities while collaborating with SOC teams to enhance network segmentation, preventing further lateral movement by attackers. In response to a ransomware outbreak, security engineers implement endpoint hardening measures, adjusting access controls and privilege settings, while working with forensic analysts to identify the malware's initial entry point.

- **Threat intelligence analyst**: Professionals who gather and analyze threat data to provide actionable insights and enhance the organization's security posture are TI analysts. Threat intelligence analysts focus on gathering and analyzing information about potential threats. Their responsibilities include the following:

  o   Collecting and analyzing threat data from various sources.

  o   Identifying emerging threats and vulnerabilities.

  o   Providing actionable intelligence to the SOC team.

  o   Developing threat profiles and risk assessments.

For example, during a nation-state cyberattack, threat intelligence analysts correlate dark web chatter with real-time attack telemetry, identifying the adversary's TTPs, then collaborate with SOC teams to refine detection rules and block further intrusions. In response to a zero-day exploit targeting financial institutions, threat intelligence analysts leverage external threat feeds to uncover emerging IOC, then work with incident responders to implement proactive defense measures before widespread compromise occurs.

- **Threat hunter**: These are experts who proactively search for hidden threats within the network, identifying vulnerabilities and potential attack vectors. Their responsibilities include:

  o   Actively search for hidden threats and vulnerabilities that may have bypassed automated defenses.

  o   Analyze APTs and sophisticated attacks to understand their behavior and impact.

  o   Conduct vulnerability assessments and penetration tests to identify potential attack vectors.

o Utilize threat intelligence to enhance detection techniques and stay ahead of emerging threats.

For example, during a cloud-based ransomware outbreak, threat hunters analyze network traffic anomalies, uncovering hidden C2 communications linked to the attack, then collaborate with SOC teams to refine detection rules and block further infiltration. In response to a zero-day exploit targeting financial transactions, threat hunters leverage behavioral analytics to detect stealthy lateral movement, then work with incident responders to implement proactive containment strategies before widespread compromise occurs.

The roles and responsibilities of a SOC team are diverse and critical for maintaining the security of an organization. Each member of the team plays a vital role in detecting, analyzing, and responding to cybersecurity threats. By understanding and fulfilling their responsibilities, SOC teams can effectively protect their organizations from a wide range of cyber threats.

Red, blue, purple teams and relevance to SOC

Red, blue, and purple teams, along with SOC, play crucial roles in protecting organizations from cyber threats. The red, blue, and purple teams each play distinct yet interconnected roles within SOC. The distinctive roles of these teams are as follows:

- Red team simulates cyberattacks to test the effectiveness of an organization's security measures, using the same tools and techniques as real attackers to identify vulnerabilities and weaknesses.

- Blue team is responsible for defending against both real and simulated attacks by monitoring systems, detecting threats, and responding to incidents to protect the organization's assets.

- Purple team acts as a bridge between the red and blue teams. They ensure that the findings from the red team are effectively used by the blue team to improve defenses. The goal is to enhance collaboration and maximize the effectiveness of both teams.

SOC is a centralized unit that continuously monitors and analyzes an organization's security posture. It is important to clarify the relationship between red, blue, and purple teams and the SOC. The SOC is a core component of the blue team. SOC analysts are definitively part of the blue team, as their primary function is defensive: monitoring, detecting, and responding to security threats. Red teams are typically separate from the day-to-day operations of the SOC. They are often internal but distinct teams or external contractors. Their role is to conduct periodic assessments, not to be constantly present within the SOC. The purple team is not necessarily a separate, standing team. Instead, purple teaming is a practice that involves close collaboration between red and blue teams. This collaboration can involve:

- Red team members working alongside SOC analysts.
- Joint exercises and simulations.
- Knowledge sharing and feedback loops.

Therefore, purple teaming is an activity that SOC members participate in, but it does not mean that there is a separate purple team that is always part of the SOC. Purple teaming is a collaborative practice that enhances the effectiveness of both red and blue teams, and SOC personal will participate in purple team activities.

Red team exercises play a crucial role in strengthening SOC operations by uncovering vulnerabilities that defenders may overlook. A recent red team exercise successfully bypassed existing firewall rules. This finding was then used by SOC analysts and security engineers to update the rules and enhance the detection capabilities for similar attack vectors. In another example, during a phishing simulation, the red team successfully bypassed email security filters, demonstrating weaknesses in user awareness and automated detection. This finding led SOC analysts to refine email filtering rules, enhance user training programs, and implement multi-factor authentication to mitigate similar attacks. A red team penetration test exposed gaps in endpoint detection, where attackers evaded traditional antivirus solutions using living-off-the-land techniques. SOC engineers responded by integrating behavioral analytics into their detection framework, improving their ability to identify anomalous activity.

Additionally, a purple team collaboration helped bridge offensive and defensive strategies when a red team privilege escalation attack revealed flaws in access control policies. SOC teams worked with security engineers to tighten role-based access controls, ensuring that unauthorized privilege escalation attempts were swiftly detected and blocked.

These real-world examples highlight how red team findings directly enhance SOC monitoring rules, refine incident response procedures, and ultimately strengthen an organization's security posture.

Tiers in SOC operations

To efficiently manage security incidents, SOCs are often structured into tiers, with each tier having specific roles and responsibilities. This tiered approach ensures that incidents are handled with the appropriate level of expertise and urgency. A typical SOC is divided into three primary tiers, as shown in the following figure:

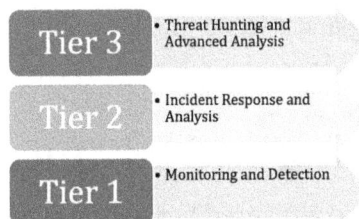

Tier 3 • Threat Hunting and Advanced Analysis

Tier 2 • Incident Response and Analysis

Tier 1 • Monitoring and Detection

Figure 9.2: Tiers of SOC

Tier 1, monitoring and detection

Tier 1 is the frontline of the SOC. The primary responsibilities of this tier include:

- **Continuous monitoring**: Monitoring security alerts generated by various tools, including SIEM systems, IDS, and EDR solutions.

- **Initial triage**: Performing initial triage on alerts to determine their validity and potential impact. This involves filtering out false positives and prioritizing genuine threats.

- **Alert escalation**: Escalating validated incidents to higher tiers for further investigation and response.

These responsibilities entail that SOC analysts working in tier 1 must have:

- Basic knowledge of cybersecurity principles and tools.

- Strong analytical and critical thinking skills.

- Ability to follow **standard operating procedures** (**SOPs**) for incident handling.

Tier 2, incident response and analysis

Tier 2 handles more complex incidents that require in-depth analysis and response. The primary responsibilities of this tier include:

- **Detailed analysis**: Conducting thorough investigations of escalated alerts to identify the root cause, scope, and impact of security incidents.

- **Incident containment**: Implementing containment measures to prevent the spread of threats within the organization.

- **Remediation**: Coordinating with other IT and security teams to remediate affected systems and restore normal operations.

- **Documentation**: Maintaining detailed records of incident investigations, response actions, and lessons learned.

These responsibilities entail that SOC analysts working in tier 2 must have:

- Intermediate to advanced knowledge of cybersecurity tools and techniques.

- Strong problem-solving and decision-making abilities.

- Effective communication skills for coordinating with other teams and stakeholders.

Tier 3, threat hunting and advanced analysis

Tier 3 is the most specialized and advanced tier within SOC. The primary responsibilities of this tier include:

- **Proactive threat hunting**: Actively searching for hidden threats within the organization's network, using advanced tools and techniques to identify potential attack vectors.

- **Advanced forensics**: Conducting deep forensic analysis to uncover sophisticated threats, malware, and APTs.

- **Threat intelligence integration**: Integrating threat intelligence feeds into the SOC's operations to enhance detection and response capabilities.

- **Root cause analysis**: Performing root cause analysis on complex incidents to identify vulnerabilities and recommend improvements to security controls.

These responsibilities entail that SOC analysts working in tier 3 must have:

- Expert-level knowledge of cybersecurity, including malware analysis, reverse engineering, and advanced threat detection.

- Proficiency with specialized tools for threat hunting and forensic analysis.

- Strong research and analytical skills to stay ahead of emerging threats.

Collaboration and communication

Effective SOC operations rely on seamless collaboration and communication among the different tiers. Key strategies for fostering collaboration include:

- Conducting regular briefings and knowledge-sharing sessions to keep all team members informed of the latest threats and incident trends.

- Providing cross-tier training opportunities to enhance the skills and knowledge of all SOC personnel.

- Utilizing centralized incident management platforms to ensure efficient coordination and documentation of incidents across tiers.

Continuous improvement

To maintain an effective SOC, continuous improvement is essential. Key strategies for continuous improvement include:

- **Performance metrics**: Establishing and tracking performance metrics to evaluate the effectiveness of SOC operations and identify areas for improvement.

- **Feedback loop**: Implementing a feedback loop to capture lessons learned from incidents and incorporate them into future operations.

- **Adapting to change**: Staying agile and adapting to changes in the threat landscape, technology advancements, and organizational needs.

The tiered structure of SOC operations ensures that security incidents are handled with the appropriate level of expertise and urgency. By clearly defining roles and responsibilities, fostering collaboration, and committing to continuous improvement, organizations can build a resilient SOC capable of defending against the ever-evolving threat landscape.

A typical flow of an incident through different SOC tiers is shown in the following figure:

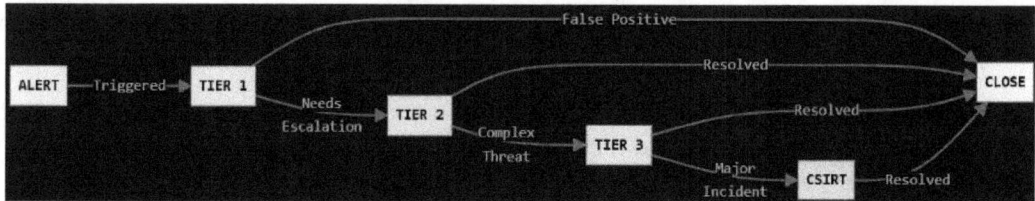

Figure 9.3: Incident workflow through different tiers of SOC

This tiered approach allows for efficient resource allocation, with the most experienced analysts focusing on the most complex threats rather than routine alerts.

SOC team and CSIRT dilemma

Organizations rely heavily on specialized teams to safeguard their digital assets and ensure operational continuity. Among these teams, the SOC and the CSIRT play pivotal roles. However, the overlapping responsibilities and distinct operational approaches of these teams often lead to a dilemma that organizations must navigate carefully.

Role of a SOC team

The SOC team serves as the nerve center of an organization's cybersecurity operations. It is a centralized unit that continuously monitors, detects, and responds to potential security threats. Equipped with advanced tools and technologies, SOC analysts sift through vast amounts of data, analyzing logs and identifying anomalies that could indicate a security breach. The primary objectives of the SOC team include:

- **Continuous monitoring**: Utilizing real-time monitoring tools to detect suspicious activities.

- **Threat detection**: Employing threat intelligence and analysis techniques to identify potential threats.

- **Incident response**: Acting swiftly to contain and mitigate security incidents.

- **Vulnerability management**: Identifying and addressing vulnerabilities in the organization's systems.

- **Reporting and documentation**: Maintaining detailed records of incidents and responses for future reference and compliance.

Role of CSIRT

While the SOC team focuses on real-time monitoring and immediate responses, CSIRT operates with a more specialized and strategic approach. The CSIRT is activated when a significant security incident occurs, requiring a coordinated and comprehensive response. The responsibilities of the CSIRT include:

- **Incident triage**: Assessing the severity and impact of security incidents.

- **Forensic analysis**: Conducting in-depth investigations to determine the cause and extent of incidents.

- **Contain and eradicate**: Implement measures to contain the incident and eliminate the threat.

- **Recovery and remediation**: Restore affected systems and ensure they are secure.

- **Post-incident review**: Analyzing incidents to learn from them and improve future responses.

SOC and CSIRT dilemma

The dilemma between SOC and CSIRT arises from the overlap in their responsibilities and the different approaches they take to incident management. Key points of contention include the following:

- **Scope of responsibilities**: SOC teams are responsible for continuous monitoring and immediate responses, while CSIRT focuses on major incidents and strategic responses. This overlap can lead to confusion about which team should handle certain incidents.

- **Operational approaches**: SOC teams often prioritize speed and efficiency, while CSIRT emphasizes thoroughness and strategic analysis. These differing approaches can result in conflicts over the best course of action during incidents.

- **Resource allocation**: Limited resources and manpower can strain both teams, leading to challenges in effectively managing incidents. Organizations must balance the allocation of resources to ensure both SOC and CSIRT can operate optimally.

- **Communication and coordination**: Effective incident response requires seamless communication and coordination between SOC and CSIRT. Miscommunication or lack of coordination can hinder response efforts and prolong incident resolution.

The SOC/CSIRT dilemma often arises when overlapping responsibilities create confusion in incident handling. For example, during a ransomware outbreak, SOC analysts may detect malicious activity and escalate the incident, expecting CSIRT to take over containment. However, if CSIRT assumes SOC will continue monitoring, gaps in response coordination can delay mitigation efforts. Similarly, in a nation-state attack, SOC may focus on real-time detection while CSIRT prioritizes forensic analysis, leading to misalignment in threat attribution and response strategy. To address the SOC and CSIRT dilemma, organizations can adopt several strategies:

- **Clear roles and responsibilities**: Establishing clear guidelines that define the roles and responsibilities of SOC and CSIRT teams can reduce confusion and ensure a more efficient incident response.

- **Integrated communication**: Implementing robust communication channels and protocols ensures that both teams are informed and can collaborate effectively during incidents.

- **Resource optimization**: Leveraging automation and advanced threat detection tools can help optimize resources and reduce the burden on both teams.

- **Regular training and drills**: Conducting joint training sessions and incident response drills can enhance the coordination and readiness of SOC and CSIRT teams.

- **Continuous improvement**: Regularly reviewing and updating incident response plans based on lessons learned from past incidents can improve the overall effectiveness of SOC and CSIRT operations.

A well-defined communication protocol can resolve the inefficiencies, such as structured handoff procedures where SOC provides detailed logs and CSIRT confirms containment actions. In one case, a financial institution streamlined its SOC-CSIRT collaboration by implementing joint tabletop exercises, ensuring clear role delineation and faster incident resolution. Establishing incident ownership frameworks and cross-team training significantly enhances response efficiency, reducing confusion and strengthening cybersecurity resilience.

The SOC and CSIRT dilemma is a critical challenge that organizations must address to ensure robust cybersecurity. By understanding these teams' distinct roles and responsibilities and implementing strategies to enhance their coordination, organizations can navigate this dilemma effectively and build a resilient cybersecurity posture.

KPIs for people in SOC

The **key performance indicators (KPIs)** are measurable values that indicate how effectively a SOC team is achieving its objectives. By tracking KPIs, SOC teams can gain insights into their operational efficiency, incident response capabilities, and overall security posture. KPIs also help in benchmarking performance against industry standards and ensuring compliance with regulatory requirements.

Some of the KPIs, like MTTD, MTTR, incident escalation rate, false positive rate, etc., will be covered in the next chapter. It is important to work out KPIs for people in SOC. Different roles within the SOC team may have specific KPIs tailored to their responsibilities. Some of the KPIs worth monitoring are as follows:

- **SOC manager**:
    - **Team performance metrics**: Monitoring team performance metrics uncovers inefficiencies in MTTD, MTTR, and incident response rates, identifying areas for enhanced alert handling, containment speed, and resource optimization. Refining these KPIs strengthens SOC efficiency, ensuring quicker threat resolution and improved overall security posture.
    - **Resource utilization**: Monitoring resource utilization helps identify inefficiencies in SOC budget allocation and tool effectiveness, revealing gaps in workflow automation, staffing, or technology investments. Optimizing this KPI ensures cost-effective operations, enhancing response efficiency while maximizing available security resources.

- **Tier 1 analyst**:
    - **Alert handling efficiency**: Number of alerts processed and the accuracy of initial triage. Monitoring alert handling efficiency reveals delays in triage accuracy and alert processing speed, helping identify gaps in analyst expertise, automation, or prioritization strategies. Refining this KPI enhances SOC responsiveness, ensuring faster threat detection and improved incident resolution.
    - **Escalation rate**: Percentage of incidents escalated to higher-tier analysts. Tracking escalation rate highlights inefficiencies in incident triage and analyst decision-making, identifying gaps in automation, detection accuracy, and workload distribution. Refining this KPI ensures balanced escalations, optimizing SOC efficiency while preventing unnecessary workload shifts.

- **Tier 2 analyst**:
    - **Incident resolution time**: Time taken to resolve incidents after escalation. Tracking incident resolution time highlights inefficiencies in response workflows, pinpointing delays in escalation, resource allocation, or analyst expertise. High-resolution times suggest gaps in forensic analysis, containment strategies, or automation tools, signaling the need for targeted training. Optimizing this KPI accelerates mitigation, reducing downtime and limiting security impact.
    - **Analysis accuracy**: Accuracy of incident analysis and the effectiveness of containment measures. Monitoring analysis accuracy identifies weaknesses in incident classification and containment, highlighting areas for improved detection techniques and forensic expertise. Enhancing this KPI ensures precise threat identification, minimizing false positives and optimizing response effectiveness.

- **Threat hunter:**

  o **Threat detection rate**: Number of threats identified through proactive hunting. Tracking threat detection rate helps uncover weaknesses in proactive threat hunting, identifying areas where analysts may require improved behavioral analysis, intelligence integration, or automation tools. Enhancing this KPI ensures quicker threat identification, minimizing dwell time and bolstering SOC effectiveness.

  o **False positive rate**: Accuracy of threat detection and the reduction of false positives. Tracking false positive rate helps pinpoint inefficiencies in detection accuracy, revealing gaps in alert tuning, rule optimization, or analyst expertise. Refining this KPI ensures precise threat identification, reducing unnecessary investigations and improving SOC efficiency.

- **Forensic analyst:**

  o **Evidence collection time**: Time taken to gather and preserve digital evidence. Tracking evidence collection time highlights inefficiencies in forensic data gathering, revealing gaps in tool proficiency, documentation practices, or chain-of-custody procedures. Optimizing this KPI ensures faster evidence preservation, strengthening investigations and compliance adherence.

  o **Analysis accuracy**: Accuracy and thoroughness of forensic analysis. Tracking analysis accuracy highlights inefficiencies in forensic examination and evidence interpretation, revealing gaps in tool proficiency, methodology, or investigative techniques. Refining this KPI ensures precise threat attribution, strengthening incident response and minimizing investigative errors.

- **Compliance officer:**

  o **Compliance audit results**: Results of internal and external compliance audits. Tracking compliance audit results highlights gaps in regulatory adherence and security controls, pinpointing areas where analysts may need enhanced policy knowledge, risk assessment skills, or procedural training. Refining this KPI ensures stronger compliance posture, reducing legal risks and improving operational integrity.

  o **Policy adherence**: Percentage of security policies and procedures followed by the organization. Tracking policy adherence highlights gaps in security compliance and procedural enforcement, identifying areas where analysts may need better training in regulatory frameworks, risk assessment, or policy implementation. Strengthening this KPI ensures consistent security practices, reducing vulnerabilities and improving organizational resilience.

Best practices for people management

Effective people management is crucial for the success of SOCs. The human element is the backbone of any SOC, and managing the team well ensures that the organization can respond swiftly and effectively to cybersecurity threats. People management in SOCs involves recruiting, training, and retaining skilled professionals and creating a supportive and collaborative work environment. Effective management practices help maintain high morale, reduce burnout, and ensure the team is equipped to handle the dynamic nature of cybersecurity threats.

Recruitment and onboarding

Hiring the right talent is critical for effective SOC. Some of the best practices for ensuring the right people are hired are:

- Clearly outline the roles and responsibilities for each position within the SOC. This helps in attracting candidates with the right skills and experience.

- Look for candidates with diverse backgrounds and skill sets, including technical expertise, analytical skills, and problem-solving abilities.

- Ensure that candidates align with the organization's culture and values. A good cultural fit can enhance teamwork and collaboration.

After hiring, it is important to have a comprehensive onboarding program to get insights into the organization's information assets and the ways they require protection.

Some key considerations are:

- Develop a structured onboarding program that includes training on the organization's security policies, tools, and procedures. After analyzing, the candidates can then factor in their expertise across their previous engagements in strengthening the policies and procedures.

- Assign mentors to new hires to provide guidance and support during their initial period in the SOC. This will prevent re-inventing the wheel.

- Encourage continuous learning and professional development through training programs, certifications, and workshops. Encourage all employees to upgrade their knowledge and skills by participating in relevant industry engagements.

Training and development

Regular training programs are effective ways to ensure continuity and maintaining currency. Some of the best practices are listed here:

- Provide regular technical training to keep the team updated on the latest cybersecurity tools, techniques, and threats. Training must include **Open Web**

Application Security Project (OWASP) top 10, MITRE frameworks, NIST standards.

- Offer training in communication, teamwork, negotiation, and leadership skills to enhance overall team performance and collaboration.

Implement cross-training programs to ensure that team members can handle multiple roles and responsibilities.

Professional development is key to upskilling and reskilling in the dynamic cyber world. Some of the best practices for professional development are:

- Encourage team members to pursue relevant certifications such as CISSP, CEH, SOC analysis, and CISM.

- Develop clear career paths and growth opportunities within the SOC to retain top talent.

- Foster a culture of knowledge sharing through regular team meetings, workshops, and collaborative projects.

Performance management

Setting clear goals is another important factor contributing to SOC effectiveness. It is worthwhile to:

- Set **Specific, Measurable, Achievable, Relevant, and Time-bound (SMART)** goals for each team member. These can then be included in the KPIs for effective monitoring.

- Provide regular feedback on performance, highlighting strengths and areas for improvement.

- Conduct periodic performance reviews to assess progress and set new goals.

Recognizing and rewarding performance clearly motivates the team members to give their best. Some of the best practices include:

- Implement recognition programs to acknowledge and reward outstanding performance, like cyber champions and cyber warriors for volunteers.

- Offer incentives such as bonuses, promotions, and professional development opportunities to motivate the team.

- Organize team-building activities to strengthen relationships and boost morale.

Fostering a positive work environment

Work-life balance is another critical element in today's fast evolving technology landscape, especially in the cybersecurity domain where impacts are far reaching and immediate. We must keep the following points in mind:

- Offer flexible work arrangements, such as remote work options and flexible hours, to promote work-life balance.

- Provide mental health support through counseling services, stress management programs, and wellness initiatives.

Collaborative culture brings additional value to this interconnected handling of security operations. Organizations must:

- Encourage open communication and transparency within the team.

- Foster an inclusive environment where all team members feel valued and respected.

- Implement effective conflict resolution strategies to address and resolve any issues promptly.

Effective people management is essential for the success of SOC. By implementing best practices in recruitment, training, and performance management and fostering a positive work environment, organizations can build a strong and resilient SOC team. A well-managed SOC team is better equipped to handle the ever-evolving cybersecurity landscape and protect the organization's assets.

Conclusion

Effective people management is the cornerstone of a successful SOC. By focusing on recruiting the right talent, providing comprehensive training and development, setting clear performance goals, and fostering a positive work environment, organizations can build a resilient and high-performing SOC team.

Investing in people management practices that support and empower SOC team members will lead to a more effective and resilient security posture, ultimately safeguarding the organization's assets and reputation.

KPIs are essential tools for measuring the performance and effectiveness of SOC teams. By tracking and analyzing these metrics, SOC teams can continuously improve their operations, demonstrate their value to stakeholders, and ensure the organization's security posture remains strong.

A well-managed SOC team not only enhances the organization's ability to detect, respond to, and mitigate cybersecurity threats but also contributes to a culture of continuous improvement and collaboration. By prioritizing the well-being and professional growth of SOC personnel, organizations can ensure that their security operations remain robust and adaptive in the face of evolving cyber threats.

In the next chapter, we will understand the processes involved in managing security operations in SOC. A well-thought-out strategy involving people, process, and technology can build a strong SOC for better cybersecurity posture management. In this chapter, we looked at People aspect. Processes play a crucial role in shaping security operations.

Points to remember

Here are some key takeaways from this chapter:

- Building and staffing a successful SOC team is a dynamic and ongoing process that requires careful planning, continuous investment in talent and technology, and a commitment to staying ahead of evolving threats.

- By defining clear roles and responsibilities, implementing effective staffing strategies, and fostering a culture of continuous improvement, organizations can establish a robust SOC capable of safeguarding their digital assets and ensuring a secure operational environment.

- Each role within the SOC team has specific KPIs that reflect their unique responsibilities, contributing to the overall success of the SOC.

Multiple choice questions

1. **What is the primary role of a security analyst in a SOC?**

    a. Developing software

    b. Monitoring and analyzing security incidents

    c. Managing financial records

    d. Designing hardware

2. **What is the main responsibility of a threat hunter in a SOC?**

    a. Treating and preventing illnesses

    b. Proactively searching for cybersecurity threats

    c. Reporting news and information

    d. Building infrastructure

3. **Which tier in the SOC is primarily responsible for threat detection and initial analysis?**

    a. Tier 1

    b. Tier 2

    c. Tier 3

    d. Tier 4

Answers

1	b
2	b
3	a

Questions

1. Discuss the key responsibilities and skills required for a security analyst in a SOC.

2. Explain the role of a SOC Manager and how they contribute to the overall security posture of an organization.

3. Describe the different tiers in an SOC and the primary responsibilities of each tier.

4. What are some KPIs used to measure the effectiveness of an SOC team? Provide examples and explain their significance.

Key terms

Some key terms used in this chapter are:

- **Security analyst**: Monitors and analyzes security incidents, ensuring timely detection and response.

- **SOC tiers**: Critical in layered structure in SOC to manage disparate security incidents.

- **SOC/CSIRT**: Balancing the roles and responsibilities of SOC and CSIRT to ensure efficient incident response and overall cybersecurity management.

- While the SOC is a blue team function, red and purple teams interact with the SOC but are not always contained within it.

Join our Discord space

Join our Discord workspace for latest updates, offers, tech happenings around the world, new releases, and sessions with the authors:

https://discord.bpbonline.com

Section 3
Implementing SOC

CHAPTER 10
Process

Introduction

In today's increasingly interconnected and digitized world, cybersecurity threats constantly evolve, becoming more sophisticated and persistent. SOCs play a critical role in defending organizations against these threats by proactively monitoring, detecting, and responding to cyberattacks. SOCs must rely on well-defined and efficient processes to effectively fulfill this mission.

This chapter will delve into the core operational aspects of a successful SOC, focusing on the critical processes that drive effective threat detection and response. It will examine key SOC processes that enhance an organization's ability to detect and respond to cyber risks, regardless of current security maturity. It will then identify measures to reduce the time to detect and respond with standard frameworks. These processes lead to better cyber resilience. This knowledge will be invaluable for security professionals, managers, and anyone building and managing a robust cybersecurity program.

Structure

In this chapter, we will cover the following topics:

- Security operations centers maturity models
- Security operations centers workflow and KPIs

- Alert levels and investigations
- Incident containment
- Remediation and reporting

Objectives

By the end of this chapter, a clear understanding of SOC processes, maturity models, and KPI will emerge. The readers will be able to grasp the best practices for alert handling, incident investigation, and containment, and highlight the importance of remediation and reporting.

Security operations centers maturity models

A SOC is more than just a collection of tools and technologies; it is a complex system of people, processes, and technology working in concert to defend an organization against cyber threats. While technology plays a crucial role, the effectiveness of a SOC hinges on well-defined and mature processes. SOC maturity models provide a framework for assessing and improving these processes, ensuring the SOC can effectively fulfill its mission. This chapter delves into the concept of SOC maturity models, focusing specifically on the process aspect and how it contributes to overall SOC effectiveness.

SOCs are fundamental to an organization's cybersecurity strategy, providing the expertise and infrastructure to detect, analyze, respond to, and recover from cyber threats. However, not all SOCs are created equal. As organizations grow and face increasingly sophisticated threats, their security operations must evolve to meet these challenges. A SOC's maturity—reflected in its processes, technologies, and capabilities—directly impacts its effectiveness and resilience against cyberattacks.

A SOC maturity model provides a structured framework for assessing and improving a SOC's processes over time. It helps identify the SOC's current state, sets a roadmap for enhancement, and provides benchmarks to measure progress.

These models typically assess various aspects of the SOC, including the following:

- **People**: The SOC team's skills, training, and organizational structure. Invest in training and development programs to enhance the expertise of SOC analysts and engineers. To improve overall security posture, foster collaboration between different teams, such as IT, network, and security. Cultivate a security-focused culture emphasizing the importance of proactive defense and continuous learning.

- **Processes**: Procedures, workflows, and methodologies used for security operations. Establish precise and repeatable procedures for incident detection, analysis, response, and recovery. Implement a feedback loop to refine and enhance processes based on lessons learned from past incidents. Ensure adherence to industry standards and regulatory requirements.

- **Technology**: Tools and technologies deployed for security monitoring, analysis, and response. Deploy and optimize SIEM solutions to enhance threat detection and response capabilities. Leverage automation tools to reduce manual workload, improve response times, and minimize human error. For SOC automation, commercial tools include Splunk Phantom, Cortex XSOAR, IBM QRadar SOAR, while open-source options feature Shuffle, Tracecat, Wazuh and MISP. Example playbooks include malware detection workflows automating IOC analysis, phishing response isolating user accounts, and failed login triage enforcing MFA for enhanced security operations. Integrate various security tools and technologies to create a cohesive and efficient security ecosystem. These will be covered in detail in *Chapter 11, Technology*.

By evaluating these areas against defined criteria, organizations can identify their current maturity level and develop a roadmap for improvement. While skilled personnel and advanced technology are essential, they are ineffective without well-defined processes. Mature processes provide several key benefits, such as:

- **Consistency and predictability**: Standardized procedures ensure consistent execution of security operations, regardless of personnel changes or workload fluctuations.

- **Efficiency and effectiveness**: Optimized workflows minimize wasted effort and maximize the impact of security activities.

- **Measurable performance**: Defined processes enable tracking key metrics, allowing for continuous improvement and demonstrating value to stakeholders.

- **Reduced risk**: Mature processes help identify and mitigate potential security gaps and vulnerabilities.

Common security operations centers maturity models

Several SOC maturity models exist, each with its structure and criteria. Some of the most widely recognized include the following:

- **Security Operations Center Capability Maturity Model (SOC-CMM)**: This model focuses on five maturity levels (initial, managed, defined, measured, and optimizing) and assesses various domains, including threat intelligence, incident response, and vulnerability management. Process maturity is evaluated based on the existence and effectiveness of documented procedures, training, and continuous improvement mechanisms.

- **The NIST cybersecurity framework**: While not specifically a SOC maturity model, the NIST framework provides a set of standards, guidelines, and best practices that can be used to assess and improve SOC processes. Its five core functions (identify, protect, detect, respond, and recover) provide a helpful structure for defining and evaluating SOC processes.

- **SANS institute maturity model**: SANS offers various maturity models and frameworks, including the critical security controls, which guide the implementation of adequate security processes.

A comparison between the SOC maturity models is covered in the following table:

Model	Focus	Key features	Maturity levels
SOC-CMM	SOC capability assessment	Evaluates threat intelligence, incident response, and vulnerability management	Initial, managed, defined, measured, optimizing
NIST framework	Cybersecurity risk management	Five core functions: identify, protect, detect, respond, recover	No fixed levels, evolves with implementation
SANS model	Practical security controls	Emphasizes measurable security improvements and operational efficiency	No predefined levels, focuses on control effectiveness

Table 10.1: Comparison between SOC maturity models

These models typically evaluate process maturity based on the following criteria:

- **Documentation**: Are processes documented and readily accessible to SOC personnel?

- **Standardization**: Are processes consistently applied across all security operations?

- **Automation**: Can processes be automated to improve efficiency and reduce human error?

- **Integration**: Are processes integrated with other security and IT operations?

- **Measurement and improvement**: Are processes regularly measured and evaluated for effectiveness, with mechanisms in place for continuous improvement?

SOC processes typically evolve through several stages of maturity, as shown in the following figure:

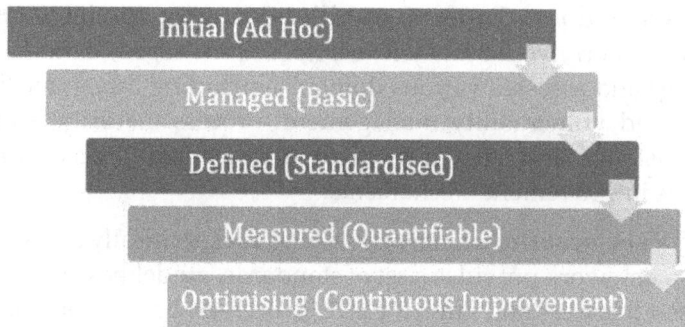

Figure 10.1: SOC maturity model stages

The distinct stages of SOC maturity can be explained as covered in the following table:

Maturity level	Description	Real-world example
0—Non-existent	No formal SOC processes or capabilities exist.	A startup without a dedicated security team relies solely on basic firewall protection.
1—Initial **(Ad-hoc)**	Processes are informal, undocumented, and inconsistent. Reliance on individual expertise is high, and outcomes are unpredictable.	A small business has an IT team handling security alerts manually without structured workflows.
2—Managed **(Basic)**	Processes are documented and basic procedures are in place. Some level of consistency is achieved, but automation and integration are limited.	A retail company implements a SIEM solution but lacks automation for incident response.
3—Defined **(Standardised)**	Processes are well-defined, documented, and standardized across the SOC. Automation and integration begin to improve efficiency and effectiveness.	A financial institution establishes formal SOC procedures, including threat intelligence integration.
4—Measured **(Quantifiable)**	Processes are regularly measured and evaluated using key metrics. Data analysis is used to identify areas for improvement and demonstrate value.	A multinational corporation tracks SOC KPIs, optimizing detection and response times.
5—Optimizing **(Continuous improvement)**	Processes are continuously monitored and improved based on data analysis and feedback. Automation and integration are maximized, and the SOC proactively adapts to evolving threats.	A government agency uses AI-driven analytics to enhance SOC efficiency and threat hunting.

Table 10.2: SOC maturity models stages

Organizations can take several initiatives to improve their SOC process maturity. A step-by-step approach to apply SOC-CMM in real-world scenarios can be as follows:

1. **Conduct a SOC-CMM self-assessment**:

    a. Use the SOC-CMM toolkit to evaluate current SOC maturity.

    b. Identify gaps in **people, processes, and technology**.

2. **Define a target maturity level**:

   a. Set realistic goals for SOC improvement.

   b. Align objectives with **business risk priorities**.

3. **Develop an action plan**:

   a. Implement structured **incident response workflows**.

   b. Integrate **automation tools** for efficiency.

4. **Measure progress and optimize**:

   a. Track SOC performance using **KPIs and metrics**.

   b. Continuously refine SOC operations based on **threat intelligence insights**.

Regular assessments are crucial to gauge the maturity of the SOC. These assessments should include the following:

- **Self-assessments**: Internal evaluations conducted by the SOC team to identify strengths and areas for improvement.

- **Third-Party audits**: External reviews by independent auditors to objectively assess SOC capabilities and processes.

- **Benchmarking**: Comparing SOC performance against industry standards and best practices to identify gaps and opportunities.

SOC-CMM toolkit

The SOC-CMM is a structured framework designed to assess and improve the maturity of SOCs. It provides organizations with a self-assessment tool to measure their SOC's capabilities across various domains, helping them identify gaps and prioritize improvements. The SOC-CMM toolkit evaluates SOC maturity across three key domains as specified in the following table:

Domain	Key areas assessed	Example application
People	Skill levels, training programs, staffing models.	A SOC team undergoes regular MITRE ATT&CK training to improve adversary detection.
Processes	Incident response workflows, threat intelligence integration, compliance adherence.	A telecom provider refines its alert triage process, reducing false positives by 30%.
Technology	SIEM solutions, automation tools, detection mechanisms.	A bank integrates Splunk Phantom for automated threat response, improving efficiency.

Table 10.3: SOC-CMM toolkit domains

SOC-CMM is widely used to enhance SOC operations. Here are some practical applications:

- **Mapping SOC-CMM to MITRE ATT&CK**: Organizations can align their SOC maturity with MITRE ATT&CK to assess detection capabilities against adversary tactics. For example:

  - A cybersecurity firm maps its SOC detection rules to MITRE ATT&CK techniques, identifying gaps in threat coverage.

  - A healthcare provider uses ATT&CK mapping to prioritize security investments based on real-world attack trends.

- **SOC Target Operating Model (SOCTOM)**: SOC-CMM helps define a strategic roadmap for SOC development, balancing operational activities with continuous improvement. For example:

  - A financial institution uses SOCTOM to transition from a reactive SOC to a proactive threat-hunting model.

  - A government agency integrates SOC automation tools to streamline incident response workflows.

- **Capability growth measurement**: SOC-CMM enables tracking of SOC evolution over time, demonstrating return on investment in security operations. For example:

  - A multinational company benchmarks its SOC improvements annually, showcasing enhanced detection accuracy and response speed.

  - A retail organization measures SOC efficiency by analyzing incident resolution times before and after automation.

The SOC-CMM toolkit is a powerful framework for assessing and improving SOC maturity. By understanding its maturity levels, assessment domains, and practical applications, we can gain valuable insights into real-world SOC operations. Implementing SOC-CMM effectively can help organizations enhance security resilience, optimize workflows, and improve threat detection capabilities.

Mature processes are the backbone of an effective SOC. Organizations can enhance their ability to detect, respond to, and prevent cyberattacks by focusing on process improvement. Utilizing SOC maturity models provides a valuable framework for assessing current capabilities, identifying areas for improvement, and developing a roadmap for achieving a higher level of security maturity. This continuous improvement of processes, combined with skilled personnel and appropriate technology, truly empowers a SOC to protect the organization it serves effectively.

Security operations centers workflow and KPIs

A well-defined workflow is the engine of a SOC, driving its efficiency and effectiveness in detecting, analyzing, and responding to security incidents. The SOC workflow outlines the step-by-step activities for identifying, investigating, responding to, and recovering from security incidents. Meanwhile, KPIs are metrics used to measure the success of the SOC in executing these processes. With relevant KPIs, SOC workflow provides a measurable framework for continuous improvement.

The SOC workflow is a series of organized steps that ensure that every cyber incident is handled appropriately. It aims to minimize detection time, reduce incident impact, and facilitate continuous improvement. The incident response lifecycle, i.e., SOC workflow stages are depicted in the following figure:

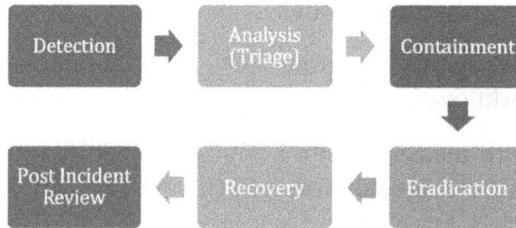

Figure 10.2: Incident response lifecycle

The key stages of the SOC workflow typically include the following:

- **Detection**: The SOC workflow's first stage constantly monitors the organization's network, endpoints, and other critical assets. This stage consists of the identification of potential security events through various monitoring tools, including SIEM systems, IDS/IPS, EDR solutions, and threat intelligence feeds. Continuous monitoring is done to identify suspicious activities, potential threats, or anomalies in real-time. This involves automated detection mechanisms combined with human analysts who investigate alerts, assess their severity, and prioritize incidents.

- **Analysis (triage)**: Once an event is detected, analysts investigate to determine its validity and potential impact. Analysts classify the alert, assess whether it is a false positive, and prioritize it based on its risk to the organization. This involves correlating data from different sources, analyzing logs, and using threat intelligence to understand the context of the event. Events are then categorized and prioritized based on their severity. Incident analysis is critical to understand the attack vectors, identify compromised systems, and evaluate the potential damage or ongoing threat. This phase may involve gathering additional data, examining network traffic, reviewing logs, and running forensic tools to determine the scope of the incident.

- **Containment**: If an event is confirmed as a security incident, containment measures are taken to limit its spread and impact and prevent further damage to the organization. This could involve isolating affected systems, blocking malicious traffic, or disabling compromised accounts. Incident response also requires communication with stakeholders, including IT teams, management, and possibly external authorities or law enforcement. The response team will also assess the impact on business operations and prioritize recovery actions.

- **Eradication**: This stage focuses on eliminating threats such as malware and correcting underlying causes like vulnerabilities or misconfigurations. This may involve patching systems, removing malicious software, reconfiguring security controls, or rebuilding compromised systems.

- **Recovery**: After eradication, systems are restored to their normal operating state while ensuring the organization is not at risk of further exploitation. This includes restoring backup data, re-enabling services, and monitoring systems for any residual activity. The recovery phase requires coordination with IT and business teams to ensure minimal disruption.

- **Post-incident review**: This phase focuses on analyzing the response, identifying lessons learned, and implementing process improvements to prevent similar incidents. This phase evaluates the response's effectiveness and identifies gaps in the process, technologies, or training. Lessons learned during the incident are used to improve the SOC's capabilities. Recommendations from the review often lead to process improvements, tool updates, and training programs designed to prepare the SOC for future incidents better. Detailed root cause analysis framework is already covered in *Chapter 7, Analysis* for reference.

A formalized workflow is crucial for consistent and efficient SOC operations. This involves the following:

- **Documentation**: Creating detailed documentation of each workflow stage, including specific procedures, roles, and responsibilities.

- **Automation**: Automating repetitive tasks, such as data collection, correlation, and initial analysis, to improve efficiency and reduce human error. SOAR platforms play a key role here.

- **Integration**: Integrating security tools and systems to streamline data flow and improve team collaboration.

- **Ticketing systems**: Utilizing ticketing systems to track incidents, assign tasks, and monitor progress.

KPIs for security operations centers workflow

KPIs are essential to evaluate the effectiveness and efficiency of the SOC workflow. They provide quantifiable data and measurable insights that help SOC managers and stakeholders understand how well the security operations function. KPIs also help identify areas for improvement and justify investments in people, processes, and technology.

Key KPIs can be categorized into several areas, such as:

- **Detection KPIs**: To properly evaluate the effectiveness of a SOC's detection capabilities, these key metrics should be tracked and incorporated:

  o **MTTD**: This KPI measures the average time from when an attack occurs to when it is detected. A low MTTD indicates that the SOC can quickly identify threats, crucial for mitigating potential damage.

  o **True positive rate (TPR)**: This KPI tracks the number of correctly identified security incidents. This measures the accuracy of detection systems.

  o **False positive rate (FPR)**: This KPI tracks the percentage of alerts incorrectly identified as legitimate threats. A high FPR can lead to alert fatigue, waste valuable resources, and impact the efficiency of the SOC, while a low FPR ensures that analysts focus on real threats.

  o **Precision**: Proportion of alerts that are true positives

  $$Precision = True\ Positives\ /\ (True\ Positives + False\ Positives)$$

  o **Recall**: Proportion of actual threats that are detected

  $$Recall = True\ Positives\ /\ (True\ Positives + False\ Negatives)$$

  o **F1 score**: Harmonic mean of precision and recall

  $$F1 = 2 * (Precision * Recall)\ /\ (Precision + Recall)$$

  o **Signal-to-noise ratio (SNR)**: Relationship between actionable alerts and false positives

  $$SNR = Count\ of\ True\ Positives\ /\ Count\ of\ False\ Positives$$

  o **Alert Fatigue Index (AFI)**: Measures potential analyst burnout risk

  $$AFI = (False\ Positive\ Rate * Alert\ Volume)\ /\ Analyst\ Capacity$$

- **Analysis and triage KPIs**:

  o **Mean time to acknowledge (MTTA)**: This measures the average time it takes for a SOC analyst to respond to an alert. The quicker the response, the faster the incident can be assessed and acted upon.

  o **Mean time to triage (MTTT)**: The average time spent analyzing an alert to determine whether it is a real or false positive incident. This is important for efficient use of resources and prompt resolution of issues.

  o **Escalation rate**: This tracks the percentage of incidents that require escalation to higher-tier analysts or specialized teams. A high escalation rate may indicate that frontline analysts lack the tools or knowledge to resolve complex threats.

- o **Alert volume**: The total number of security alerts generated by monitoring systems. Monitoring trends in alert volume can help identify potential issues with detection rules or system configurations.

- **Response KPIs**:

  - o **Mean time to respond (MTTR)**: This KPI tracks the average time it takes from detecting an incident to implementing the first response actions, such as blocking malicious traffic or isolating compromised systems.

  - o **Containment time**: It takes the SOC to contain the incident and prevent further damage. This is a critical metric that indicates the speed and effectiveness of the response team.

  - o **Number of incidents handled per analyst**: This measures the productivity of SOC analysts. It can help determine whether the team is staffed correctly or additional resources are needed.

- **Containment, eradication, and recovery KPIs**:

  - o **Mean time to contain (MTTC)**: The average time to contain a security incident.

  - o **Mean time to recover (MTTR)**: This measures the time it takes to restore systems and services after a successful attack, including containment, eradication, and recovery. A lower MTTR indicates better recovery processes and a quicker return to normal business operations.

  - o **Impact of incidents**: Measuring the business impact of security incidents, such as downtime, data loss, or financial losses.

- **Post-incident activity KPIs**:

  - o **Number of lessons learned implemented**: This tracks the number of recommendations from post-incident reviews that are implemented to improve processes and prevent future incidents.

  - o **Recurrence rate of incidents**: This monitors the frequency of similar incidents occurring over time. A decreasing recurrence rate indicates effective incident response and process improvement.

- **Overall SOC performance KPIs**:

  - o **Security posture improvement**: Measuring the overall improvement in the organization's security posture over time based on vulnerability assessments, penetration testing, and other security metrics.

  - o **Employee training completion rate**: Since human error is a significant factor in security breaches, continuous training is essential. This KPI tracks the percentage of SOC analysts and staff completing required training programs.

  o **Cost of security operations**: Tracking the cost of running the SOC, including personnel, technology, and other expenses.

The relationship between workflow and KPIs is symbiotic. A well-defined workflow provides the framework for collecting the data needed to measure KPIs. Conversely, KPIs offer feedback on the effectiveness of the workflow, highlighting areas that need improvement. The mapping of KPIs across different SOC functions is brought out in following table:

KPI type	Time-based metrics	Accuracy metrics	Operational efficiency metrics
Detection	MTTD	TPR, FPR, precision, recall, F1 score	SNR, AFI
Analysis and triage	MTTA, MTTT	Alert volume, escalation rate	Escalation rate
Response	MTTR	Number of incidents handled per analyst	Containment time
Containment and recovery	MTTC, MTTR	Impact of incidents	Recovery time
Post-incident activity	-	Recurrence rate of incidents	Lessons learned implemented
Overall SOC performance	-	Security posture improvement	Employee training completion rate, cost of security operations

Table 10.4: SOC KPI mapping table

For example, a high MTTR might indicate inefficiencies in the containment or eradication stages of the workflow. By analyzing the workflow in detail, the SOC team can identify bottlenecks and implement improvements, such as automating specific tasks or improving team communication.

The SOC workflow and KPIs should be continuously reviewed and updated to reflect changes in the threat landscape, technology, and business requirements. This involves the following:

- **Regular workflow reviews**: Conducting periodic reviews of the SOC workflow to identify areas for improvement.

- **KPI monitoring and analysis**: Regularly monitoring and analyzing KPIs to track performance and identify trends.

- **Feedback loops**: Establishing feedback loops between SOC analysts, management, and other stakeholders to ensure the workflow and KPIs align with business needs.

Some of the industry benchmark ranges for key SOC KPIs like MTTD, MTTR, along with role expectations across different SOC tiers, are covered in the *Tables 10.5* and *10.6* :

KPI	Definition	Industry benchmark range
MTTD	Time taken to identify a security incident after it occurs.	**Minutes to Hours** (Best-in-class SOCs aim for **<30 minutes** detection time)
MTTR	Time taken to contain and remediate an incident after detection.	**Hours to Days** (Efficient SOCs target **<4 hours** for critical incidents)
MTTI	Time taken to analyze an alert and determine its severity.	**Minutes to Hours** (SOC analysts aim for **<60 minutes** for high-priority alerts)
False positive rate	Percentage of alerts incorrectly flagged as threats.	**10-30**% (Lower rates indicate better tuning of detection rules)
False negative rate	Percentage of actual threats missed by detection systems.	**<5**% (Critical for ensuring comprehensive threat coverage)

Table 10.5: *Key SOC KPIs and industry benchmarks*

SOC Tier	Responsibilities	Key metrics and expectations
Tier 1—Alert triage and monitoring	First-line analysts responsible for reviewing alerts and escalating incidents.	**MTTD**: <30 minutes for critical alerts **MTTI**: <60 minutes for high-priority cases **Escalation Rate**: ~30-50% of alerts
Tier 2—Incident investigation and response	Analysts who conduct deeper investigations and initiate containment actions.	**MTTR**: <4 hours for critical incidents **Threat Hunting**: Proactive identification of hidden threats **False Positive Reduction**: Continuous tuning of detection rules
Tier 3—Threat intelligence and advanced response	Senior analysts responsible for threat intelligence, forensic analysis, and strategic improvements.	**Threat attribution**: Mapping incidents to known adversary tactics **SOC automation**: Implementing playbooks for efficiency **Detection coverage**: Ensuring alignment with **MITRE ATT&CK** framework

Table 10.6: *SOC tier role expectations*

Some real-world applications of KPI utilisation are as follows:

- A financial institution optimized its SOC by reducing MTTD from 45 minutes to 20 minutes using automated threat correlation.

- A telecom provider improved MTTR from 6 hours to 3 hours by integrating SOAR playbooks for rapid containment.

- A government agency enhanced tier 3 threat intelligence by mapping SOC detections to MITRE ATT&CK, improving adversary tracking.

A robust SOC workflow and relevant KPIs are essential for effective security operations. Organizations can improve their ability to detect, respond to, and prevent cyberattacks by formalizing the workflow, automating tasks, and tracking key metrics. Continuous monitoring, analysis, and improvement of workflow and KPIs are crucial for maintaining a strong security posture in the face of evolving threats.

Alert levels and investigations

Effective security operations hinge on rapidly and accurately identifying, prioritizing, and investigating security events. This section delves into the crucial concepts of alert levels and investigations, which form the core of daily SOC operations. We will explore how these elements work together to ensure timely responses to potential threats. A security alert is a notification from a security monitoring system indicating a possible security event or anomaly. Integrating MITRE ATT&CK mapping with security alerts enhances a SOC's ability to correlate detections with adversary TTPs. Security alerts are generated from various sources, SIEM platforms, IDS/IPS systems, EDR solutions, firewalls, and vulnerability scanners, but these alerts often lack context, making triage and response challenging. By aligning alerts with the MITRE ATT&CK framework, SOC teams can map each detection to a specific attack technique used by real-world adversaries. This helps analysts prioritize investigations, reduce false positives, and identify patterns across multiple attack stages. For example, alerts triggered by a combination of failed authentication attempts, suspicious PowerShell execution, and abnormal process creation can be mapped to Credential Access (T1078), Execution (T1059), and Defense Evasion (T1218) in ATT&CK, indicating possible credential theft activity. Additionally, automation tools like Splunk Phantom and Cortex XSOAR can further enrich alerts by integrating threat intelligence feeds, automatically mapping incoming incidents to adversary behaviors, and generating contextual playbooks for rapid response. This approach not only improves incident correlation and detection accuracy but also empowers SOC teams with a structured method to defend against APTs.

Not all security alerts are created equally. Some indicate minor anomalies, while others suggest active attacks. Establishing a transparent alert level system is crucial for effectively prioritizing investigations and allocating resources.

A typical alert-level system might include the following categories:

- **Informational**: These alerts provide information about system activity or minor anomalies. They typically do not require immediate action but can be helpful to for trend analysis and proactive monitoring.

- **Low**: These alerts indicate potentially suspicious activity that warrants further investigation but does not pose an immediate threat.

- **Medium**: These alerts suggest a higher likelihood of malicious activity and require prompt investigation. They may indicate attempted intrusions, suspicious network connections, or other potentially harmful events.

- **High (critical)**: These alerts indicate an active attack or a confirmed security breach. They require immediate attention and escalation to the appropriate teams.

The specific criteria for each alert level should be clearly defined and documented, considering factors such as the severity of the potential impact, the likelihood of the event occurring, and the criticality of the affected systems. A typical alert classification with specific real-world examples is covered in the following table:

Alert level	Description	Real-world example	Remarks
Informational	System activities or minor irregularities that are useful for monitoring trends but do not require immediate action	Regular login attempts, scheduled system updates	Roughly 70% of alerts fall into this category, serving as useful operational insights
Low	Activities that may be unusual or slightly suspicious, requiring further review but not posing an immediate risk	Login attempts at odd hours, minor policy deviations	About 20% of alerts warrant analysis to determine legitimacy
Medium	More concerning security events that signal potential threats, necessitating prompt attention	Multiple failed login attempts, unfamiliar network activity	Around 8% of alerts indicate potential security breaches
High (Critical)	Active cyber threats or confirmed breaches that demand urgent intervention	Ransomware outbreaks, unauthorized access to confidential systems	Approximately 2% of alerts require immediate escalation and incident response

Table 10.7: Alert classification examples

This alert classification framework enables security teams to prioritize incidents effectively, ensuring timely responses based on severity. By categorizing alerts from informational to critical, organizations can optimize resource allocation and enhance threat mitigation strategies.

Investigation process

Once an alert is generated, the SOC team investigates its validity and potential impact. The investigation process typically involves the following steps:

1. **Triage**: The initial assessment of the alert to determine its priority and assign it to the appropriate analyst. This involves reviewing the alert details, correlating data from other sources, and using threat intelligence to understand the context of the event.

2. **Data collection and analysis**: Additional information related to the alert, such as logs, network traffic captures, and endpoint activity data, is gathered. This data is then analyzed to identify patterns, anomalies, and evidence of malicious activity.

3. **Correlation and contextualization**: Correlating the collected data with other security events and threat intelligence to build a complete picture of the incident. This helps determine the scope and impact of the incident and identify potential attack vectors.

4. **Containment (if necessary)**: If the investigation confirms a security incident, containment measures are taken to limit its spread and impact. This could involve isolating affected systems, blocking malicious traffic, or disabling compromised accounts.

5. **Escalation (if necessary)**: If the investigation reveals a serious security incident, the SOC team escalates the issue to the appropriate teams, such as the incident response team or management.

6. **Documentation**: All actions and findings discovered are documented throughout the investigation. This documentation is crucial for future analysis, reporting, and lessons learned.

Adequate alert levels and investigations are essential for a successful SOC. By establishing a transparent alert level system, implementing a robust investigation process, and utilizing appropriate tools and technologies, organizations can significantly improve their ability to detect, respond to, and mitigate security threats. Continuous improvement of these processes, along with ongoing training and development for SOC analysts, is crucial for maintaining a strong security posture in the face of evolving threats.

Incident containment

Once a security incident has been confirmed through investigation, the immediate priority shifts to containment. Effective containment aims to limit the scope and impact of the incident, preventing further damage and minimizing disruption to business operations. Containment is a crucial step in the incident response lifecycle.

Let us look at the primary objectives of incident containment:

- **Preventing further damage**: Stopping the spread of malware, preventing data exfiltration, and limiting the impact on affected systems.

- **Preserving evidence**: Maintaining the integrity of forensic data for later analysis and investigation.

- **Minimizing business disruption**: Reducing downtime and ensuring business continuity.

- **Protecting reputation**: Limiting the negative impact on the organization's reputation and customer trust.

- A swift and effective containment strategy can significantly reduce the overall cost and impact of a security incident.

Developing a containment strategy

A well-defined containment strategy is essential for a coordinated and effective response. This strategy should be documented in incident response plans and playbooks and should consider the following factors:

- **Type of incident**: Different types of incidents require different containment strategies. For example, containing a malware infection will differ from containing a denial-of-service attack.

- **Impact on business operations**: The containment strategy should balance the need to stop the incident with the need to maintain essential business functions.

- **Available resources**: The availability of personnel, tools, and other resources will influence the choice of containment methods.

- **Legal and regulatory requirements**: Containment actions should comply with relevant legal and regulatory obligations.

Several techniques can be used for incident containment, depending on the nature of the incident. Let us look at a few of them in detail:

- **Network segmentation**: Isolating affected systems or networks from the rest of the organization's network to prevent the spread of malware or other malicious activity. This can be achieved through firewall rules, VLAN, or **network access control** (**NAC**).

- **System isolation**: Disconnecting affected systems from the network entirely to prevent further communication or data exfiltration. This is a drastic measure but may be necessary in severe cases.

- **Account disablement**: Disabling compromised user accounts to prevent further unauthorized access.

- **Application shutdown**: In critical situations, affected applications may be temporarily shut down to prevent further exploitation, especially when no safer containment option exists.

- **Data removal or modification**: Removing or modifying malicious data or configurations to prevent further damage. This should be performed carefully to avoid data loss or corruption.

- **Content filtering/blocking**: Blocking malicious traffic or URLs at the network perimeter or on individual systems.

- **Honeypots and decoys**: Deploying honeypots or decoys to attract attackers and gather intelligence about their tactics and techniques can help contain the attack by diverting the attacker's attention.

In many cases, multiple containment actions may be necessary. It is crucial to prioritize these actions based on the severity of the incident and the potential impact on business operations. A typical prioritization approach might include the following:

- **Stop the bleeding**: Focus on actions that will immediately stop the spread of the incident and prevent further damage.

- **Preserve evidence**: Preserve forensic evidence by capturing memory, system images, logs, and network traffic in accordance with incident response and legal guidelines for later analysis.

- **Restore essential services**: Prioritize the restoration of critical business functions.

- **Implement long-term fixes**: Implement permanent solutions to prevent similar incidents in the future.

Incident-specific containment playbooks are essential for guiding SOC teams through structured response actions tailored to different attack scenarios. Here is an overview of containment strategies for ransomware, phishing, and insider threats, along with their connection to MITRE ATT&CK mapping for better alert correlation.

- **Ransomware containment playbook**

  - **Detection**: Identify unusual encryption activity, mass file modifications, or ransom notes.

  - **Containment actions**:

    - **Network segmentation**: Isolate infected endpoints to prevent lateral movement.

    - **Account lockdown**: Disable compromised user accounts to limit attacker persistence.

- **Backup protection**: Ensure backups are offline and immutable to prevent encryption.

  o MITRE ATT&CK mapping:

    - **Initial access (T1078)**: Use of stolen credentials.

    - **Execution (T1059)**: Malicious script execution.

    - **Impact (T1486)**: Data encryption for ransom.

- **Phishing containment playbook:**

  o **Detection**: Identify suspicious emails, credential harvesting attempts, or unauthorized login attempts.

  o **Containment actions**:

    - **Email filtering**: Block malicious domains and sender addresses.

    - **Credential reset**: Force password changes for affected accounts.

    - **User awareness**: Notify employees and conduct phishing simulations.

  o MITRE ATT&CK mapping:

    - **Initial access (T1566)**: Spear phishing via email.

    - **Credential access (T1078)**: Stolen credentials used for unauthorized access.

    - **Persistence (T1136)**: Creation of rogue accounts for long-term access.

- **Insider threat containment playbook:**

  o **Detection**: Monitor abnormal data access patterns, privilege escalations, or unauthorized file transfers.

  o **Containment actions**:

    - **Access revocation**: Restrict access to sensitive systems for suspicious users.

    - **Data loss prevention (DLP)**: Block unauthorized data exfiltration attempts.

    - **Behavioral analytics**: Use UEBA to detect anomalies.

  o MITRE ATT&CK mapping:

    - **Privilege escalation (T1078)**: Abuse of elevated permissions.

    - **Exfiltration (T1020)**: Unauthorized data transfers.

    - **Defense evasion (T1070)**: Log deletion to cover tracks.

Integrating MITRE ATT&CK mapping into containment playbooks helps SOC teams correlate alerts with known adversary behaviors, enabling faster and more effective incident response. By aligning detection signals with ATT&CK techniques, SOC analysts can prioritize containment actions, automate response workflows, and enhance threat intelligence-driven decision-making.

Documentation and communication

Thorough documentation of all containment actions is essential. This documentation should include the following:

- **Date and time of actions**: Recording the precise time of each action taken.

- **Description of actions**: Clearly describe the actions taken.

- **Personnel involved**: Identifying the individuals responsible for each action.

- **Impact of actions**: Documenting any impact of the containment actions on business operations.

Effective communication is also crucial during the containment phase. Relevant stakeholders, including management, IT teams, and legal counsel, should be kept informed of the incident and the containment actions being taken.

Challenges in containment

Several challenges can complicate incident containment. Let us take a look at some of them:

- **Lack of visibility**: Limited visibility into network traffic or endpoint activity can make it difficult to identify the scope of the incident and implement effective containment measures.

- **Complex IT environments**: Complex and distributed IT environments can make isolating affected systems or networks challenging.

- **APTs**: APTs often use sophisticated techniques to evade detection and maintain persistence, making containment difficult.

- **Balancing security and business operations**: It can be challenging to find the right balance between containing the incident and minimizing disruption to business operations.

Post-containment activities

Once the incident is contained, it is essential to perform the following:

- **Verify containment**: Confirm that the containment actions have been effective and that the incident is no longer spreading.

- **Monitor affected systems**: Monitor affected systems for any residual activity.

- **Begin eradication and recovery**: Move on to the next phases of incident response, focusing on eradicating the root cause and restoring systems to their normal operating state.

Effective incident containment is a critical component of a robust security operations program. By developing a well-defined containment strategy, utilizing appropriate techniques, and prioritizing actions, organizations can significantly limit the damage caused by security incidents and minimize disruption to business operations. Thorough documentation, effective communication, and continuous improvement of containment processes are essential for maintaining a strong security posture.

Remediation and reporting

After containment has halted an incident's immediate spread, the focus shifts to remediation and reporting. Remediation involves eradicating the incident's root cause and restoring affected systems to a secure state. Reporting ensures that stakeholders are informed of the incident, its impact, and the actions taken. This chapter explores the key aspects of remediation and reporting within SOC processes.

Remediation aims to eliminate the root cause of the security incident and prevent its recurrence. This involves more than just removing the immediate symptoms; it requires identifying and addressing the underlying vulnerabilities or weaknesses that allowed the incident to occur in the first place. The key objectives of remediation include the following:

- **Eradicating the root cause**: Removing malware, patching vulnerabilities, correcting misconfigurations, and addressing other underlying issues.

- **Restoring affected systems**: Rebuilding or restoring compromised systems to a known good state.

- **Preventing recurrence**: Implementing security controls and processes to prevent similar incidents in the future.

The remediation process typically involves the following steps:

1. **Vulnerability analysis**: Identifying the vulnerabilities or weaknesses that were exploited during the incident. This may involve reviewing logs, analyzing system configurations, and conducting vulnerability scans.

2. **Patching and updates**: Applying security patches and updates to address known vulnerabilities in operating systems, applications, and other software.

3. **Malware removal**: Removing any malware or malicious code that was installed on affected systems. This may involve using anti-malware software, manual removal techniques, or reimaging systems.

4. **Configuration changes**: Correcting any misconfigurations that contributed to the incident, such as weak passwords, open ports, or incorrect access controls.

5. **Security control implementation**: Organizations can strengthen SOC security by implementing NIST SP 800-53, ISO/IEC 27001, and CIS Controls, focusing on access control (NIST AC-1, ISO A.9, CIS Control 6), continuous monitoring (NIST CA-7, ISO A.12, CIS Control 8), and incident response (NIST IR-4, ISO A.16, CIS Control 19). Additional defenses include endpoint protection (NIST SI-3, ISO A.12, CIS Control 7), network segmentation (NIST SC-7, ISO A.13, CIS Control 12), and audit logging (NIST AU-6, ISO A.12, CIS Control 8) to enhance resilience and compliance. Security awareness training (NIST AT-2, ISO A.7, CIS Control 14) further mitigates human-related risks, ensuring proactive prevention of future incidents.

6. **Testing and validation**: Thoroughly testing and validating the remediated systems to ensure that the root cause has been addressed and that the systems are functioning correctly.

7. **Documentation**: Documenting all remediation actions taken, including the vulnerabilities addressed, the patches applied, and the configurations changed.

Remediation can present several challenges, such as:

- **Identifying the root cause**: Determining the precise root cause of an incident can be difficult, especially in complex IT environments.

- **System downtime**: Remediation actions may require system downtime, which can disrupt business operations.

- **Resource constraints**: Implementing remediation actions may require significant resources, including personnel, time, and budget.

- **Legacy systems**: Remediating vulnerabilities in legacy systems can be particularly challenging, as patches may not be available or compatible.

Reporting is a crucial aspect of the incident response lifecycle. It ensures that relevant stakeholders are informed of the incident, its impact, and the actions taken. Effective reporting should keep the following points in mind:

- **Timely**: Reports should be provided promptly to ensure stakeholders know the situation and can take appropriate action.

- **Accurate**: Reports should be based on accurate and verified information.

- **Clear and concise**: Reports should be easy to understand and avoid technical jargon.

- **Actionable**: Reports should provide clear recommendations for action.

Different types of reports may be required depending on the audience and the nature of the incident. Let us look at a few examples:

- **Initial incident report**: A brief summary of the incident, its impact, and the initial containment actions taken.

- **Technical report**: A detailed report of the technical aspects of the incident, including the attack vector, the vulnerabilities exploited, and the remediation actions taken.

- **Management report**: A summary of the incident, business impact, and the overall response effort. This report should focus on the business implications and avoid technical details.

- **Post-incident review report**: A comprehensive analysis of the incident response process, including lessons learned and recommendations for improvement.

A typical incident report should include the following elements:

- **Executive summary**: A brief overview of the incident and its key findings.

- **Incident description**: A detailed description of the incident, including the timeline of events, the attack vector, and the affected systems.

- **Impact assessment**: An assessment of the impact of the incident on business operations, including data loss, downtime, and financial losses.

- **Containment and remediation actions**: A description of the containment and remediation actions taken.

- **Lessons learned**: An analysis of the incident response process, including lessons learned and recommendations for improvement.

- **Recommendations**: Specific recommendations for preventing similar incidents in the future.

- **Communication channels**: For structured incident reporting, NIST SP 800-61 follows a four-phase approach, preparation, detection and analysis, containment and eradication, and recovery, ensuring clear escalation and communication. The CERT/CC model streamlines incident classification, severity assessment, and response coordination for efficient notification workflows. Both frameworks help define severity levels, escalation timelines, and communication channels, ensuring regulatory compliance and timely stakeholder updates.

- **Email**: For routine updates and less urgent reports.

- **Phone calls**: For urgent updates and critical incidents.

- **Incident management platforms**: These are used to track incidents and collaborate with stakeholders.

- **Meetings**: For discussing complex issues and presenting detailed reports.

Remediation and reporting are essential for effectively closing the loop on security incidents. Organizations can prevent recurrence and minimize future risks by thoroughly eradicating the root cause and restoring affected systems. Effective reporting ensures that stakeholders are informed and can learn from the incident. Continuous improvement of remediation and reporting processes is crucial for maintaining a strong security posture and effectively managing security incidents.

Conclusion

The SOC workflow is a complex but critical process for maintaining the security and integrity of an organization's digital environment. Understanding each stage of the workflow and the associated KPIs allows SOC teams to monitor their performance, identify areas for improvement, and better prepare for future incidents. By continually refining the workflow and ensuring that KPIs align with organizational goals, a SOC can be a highly effective and proactive force against cyber threats.

In this chapter, we have explored the fundamental components of the SOC workflow and the KPIs that help to measure its effectiveness. Subsequent chapters will look into technology aspects, covering log collecting tools, SIEM/SOAR, EDR/XDR, threat hunting, etc.

Points to remember

Here are some key takeaways from this chapter:

- Achieving and maintaining a high level of SOC maturity is an ongoing journey that requires a commitment to continuous improvement, investment in advanced technologies, and a focus on developing skilled personnel.

- Understanding SOC workflow and KPIs is critical for optimizing SOC performance, ensuring timely responses, and improving overall security posture.

Multiple choice questions

1. **Which SOC maturity level involves proactive monitoring and refined processes?**
   a. Initial
   b. Defined
   c. Managed
   d. Optimized

2. **Which of the following is a key component of SOC processes?**
   a. Continuous improvement
   b. Annual budget planning
   c. Marketing strategies
   d. Product development

3. **Which of the following is a common containment strategy?**

    a. Isolating affected systems from the network

    b. Conducting a forensic analysis

    c. Installing software updates

    d. Informing customers about the breach

Answers

1	c
2	a
3	a

Questions

1. Discuss the importance of SOC maturity models in enhancing an organization's cybersecurity posture. Explain the different levels of maturity and key components that contribute to the growth and effectiveness of SOC.

2. Discuss the significance of KPIs in an SOC. Identify and explain key SOC KPIs, how they are measured, and their impact on enhancing the effectiveness and efficiency of SOC operations.

3. Discuss the significance of remediation and reporting in the incident response process within a SOC. Explain the key steps involved in each phase, the challenges faced, and the impact on the overall security posture of an organization.

Key terms

- **SOC-CMM**: Capability maturity models for SOC operations.
- **MTTD, MTTA, MTTR, MTTC**: Key KPIs for monitoring SOC effectiveness.

Join our Discord space

Join our Discord workspace for latest updates, offers, tech happenings around the world, new releases, and sessions with the authors:

https://discord.bpbonline.com

CHAPTER 11
Technology

Introduction

The modern SOC is a dynamic and technology-driven hub responsible for monitoring, detecting, and responding to cyber threats. The technologies employed decisively decide the effectiveness of an SOC. This chapter examines the crucial role of technology in SOC infrastructure, highlighting the diverse tools and platforms that enable security analysts to effectively combat the ever-evolving threat landscape.

We will examine the core technologies that form the foundation of a robust SOC, including SIEM systems, EDR solutions, SOAR platforms, threat intelligence platforms, and cloud security solutions. Furthermore, we will discuss the importance of data analytics, AI, and ML in enhancing threat detection and response capabilities. By understanding the intricacies of these technologies and their effective integration, organizations can build a resilient and proactive security posture.

In 2024, a major financial institution experienced a sophisticated cyberattack that bypassed traditional security measures. The attackers used advanced techniques to infiltrate the network, highlighting the need for robust SOC technologies to detect and respond to such threats. The attackers exploited vulnerabilities in the institution's outdated software, gaining access to sensitive data and causing significant financial and reputational damage. The incident underscored the importance of integrating advanced technologies like SIEM, SOAR, and EDR in SOC operations. This incident demonstrates the critical role of modern SOC technologies in detecting and responding to sophisticated cyber threats. By understanding and effectively integrating these technologies, organizations can build a resilient and proactive security posture.

Technology is the key element on which the defenses are built. The tools and technologies used for collecting logs, correlating and analyzing them to facilitate real-time threat detection will make the organizations vigilant and well-prepared to tackle the cyberattacks.

Structure

In this chapter, we will discuss the following topics:

- Log collecting tools
- Wireshark monitoring
- SIEM and SOAR
- SIEM operations
- EDR or XDR
- EDR monitoring for user and entity behavior analysis
- Vulnerability management
- Cyber threat hunting

Objectives

By the end of this chapter, readers will get a comprehensive overview of the key technologies utilized in modern SOCs and the role of each technology in the threat detection and response lifecycle. Readers will be able to analyze the importance of data analytics, AI, and ML in enhancing SOC capabilities and understand the criticality of integration and interoperability among different technologies. It will offer insights into the future of technology in SOCs, including emerging trends and advancements.

Log collecting tools

In the ever-evolving landscape of cybersecurity, the ability to collect, analyze, and respond to security events is paramount. In *Chapter 6, Incident Response*, we understood the log management aspect of SOC operations. Central to this log management process are log collecting tools, i.e., software solutions designed to gather and manage logs generated by various systems, applications, and devices. These logs provide a detailed account of activities and can be crucial in identifying and mitigating security threats.

Logs are records of events that occur within an information system or network. They serve as an audit trail, capturing detailed information about user activities, system operations, errors, and other events. In a SOC, log collecting tools play a vital role in centralizing these logs for analysis and response.

To effectively manage and analyze logs, a good log collecting tool should possess the following features:

- **Centralized log collection**: Ability to collect logs from multiple sources and centralize them in a single repository.

- **Real-time monitoring**: Continuous monitoring of logs to detect and respond to security incidents promptly.

- **Scalability**: Capability to handle large volumes of log data without performance degradation.

- **Security**: Ensuring the integrity and confidentiality of collected logs.

- **Integration**: Compatibility with other security tools and systems.

Let us look into some of the most popular log collecting tools used in SOCs. The most popular tools are ELK Stack, Splunk, Graylog, and Syslog. The basic features provided by these tools are covered in the following table:

Feature	ELK Stack	Splunk	Graylog	Syslog
Open-source	**Yes**, Open-source, freely available	**No**, Proprietary, requires licensing	**Yes,** Community-driven	**Yes,** Supports open standards
Deployment options	**On-premise**, Cloud, Flexible installation across environments	**On-premise**, Cloud, Supports enterprise-level scaling	**On-premise**, Cloud, Primarily self-managed	**On-premise**, Limited cloud support
Scalability	**High**, Elasticsearch scales horizontally, handling terabytes of logs	**High**, Optimized for large-scale enterprise environments	**Moderate**, Suitable for mid-sized organizations	**Low**, Designed for small-scale logging needs
Ease of use	**Moderate**, Requires setup for log parsing, visualization	**High**, User-friendly UI with point-and-click configurations	**High**, Intuitive interface, easier setup than ELK	**Low**, Requires manual configuration
Data visualization	**Kibana**, Provides rich dashboards, anomaly detection, ML integration	**Splunk UI**, Advanced visualizations, predictive analytics	**Graylog UI**, Custom dashboards, quick filtering	**Limited**, Only basic text-based log reports
Log management	**Excellent**, Powerful indexing, full-text search	**Excellent**, Handles structured / unstructured logs efficiently	**Good**, Strong log parsing but fewer integrations	**Basic**, Primarily for message-based logging

Feature	ELK Stack	Splunk	Graylog	Syslog
Integration	**Extensive**, Supports various log formats (Syslog, JSON, etc.), cloud apps	**Extensive**, Works with SIEM tools, third-party security services	**Good**, Native support for security logs, APIs	**Basic**, Mainly integrates with Unix-based systems
Cost	**Free (open-source)** – Only requires infrastructure costs	**High**, Paid licensing model, costly for large deployments	**Moderate**, Free core version, paid enterprise features	**Low**, Minimal infrastructure requirements
Community support	**Strong**, Large open-source community, extensive documentation	**Strong**, Dedicated enterprise support, commercial assistance	**Moderate**, Growing community, active development	**Low**, Limited forums and vendor support
Incident management	**Good**, Real-time alerting, integration with SIEM tools	**Excellent**, Built-in analytics, threat intelligence	**Good**, Supports alerts, workflows	**Basic**, Primarily for event logging without advanced detection

Table 11.1: Basic features of log collecting tools

Elasticsearch, Logstash and Kibana

The ELK Stack is a powerful suite of open-source tools for searching, analyzing, and visualizing log data in real time. For example, a company might use ELK Stack to monitor and analyze logs from its web servers, identifying unusual traffic patterns that could indicate a DDoS attack. It comprises Elasticsearch, a distributed search and analytics engine; Logstash, a server-side data processing pipeline that ingests data from multiple sources, transforms it, and then sends it to Elasticsearch; and Kibana, a data visualization tool that provides a front-end interface for querying and visualizing logs stored in Elasticsearch. Specific features are mentioned in the following list:

- **Data ingestion**: It supports a wide range of input plugins to collect data from various sources, including logs, metrics, and events. It also supports data streams for real-time data ingestion and analysis.

- **Data exploration**: It offers graph analytics for visualizing relationships between different data points for exploring and analyzing data, including histograms, pie charts, line graphs, and maps.

- **Alerts and anomalies**: It supports alerting, anomaly detection and forecasting, enabling proactive monitoring and response to unusual events using machine learning capabilities. It provides a highly scalable and configurable alerting system with integrations for various notification channels.

- **Visualization plugins**: It offers a range of plugins for creating specialized visualizations and reports.

Splunk

Splunk is a powerful platform for searching, monitoring, and analyzing machine-generated data in real time. For instance, a retail company might use Splunk to analyze transaction logs, detecting fraudulent activities and generating alerts for further investigation. It is widely used in SOCs for its comprehensive capabilities. Here are some of its key features:

- **Augmented reality (AR)**: Splunk offers AR features to visualize data on physical objects. Splunk offers customizable dashboards and visualizations to present data in a clear and actionable manner.

- **Alerting and reporting**: Splunk can be configured to generate alerts and reports based on specific conditions or thresholds. This proactive feature helps in early detection of anomalies and potential security threats. It provides mobile-friendly dashboards. It also provides tools for managing mobile devices at scale with end-to-end encryption.

- **ML and predictive analytics**: Splunk incorporates machine learning capabilities to identify patterns and anomalies in data. It can perform predictive analytics to forecast future trends and detect potential issues before they occur. It has a strong focus on SIEM with threat detection and response.

- **App ecosystem**: Splunk has an extensive app ecosystem with numerous apps and add-ons available to extend its functionality. These apps provide pre-built solutions for various use cases, including security, IT operations, and business analytics.

- **Data correlation and enrichment**: Splunk enables data correlation and enrichment, allowing users to link related data points and derive more profound insights. This feature is particularly useful for identifying the root causes of incidents and understanding the context of security events.

Graylog

Graylog is another powerful open-source log management tool that offers flexibility and ease of use. A healthcare provider might use Graylog to monitor access logs, ensuring compliance with data protection regulations and detecting unauthorized access to patient records. It provides a centralized log collection and analysis platform, with features such as the following:

- **Extensible architecture**: Graylog's modular architecture allows for easy integration with other tools and systems through plugins and extensions. This extensibility ensures that it can be tailored to meet specific needs. It supports **Graylog Extended Log Format (GELF)** for more efficient and flexible log data handling.

- **Alerting and notification**: Graylog can be configured to send alerts and notifications based on specific log events or conditions. This feature helps in proactive monitoring and prompt incident response.

- **Flexible log storage**: Graylog supports various storage backends, enabling organizations to select the storage solution that best suits their needs. Logs can be stored locally or in distributed environments. It supports the automatic archiving of log messages to compressed flat files for long-term storage.

Syslog

Syslog is a fundamental tool for log collection, particularly in UNIX and Linux environments. For example, a university might use Syslog to collect and store logs from its network devices, facilitating troubleshooting and performance analysis. Syslog, short for system logging protocol, is a standard protocol used for message logging. It allows devices, applications, and systems to send event messages to a designated log server, making it a critical component for centralized log management. This versatile tool provides the following specific features:

- **Centralized logging**: Enables the collection and storage of log messages from multiple sources into a single, centralized log server. This centralization facilitates easier management, analysis, and correlation of logs. Syslog allows for customizable logging configurations. Administrators can define which events to log, where to store them, and how long to retain them, tailoring the system to meet specific requirements. Syslog can store logs in various formats and locations, including local files, remote servers, or databases. This flexibility enables seamless integration with existing IT infrastructures.

- **Standardized format**: Syslog messages adhere to a standardized format, ensuring consistency across logs from various devices and applications. This uniformity simplifies log parsing and analysis. It uses a simple and lightweight protocol for the secure transmission of log messages.

- **Compatibility**: Syslog is widely supported by many devices, applications, and operating systems. Its widespread adoption ensures compatibility and interoperability across different systems.

- **Built-in alerting**: Syslog can be configured to trigger alerts based on specific log events or thresholds. This proactive approach aids in early detection and response to potential issues. It tracks events, errors, and system performance for troubleshooting.

Based on the parameters and functionalities, the recommendations for organizations are as follows:

- **ELK stack**: This is ideal for enterprises looking for a cost-effective, highly scalable solution with extensive community support. It is suitable for organizations with strong DevOps practices and the technical expertise to manage open-source tools.

- **Splunk**: This is best for enterprises that require robust log management and advanced analytics capabilities. It is a great choice if budget is not a constraint and you need comprehensive incident management and real-time monitoring.

- **Graylog**: This is a good balance between cost and functionality, suitable for enterprises that need a user-friendly interface and moderate scalability. It is a solid choice for organizations that prefer open-source solutions but require some commercial support.

- **Syslog**: This is recommended for smaller enterprises or those with more straightforward log management needs. It is a basic, cost-effective solution for collecting and storing logs without advanced features.

The tools covered in this chapter are for understanding purposes. There are numerous other tools available on the market. Each tool has its strengths and unique features, so the best choice depends on your specific needs and use cases. By centralizing and analyzing logs, these tools help SOC teams detect, investigate, and respond to security incidents more effectively. As cybersecurity threats continue to evolve, so too will the capabilities of log collecting tools, ensuring that SOCs remain at the forefront of defense.

Wireshark monitoring

Having explored various log management and collection systems like ELK Stack, Splunk, Graylog, and Syslog, it is essential to consider another critical tool in network monitoring: Wireshark. Unlike traditional log management systems, Wireshark provides a detailed and granular view of network traffic. Wireshark is primarily a network protocol analyzer and packet sniffer. It captures and analyzes network traffic in real time, providing detailed information about the packets transmitted over a network. While it does not collect logs in the traditional sense, it is invaluable for network troubleshooting, performance analysis, and security investigations.

This section will guide you through a hands-on practical on using Wireshark for network monitoring, complete with relevant screenshots for clarity. Follow these steps:

1. **Setting up Wireshark**: Install Wireshark and follow on-screen instructions. After installing Wireshark, it will open as shown in the following figure:

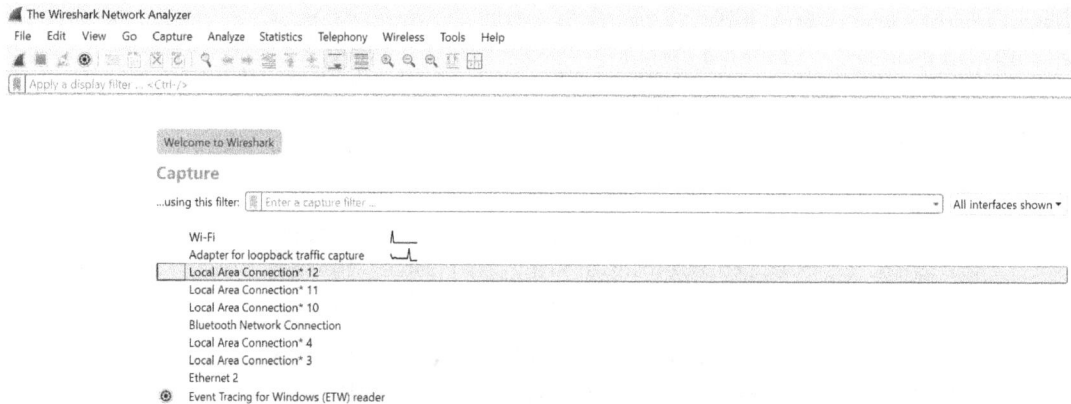

Figure 11.1: Wireshark

2. **Launch Wireshark**: Begin by launching Wireshark on your system. Upon opening, you will be presented with the main interface where you can see a list of available network interfaces as shown in *Figure 11.1* above.

3. **Choose the network interface**: Select the network interface you wish to monitor. This choice is crucial as it determines which segment of your network traffic will be captured. For example, if you are monitoring a wired connection, select the Ethernet interface.

4. **Start capturing packets**: Click on the blue shark fin icon on the toolbar to start capturing packets. Wireshark will immediately begin displaying real-time packet data as they are captured from the selected network interface, as shown in the following figure:

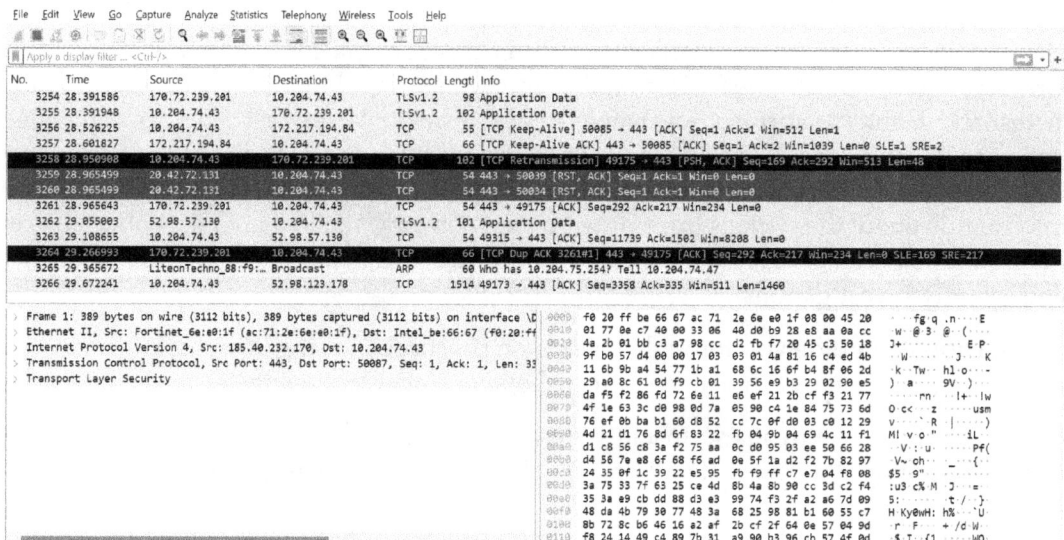

Figure 11.2: Wireshark network capture

5. **Filter the traffic**: To focus on specific types of traffic, apply filters.

6. For instance, to view only ARP packets, type **arp** in the filter bar and press *Enter*. Filters help you narrow down the data to the most relevant information for your analysis:

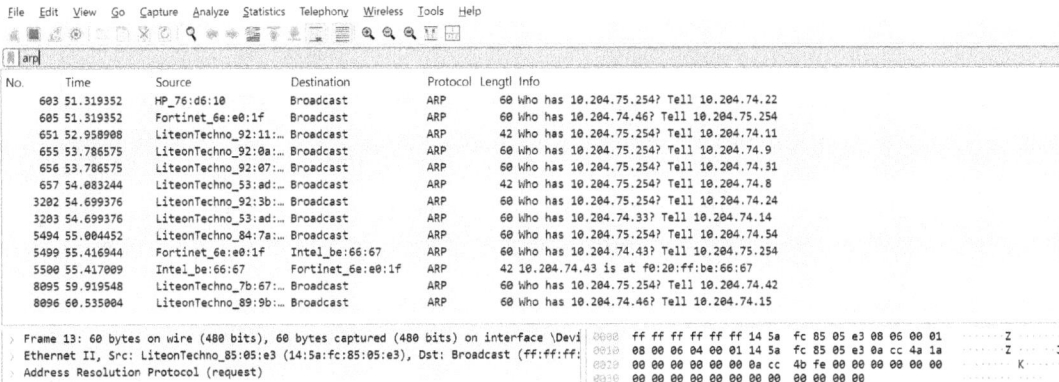

Figure 11.3: *Wireshark filter with ARP packets*

7. **Inspect packet details**: Click on any packet in the capture list to see detailed information about it.

8. The packet details pane provides a breakdown of the packet structure, including headers and payload data, allowing you to diagnose issues or investigate anomalies:

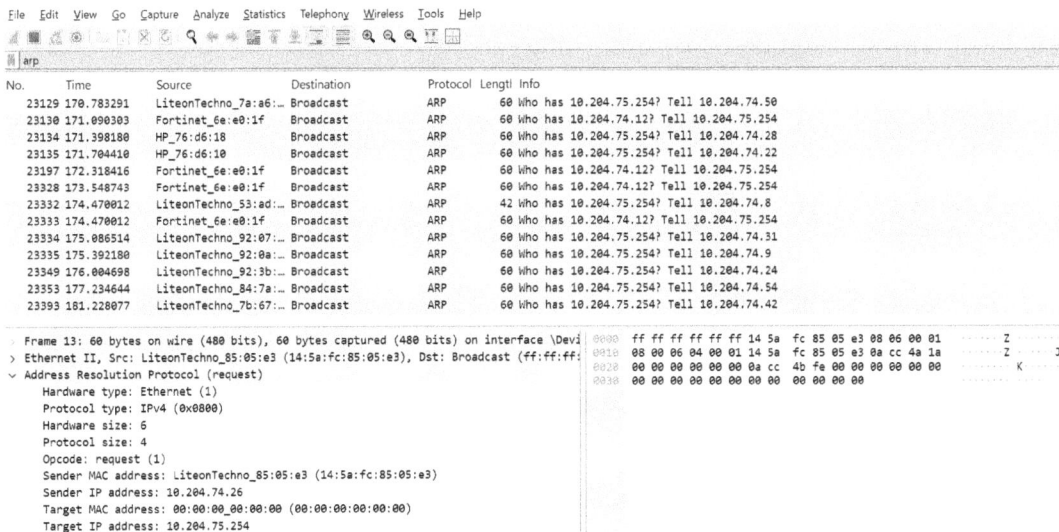

Figure 11.4: *Packet breakdown structure in Wireshark*

9. **Follow TCP stream**: For a more in-depth analysis, you can follow a specific TCP stream. Right-click on a TCP packet and select **Follow | TCP Stream**. This feature

shows the entire conversation between the client and server, which is useful for troubleshooting and security investigations.

10. **Export captured data**: To share your findings or conduct further analysis, export the captured data. Click on **File** | **Export Specified Packets** to save the capture data in various formats. This functionality is crucial for documentation and collaboration with your team.

Wireshark is a powerful tool that complements traditional log management systems by providing deep insights into network traffic at the packet level. Through this practical guide, you have learned how to set up Wireshark, capture and filter network traffic, analyze packets, and export data for reporting. Mastering Wireshark equips you with the skills to monitor and troubleshoot your network effectively, enhancing the capabilities of SOC.

SIEM and SOAR

The modern SOC faces an ever-increasing volume of security alerts, sophisticated attacks, and a persistent skills gap. To effectively combat these challenges, SOCs rely on a powerful combination of technologies, SIEM and SOAR.

SIEM

At the heart of any SOC lies the SIEM. SIEM systems are designed to provide a comprehensive view of an organization's security posture by aggregating and analyzing log data from various sources. By correlating security events, SIEM solutions help detect anomalies, identify potential threats, and generate alerts. It acts as the central nervous system, collecting and analyzing security logs and events from a multitude of sources across the IT infrastructure. These sources can include the following:

- **Network devices**: Firewalls, routers, **intrusion detection/prevention systems (IDS/IPS)**.

- **Security appliances**: Antivirus servers, web proxies, vulnerability scanners.

- **Servers and endpoints**: Operating systems, applications, databases.

- **Cloud services: Infrastructure as a service (IaaS), platform as a service (PaaS), software as a service (SaaS)**.

SIEM performs several key functions, such as:

- **Data aggregation**: It gathers logs from disparate sources into a centralized repository, normalizing them into a common format for consistent analysis.

- **Log management**: SIEM systems collect and centralize log data from diverse sources such as firewalls, antivirus solutions, and intrusion detection systems.

It provides secure storage, indexing, and retrieval of log data, enabling efficient searching and reporting for compliance and investigations.

- **Real-time analysis**: Continuous monitoring of network traffic and security events enables the timely detection of threats. Advanced correlation engines correlates events from different sources to identify suspicious patterns and potential security threats in real time.

- **Alerting**: Automated alerts notify SOC analysts of potential security breaches, facilitating prompt investigation and response. It generates alerts based on predefined rules or anomalies, notifying security analysts of possible incidents.

- **Reporting and visualization**: It provides dashboards and reports that offer a comprehensive overview of the security posture, enabling trend analysis and performance monitoring. SIEM solutions generate detailed reports to demonstrate compliance with regulatory requirements such as GDPR, HIPAA, and PCI-DSS.

A SIEM system in a banking institution detects failed login attempts from multiple locations within minutes. The system correlates logs and raises an alert for a possible brute-force attack, allowing SOC teams to investigate and block malicious IPs.

By providing a consolidated view of security events and enabling rapid threat detection, SIEM empowers security analysts to identify and respond to security threats proactively.

Security orchestration automation and response

SOAR platforms augment SIEM capabilities by automating and orchestrating incident response processes. These solutions enable SOC teams to streamline workflows, reduce response times, and enhance overall operational efficiency. While SIEM excels at threat detection and alerting, SOAR takes it a step further by automating and orchestrating incident response workflows. SOAR platforms integrate with various security tools and systems, enabling automated actions based on SIEM alerts or other triggers.

Key capabilities of SOAR include the following:

- **Orchestration**: SOAR connects disparate security tools and systems, enabling them to work together seamlessly across the security stack. It automates tasks such as retrieving threat intelligence, enriching alerts with contextual information, and executing predefined response actions.

- **Automation**: SOAR automates repetitive and time-consuming tasks, such as:

  o **Alert triage**: Automatically classifying and prioritizing alerts based on severity and context.

  o **Enrichment**: SOAR solutions leverage threat intelligence feeds to enrich incident data about an alert, such as threat intelligence data, asset information, and user details, providing context and aiding in threat prioritization.

- ○ **Containment**: Isolating infected endpoints, blocking malicious IP addresses, and disabling compromised accounts.

- ○ **Investigation**: Automatically gathering forensic data, running diagnostic scripts, and generating reports. Comprehensive case management features help track and document incident investigations, facilitating collaboration and knowledge sharing.

- **Response**: SOAR enables automated or semi-automated responses to security incidents, reducing response times and minimizing the impact of attacks. SOAR automates repetitive and manual tasks, freeing up SOC analysts to focus on more complex investigations. Predefined playbooks guide the automated response to common security incidents, ensuring consistency and accuracy.

A healthcare provider experiences a ransomware attack. The SOAR system automatically isolates infected endpoints, blocks malicious IPs, and generates a response report. Simultaneously, it notifies SOC teams and regulatory authorities, ensuring faster mitigation.

By automating incident response workflows, SOAR significantly enhances the efficiency and effectiveness of the SOC, enabling analysts to concentrate on more complex tasks and strategic initiatives.

SIEM and SOAR are not mutually exclusive; they are complementary technologies that work together to enhance the overall security posture.

The synergy between them can be summarized as follows:

- **SIEM detects, SOAR responds**: SIEM identifies potential threats and generates alerts, while SOAR automates the response to those alerts.

- **SIEM provides context, SOAR acts**: SIEM provides valuable context about security events, which SOAR uses to execute appropriate response actions.

- SIEM reduces noise, while SOAR improves efficiency: SIEM filters out irrelevant events, reducing alert fatigue, and SOAR automates tasks, enhancing analyst efficiency.

By integrating SIEM and SOAR, SOCs can achieve significant improvements in threat detection, incident response, and overall security operations. Implementing SIEM and SOAR requires careful planning and execution. Key considerations include the following:

- **Defining clear objectives**: Determine the specific goals and objectives for implementing SIEM and SOAR, such as improving threat detection, reducing response times, or automating particular tasks.

- **Selecting the right tools**: Choose SIEM and SOAR platforms that meet the specific needs and requirements of the organization, considering factors such as scalability, integration capabilities, and cost.

- **Developing use cases and playbooks**: Define specific use cases for threat detection and incident response and develop corresponding SOAR playbooks to automate the response actions.

- **Integrating with existing tools**: Integrate SIEM and SOAR with other security tools and systems, such as threat intelligence platforms, vulnerability scanners, and EDR solutions.

- **Continuous improvement**: Regularly review and update SIEM rules, SOAR playbooks, and integration configurations to ensure they remain effective and aligned with evolving threats.

SIEM and SOAR are essential technologies for building a modern and effective SOC. SIEM provides the foundation for threat detection and analysis, while SOAR automates and orchestrates incident response workflows. By working together, they empower security teams to proactively identify and respond to security threats, minimizing the impact of attacks and improving the overall security posture. As the threat landscape continues to evolve, the synergy of SIEM and SOAR will remain a cornerstone of effective security operations.

Case study: Consider an organization that has implemented both SIEM and SOAR solutions as real-world applications. When a suspicious login attempt is detected by the SIEM system, it triggers an automated response workflow in the SOAR platform. The SOAR system cross-references the login attempt with threat intelligence feeds, blocks the suspicious IP address, and generates a detailed incident report. SOC analysts can then review the incident, conduct a more thorough investigation, and implement additional security measures if necessary.

SIEM operations

For practical SIEM operations, we will consider Wazuh, an open-source security platform that provides both SIEM and EDR capabilities. Here are the components of Wazuh:

- **Wazuh server**: The central component that receives logs from agents, processes them, and generates alerts.

- **Wazuh agents**: Installed on endpoints to collect logs and send them to the Wazuh Server.

- **Wazuh indexer**: Stores alerts for real-time data search and analytics.

- **Wazuh dashboard**: User interface for searching, analyzing, and visualizing data.

Perform the following practical using Wazuh:

- **Install Wazuh Server**: Download the installation script from the Wazuh website and run it on your server.

- **Configure agents**: Install Wazuh agents on endpoints and configure them to send logs to the Wazuh Server.

- **Set up indexer**: Configure the Wazuh Indexer to store and manage alerts.

- **Collect logs**: Configure log collection from following sources

  o **Windows event logs**: Collect logs from Windows operating systems.

  o **Linux logs**: Collect logs from Linux systems.

  o **Firewall logs**: Collect logs from Firewalls.

- **Process logs**: Ensure converting raw logs into a structured format and define rules to identify and generate alerts based on specific log patterns.

- **Monitor in real-time and configure alerts**: Create specific use cases for common attack scenarios (e.g., brute-force attacks, malware infections). Configure alert thresholds and escalation procedures.

- **Custom dashboards**: Create customizable dashboards to provide real-time visibility into key security metrics.

- **Incident response and investigation**:

  o **Prioritize alerts**: Assess and prioritize alerts based on severity and potential impact.

  o **Playbooks**: Use predefined playbooks and SOPs to guide the initial response.

  o **Event correlation**: Correlate events across multiple data sources to reconstruct the attack timeline.

  o **Root cause analysis**: Identify the root cause of the incident and take corrective actions.

- **Reporting and compliance**:

  o **Compliance reports**: Generate automated reports for compliance audits (e.g., GDPR, PCI DSS).

  o **Custom reports**: Create custom reports to meet specific organizational requirements.

- **Maintain logs**: Keep detailed audit logs of all SIEM activities for accountability and transparency.

- **Continuous improvement**: Ensure following key issues:

  o **Software updates**: Keep Wazuh software and threat intelligence feeds up to date.

  o **Rule tuning**: Continuously refine correlation rules to improve detection capabilities.

- **SOC analyst training**: Regularly train SOC analysts on new threats, attack techniques, and SIEM features.

By following these practical steps, organizations can effectively implement and manage SIEM operations using Wazuh, enhancing their overall security posture.

EDR or XDR

In the ever-evolving threat landscape, traditional security solutions often fall short in detecting and responding to sophisticated attacks that bypass perimeter defenses. EDR and its more comprehensive evolution, XDR, have emerged as critical components of a modern SOC, providing deep visibility and advanced response capabilities across the IT environment.

Endpoint Detection and Response

EDR focuses specifically on endpoint devices (e.g., desktops, laptops, servers, mobile devices), providing real-time visibility into endpoint activity and enabling rapid threat detection and response.

Key capabilities of EDR include the following:

- **Endpoint data collection**: EDR agents continuously collect detailed data from endpoints, such as:

  - **Process activity**: Executed processes, command-line arguments, parent-child process relationships.

  - **File system activity**: File creation, modification, deletion, and access.

  - **Network connections**: Inbound and outbound network connections, protocols, and destination IP addresses.

  - **Registry changes (Windows)**: Modifications to registry keys and values.

  - User logins and logoffs.

- **Threat detection**: EDR platforms use various techniques to detect malicious activity, such as:

  - **Signature-based detection**: Identifying known malware based on signatures or hashes.

  - **Behavioral analysis**: Detecting suspicious patterns of activity that deviate from normal behavior.

  - **ML**: Using ML algorithms to identify anomalies and predict potential threats.

  - **Threat intelligence integration**: Leveraging threat intelligence feeds to identify known malicious indicators.

- **Alerting and investigation**: EDR generates alerts when suspicious activity is detected, providing security analysts with detailed information about the event.

Analysts can then investigate the alert, pivoting on different data points to understand the scope and impact of the potential threat.

- **Response capabilities**: EDR provides various response options, including:

  ○ **Endpoint isolation**: Isolating an infected endpoint from the network to prevent further spread of the threat.

  ○ **Process termination**: Terminating malicious processes running on the endpoint.

  ○ **File quarantine and deletion**: Quarantining or deleting malicious files.

  ○ **Rollback**: Reverting an endpoint to a previous clean state.

- **Forensic analysis**: EDR collects detailed forensic data that can be used for post-incident analysis and investigations.

By providing deep visibility into endpoint activity and enabling rapid response, EDR empowers security teams to proactively identify and contain threats before they can cause significant damage.

Extended Detection and Response

XDR takes the core principles of EDR and extends them beyond the endpoint to encompass other security layers, such as:

- **Network**: Network traffic analysis, IDS/IPS logs, and firewall logs.

- **Email**: Email security gateway logs, phishing detection data, and email content analysis.

- **Cloud**: **Cloud security posture management (CSPM)** data, **cloud workload protection platform (CWPP)** logs, and **cloud access security broker (CASB)** data.

- **Identity**: **Identity and access management (IAM)** logs, user authentication data, and **privileged access management (PAM)** activity.

XDR platforms correlate data from these various sources to provide a more holistic view of the security landscape and enable more effective threat detection and response.

Key benefits of XDR include the following:

- **Improved threat detection**: By correlating data from multiple sources, XDR can detect more complex and sophisticated attacks that might evade detection by individual security tools.

- **Faster incident response**: XDR automates many incident response tasks, such as investigation, containment, and remediation, significantly reducing response times.

- **Reduced complexity**: XDR consolidates security data and management into a single platform, simplifying security operations and reducing the burden on security teams.

- **Enhanced visibility**: XDR provides a unified view of security data across the entire IT environment, improving overall visibility and situational awareness.

While both EDR and XDR aim to improve threat detection and response, there are key differences between them, which are covered in the following table:

Feature	EDR	XDR
Scope	Endpoint devices only	Multiple security layers (endpoint, network, email, cloud, etc.)
Data sources	Endpoint data	Data from multiple security tools
Focus	Endpoint-centric threat detection and response	Cross-layer threat detection and response
Correlation	Primarily within endpoint data	Across multiple security layers
Complexity	Less complex to implement	More complex to implement

Table 11.2: Key differences between EDR and XDR

Implementing EDR and XDR requires careful planning and execution. Key considerations include the following:

- **Defining clear objectives**: Determine the specific goals and objectives for implementing EDR or XDR, such as improving threat detection, reducing response times, or enhancing visibility.

- **Selecting the right tools**: Choose EDR or XDR platforms that meet the specific needs and requirements of the organization, considering factors such as scalability, integration capabilities, and cost.

- **Integrating with existing tools**: Integrate EDR and XDR with other security tools and systems, such as SIEM, threat intelligence platforms, and SOAR.

- **Developing use cases and playbooks**: Define specific use cases for threat detection and incident response and develop corresponding playbooks to automate response actions.

- **Training and staffing**: Ensure that the SOC team has the necessary skills and training to effectively use EDR and XDR.

EDR and XDR are essential technologies for building a modern and effective SOC. EDR provides deep visibility and response capabilities at the endpoint level, while XDR extends these capabilities across multiple security layers, providing a more holistic view of the security landscape. As the threat landscape continues to evolve, EDR and XDR will remain crucial components of a robust and proactive security strategy.

EDR monitoring for user and entity behavior analysis

Traditional security solutions often rely on signatures, rules, or known **indicators of compromise (IOC)** to detect threats. However, sophisticated attackers are adept at evading these defenses by using novel techniques and zero-day exploits. This is where behavioral analysis tools become crucial. These tools focus on detecting anomalous or suspicious behavior, regardless of whether a specific signature or rule exists, enabling the SOC to identify and respond to previously unknown threats.

Behavioral analysis, also known as anomaly detection or **user and entity behavior analytics (UEBA)**, focuses on establishing a baseline of normal behavior for users, devices, applications, and network traffic. It then monitors activity and flags deviations from this baseline as potentially suspicious. This approach offers several advantages such as:

- **Detection of unknown threats**: By focusing on behavior rather than signatures, behavioral analysis can detect zero-day exploits, **advanced persistent threats (APTs)**, and other novel attacks.

- **Reduced false positives**: By understanding normal behavior, these tools can reduce the number of false positive alerts compared to signature-based systems.

- **Insider threat detection**: Behavioral analysis can effectively detect insider threats by identifying unusual activity by authorized users.

- **Contextual awareness**: These tools provide valuable context about security events by correlating different data points and identifying patterns of behavior.

Several techniques are used to implement behavioral analysis. Let us look at some of them:

- **Statistical analysis**: This involves using statistical methods to identify deviations from normal behavior. For example, a sudden spike in network traffic from a specific user could be flagged as suspicious.

- **Machine learning**: Machine learning algorithms are used to build models of normal behavior and detect anomalies. These algorithms can learn from data and adapt to changing behavior patterns.

- **Time-series analysis**: This involves analyzing data over time to identify trends and anomalies. For example, a sudden change in login time for a user could be flagged as suspicious.

- **Rule-based analysis (with behavioral context)**: While the core of behavioral analysis is anomaly detection, rules can be used to refine and enhance the detection process. These rules are often based on observed behavioral patterns and can help to reduce false positives.

Several types of tools leverage behavioral analysis to enhance security. These are listed as follows:

- **UEBA**: UEBA focuses on analyzing user and entity behavior, such as login patterns, access to sensitive data, and network activity. It uses machine learning and statistical modeling to establish baselines and detect anomalies. UEBA can identify compromised accounts, insider threats, and other suspicious user activity.

- **NTA**: NTA tools analyze network traffic patterns to detect anomalies and potential threats. They can identify unusual communication patterns, data exfiltration attempts, and other suspicious network activity. NTA often uses flow data (NetFlow, IPFIX) and **packet capture** (**PCAP**) for analysis.

- **EDR with behavioral analysis**: Modern EDR solutions incorporate behavioral analysis to detect malicious activity on endpoints. They monitor process execution, file system activity, and network connections to identify suspicious patterns.

- **SIEM with UEBA integration**: Some SIEM platforms integrate UEBA capabilities to enhance their threat detection capabilities. They correlate security events with behavioral data to identify more complex and sophisticated attacks.

- **CASB with behavioral analysis**: CASBs often include behavioral analysis to monitor user activity in cloud applications and detect suspicious behavior, such as unauthorized data access or unusual download patterns.

Implementing behavioral analysis in SOC

Implementing behavioral analysis tools requires careful planning and execution, such as:

- **Data collection and normalization**: Ensure that the necessary data is being collected from relevant sources and normalized into a consistent format.

- **Baseline establishment**: Establish a baseline of normal behavior for users, devices, and network traffic. This may require a period of data collection and analysis.

- **Tuning and calibration**: Fine-tune the behavioral analysis models and rules to minimize false positives and maximize detection accuracy.

- **Integration with other security tools**: Integrate behavioral analysis tools with other security tools, such as SIEM, SOAR, and threat intelligence platforms.

- **Alerting and response workflows**: Define clear alerting and response workflows for handling behavioral analysis alerts.

- **Continuous monitoring and improvement**: Continuously monitor the performance of the behavioral analysis tools and adjust as needed.

Use cases for behavioral analysis

Behavioral analysis can be used for a variety of use cases in the SOC. Let us look at them:

- **Compromised account detection**: Identifying accounts that have been compromised by attackers.

- **Insider threat detection**: Detecting malicious activity by authorized users.

- **Data exfiltration detection**: Identifying attempts to steal sensitive data.

- **Lateral movement detection**: Detecting attackers moving laterally within the network.

- **Malware detection**: Identifying malware that uses novel techniques to evade traditional defenses.

Challenges of behavioral analysis

While behavioral analysis offers significant advantages, there are also some challenges such as:

- **Data volume and complexity**: Analyzing large volumes of data can be challenging and require significant computing resources.

- **Baseline drift**: Normal behavior can change over time, requiring continuous tuning and recalibration of the models.

- **False positives**: While behavioral analysis generally reduces false positives compared to signature-based systems, they can still occur.

- **Explainability**: Understanding why a specific event was flagged as suspicious can be difficult, especially with complex machine learning models.

Behavioral analysis tools are essential for building a modern and effective SOC. By focusing on detecting anomalous behavior, these tools can identify previously unknown threats and enhance the overall security posture. As attackers continue to evolve their tactics, behavioral analysis will play an increasingly important role in protecting organizations from cyberattacks. By understanding the principles, techniques, and challenges of behavioral analysis, SOC teams can effectively leverage these tools to detect and respond to the ever-evolving threat landscape.

Vulnerability management

Vulnerability management is a proactive defense within an SOC. It is a crucial process for any organization seeking to maintain a strong security posture. It involves identifying, assessing, prioritizing, and remediating vulnerabilities in IT systems and applications before attackers can exploit them.

Vulnerability management is a cyclical process, not a one-time activity, as shown in the following figure:

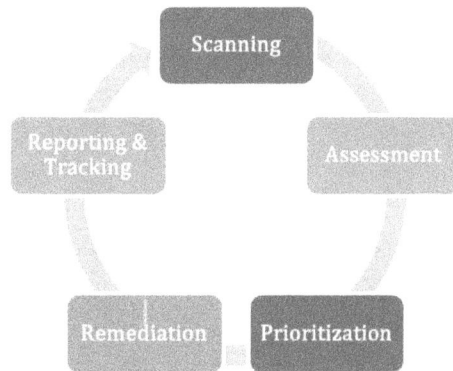

Figure 11.5: Vulnerability management cycle

It is a continuous effort to reduce the attack surface and minimize the risk of exploitation. The core components of vulnerability management include the following:

- **Vulnerability scanning**: The process of automatically identifying known vulnerabilities in systems, applications, and network devices. This is typically done using automated scanning tools that check for known weaknesses based on vulnerability databases like the **National Vulnerability Database** (**NVD**) and **Common Vulnerabilities and Exposures** (**CVE**). Several techniques are used for vulnerability scanning:

  o **Network scanning**: Scanning network devices and systems for open ports, running services, and known vulnerabilities.

  o **Host-based scanning**: Scanning individual systems for vulnerabilities in operating systems, applications, and configurations.

  o **Web application scanning**: Scanning web applications for vulnerabilities such as SQL injection, **cross-site scripting** (**XSS**), and **cross-site request forgery** (**CSRF**).

  o **Database scanning**: Scanning databases for vulnerabilities such as SQL injection and weak authentication.

  o **Cloud scanning**: Scanning cloud environments (IaaS, PaaS, SaaS) for misconfigurations and vulnerabilities.

- **Vulnerability assessment**: A more in-depth analysis of identified vulnerabilities to determine their potential impact and likelihood of exploitation. This involves considering factors such as the severity of the vulnerability, the exploitability of the vulnerability, and the criticality of the affected system. Various methodologies are used for vulnerability assessment:

- o **CVSS**: A standardized scoring system for assessing the severity of vulnerabilities. It provides a numerical score that represents the base, temporal, and environmental characteristics of a vulnerability.

- o **Penetration testing (Pen testing)**: Simulated attacks against systems and applications to identify exploitable vulnerabilities. Pen testing goes beyond simply identifying vulnerabilities; it attempts to exploit them to demonstrate the potential impact.

- o **Risk assessment**: Evaluating the likelihood and impact of a vulnerability being exploited. This involves considering factors such as the vulnerability's severity, exploitability, and the value of the affected assets.

- **Vulnerability prioritization**: Ranking identified vulnerabilities based on their risk level. This helps organizations focus their remediation efforts on the most critical vulnerabilities first. Risk is often calculated using a combination of severity and exploitability scores, along with business impact. Effective vulnerability prioritization is essential for efficient remediation. Common strategies include:

  - o **Risk-based prioritization**: Prioritizing vulnerabilities based on their calculated risk score (e.g., CVSS score multiplied by business impact).

  - o **Exploitability-based prioritization**: Prioritizing vulnerabilities for which known exploits exist.

  - o **Asset criticality prioritization**: Prioritizing vulnerabilities affecting critical business systems and data.

  - o **Compliance-driven prioritization**: Prioritizing vulnerabilities based on regulatory requirements and compliance standards.

- **Vulnerability remediation**: The process of fixing or mitigating identified vulnerabilities. This can involve patching software, configuring systems, or implementing compensating controls. Several approaches can be used for vulnerability remediation:

  - o **Patching**: Applying software updates or patches to fix known vulnerabilities.

  - o **Configuration changes**: Modifying system or application configurations to mitigate vulnerabilities.

  - o **Compensating controls**: Implementing alternative security measures to reduce the risk of exploitation when patching or configuration changes are not feasible.

  - o **Vulnerability mitigation**: Reducing the impact of a vulnerability without completely fixing it.

  - o **Acceptance of risk**: In some cases, the cost or effort of remediation may outweigh the risk of exploitation. In such cases, the risk may be accepted, but this decision should be documented and justified.

- **Vulnerability reporting and tracking**: Documenting and tracking identified vulnerabilities, their remediation status, and any associated risks. This provides a clear overview of the organization's vulnerability posture and enables effective management of remediation efforts. The SOC plays a critical role in vulnerability management:

  o **Integrating vulnerability scan data**: The SOC integrates vulnerability scan data from various sources into the SIEM or other security information management systems.

  o **Correlating vulnerability data with security events**: The SOC correlates vulnerability data with security events to identify potential attacks that are exploiting known vulnerabilities.

  o **Prioritizing vulnerability remediation efforts**: The SOC works with IT teams to prioritize vulnerability remediation efforts based on risk and business impact.

  o **Monitoring remediation progress**: The SOC monitors the progress of vulnerability remediation efforts and tracks the status of identified vulnerabilities.

  o **Reporting on vulnerability posture**: The SOC provides regular reports on the organization's vulnerability posture to management and other stakeholders.

Challenges in vulnerability management

Several challenges can hinder effective vulnerability management, such as:

- **Vulnerability overload**: The sheer number of vulnerabilities discovered can overwhelm security teams.

- **Lack of visibility**: Limited visibility into all IT assets can make it challenging to identify all vulnerabilities.

- **Remediation complexity**: Remediation can be complex and time-consuming, especially for large and complex IT environments.

- **False positives**: Inaccurate vulnerability scan results can lead to wasted time and effort.

- **Lack of automation**: Manual vulnerability management processes can be inefficient and error prone.

Here are some best practices for vulnerability management:

- **Establish a formal vulnerability management program**: Define clear roles, responsibilities, and processes for vulnerability management.

- **Use automated scanning tools**: Automate vulnerability scanning to ensure regular and consistent coverage.

- **Prioritize vulnerabilities based on risk**: Focus remediation efforts on the most critical vulnerabilities first.

- **Develop a remediation plan**: Create a plan for remediating identified vulnerabilities, including timelines and responsibilities.

- **Track remediation progress**: Monitor the progress of remediation efforts and track the status of identified vulnerabilities.

- **Perform regular vulnerability assessments**: Conduct regular vulnerability assessments to identify new vulnerabilities and validate the effectiveness of remediation efforts.

- **Integrate vulnerability management with other security processes**: Integrate vulnerability management with incident response, change management, and other security processes.

Effective vulnerability management is a critical component of a proactive security strategy. By consistently identifying, assessing, prioritizing, and remediating vulnerabilities, organizations can significantly reduce their attack surface and minimize the risk of exploitation. The SOC plays a crucial role in coordinating and managing this process, ensuring that vulnerabilities are addressed promptly and effectively. As the threat landscape continues to evolve, a robust vulnerability management program is essential for maintaining a strong security posture.

Cyber threat hunting

While traditional security measures like firewalls, **intrusion detection systems** (**IDS**), and antivirus software provide a crucial first line of defense, they are often reactive, responding to known threats. Cyber threat hunting takes a more proactive approach, actively searching for hidden threats that have bypassed existing security controls for much-needed defense in depth.

Cyber threat hunting is a proactive and iterative process of searching for and identifying **advanced persistent threats** (**APTs**), insider threats, and other malicious activities that have evaded traditional security solutions. Unlike automated security systems that rely on predefined rules and signatures, threat hunting relies on human intuition, expertise, and a deep understanding of attacker **tactics, techniques, and procedures** (**TTPs**).

Some key characteristics of threat hunting include the following:

- **Proactive**: Threat hunting actively seeks out threats before they can cause significant damage.

- **Hypothesis-driven**: Hunters develop hypotheses about potential attack scenarios and then use various techniques to validate or disprove them.

- **Iterative**: Threat hunting is an ongoing process of searching, analyzing, and refining hypotheses.

- **Human-centric**: Threat hunting relies on the skills and expertise of security analysts.

- **Data-driven**: Threat hunters use various data sources, including logs, network traffic, and endpoint data, to identify suspicious activity.

Threat hunting process

A typical threat hunting process involves the following steps:

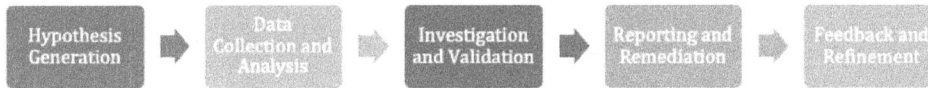

Figure 11.6: Threat hunting process

Let us understand this in detail:

- **Hypothesis generation**: The process begins with forming a hypothesis about a potential attack scenario. Hypotheses can be based on the following factors:

  o **Threat intelligence**: Information about known threat actors and their TTPs.

  o **Anomaly detection**: Identifying unusual activity that might indicate a compromise.

  o **Internal events**: Suspicious events observed within the organization's network.

  o **Industry trends**: Emerging threats and attack vectors.

- **Data collection and analysis**: Once a hypothesis is formulated, the hunter gathers relevant data from various sources, such as:

  o SIEM logs.

  o EDR data.

  o NTA data.

  o Firewall logs.

  o Threat intelligence platforms.

  The collected data is then analyzed using various techniques, such as statistical analysis, behavioral analysis, pattern matching, data visualization.

- **Investigation and validation**: If the analysis reveals suspicious activity, the hunter investigates further to confirm whether it is indeed malicious. This may involve the following:

  o Examining affected systems and endpoints.

  o Analyzing malware samples.

  o Conducting forensic analysis.

- **Reporting and remediation**: Once a threat is confirmed, the hunter reports their findings to the appropriate teams for remediation. This may involve the following:

  o Containing the threat.

  o Removing malware.

  o Patching vulnerabilities.

  o Improving security controls.

- **Feedback and refinement**: The results of the threat hunt are used to refine future hunts and improve overall security posture. This includes the following:

  o Updating threat intelligence.

  o Improving detection rules and signatures.

  o Enhancing security processes.

Threat hunting methodologies

Several methodologies are used in threat hunting. Let us look at a few of them:

- **Intelligence-driven hunting**: This approach uses threat intelligence to inform the hunting process. Hunters use information about known threat actors, their TTPs, and their targets to develop hypotheses and focus their search.

- **Anomaly-driven hunting**: This approach focuses on identifying unusual activity that deviates from established baselines. Hunters use statistical analysis and machine learning to detect anomalies in network traffic, user behavior, and system activity.

- **TTP-based hunting**: This approach focuses on identifying specific attacker TTPs, such as lateral movement, data exfiltration, or command-and-control communication. Hunters use their knowledge of attacker behavior to develop hypotheses and search for evidence of these TTPs.

Threat hunters utilize a variety of tools to support their activities:

- **SIEM**: SIEM platforms are essential for collecting, correlating, and analyzing security logs from various sources.

- **EDR**: EDR solutions provide deep visibility into endpoint activity and enable hunters to investigate suspicious processes, file activity, and network connections.

- **NTA**: NTA tools analyze network traffic patterns and identify suspicious communication.

- **Threat intelligence platforms**: These platforms provide access to threat intelligence feeds and enable hunters to research known threat actors and their TTPs.

- **Forensic tools**: These tools are used to analyze digital evidence and investigate security incidents.

- **Scripting and automation tools**: These tools are used to automate repetitive tasks and improve efficiency.

Integrating threat hunting into SOC

Integrating threat hunting into the SOC requires:

- **Dedicated threat hunting team (or function)**: While not every SOC can have a dedicated team, having personnel with the skills and time to dedicate to hunting is important. However, threat hunting requires experienced security analysts with a deep understanding of attacker TTPs and security technologies.

- **Defined processes and procedures**: Threat hunting can be a time-consuming process, requiring significant effort and resources. Establish clear processes and procedures for conducting threat hunts, including hypothesis generation, data collection, analysis, and reporting.

- **Collaboration with other teams**: Analyzing large volumes of data from various sources can be challenging. Threat hunters should collaborate closely with other SOC teams, such as incident response and vulnerability management, to share information and improve overall security posture.

- **Continuous improvement**: While threat hunting aims to reduce false positives, they can still occur. Regularly review and refine the threat hunting process based on lessons learned and evolving threats.

Cyber threat hunting is an essential component of a proactive security strategy. By actively searching for hidden threats, organizations can significantly improve their ability to detect and respond to advanced attacks. While it requires skilled personnel and dedicated resources, the benefits of threat hunting in terms of early threat detection and improved security posture make it a worthwhile investment for any organization seeking to enhance its cybersecurity defenses.

Conclusion

The technologies discussed in this chapter—SIEM, SOAR, EDR/XDR, behavioral analysis tools, vulnerability management platforms, and the methodologies of cyber threat hunting- form the technological backbone of a modern, effective SOC. They represent a shift from reactive to proactive security, enabling organizations to not only detect and respond to known threats but also to anticipate and prevent emerging ones. By effectively integrating and leveraging these tools, the SOC transforms from a simple monitoring center into a dynamic hub of threat intelligence, incident response, and continuous security improvement. This technological foundation, combined with skilled personnel and well-defined processes, enables the SOC to defend against the increasingly complex and persistent cyber threats present in today's digital landscape effectively.

In the next chapter, we will delve into building SOC infrastructure. The key components of SOC—people, process, and technology—have been covered earlier. From an implementation perspective, we will understand how hyper-converged infrastructure can aid in building an SOC. It will cover other aspects of data protection, facility management, and IAM.

Points to remember

Here are some key takeaways from this chapter:

- Log collection tools are indispensable in the operation of a SOC.

- By strategically implementing and integrating SIEM and SOAR, organizations can establish a robust and efficient SOC that is well-equipped to defend against modern cyber threats.

- By strategically implementing and integrating EDR/XDR technologies, organizations can significantly improve their ability to detect and respond to sophisticated cyber threats.

- Cyber threat hunting identifies threats that have bypassed existing security controls before they can cause significant damage, providing valuable insights into attacker TTPs that can improve incident response effectiveness.

Multiple choice questions

1. **What does SIEM stand for?**
   a. Security Integration and Event Management
   b. System Information and Event Monitoring
   c. Security Information and Event Management
   d. System Integration and Event Monitoring

2. **Which of the following is an example of a log collection source for an SIEM system?**
   a. Firewall logs
   b. Network switches
   c. Antivirus software
   d. All of the above

3. **Which of the following is not typically part of the threat hunting process?**
   a. Formulating hypothesis
   b. Investigating alerts

c. Monitoring user activity

d. Developing malware

Answers

1	c
2	d
3	d

Questions

1. Discuss the role of SOAR platforms in automating incident response and the impact it has on the efficiency of a SOC.

2. How can threat hunting improve the detection of advanced threats, and what techniques are commonly used in the process?

3. Discuss the role of vulnerability management tools in a SOC.

Key terms

Some key terms used in this chapter are:

• **SIEM/SOAR/EDR/XDR**: Key technologies in effective SOC.

• **Threat hunting**: Critical in proactive cyber defense strategy.

Join our Discord space

Join our Discord workspace for latest updates, offers, tech happenings around the world, new releases, and sessions with the authors:

https://discord.bpbonline.com

CHAPTER 12

Building Security Operations Centers Infrastructure

Introduction

As cyber threats continue to evolve in complexity and frequency, the need for a robust **security operations centers** (**SOC**) infrastructure becomes vital. From understanding what constitutes a SOC to exploring the network, compute, and storage requirements, this chapter provides a comprehensive guide to building a SOC infrastructure that can withstand the ever-evolving threat landscape. Special attention is required to facilities management, IAM, data protection, and the technology stack that collectively empower the SOC to perform its vital functions.

In 2024, a major healthcare provider experienced a data breach that compromised sensitive patient information. The attackers exploited vulnerabilities in the provider's network infrastructure, highlighting the need for a robust SOC infrastructure to detect and respond to such threats. The attackers gained access to the network through a misconfigured firewall, allowing them to exfiltrate sensitive data. The breach underscored the importance of having a well-designed SOC infrastructure with strong network, compute, and storage requirements. This incident demonstrates the critical role of a robust SOC infrastructure in protecting sensitive information. By understanding and effectively implementing the key components of a SOC, organizations can build a resilient security posture.

This chapter aims to provide a comprehensive guide to building a SOC infrastructure that can withstand the ever-evolving threat landscape. It will cover the essential components, network, compute, and storage requirements, facilities management, IAM, data protection, and the technology stack. SOC services must be accessed securely and reliably. The **confidentiality, integrity and availability (CIA)** triad needs to be ensured at all times through effective measures in physical infrastructure. Cloud hosting adds complexity to security management. Building an SOC infrastructure that encompasses all these facets is crucial for creating a robust security posture for any organization.

Structure

In this chapter, we will discuss the following topics:

- Understanding constitutes of SOC
- Network, storage and compute requirements
- Facilities management and IAM
- Data protection
- Technology stack

Objectives

By the end of this chapter, readers will be equipped with a thorough understanding of the essential elements involved in building a SOC infrastructure. Readers will comprehend the key components that constitute a SOC and their respective roles, recognize the critical network, compute, and storage requirements necessary for SOC operations, understand the importance of facilities management, IAM and how it contributes to the SOC's effectiveness, learn about data protection measures that safeguard sensitive information and ensure regulatory compliance.

Understanding constitutes of security operations centers

A SOC is the central unit within an organization critical for defense against cyber threats. It is the command center where skilled professionals and sophisticated technologies converge to detect, analyze, respond to, and mitigate security incidents. Understanding what constitutes a SOC is crucial when building SOC infrastructure. The SOC is staffed by skilled security analysts who work together to manage and improve the organization's security posture. A SOC is composed of several critical elements that work harmoniously to ensure the security and integrity of an organization's digital assets.

These components include the following:

- **Team of analysts**: As we have seen in *Chapter 9, People*, security analysts, incident responders, threat hunters, and forensic investigators, each one of these analysts plays a crucial role as mentioned here:

- o Security analysts are the front-line defenders who monitor and analyze security data to detect threats. They are responsible for responding to incidents and escalating them when necessary. For example, during a ransomware attack, security analysts would identify the malicious activity and initiate the incident response process.

- o Incident responders handle the response to security incidents, ensuring that threats are mitigated and normal operations are restored quickly.

- o Threat Hunters proactively seek out hidden threats within the organization's environment by analyzing data and identifying patterns that indicate malicious activity.

- o Forensic Investigators analyze security breaches to understand the TTPs used by attackers, providing insights to improve defenses.

- **Processes and procedures**: As we have seen in *Chapter 10, Process*, these include well-defined workflows for incident response, threat hunting, and security monitoring covering the following activities:

  - o Incident response plans are the detailed plans outlining the steps to be taken when a security incident occurs. For instance, an incident response plan might include procedures for detecting, analyzing, containing, eradicating, and recovering from a malware infection.

  - o Threat intelligence and hunting methodologies entail structured approaches for proactively searching for threats within the network.

  - o Security monitoring involves continuous monitoring of the organization's environment to identify potential security threats in real-time.

- **Technological infrastructure**: As we have seen in *Chapter 11, Technology*, SIEM systems, IDS/IPS, EDR tools, and threat intelligence platforms are important to address the threats. For example, a SIEM system might correlate firewall logs, antivirus logs, and IDS logs to detect a coordinated attack on the network.

- **Effective communication and collaboration**: These are essential for SOC operations. This includes the following:

  - o **Collaboration tools**: Secure communication channels, such as encrypted messaging apps and collaborative platforms, to facilitate information sharing among SOC personnel.

  - o **Regular training and drills**: Continuous training programs and simulated exercises to ensure SOC personnel are prepared to handle a wide range of security incidents.

Building an SOC infrastructure involves more than just acquiring the right tools and technologies. It requires a holistic approach that integrates skilled personnel, well-defined processes, robust technological infrastructure, and stringent security measures. By understanding what constitutes a SOC, organizations can establish a strong foundation for their security operations and effectively defend against evolving cyber threats.

Network, storage, compute requirements

Building a robust SOC requires careful consideration of the network, compute, and storage infrastructure. These components are the backbone of the SOC, enabling it to operate efficiently and effectively in detecting, analyzing, and responding to security threats. The essential requirements for network, compute, and storage are as follows:

- **Network requirements**: A robust network infrastructure forms the backbone of an effective SOC, enabling security monitoring, incident response, and threat hunting activities. A reliable and secure network infrastructure is critical for the smooth operation of the SOC. For example, a financial services SOC might implement dual 40 Gbps connections with automatic failover and 99.999% uptime SLAs. Key considerations for planning such a network include:

  - **Redundancy and high availability**: The network must be designed with redundancy to ensure high availability. This includes multiple network paths, redundant links, and failover mechanisms to prevent single points of failure. Minimum 1 Gbps network backbone is envisaged to handle the volume of security telemetry. Also, prioritize security monitoring traffic over standard business traffic.

  - **Network segmentation**: Implement network segmentation (e.g., security management servers, threat intelligence feeds) to isolate critical systems and reduce the attack surface. This involves creating distinct network zones for different security levels and ensuring controlled access between them. Place public-facing services in a demilitarized zone separate from internal resources. Implement *never trust, always verify* access controls regardless of location. For example, a healthcare SOC might create separate network segments for patient data systems, administrative functions, and security monitoring infrastructure.

  - **Secure connectivity**: Implement robust firewalls to control network traffic, filter out malicious packets, and protect the SOC environment from external threats. Secure connectivity options such as **Virtual Private Networks (VPNs)** are essential for remote access to the SOC. Encrypted communication channels should be used to protect data in transit. Implement jump servers for accessing critical systems. Use dedicated hardened systems for administrative access. For example, a global SOC with analysts in multiple locations might deploy regional secure access points with step-up authentication for critical systems.

  - **Bandwidth and latency**: Adequate bandwidth and low latency are necessary to support the real-time monitoring and analysis of security events. The network should be capable of handling large volumes of data between security devices, servers, and storage without performance degradation.

o **Network monitoring and visibility**: Utilize network monitoring tools to gain visibility into network traffic and detect anomalies. This includes deploying IDS and IPS to monitor and block malicious activities.

- **Storage requirements**: Effective security operations depend on comprehensive data collection and retention capabilities to support detection, investigation, and compliance needs. Adequate storage capacity is vital for retaining security data, logs, and forensic evidence. This may involve a combination of on-premises and cloud-based storage solutions. Key considerations for storage include the following:

  o **Capacity and scalability**: Choose a storage solution that can easily retain large volumes of data, typically 50-100 GB per day per 1,000 endpoints, over extended periods. Scale to accommodate growing data volumes as your organization expands, plan for 25-40% annual growth in data collection. **Network attached storage** (**NAS**), centralized storage over network, **storage area network** (**SAN**), high-performance storage network optimized for demanding applications or cloud storage services (e.g., AWS S3, Azure Blob Storage, Google Cloud Storage, OCI Cloud Storage) can be leveraged for scalability, data durability, and cost-effectiveness.

  o **Performance**: High-performance storage systems are necessary for quick access to security data. **Solid-state drives** (**SSDs**) are essential for high-performance applications like threat hunting, log analysis, and real-time threat detection as they offer significantly faster read/write speeds compared to traditional hard drives. While deciding storage, a minimum of 5,000 IOPS for active security analytics must be taken in to consideration. Tiered storage architecture like the following can be considered:

    ▪ **Hot tier**: NVMe storage for active investigations (7-30 days).

    ▪ **Warm tier**: SSD storage for recent data (30-90 days).

    ▪ **Cold tier**: HDD/object storage for historical data (90+ days).

  o **Data retention policies**: Establish data retention policies that align with regulatory requirements and organizational needs. Determine the retention periods for various types of data and ensure compliance with relevant policies. Typically, plan for a minimum of 1 year for compliance logs, 90 days for full packet capture. For example, a medium enterprise (5,000 endpoints) might need 250-500 TB storage capacity for one year of logs.

  o **Backup and recovery**: Implement robust backup and recovery solutions to protect against data loss. Regular backups should be performed, and disaster recovery plans should be in place to restore data in the event of a breach or failure. 3-2-1 backup rule (3 copies, 2 different media types, 1 offsite) must be implemented. For example, a SOC might implement daily incremental and weekly full backups with 256-bit AES encryption and an air-gapped quarterly archive.

o **Data encryption**: Ensure that all sensitive data stored within the SOC is encrypted to protect it from unauthorized access and tampering. This includes both data at rest and data in transit.

o **Cloud storage**: Consider utilizing cloud storage solutions for flexibility and scalability. Hybrid storage architectures that combine on-premises and cloud storage can provide the best of both worlds.

o **Data management**: Automated tiering, compression, and archiving must be included in data lifecycle policies. The storage must be optimized for rapid threat hunting and investigation. Mechanism must be thought to preserve relevant data for investigations from legal hold perspective. For example, implementing automatic compression of logs older than 30 days while maintaining searchability through advanced indexing can be a good data management practice.

- **Compute requirements**: The SOC requires powerful computing resources to process and analyze large volumes of security data in real time. This includes servers, workstations, and virtualized environments to support various security tools and applications. The compute infrastructure is the engine that powers the SOC, enabling it to process and analyze security data. Important factors include the following:

  o **Processing capacity**: Deploy high-performance servers with ample CPU cores, RAM to handle the demands of security analytics. Multi-core processors and large amounts of RAM are essential for real-time data processing. The compute resources envisaged are a minimum of 16-32 cores per 10,000 **events per second (EPS)**. Further, 2-4 GB RAM per 1,000 EPS must be catered for real-time analytics. For machine learning and behavioral analytics workloads, GPU acceleration is a must. For example, a large enterprise SOC processing 50,000 EPS might deploy multiple servers with 128+ CPU cores and 512GB RAM.

  o **Scalability**: The compute resources must be scalable to accommodate the growing volume of security data. This includes the ability to add more servers and virtual machines as needed.

  o **Virtualization**: Utilize virtualization technologies (e.g., VMware, KVM, Xen, Hypervisor) to create flexible and efficient compute environments. Virtual machines can be easily provisioned, managed, and scaled to meet the needs of the SOC. Use elastic infrastructure with the ability to scale resources during security incidents. Enhance security by isolating critical security functions in separate virtual environments. Containerization microservices architecture can be exploited for security tools. Orchestration for automated resource allocation can be considered based on threat levels. For example, implementing Kubernetes clusters for security analytics with automatic scaling during detected attack campaigns can be best practice.

o **Load balancing**: Implement load balancing to distribute workloads evenly across compute resources, preventing bottlenecks and ensuring optimal performance. Cater for failover clusters, i.e. N+1 or N+2 redundancy for critical systems. Geographic distribution can be planned for better resilience. For example, a SOC might implement active-active clustering across two data centers with automatic workload balancing.

o **Security hardened systems**: Ensure that all compute systems are hardened against security threats. This includes regular patching, secure configurations, and monitoring for vulnerabilities.

Integration and interoperability

Seamless integration and interoperability of network, compute, and storage components are essential for the efficient functioning of the SOC. Key issues in integration include the following:

- **Unified management**: Implement unified management platforms that provide a single pane of glass for monitoring and managing the entire SOC infrastructure.

- **Standardized protocols**: Use standardized protocols and interfaces to ensure compatibility and interoperability between different components.

- **Automation and orchestration**: Leverage automation and orchestration tools to streamline workflows, reduce manual intervention, and improve the efficiency of SOC operations.

Establishing a robust network, compute, and storage infrastructure is foundational to the success of a SOC. **Hyper-converged infrastructure (HCI)** provides reliable solutions by the service providers to effectively meet these converged requirements as a single pane for effective management. By carefully planning and implementing these requirements, organizations can establish a resilient and efficient SOC that effectively defends against the ever-evolving cyber threat landscape.

Facilities management and IAM

A robust SOC requires more than just powerful hardware and sophisticated software. Effective facilities management for a SOC goes beyond basic office space, focusing on specialized requirements for security, reliability, and operational effectiveness. Effective facility management and a robust IAM strategy are crucial for ensuring the physical and logical security of the SOC environment.

Facility management encompasses a wide range of activities aimed at creating and maintaining a safe, comfortable, and productive working environment for SOC analysts. Key aspects of facility management include:

- **Physical security**: The SOC facility must have strict physical security measures such as biometric authentication, card readers, security guards, and surveillance cameras in place to restrict unauthorized entry into the SOC. Multi-layered access control must include perimeter security with fencing and vehicle barriers. Mantrap/security airlock entrances for the most sensitive areas must be planned. Conduct regular physical security audits to identify and address potential vulnerabilities. For example, A financial sector SOC might implement fingerprint scanners for the outer perimeter, retina scanners for the SOC floor, and PIN + card for secure storage areas.

- **Surveillance systems**: The SOC facility must have 24/7 CCTV coverage with a minimum of 90-day retention. The CCTV cameras should have motion detection with automated alerts and pan-tilt-zoom capabilities covering all entry points and critical assets. For example, implementing AI-enhanced video analytics to detect suspicious behavior like tailgating or unauthorized access attempts is best practice.

- **Environmental controls**: The SOC facility must be equipped with proper **heating, ventilation, and efficient air conditioning (HVAC)** systems to prevent equipment failures and ensure uninterrupted operations. The recommended HVAC is precision cooling, maintaining temperatures in the optimal range of 68-75°F and humidity in the optimal range of 45-55%. Very early smoke detection systems must be implemented for fire suppression. A SOC might implement pre-action dry pipe systems with dual-stage alarms to prevent accidental discharge.

- **Redundancy and resilience**: The SOC facility must have reliable power supply, backup power supplies, such as **uninterruptible power supplies (UPS)** and generators, to ensure continuous operations during power outages. It must have redundant power feeds from different substations with generator backup, with a minimum 72-hour runtime. N+1 or 2N UPS configuration must be planned with automated testing and maintenance schedules. For example, a critical infrastructure SOC might implement dual power paths with automatic transfer switches and weekly generator load testing as the best practice.

A robust IAM framework is essential for SOC operations, ensuring appropriate access controls while enabling efficient security operations. It involves managing user identities, authenticating users, and authorizing access to resources based on their roles and responsibilities. Key aspects of IAM in an SOC are listed as follows:

- **User authentication, authorization**: The SOC must implement strong authentication mechanisms, such as **multi-factor authentication (MFA)**, to verify the identity of users accessing SOC resources. Define and enforce least privilege access controls, granting users only the necessary permissions to perform their job functions. Efficiently create, modify, and delete user accounts, ensuring that access rights are granted and revoked promptly.

- **Role-based access control (RBAC)**: Access to SOC systems and data must be granted based on the principle of least privilege, with role-based access controls to restrict access to only those who need it. Implement controls for managing privileged accounts, such as administrative accounts, to minimize the risk of misuse. Split administrative functions across multiple roles with four-eyes principle for critical changes. For example, implementing controls where one team member can create firewall rules while a different team member must approve and implement them.

- **Monitoring and auditing**: Continuous monitoring and auditing of access activities are essential to detect and respond to unauthorized access attempts. A data wall with various dashboards displaying KPIs can be a valuable monitoring tool. All the critical alerts can be highlighted to draw specific attention of the SOC responders.

Facility management and IAM are closely intertwined. For example, physical access control systems can be integrated with IAM systems to ensure that only authorized personnel can access the SOC. Similarly, IAM can be used to manage access to physical security systems, such as surveillance cameras and intrusion detection systems. By implementing appropriate physical security measures, maintaining a reliable infrastructure, and effectively managing user identities and access rights, organizations can significantly reduce the risk of cyberattacks and ensure the confidentiality, integrity, and availability of their critical security data.

Data protection

In the construction of a SOC, data protection is paramount. Ensuring the **confidentiality, integrity, and availability** (**CIA**) of data is critical for maintaining trust and securing sensitive information.

Key components of data protection within the SOC infrastructure include the following:

- **Encryption**: Encryption is a fundamental measure for protecting data, both in transit and at rest. By encrypting data, organizations can prevent unauthorized access and ensure that even if data is intercepted or stolen, it remains unreadable without the appropriate decryption keys.

- **Data classification**: Implementing data classification policies helps organizations categorize data based on its sensitivity and criticality. This allows for the application of tailored protection measures, ensuring that highly sensitive data receives the highest level of security. **Data loss prevention** (**DLP**) solutions help organizations detect and prevent the unauthorized transfer of sensitive data. By monitoring data flows and applying policies to block or alert on suspicious activities, DLP helps mitigate the risk of data breaches.

- **Backup and recovery**: Regular backups of critical data are crucial for ensuring business continuity in the event of a data breach, hardware failure, or other disaster. Robust disaster recovery plans must be in place to restore data quickly and minimize downtime.

- **Monitoring and auditing**: Continuous monitoring and auditing of data access and usage are vital for detecting potential security incidents. By maintaining detailed logs and conducting regular audits, organizations can identify and respond to anomalies that may indicate a breach.

- **Compliance and regulations**: Adhering to relevant data protection regulations and industry standards is essential for ensuring legal compliance and protecting the organization's reputation. This includes staying up-to-date with regulations such as the GDPR, CCPA, and other applicable laws that may impact the organization's operations.

By implementing these data protection measures, organizations can establish a secure SOC infrastructure that safeguards sensitive information, ensures regulatory compliance, and maintains the ongoing integrity and availability of critical data.

Technology stack

The technology stack forms the backbone of a SOC, providing the tools and platforms necessary for effective threat detection, analysis, and response. We have explored in detail about the technology aspect in *Chapter 11, Technology*. By integrating these technologies like SIEM/SOAR, EDR/XDR, IPS/IDS, threat intelligence platforms, log management, analysis and network monitoring tools, DLP systems into a cohesive stack, the SOC can achieve comprehensive visibility, rapid detection, and effective response to security threats. The right combination of tools and platforms ensures that the SOC is well-equipped to defend against a wide range of cyber threats, maintaining the organization's security posture and protecting critical assets.

Conclusion

Building a SOC infrastructure is a complex and multifaceted endeavor that demands a comprehensive approach. By carefully considering the core components of a SOC, i.e., personnel, processes, and technology, organizations can create a robust and resilient defense against the ever-evolving landscape of cyber threats.

Ensuring the right network, compute, and storage requirements are met is crucial for the SOC to function effectively and efficiently. Moreover, implementing stringent data protection measures safeguards sensitive information and maintains the integrity and availability of critical data. A well-designed technology stack further enhances the SOC's capabilities, enabling rapid detection, analysis, and response to threats. The success of a SOC hinges on the integration of skilled professionals, advanced technologies, and well-defined processes. By building a strong SOC infrastructure, organizations can proactively defend against cyber threats, mitigate risks, and safeguard their valuable assets, ensuring a secure and resilient operational environment.

In the next chapter, we will understand the practical implementation aspects in terms of business continuity.

Points to remember

Here are some key takeaways from this chapter:

- People, processes, and technology are crucial in building a secure, reliable SOC in mitigating the evolving cyber threats. Ensure proper network, storage and compute resources are made available with adequate access controls for building the SOC. With thorough data protection practices, the SOC can effectively defend against the evolving cyber threats that target an organization's most valuable data.

Multiple choice questions

1. **Which of the following is a key component of data protection in a SOC?**
   a. Network latency
   b. Encryption
   c. Software development
   d. Customer feedback

2. **Why is data classification important in a SOC?**
   a. To organize data alphabetically
   b. To apply appropriate protection measures based on data sensitivity and criticality
   c. To increase data storage capacity
   d. To simplify data retrieval processes

3. **What is a critical component of physical security in a SOC?**
   a. High-speed internet connection
   b. Bright interior lighting
   c. Secure entry points and access controls
   d. Comfortable seating arrangements

Answers

1	b
2	b
3	c

Questions

1. Explain the role of physical and logical security in building a SOC infrastructure.

2. Discuss the importance of data protection measures in the context of SOC operations.

3. Describe the key components of a SOC.

Key terms

Some key terms used in this chapter are:

- **Compute, storage, network, IAM, data protection**: Key elements for SOC setup

- **People, process, technology**: These are crucial in building SOC infrastructure for any organization.

- **HCI**: Converged solution for network, storage, and compute requirements in a single pane.

Join our Discord space

Join our Discord workspace for latest updates, offers, tech happenings around the world, new releases, and sessions with the authors:

https://discord.bpbonline.com

CHAPTER 13
Business Continuity

Introduction

Resilience is the cornerstone of sustained success in an increasingly interconnected and dynamic business landscape. Business continuity, as a discipline, transcends the mere restoration of operations after disruptions; it embodies a proactive approach to safeguarding organizational stability, ensuring that businesses remain functional even in the face of adversity. SOCs play a vital role in ensuring business continuity.

For **security operations centers (SOC)**, business continuity is an operational necessity with a strategic priority. A SOC is the heartbeat of an organization's cybersecurity framework, responsible for monitoring, detecting, and responding to threats. However, we must try and answer this question: *What happens when the SOC itself encounters disruptions?* The SOC must be prepared to maintain its critical functions without compromise, whether due to natural disasters, cyberattacks, or unforeseen internal challenges.

Imagine a global e-commerce company on the brink of disruption due to a sophisticated ransomware attack. As malicious encryption spreads across critical systems, threatening to halt transactions and customer access, the SOC springs into action. Leveraging real-time threat intelligence, SOC analysts detect the attack in its early stages, swiftly isolating affected endpoints and deploying automated containment measures. By proactively identifying vulnerabilities before exploitation, the SOC ensures uninterrupted business operations, preventing financial losses and reputational damage.

This chapter explores how SOC teams safeguard organizations against cyber threats, reinforcing business continuity through rapid detection, strategic mitigation, and resilient security frameworks. It further explores the principles, strategies, and best business continuity practices within the SOC ecosystem. From understanding risk assessments and crafting robust continuity plans to implementing failover systems and conducting regular drills, this chapter aims to equip organizations with the tools needed to build resilience. It emphasizes the importance of integrating business continuity into the very fabric of SOC operations, fostering a culture of preparedness that can withstand the tests of an unpredictable world. ESG concerns are increasingly becoming inescapable and important aspects of holistic BCP. This chapter also covers key aspects of ESG concerns.

Structure

In this chapter, we will discuss the following topics:

- Role of SOC in ensuring business continuity
- Proactive measures for BCP
- Employee awareness
- Balancing cybersecurity and business growth
- Audits and assessments
- Collaboration with other agencies
- ESG concerns

Objectives

By the end of this chapter, readers will get a comprehensive understanding of how to ensure the uninterrupted operation of SOC during unexpected disruptions or crises. This chapter aims to equip readers with the knowledge and tools to assess risks, design effective continuity plans, and implement strategies to sustain critical SOC functions.

 By emphasizing proactive measures, resilience-building, and adaptability, it highlights the importance of maintaining seamless security operations even amidst adverse conditions. Ultimately, the chapter aims to foster a culture of preparedness within SOC environments, enabling organizations to continue protecting their assets and responding to threats effectively, regardless of the challenges they face.

Role of SOC in ensuring business continuity

Organizations today are more prone to threats that can disrupt their operations. From cyberattacks and natural disasters to technical failures and human errors, maintaining business continuity has become an operational necessity rather than a luxury. At the heart of an organization's resilience strategy lies the SOC, a critical entity responsible for safeguarding the organization's digital assets and ensuring uninterrupted operations during crises.

The primary mission of a SOC is to monitor, detect, analyze, and respond to cybersecurity threats in real time. While this reactive approach forms the cornerstone of SOC operations, its role in business continuity extends far beyond traditional cybersecurity tasks. A well-structured SOC serves as a proactive defense mechanism, identifying vulnerabilities and mitigating risks before they escalate into significant disruptions. It ensures that critical business functions remain operational, even in the face of unforeseen adversities.

A SOC's involvement in business continuity planning begins with comprehensive risk assessments. By identifying potential threats, ranging from cyberattacks to physical disasters, the SOC provides valuable insights into the organization's risk landscape. These assessments inform the development of robust **business continuity plans** (**BCP**) that outline procedures for maintaining essential operations during and after a crisis.

The core functions of SOC in business continuity are mentioned as follows:

- **Risk identification and management**: The SOC continuously analyzes internal and external environments to identify potential risks. Using advanced tools and threat intelligence, it predicts and prepares for scenarios that could impact business operations.

- **Incident response and recovery**: In the event of an incident, the SOC is the first line of defense. Its incident response capabilities ensure that threats are contained and neutralized swiftly, minimizing downtime and preventing further damage.

- **Data protection and availability**: Ensuring the security and availability of data is a critical aspect of business continuity. The SOC implements robust measures such as encryption, backup solutions, and access controls to protect sensitive information and ensure its availability when needed.

- **Disaster recovery support**: The SOC plays a vital role in disaster recovery efforts by monitoring the restoration process, ensuring that systems are brought back online securely, and verifying the integrity of recovered data.

- **Communication and coordination**: During a crisis, the SOC acts as a hub for communication and coordination. It collaborates with other departments, stakeholders, and external partners to ensure a unified response to disruptions.

- **Monitoring and reporting**: The SOC continuously monitors critical systems and provides real-time updates on the operational status. Its reporting capabilities enable decision-makers to make informed choices during emergencies.

The SOC's role in business continuity extends beyond crisis management to include building long-term resilience. By fostering a culture of vigilance and preparedness, the SOC ensures that the organization is not only equipped to handle current threats but also adaptable to future challenges. Moreover, the SOC's integration with business continuity planning enhances its effectiveness. Collaborative efforts between the SOC and other departments ensure that continuity plans are comprehensive and aligned with organizational goals. For example, the SOC can work with IT teams to implement failover systems or with human resources to establish protocols for employee safety during emergencies.

The SOC also contributes to regulatory compliance by adhering to industry standards and legal requirements for data protection and operational continuity. Compliance protects the organization from legal repercussions and strengthens stakeholder trust.

While the SOC is critical in ensuring business continuity, it has challenges. Resource constraints, evolving threat landscapes, and the complexity of modern IT environments can hinder its effectiveness. However, these challenges also present opportunities for innovation. By leveraging advanced technologies such as artificial intelligence, machine learning, and automation, SOCs can enhance their capabilities and stay ahead of emerging threats.

Business continuity and disaster recovery are closely related concepts, often considered one concept; yet they serve distinct purposes within an organization. Business continuity focuses on ensuring that critical business operations can continue seamlessly during and after a disruption, encompassing strategies to maintain essential services like customer support, supply chain management, and overall operations.

On the other hand, disaster recovery explicitly addresses the restoration of IT systems, data, and infrastructure following an incident, such as a cyberattack or natural disaster. While disaster recovery is a key component of business continuity, the latter takes a more holistic approach, considering not just technology but also personnel, processes, and communication. Together, these practices ensure resilience, minimize downtime, and safeguard an organization's ability to thrive in unexpected challenges.

Proactive measures for BCP

BCP is vital for ensuring that organizations can withstand and recover from disruptions. While reactive measures focus on responding to incidents after they occur, proactive measures aim to identify and mitigate risks before they escalate, safeguarding operations and minimizing the likelihood of disruptions. In the context of SOC, proactive measures are significant given the critical role the SOC plays in maintaining organizational security.

Disruptions to SOC operations can have far-reaching consequences, affecting the entire organization. Proactive measures are designed to anticipate potential threats, evaluate vulnerabilities, and implement safeguards. By addressing risks before they materialize, the SOC not only ensures its own continuity but also supports the organization's broader business continuity objectives.

Proactive measures are rooted in a preventive mindset, emphasizing preparedness and vigilance. These measures align with the SOC's overarching mission of risk management and threat mitigation, reinforcing its ability to maintain seamless operations under any circumstances.

Key proactive measures for BCP in the SOC are:

- Comprehensive risk assessments constitute the first step in the planning. Important elements in this process are:

  o Proactive BCP begins with identifying and understanding potential risks to SOC operations.

  o Risk assessments should consider various scenarios, including cyberattacks, natural disasters, equipment failures, and human errors.

  o Tools such as vulnerability scans, threat intelligence, and penetration testing can help identify weak points in the SOC's infrastructure.

  This foundational step allows the SOC to understand potential threats specific to its operations and the organization, enabling it to prioritize safeguards effectively. A well-executed risk assessment can be the difference between a minor security event and a full-scale crisis. Take, for example, a financial institution that proactively conducted penetration testing on its SOC infrastructure. During the test, ethical hackers uncovered a misconfigured firewall rule, which could have allowed attackers to bypass security controls and access sensitive transaction data. By identifying this vulnerability early, the SOC team swiftly patched the misconfiguration, preventing a potential breach that could have led to financial fraud and reputational damage. Similarly, a cloud service provider leveraged threat intelligence to detect an emerging zero-day exploit targeting its authentication systems. By analyzing attack patterns and implementing preemptive security measures, the SOC successfully mitigated the risk before adversaries could exploit it. These examples underscore the importance of proactive risk assessments, ensuring SOC teams stay ahead of evolving threats and maintain operational resilience.

- Redundancy and failover systems follow the risk assessments. Key measures include the following:

  o Establishing redundancy in critical systems is essential to ensure continuous operation.

  o Failover systems, such as secondary data centers or backup servers, can be activated seamlessly in case of primary system failure.

  o Regular testing of these systems ensures their effectiveness when needed.

  For example, when a major financial institution experienced a sudden server failure during peak transaction hours, the primary system, responsible for processing millions of transactions, unexpectedly went offline due to a hardware malfunction. However, thanks to a redundant failover system, operations seamlessly transitioned to a backup server within seconds, ensuring uninterrupted service. Customers remained unaware of the issue, and financial transactions continued without disruption. This proactive measure not only prevented revenue loss but also reinforced trust in the institution's reliability. Such failover strategies are critical in maintaining business continuity, minimizing downtime, and safeguarding against unexpected failures.

- The next steps constitute data backup and recovery planning. Key measures include the following:

  o   Regular data backups are a cornerstone of proactive BCP.

  o   The SOC should implement automated backup schedules and ensure that backups are stored in secure, offsite locations.

  o   A well-defined data recovery plan ensures quick restoration of operations in case of data loss or corruption.

A well-structured data backup and recovery plan can be the difference between a minor inconvenience and a catastrophic business disruption. Consider a healthcare provider that suffered a ransomware attack, encrypting patient records and operational data. Because the SOC had automated daily backups stored securely offsite, they swiftly restored critical systems without paying the ransom, ensuring uninterrupted patient care. Similarly, a financial institution experienced a sudden database corruption due to a software failure. Thanks to a well-defined recovery plan, SOC analysts quickly identified the latest clean backup and restored operations within hours, preventing transaction failures and customer dissatisfaction. These examples highlight the importance of proactive backup strategies, ensuring resilience against cyber threats and system failures.

- Next important aspect is patch management and system updates, which entails the following:

  o   Keeping systems and software up to date is a proactive measure to prevent vulnerabilities.

  o   The SOC should have a robust patch management process in place to address security flaws promptly.

  o   Regular system audits help identify outdated or unsupported technologies that may pose risks.

A well-structured patch management process can be the difference between a secure system and a major breach. Consider a financial institution that failed to update a critical server, leaving it vulnerable to a known exploit. Attackers leveraged this weakness to gain unauthorized access, leading to data theft and financial losses. Had the SOC implemented timely patching, the breach could have been prevented. In contrast, a healthcare provider proactively conducted regular system audits, identifying outdated software that lacked security updates. By replacing unsupported technologies and enforcing automated patch deployment, they mitigated potential vulnerabilities, ensuring patient data remained secure. These examples highlight the importance of patch management and system updates in maintaining cybersecurity resilience.

- Physical security enhancements further contribute to effective BCP. Key measures include the following:

  o The SOC's physical premises should be safeguarded against unauthorized access and environmental threats.

  o Measures such as access controls, surveillance systems, and climate control solutions contribute to operational continuity.

  o Physical security audits can help identify and address potential vulnerabilities.

A well-implemented physical security strategy can prevent disruptions that might otherwise compromise SOC operations. For instance, a data center housing critical SOC infrastructure faced an attempted unauthorized entry when an individual tried to bypass security checkpoints. Thanks to biometric access controls and 24/7 surveillance, security personnel swiftly identified and neutralized the threat before any damage occurred. Similarly, a financial institution experienced a server overheating issue due to a malfunctioning cooling system. Because the SOC had climate control solutions in place, automated alerts triggered immediate intervention, preventing hardware failure and ensuring uninterrupted operations. These examples highlight the importance of physical security enhancements in maintaining business continuity and safeguarding critical assets.

- A skilled and versatile workforce is critical for SOC continuity. Another key measure is the workforce cross-training and succession planning which can be achieved through the following:

  o Cross-training SOC staff in multiple roles ensures that operations can continue even if key personnel are unavailable.

  o Succession planning identifies backup staff for critical positions, reducing dependency on individual team members.

A well-executed cross-training strategy ensures SOC operations remain resilient even when key personnel are unavailable. For instance, a financial institution faced a sudden staffing shortage when a senior threat analyst unexpectedly left. Because junior analysts had been cross-trained in threat intelligence workflows, they seamlessly took over critical tasks, preventing disruptions in incident detection and response. Similarly, a technology firm implemented succession planning by identifying backup staff for key SOC roles. When a lead forensic investigator transitioned to another department, a trained successor stepped in without delays, ensuring ongoing investigations remained uninterrupted. These proactive measures strengthen SOC continuity, minimizing operational risks and maintaining security effectiveness.

- Incident simulation and drills further adds to maintaining currency. These measures entail the following:
  - Conducting regular incident simulation exercises prepares the SOC for real-world disruptions.
  - Simulations can include scenarios such as ransomware attacks, power outages, or communication breakdowns.
  - Lessons learned from these exercises should be incorporated into the SOC's BCP to enhance preparedness.

Think of these as fire drills for the cybersecurity world. By practicing responses to various scenarios, the SOC team becomes better prepared and more efficient when a real incident occurs, minimizing potential downtime. Conducting incident simulations helps SOC teams stay prepared for real-world cyber threats and operational disruptions. For instance, a ransomware drill at a financial institution tested analysts' ability to contain and mitigate an encryption attack on customer databases. The exercise exposed weaknesses in communication and escalation protocols, leading to refinements that improved coordination during actual security incidents. Similarly, a power outage simulation at a technology firm assessed how well SOC operations could continue under infrastructure failures. The drill revealed gaps in backup power and failover systems, prompting enhancements to prevent downtime. These proactive simulations ensure SOC teams remain resilient, strengthening response strategies and minimizing operational risks.

- Third-party vendor management has evolved into a critical aspect of BCP. This is crucial due to the following reasons:
  - Many SOCs rely on external vendors for tools, services, or support.
  - Proactively assessing and managing vendor risks ensures that third-party dependencies do not become single points of failure.
  - Vendor agreements should include provisions for continuity support during disruptions.

Managing third-party vendors is essential for maintaining SOC resilience, as external dependencies can introduce operational risks. For example, a financial institution relied on a third-party cloud security provider for monitoring threats. When the provider experienced an unexpected service interruption, SOC operations were briefly affected. However, due to pre-established contingency agreements, the vendor swiftly deployed a backup system, ensuring uninterrupted security monitoring. Similarly, a technology firm performed vendor risk assessments and discovered that a critical endpoint security provider had delayed patching for emerging vulnerabilities. By renegotiating service contracts to enforce timely security updates, the firm safeguarded its SOC against potential threats. These scenarios highlight the importance of vendor risk management, helping organizations mitigate vulnerabilities and ensure continuity in security operations.

Implementing proactive measures requires a holistic approach that integrates BCP into the SOC's daily operations. This involves fostering a culture of preparedness, where every team member understands the importance of continuity planning and their role in achieving it. Collaboration across departments is also crucial, as the SOC must align its continuity strategies with the organization's broader BCP efforts.

Regular reviews and updates to the BCP ensure its relevance in the face of evolving threats and organizational changes. Proactive measures should be seen as an ongoing effort with continuous monitoring, testing, and refinement. Adopting proactive measures for BCP in the SOC offers numerous benefits, like reduced downtime, enhanced security posture, improved stakeholder confidence, and significant cost savings. From comprehensive risk assessments to cross-training staff and testing failover systems, these measures empower the SOC to confidently navigate uncertainties.

Employee awareness

In the intricate ecosystem of SOC, advanced technologies and robust processes play a significant role in ensuring business continuity. However, one often-overlooked yet vital element of resilience lies in the people, the employees, who form the backbone of any organization. Employee awareness is the linchpin of a successful BCP. Without the understanding, involvement, and cooperation of staff, even the most meticulously designed continuity strategies can falter.

Imagine a well-meaning SOC analyst receiving an email that appears to be from a trusted vendor, requesting urgent access to internal systems. Without adequate security awareness training, they click the link and unknowingly provide credentials to an attacker. Within minutes, the adversary gains access to sensitive SOC infrastructure, bypassing defenses and escalating privileges. This seemingly small mistake jeopardizes incident response capabilities, disrupts monitoring operations, and exposes critical data to exploitation.

To prevent such incidents, organizations must implement continuous security awareness programs, including phishing simulations, role-based training, and real-time threat intelligence briefings. By reinforcing employee vigilance, SOC teams can proactively identify deceptive tactics, reducing the risk of human error and strengthening overall business continuity. Investing in structured awareness initiatives ensures that personnel remain the first line of defense against evolving cyber threats.

A SOC functions as a highly interconnected unit, requiring every team member to be aligned with its goals and procedures. Business continuity in this environment is not solely the responsibility of leadership or IT personnel; it is a collective effort that requires the active participation of all employees.

Here are some key reasons why employee awareness is indispensable:

- When employees are aware of potential risks and continuity protocols, they are better equipped to respond swiftly and effectively during disruptions. This reduces downtime and mitigates the impact of incidents.

- Lack of awareness can lead to mistakes that exacerbate crises. Educated employees are less likely to compromise operations or deviate from continuity procedures inadvertently.

- An informed workforce contributes to a culture of resilience, where proactive thinking and problem-solving become second nature.

- Awareness fosters coordination and clarity, ensuring that employees understand their roles and responsibilities during a crisis, thereby minimizing confusion and delays.

Some strategies for building employee awareness are listed here. Let us look at them:

- Comprehensive training programs create a conducive environment for better awareness. Key measures include:

  o Conduct regular training sessions focused on business continuity concepts, the SOC's continuity plan, and employees' roles during disruptions.

  o Include hands-on exercises, such as disaster simulations and tabletop exercises, to reinforce learning.

  o Tailor training to specific roles, ensuring that each employee understands their unique responsibilities.

- Clear and accessible documentation creates a robust environment for effective training programs. It essentially helps in:

  o Providing employees with concise and easy-to-understand documentation outlining the SOC's continuity plan.

  o Ensuring the information is readily accessible, whether through a centralized portal or printed materials.

  o Using visual aids, such as flowcharts and checklists, to simplify complex processes.

- Regular communication and updates ensure the currency of employees. This entails:

  o Keeping employees informed about updates to the continuity plan or changes in protocols.

  o Using multiple channels, such as emails, newsletters, and team meetings, to communicate effectively.

  o Encouraging open dialogue, allowing employees to ask questions and provide feedback.

- Leadership engagement and advocacy aid in creating a supportive environment. Here are some points to keep in mind while focusing on leadership:

- o Leadership should actively promote the importance of BCP awareness, setting an example for the rest of the organization.

- o Managers and team leads should reinforce continuity principles in day-to-day interactions with employees.

- Incentives and recognition play a vital role in the continuation of the training efforts. This can be achieved through the following measures:

  - o Recognize and reward employees who demonstrate exceptional commitment to BCP awareness and preparedness.

  - o Offer incentives for completing training programs or participating in exercises, fostering enthusiasm and engagement.

- Regular testing and drills keep the momentum in BCP efforts. This can be achieved through the following measures:

  - o Conduct periodic drills to evaluate employees' understanding of continuity procedures.

  - o Use these exercises to identify gaps in awareness and address them through targeted interventions.

- Periodic awareness campaigns ensure that employees are never out of sync with the situation. This can be achieved through the following measures:

  - o Launch campaigns to promote continuity awareness utilizing posters, videos, and newsletters to effectively convey key messages.

  - o Incorporate themes and slogans that resonate with employees, making the concept of continuity relatable and memorable.

While fostering awareness is crucial, it is not without challenges. Common obstacles include employee resistance to change, lack of time for training, and information overload.

To overcome these barriers, we can implement the following measures:

- Emphasize the practical benefits of awareness, showing employees how it directly impacts their roles and the organization's success.

- Integrate continuity concepts into existing workflows, making training and communication less intrusive.

- Use engaging and interactive training methods, such as gamification or scenario-based learning, to capture employees' interest.

Employee awareness is the bedrock of an effective BCP in SOC. By investing in education, communication, and engagement, organizations can cultivate a workforce that is not only prepared to respond to disruptions but also contributes to a culture of resilience and vigilance.

Balancing cybersecurity and business growth

In the modern business ecosystem, organizations are under increasing pressure to achieve rapid growth, embrace innovation, and adopt cutting-edge technologies. However, this pursuit of progress often introduces new vulnerabilities and risks, making cybersecurity a critical priority. For SOC, the challenge lies in striking the right balance between enabling business growth and maintaining a robust cybersecurity posture. This balance is not a zero-sum game; with the right strategies, organizations can achieve both goals in harmony.

Cybersecurity and business growth are inherently interconnected. While strong cybersecurity practices safeguard the organization against potential threats, they also create a foundation of trust for customers, partners, and stakeholders. On the other hand, business growth initiatives, such as digital transformation and global expansion, often expose organizations to new attack vectors.

The SOC plays a pivotal role in navigating this complex relationship. By integrating cybersecurity into business strategies, the SOC ensures that growth does not come at the expense of security. Conversely, by aligning its operations with business objectives, the SOC supports innovation and competitiveness.

Some of the challenges one might face in balancing cybersecurity and growth are listed here:

- **Rapid technological advancements**: The adoption of emerging technologies, such as cloud computing, IoT, and artificial intelligence, introduces new risks that the SOC must address. The pace of technological change often outstrips the development of cybersecurity measures, creating a gap that can be exploited by adversaries.

- **Resource constraints**: Balancing cybersecurity and growth requires significant investment in tools, talent, and infrastructure. Limited budgets or competing priorities can hinder the SOC's ability to fully address both objectives.

- **Evolving threat landscape**: As businesses grow, they become more attractive targets for cybercriminals. The SOC must constantly adapt to new and sophisticated attack methods, requiring agility and vigilance.

- **Cultural resistance**: Employees and leadership may view cybersecurity measures as obstacles to growth, leading to resistance or non-compliance. Bridging this gap requires effective communication and education.

- **Alert fatigue:** One of the most pressing concerns is alert fatigue, where analysts struggle to sift through a relentless flood of security notifications. This constant barrage increases the likelihood of critical alerts being overlooked, potentially exposing the organization to undetected threats.

To overcome these challenges, here are some key strategies for achieving balance:

- **Integrating cybersecurity into business planning**: Cybersecurity should be a core component of business planning and decision-making processes. The SOC must work closely with leadership and other departments to align security objectives with business goals.

- **Risk-based approach**: Not all risks are equal; the SOC should prioritize efforts based on the potential impact and likelihood of threats. This approach ensures that resources are allocated effectively, addressing the most critical risks first.

- **Implementing scalable security solutions**: As businesses grow, their cybersecurity needs evolve. The SOC should adopt scalable and flexible solutions that can adapt to changing requirements without hindering growth.

- **Promoting a security-first culture**: A culture of security awareness and accountability is essential for balancing growth and cybersecurity. The SOC should lead efforts to educate employees about best practices and the importance of security in achieving business objectives.

- **Leveraging automation and innovation**: Automation can help the SOC streamline operations, reduce manual workload, and respond to threats more efficiently. Investing in innovative tools and technologies enables the SOC to stay ahead of emerging threats while supporting business growth. By automating routine tasks, the SOC can free up analysts to focus on more critical issues, effectively doing more with the same or fewer resources.

- **Building strategic partnerships**: Collaboration with trusted vendors, industry peers, and government agencies can enhance the SOC's capabilities. Sharing threat intelligence and best practices strengthens the organization's overall security posture.

- **Implement intelligent alert prioritization**: Leveraging machine learning-driven filtering and automated correlation to reduce false positives. By refining alert accuracy, analysts can devote their attention to genuine security incidents, improving response times, and overall operational effectiveness.

- **Align security metrics with business KPIs**: Demonstrate the value of cybersecurity by linking its impact to KPIs that matter to the business.

- **Adopt agile methodologies**: Use agile practices to ensure that security initiatives are implemented quickly and effectively, keeping pace with business demands.

- **Conduct continuous monitoring and improvement**: Regularly assess the effectiveness of security measures and adjust strategies to address new challenges.

- **Focus on customer trust**: Strong cybersecurity practices enhance customer confidence, a critical driver of business growth.

By adopting a proactive, collaborative, and strategic approach, the SOC can help organizations thrive in a competitive and rapidly evolving environment while maintaining a robust security posture. Ultimately, integrating cybersecurity into the fabric of business growth is not just a necessity; it is a competitive advantage.

Audits and assessments

Business continuity planning is not static; it requires continuous validation, improvement, and adaptation to evolving risks and operational dynamics. In the context of SOCs, audits and assessments play a critical role in ensuring the robustness and effectiveness of business continuity strategies. These processes identify gaps and vulnerabilities and provide actionable insights to strengthen the SOC's readiness to handle disruptions.

Audits and assessments are essential for ensuring that SOCs remain resilient against disruptions. Each type of audit serves a distinct purpose, uncovering vulnerabilities that could impact business continuity. Let us look at some specific examples:

- **Compliance audits**: A financial institution undergoes a compliance audit and discovers that its incident response documentation is outdated, leading to potential regulatory violations. As a result, the SOC updates its protocols to align with the latest industry standards, ensuring adherence to legal requirements.

- **Penetration testing**: A technology firm performs a penetration test and finds that its privileged access management system has weak authentication controls. This insight prompts the SOC to enforce multi-factor authentication, reducing the risk of unauthorized access.

- **Operational audits**: A retail company's SOC conducts an operational audit and discovers inefficiencies in alert triage workflows, causing delays in incident response. By optimizing automation and refining escalation procedures, the SOC improves response times and minimizes downtime.

Audits and assessments are integral to maintaining the integrity of business continuity planning. They serve as mechanisms to evaluate the effectiveness of continuity measures, ensuring that the SOC is prepared to manage crises with minimal operational impact.

Key stages in audits and assessments include the following:

- **Validation of plans and protocols**: Audits verify that the SOC's BCP aligns with industry standards, regulatory requirements, and organizational goals. Assessments ensure the plan remains relevant to the SOC's current risk landscape and operational priorities.

- **Identification of gaps and weaknesses**: By scrutinizing existing measures, audits, and assessments highlight vulnerabilities that may compromise the SOC's ability to respond to disruptions. These findings inform targeted improvements to address identified deficiencies.

- **Performance measurement**: Assessments evaluate the effectiveness of continuity strategies, such as response times, recovery capabilities, and employee readiness. Metrics and KPIs derived from these evaluations provide a basis for continuous improvement.

- **Regulatory and compliance assurance**: Regular audits ensure that the SOC adheres to legal and industry-specific requirements related to business continuity and cybersecurity. Compliance audits demonstrate accountability and build trust with stakeholders.

Types of audits and assessments

Audits and assessments for SOC business continuity are shown in the following figure:

Figure 13.1: Audits and assessments for BCP in SOC

Different audits and assessments are crucial for ensuring BCP. Some of the audits and assessments are mentioned here:

- **Internal audits**: These are conducted by the organization itself; internal audits focus on evaluating the SOC's adherence to its own business continuity protocols. These audits are often more flexible and can be customized to address specific concerns or objectives. For example, during an internal audit, a financial institution discovered that its incident response playbooks were outdated, leading to inconsistencies in escalation procedures. This finding prompted a revision of response workflows, ensuring analysts followed standardized protocols during security incidents. Similarly, a technology firm conducted an internal audit and identified gaps in backup testing procedures—while backups were regularly created, they had never been tested for integrity. As a result, the SOC implemented routine recovery drills, ensuring that backups could be restored efficiently in case of a cyberattack or system failure.

- **External audits**: These are performed by independent third parties; external audits provide an objective evaluation of the SOC's continuity measures. External auditors may use established frameworks, such as ISO 22301 (business continuity management), or NIST SP 800-34, SOC2, as benchmarks. For instance, a SOC 2 audit conducted on a cloud service provider uncovered gaps in encryption protocols used to protect customer data. In response, the provider enhanced its security framework by implementing stronger encryption standards, reinforcing data protection, and ensuring regulatory compliance. Similarly, an ISO 22301 audit at a financial institution exposed insufficient redundancy in disaster recovery planning, leaving critical systems vulnerable during disruptions. To mitigate this risk, the organization strengthened its failover mechanisms, ensuring operational continuity even in the event of infrastructure failures.

- **Risk assessments**: These assessments identify potential threats to the SOC's operations, such as cyberattacks, natural disasters, or hardware failures. They prioritize risks based on likelihood and impact, enabling the SOC to focus its resources on the most critical areas. For instance, a healthcare provider conducts a risk assessment and identifies that its backup data storage is located in the same geographic region as its primary servers. This poses a risk in case of natural disasters. The SOC implements geo-redundant backups, ensuring data availability even in catastrophic events.

- **Gap analyses**: Gap analyses compare the SOC's current continuity practices against best practices, standards, or organizational goals. They identify discrepancies and provide recommendations for bridging these gaps. For instance, a gap analysis might reveal that the SOC's current data backup procedures do not meet the industry best practice of having an air-gapped offline backup, highlighting a critical vulnerability.

- **Business impact analyses (BIA)**: A BIA evaluates the potential consequences of disruptions on the SOC's operations and the broader organization. It identifies critical functions and resources, informing the development of priority-focused continuity strategies. A BIA might determine that the SOC's SIEM system is a mission-critical function, and any downtime would severely impact the organization's ability to detect and respond to threats, thus emphasizing the need for robust redundancy for this system.

- **Simulation exercises and drills**: These assessments test the SOC's readiness to handle real-world disruptions. Scenarios such as ransomware attacks, power outages, or communication breakdowns are simulated to evaluate response effectiveness.

By integrating these audits and assessments into the business continuity lifecycle, the SOC achieves enhanced preparedness, informed decision making, regulatory compliance, and stakeholder confidence. Audits and assessments are not merely checkpoints in the business continuity planning process; they are critical enablers of resilience and readiness within the SOC. By systematically evaluating and improving continuity measures, these processes ensure that the SOC can withstand disruptions and continue to safeguard the organization's operations.

Collaboration with other agencies

In the realm of business continuity, no organization operates in isolation. The complexity and interconnectedness of today's digital and physical landscapes demand a collaborative approach to building resilience. For SOC, collaboration with external agencies, such as law enforcement, government bodies, industry organizations, and third-party service providers, is crucial in ensuring the success of business continuity strategies. These partnerships enhance the SOC's ability to anticipate, mitigate, and respond to disruptions effectively. Collaboration with external agencies brings unique advantages to the SOC's business continuity efforts.

These benefits include the following:

- **Access to expertise and resources**: External agencies often possess specialized knowledge, tools, and experience that complement the SOC's internal capabilities. Collaboration provides access to resources such as threat intelligence, technical expertise, and crisis management frameworks.

- **Enhanced situational awareness**: Partnering with agencies allows the SOC to stay informed about emerging threats, trends, and best practices. This situational awareness strengthens the SOC's ability to anticipate and prepare for potential disruptions.

- **Shared responsibility**: Collaboration ensures that responsibilities for managing and mitigating risks are distributed across multiple stakeholders. This shared approach reduces the burden on the SOC and enhances overall resilience.

- **Regulatory compliance and support**: Government and regulatory agencies can provide guidance on compliance requirements and industry standards. Collaboration ensures that the SOC meets legal and regulatory expectations, reducing the risk of penalties or reputational damage.

Consider a scenario where a financial institution detects unusual network activity indicative of a nation-state cyberattack. The SOC quickly escalates the incident to law enforcement and government cybersecurity agencies, enabling access to classified threat intelligence and advanced forensic capabilities.

Through this partnership, the SOC gains insights into attack attribution, allowing analysts to refine detection rules and implement countermeasures before the threat escalates. Additionally, government agencies provide legal guidance on handling sensitive data breaches, ensuring compliance with regulatory frameworks. This collaboration not only mitigates immediate risks but also enhances the SOC's ability to anticipate future threats, reinforcing business continuity strategies.

Agencies involved in SOC collaboration

The agencies involved in the collaboration are diverse. These agencies are critical to the effective BCP in security operations.

These are the agencies involved:

- **Government and regulatory bodies**: Agencies such as national cybersecurity centers or data protection authorities provide guidance on regulatory compliance and cybersecurity best practices. Partnerships with these entities ensure that the SOC aligns with legal requirements and benefits from governmental support during crises. Collaboration with government and regulatory bodies strengthens SOC resilience by ensuring compliance with legal frameworks and leveraging governmental support during crises. Consider a scenario where a financial institution detects signs of a nation-state cyberattack targeting its payment processing systems. The SOC immediately escalates the incident to the national cybersecurity center, which provides classified threat intelligence on the attacker's TTPs. With this intelligence, the SOC refines its detection rules, blocking further intrusion attempts while coordinating with data protection authorities to ensure compliance with breach notification laws. Additionally, government agencies assist in forensic analysis, helping attribute the attack and advising on legal countermeasures. This collaboration not only mitigates immediate risks but also strengthens the institution's long-term security posture, ensuring business continuity and regulatory adherence.

- **Law enforcement agencies**: Collaboration with law enforcement is critical in investigating and responding to cyberattacks, particularly in cases involving criminal activities. Law enforcement agencies can assist in tracing attackers, gathering evidence, and prosecuting perpetrators. Imagine the SOC detecting a large-scale data breach. By immediately collaborating with law enforcement, they can gain access to specialized forensic expertise and legal guidance on how to proceed with the investigation and potential prosecution of the attackers, which is beyond the typical capabilities of the SOC alone.

- **Industry organizations and forums**: Industry groups, such as ISAC, facilitate the exchange of threat intelligence and best practices among peers. Participation in these forums enhances the SOC's understanding of industry-specific risks and solutions. Consider a scenario where a global financial institution detects a new strain of malware targeting its payment processing systems. The SOC analysts, unsure of the malware's full capabilities, share their findings with an ISAC specializing in financial sector cybersecurity. Within hours, peer organizations contribute real-time intelligence, revealing that the malware has been observed in multiple attacks across different institutions. Armed with this collective knowledge, the SOC refines its detection rules, implements proactive mitigation strategies, and alerts other financial entities to prevent further infections. This collaboration not only strengthens the institution's defenses but also enhances industry-wide resilience, ensuring that organizations can collectively respond to emerging threats more effectively.

- **Third-party service providers: Managed security service providers (MSSPs)**, cloud providers, and technology vendors play a key role in supporting SOC operations. Collaboration ensures that these third parties align with the SOC's business continuity objectives and provide reliable support during disruptions. Consider a scenario where a financial institution relies on a MSSP for 24/7 threat monitoring. One evening, the MSSP detects an anomalous spike in network traffic, indicating a potential DDoS attack targeting the institution's online banking platform. Thanks to real-time threat intelligence sharing, the MSSP immediately alerts the SOC, allowing analysts to activate mitigation protocols, reroute traffic, and deploy rate-limiting measures to prevent service downtime. Meanwhile, the cloud provider supporting the institution's infrastructure scales up server capacity, ensuring uninterrupted access for customers. This seamless coordination between the SOC and its third-party partners not only neutralizes the attack but also reinforces business continuity, preventing financial losses and reputational damage. Such strategic partnerships ensure that SOC teams can leverage external expertise, advanced technologies, and scalable solutions to maintain security effectiveness.

- **Emergency response agencies**: Agencies such as disaster response teams or emergency management authorities provide critical support during natural disasters or large-scale crises. These partnerships enhance the SOC's ability to coordinate recovery efforts and minimize operational downtime. Collaboration with emergency response agencies is crucial for ensuring SOC resilience during large-scale crises. Consider a scenario where a data center supporting critical financial transactions is impacted by a natural disaster, such as severe flooding. As water levels rise, power systems fail, threatening to disrupt banking operations nationwide. The SOC immediately activates its business continuity plan, coordinating with emergency management authorities to secure backup power and relocate essential personnel. Disaster response teams assist in physical infrastructure protection, ensuring that critical servers remain operational. Meanwhile, emergency agencies provide real-time situational updates, allowing the SOC to adjust its mitigation strategies accordingly. Thanks to this collaborative effort, financial services remain uninterrupted, preventing economic disruptions and ensuring customer trust. This example highlights how proactive coordination with emergency response agencies strengthens SOC resilience, enabling swift recovery and minimizing downtime during crises.

Here are some strategies for effective collaboration with all relevant stakeholders:

- Define protocols for sharing information and coordinating actions with external agencies. Use secure and reliable communication tools to facilitate real-time collaboration.

- Develop strong working relationships with key stakeholders through regular engagement and collaboration on joint initiatives. Trust is essential for sharing sensitive information, such as threat intelligence or incident details.

- Document partnerships through **memorandums of understanding** (MOUs), **service-level agreements** (SLAs), or contracts. Clearly define the roles, responsibilities, and expectations of each agency involved.

- Conduct collaborative simulation exercises to test response capabilities and identify areas for improvement. These exercises build familiarity and coordination among all stakeholders.

- Collaborate with agencies to pool resources, such as threat intelligence platforms, incident response tools, or training programs. Shared resources reduce duplication of effort and enhance overall efficiency.

- Schedule periodic meetings or briefings with external agencies to discuss developments, share updates, and review collaborative strategies. Ongoing engagement ensures that partnerships remain active and relevant.

These partnerships bring valuable expertise, resources, and support that enhance the SOC's ability to manage risks and recover from disruptions. By fostering strong relationships, maintaining clear communication, and leveraging shared resources, the SOC can create a collaborative network that underpins its resilience and operational stability.

ESG concerns

In an era where organizations are increasingly held accountable for their ESG practices, business continuity planning has transcended its traditional focus on operational resilience. For SOC, ESG considerations are no longer peripheral concerns. They are integral to the strategies that safeguard the organization's future. By aligning business continuity efforts with ESG principles, the SOC contributes to organizational sustainability, ethical responsibility, and stakeholder trust.

ESG principles provide a framework for addressing critical issues that extend beyond the immediate scope of business continuity. While traditional business continuity focuses on mitigating risks and maintaining operations, ESG emphasizes the broader impact of organizational practices on the environment, society, and governance. Integrating ESG concerns into the SOC's business continuity planning ensures a holistic approach that balances operational resilience with ethical responsibility.

Reducing environmental impact is the need of the hour. While planning SOC, the following measures can be effective:

- Continuity strategies should consider the environmental footprint of SOC operations, including energy consumption, waste generation, and carbon emissions.

- Implementing energy-efficient technologies and adopting green practices reduces the environmental impact of maintaining SOC functionality. A SOC could implement energy-efficient hardware and optimize cooling systems in its data center to reduce its carbon footprint.

- During disruptions, sustainable practices should guide resource allocation and recovery efforts. For example, prioritizing renewable energy sources for backup systems minimizes the reliance on fossil fuels.

- The SOC must address climate-related risks, such as natural disasters and extreme weather events, in its continuity planning. Proactive measures, such as resilient infrastructure and disaster recovery sites in low-risk areas, enhance environmental preparedness.

Social concerns in business continuity can be addressed through:

- The SOC's continuity plans should prioritize the safety, health, and well-being of its employees during crises.

- Provisions such as remote work options, mental health support, and clear communication protocols ensure that staff are supported throughout disruptions.

- The SOC can play a role in supporting local communities during emergencies, such as by sharing resources or expertise. Collaboration with community organizations enhances the SOC's social impact and strengthens relationships with stakeholders.

- Continuity planning should reflect the organization's commitment to diversity, equity, and inclusion. Ensuring equitable access to resources and support during crises demonstrates social responsibility.

Governance concerns in business continuity can be mitigated through the following:

- Governance frameworks should guide ethical decision-making in continuity planning and crisis response.

- Transparent and accountable practices build trust with employees, customers, and regulators. The SOC could establish transparent reporting mechanisms on its business continuity preparedness and incident response activities, demonstrating accountability to stakeholders.

- The SOC must ensure compliance with ESG-related regulations and standards, such as data protection laws and environmental guidelines. Regular audits and assessments verify adherence to these requirements.

- Engaging stakeholders in the development and review of continuity plans enhances governance practices. This includes communicating the organization's commitment to ESG principles and integrating stakeholder feedback.

Integrating ESG concerns into SOC business continuity plans can provide a practical and holistic approach to sustainable security operations. Here are some measures for a seamless integration of ESG in SOC:

- Incorporate ESG-specific metrics into the SOC's continuity planning process to track progress and measure impact. Examples include carbon footprint reduction, employee satisfaction, and community engagement levels.

- Ensure that the SOC's continuity strategies are aligned with the broader ESG objectives of the organization. This alignment demonstrates a unified commitment to sustainability and responsibility.

- Engage with the organization's ESG leaders and teams to incorporate their expertise into continuity planning. This collaboration fosters a cohesive approach to addressing ESG concerns.

- Evaluate the ESG impact of continuity measures to identify areas for improvement. These assessments ensure that the SOC's strategies contribute positively to environmental, social, and governance goals.

Integrating ESG concerns into the SOC's business continuity planning yields significant advantages. Demonstrating a commitment to ESG principles builds confidence among employees, customers, and investors. Proactively addressing ESG concerns ensures compliance with evolving regulations and standards. Organizations that prioritize ESG gain a reputation as responsible and forward-thinking, attracting talent and business opportunities.

For the SOC, aligning continuity strategies with ESG principles ensures a holistic approach that addresses environmental, social, and governance challenges. By doing so, the SOC not only safeguards its operations but also contributes to a sustainable, equitable, and ethically governed future.

Conclusion

SOC's role in ensuring business continuity is indispensable in an era where disruptions are a constant reality. Through its proactive risk management, rapid incident response, and strategic contributions to resilience building, the SOC serves as a cornerstone of organizational stability. By identifying and addressing risks before they manifest, the SOC can ensure that it remains a reliable and resilient guardian of organizational security.

This chapter has underscored the vital importance of planning, preparing, and implementing strategies that ensure seamless operations in the face of disruptions. From proactive risk management and employee awareness to collaboration with external agencies and alignment with ESG concerns, business continuity requires a holistic and adaptable approach.

As the threat landscape evolves and challenges grow more complex, the SOC must continuously refine its continuity strategies, leveraging emerging technologies and global best practices. Ultimately, business continuity is not just a defensive mechanism; it is a strategic enabler of security, stability, and success. Through dedication, collaboration, and foresight, the SOC can rise as a beacon of operational resilience, ensuring the organization thrives in an unpredictable world.

In the next chapter, we will explore the frameworks and regulations that govern security operations. Compliance management is crucial to the success of SOC operations.

Points to remember

Here are some key takeaways from this chapter:

- By integrating business continuity into its core functions, the SOC not only safeguards the organization's operations but also reinforces its ability to thrive in an unpredictable world.

- Employees are partners in continuity efforts, highlighting that an aware and empowered workforce is key to maintaining seamless SOC operations in an unpredictable world.

- Balancing cybersecurity and business growth is a complex yet achievable goal for organizations. As threats and challenges evolve, the importance of regular and thorough audits and assessments cannot be overstated. They are the foundation upon which a resilient and adaptive SOC is built.

- Incorporating ESG concerns into business continuity planning is an essential aspect of organizational resilience and responsibility.

Multiple choice questions

1. **What is the primary goal of a BCP?**

   a. Increase sales

   b. Ensure essential functions continue during and after a disaster

   c. Improve employee performance

   d. Enhance marketing strategies

2. **What is a BIA?**

   a. A financial analysis of profits

   b. A study to determine the effects of disruptions on business operations

   c. A market research analysis

   d. A performance review of employees

3. **What is the primary focus of the social aspect in ESG?**

   a. Financial performance

   b. Employee well-being and community impact

   c. Regulatory compliance

   d. Technological advancements

Answers

1	b
2	b
3	b

Questions

1. What is the role of a BCP in ensuring the resilience of a SOC during unexpected disruptions?

2. What are different audits and assessments? How are they relevant in BCP in SOC?

3. Explain how ESG concerns play vital role in BCP.

Key terms

Some key terms used in this chapter are:

*   Audits and assessments are crucial to BCP continuity.

*   Collaboration with external agencies is a cornerstone of effective business continuity planning for SOCs.

*   ESG-aligned strategies contribute to long-term sustainability and adaptability.

Join our Discord space

Join our Discord workspace for latest updates, offers, tech happenings around the world, new releases, and sessions with the authors:

https://discord.bpbonline.com

Section 4
Practical Implementation Aspects

CHAPTER 14

Frameworks

Introduction

Frameworks are the backbone of effective operations within **security operations centers (SOC)**. This chapter explores the critical role frameworks play in standardizing processes, ensuring compliance, and strengthening an organization's overall security posture. By providing structured guidelines, these frameworks help SOC teams efficiently detect, respond to, and mitigate security incidents while aligning with industry standards and best practices. From **National Institute of Standards and Technology (NIST)** cybersecurity framework to ISO/IEC 27001, this chapter looks into widely recognized models, illustrating their application in SOC operations. Understanding these frameworks empowers organizations to build scalable, adaptable, and resilient security strategies in an ever-evolving thre at landscape.

The frameworks provide a structured approach to managing SOC operations, encompassing people, processes, and technology. Compliance management, encompassing all three aspects, is also a key component of SOC operations. Regulations are specific to the industry, domain, or location. These are crucial from a compliance standpoint in ensuring stakeholders are informed about information security posture management. This chapter also covers all associated regulations.

Structure

In this chapter, we will discuss the following topics:

- Key components of frameworks
- Activities governed by frameworks
- Leading frameworks
- COBIT framework
- SANS incident response framework
- Kill Chain framework
- Information technology infrastructure library
- HITRUST framework
- Compliance management
- Regulations

Objectives

By the end of this chapter, readers will have a comprehensive understanding of the foundational models and guidelines that govern SOC operations. This chapter aims to illustrate how frameworks standardize security practices, ensure compliance with regulatory requirements, and enhance the efficiency and effectiveness of SOC processes. By exploring widely recognized frameworks, such as the NIST cybersecurity framework, MITRE ATT&CK, and ISO/IEC 27001, the chapter aims to equip readers with the knowledge to design, implement, and maintain robust security practices. Ultimately, the goal is to help readers understand how to manage risks proactively, adapt to evolving threats, and achieve a resilient security infrastructure.

Key components of frameworks

Frameworks serve as guiding principles to standardize operations, ensure regulatory compliance, and effectively mitigate risks. The essential components that form the backbone of such frameworks are:

- **Governance and leadership**: Governance is the cornerstone of any framework, establishing the policies, procedures, and oversight mechanisms necessary for SOC's smooth functioning. Key elements in governance include the following:
  - o Clear documentation of security policies aligned with organizational goals.
  - o Defined leadership roles and accountability at every level of the SOC hierarchy.
  - o Ensuring alignment with regulatory standards like GDPR, HIPAA, or ISO/IEC 27001.

- **Risk management**: Effective risk management is vital for identifying and mitigating potential threats. The risk management framework must encompass the following:

  o Periodic evaluations to identify vulnerabilities and prioritize risks.

  o Implementation of controls to reduce identified risks.

  o Ongoing observation to adapt to emerging threats.

- **Incident management**: Incident management ensures a coordinated response to security events. Key components include the following:

  o Leveraging tools like SIEM to identify anomalies.

  o Documented processes for handling incidents, including containment, eradication, and recovery.

  o Analysis of past incidents to improve future responses.

- **Technology and tools**: A robust SOC framework integrates advanced technology to enhance efficiency and effectiveness. Let us understand this point in further detail:

  o Deployment of AI and machine learning to streamline repetitive tasks.

  o Tools to collect, analyze, and act upon threat data.

  o Centralized systems for tracking and analyzing security logs.

- **Workforce and training**: A well-trained SOC team is crucial to the success of any framework. Essential components include:

  o Regular training and certifications for SOC analysts.

  o Encouraging cross-functional collaboration for holistic security management.

  o Organization-wide efforts to promote a security-conscious culture.

- **Performance metrics and reporting**: Measurement and reporting ensure the framework's effectiveness. Key aspects that help us measure performance include the following:

  o KPIs to assess the SOC's efficiency, such as **mean time to detect (MTTD)** and **mean time to respond (MTTR)**.

  o Dashboards and visualization tools for real-time monitoring and reporting of security metrics.

  o Regular reporting to stakeholders to maintain transparency and trust.

Activities governed by frameworks

Frameworks serve as guiding blueprints for SOCs, standardizing their processes and ensuring that activities align with the industry's best practices, regulatory requirements, and organizational goals. By structuring these activities, frameworks help SOCs achieve consistency, efficiency, and resilience in tackling cybersecurity challenges.

Here are some key activities of SOC governed by frameworks:

- Incidence response and management
- Threat detection and analysis
- Vulnerability management
- Compliance and audit
- Log management and monitoring
- Incident reporting and documentation
- Threat intelligence and integration
- Training and awareness

Leading frameworks

In the ever-evolving cybersecurity landscape, SOCs rely on established frameworks to ensure consistent, efficient, and effective operations. These frameworks provide guidelines for implementing robust security measures, fostering operational resilience, and aligning with the industry's best practices.

NIST cybersecurity framework

The NIST cybersecurity framework is one of the most widely adopted frameworks in the SOC domain. It is designed to help organizations effectively manage and mitigate cybersecurity risks. The key components of NIST CSF are to identify, protect, detect, respond, and recover.

CSF helps SOCs establish a lifecycle approach to cybersecurity by guiding activities such as risk assessment, threat monitoring, and incident response. It is flexible and adaptable to various industries and organization sizes.

MITRE ATT&CK framework

MITRE ATT&CK, encompassing adversarial tactics, techniques, and common knowledge, is a globally recognized framework that provides insights into adversarial behavior as covered in detail in *Chapter 5, Modern Developments in Security Operations Centers.* It enhances threat detection, investigation, and response by mapping real-world attack scenarios to detection methods. It also promotes proactive defense and enriches threat intelligence.

ISO/IEC 27001

ISO/IEC 27001 is an international **Information Security Management System (ISMS)** standard. It provides a structured approach to managing and protecting sensitive information. It covers risk assessment, information security controls, and continual improvement processes. It primarily governs policies, processes, and technical controls, ensuring a secure environment for SOC operations. It is a globally accepted certification that enhances credibility and compliance.

CIS Controls

The **Center for Internet Security (CIS)** Controls provide a prioritized set of best practices to defend against cyber threats. The key components of CIS Controls encompass safeguards across various areas, including asset management, vulnerability management, and access control. It guides SOC teams in implementing foundational controls for effective monitoring and incident response. It provides a simplified approach to security that is practical for organizations of varying sizes.

COBIT framework

The **Control Objectives for Information and Related Technologies (COBIT)** framework focuses on the governance and management of enterprise IT. It consists of processes, organizational structures, and best practices for aligning IT goals with business objectives. It ensures that SOC operations are integrated with broader enterprise IT governance, balancing risk and optimizing resources. It promotes accountability and regulatory compliance.

SANS incident response framework

The SANS framework offers a comprehensive guide to incident handling and response. The key components of this framework include preparation, identification, containment, eradication, recovery, and lessons learned. It facilitates structured and effective responses to cybersecurity incidents, minimizing damage and downtime. It provides a practical approach to incident management, facilitating ongoing improvement.

Kill Chain framework

Developed by *Lockheed Martin*, the Cyber Kill Chain framework identifies the phases of a cyberattack to disrupt adversaries' actions, as covered in *Chapter 5, Modern Developments in Security Operations Centers*. The key components include reconnaissance, weaponization, delivery, exploitation, installation, command and control, and actions on objectives. It helps SOC teams understand attack patterns and implement countermeasures to interrupt the chain. It is focused on proactive threat hunting and detection.

Information technology infrastructure library

ITIL is a framework for IT service management that guides aligning IT services with business needs. It includes service strategy, design, operation, and continual service improvement. It basically enhances the management of SOC services, ensuring efficiency and alignment with organizational objectives. It has broad applicability across IT and security operations.

HITRUST framework

The HITRUST **common security framework (CSF)** is a comprehensive and certifiable framework designed to unify various regulatory and industry standards for cybersecurity and compliance. In the context of SOC, the HITRUST framework plays a pivotal role in streamlining risk management and ensuring adherence to security and privacy regulations.

By harmonizing controls from multiple authoritative sources such as HIPAA, GDPR, and NIST, it provides a structured approach to safeguarding sensitive information. SOCs leveraging the HITRUST framework can enhance their operational efficiency, reduce vulnerabilities, and demonstrate a strong commitment to data protection and compliance. This makes it an invaluable tool for organizations aiming to maintain robust security postures in an ever-evolving threat landscape.

Systems and organization controls

SOC frameworks are standardized reporting structures developed by the **American Institute of Certified Public Accountants (AICPA)**.

It has three different types for organizations to comply with. Let us look at them:

- SOC 1 focuses on controls relevant to an organization's financial reporting. It is primarily designed for service organizations whose operations impact the financial statements of their clients, such as payroll processors or financial service providers. It addresses **Internal Controls over Financial Reporting (ICFR)**.

  It aids clients in complying with regulations like the **Sarbanes-Oxley Act (SOX)**. SOC1 typically includes Type 1 (point-in-time review) and Type 2 (ongoing operational effectiveness) reports. For example, a payroll service provider uses SOC 1 to assure clients that their processes for calculating payroll, withholding taxes, and issuing payments are accurate and compliant with financial regulations.

- SOC 2 focuses on controls related to the **trust services criteria (TSC)** involving security, availability, processing integrity, confidentiality, and privacy. It is widely used by technology and SaaS companies to demonstrate the security and reliability of their systems. It is applicable to organizations managing customer data.

It is based on criteria such as encryption, data backup, and access controls. SOC2 also provides both Type 1 and Type 2 reports, with Type 2 emphasizing ongoing compliance. For example, a cloud service provider uses SOC 2 to demonstrate that customer data hosted on its platform is secure, available, and processed accurately, addressing concerns related to regulations like GDPR or CCPA.

- SOC 3 is essentially a summary of SOC 2 but is designed for public distribution. It focuses on providing assurance to a broader audience about an organization's compliance with the trust services criteria without disclosing sensitive details. It offers a high-level report suitable for marketing or public disclosure.

  It is specifically ideal for organizations that want to demonstrate trustworthiness without revealing proprietary or operational details, as it is easier to understand for non-technical stakeholders. For example, an e-commerce platform shares its SOC 3 report on its website to assure customers that their personal and payment information is secure and managed responsibly.

SOC frameworks provide confidence and transparency in a world where trust is a key differentiator. They enable organizations to meet regulatory standards by aligning with SOX, GDPR, HIPAA, and more laws. It builds trust with existing and prospective customers while safeguarding sensitive data and processes from breaches.

SOC frameworks, such as SOC 1, SOC 2, and SOC 3, are designed to align with regulatory requirements and ensure organizations meet legal and ethical standards.

Some of the best practices for regulatory compliance in SOC include the following:

- Identify potential regulatory risks and their impact on the organization.

- Design and implement controls that align with both SOC criteria and regulatory requirements.

- Monitor changes in regulations to ensure ongoing compliance.

- Use compliance tools to automate monitoring, reporting, and risk assessment processes.

- Collaborate with external auditors to validate compliance with SOC frameworks and regulatory standards.

A comprehensive framework can ensure effective security posture management. The different frameworks covered previously address the specific needs of their respective domains. A comparison of the impacts and relevance of these frameworks is covered in the following table:

Framework	Impact	Relevance
NIST CSF	Provides a comprehensive risk management framework.	Widely adopted across industries for its flexibility and adaptability.

Framework	Impact	Relevance
MITRE ATT&CK	Offers a detailed matrix of tactics and techniques used by adversaries.	Essential for threat intelligence and understanding adversary behavior.
ISO/IEC 27001	Establish an **Information Security Management System (ISMS)**.	Crucial for organizations needing certification and compliance with international standards.
CIS Controls	Provides prioritized actions to mitigate cyber threats.	Practical and hands-on guidance for improving cybersecurity posture.
COBIT	Focuses on IT governance and management.	Aligns IT strategy with business goals, covering strategy, risk management, and performance.
SANS incident response framework	Guides incident response processes.	Vital for structured and effective incident handling and response.
Kill Chain framework	Describes stages of a cyberattack.	Useful for understanding and disrupting adversary activities.
ITIL	Provides best practices for IT service management.	Enhance service delivery and management within SOC operations.
HITRUST framework	Combines various standards and regulations.	It is important for healthcare organizations to have a comprehensive compliance framework.
Systems and Organization Controls (SOC)	Focuses on data security and privacy.	Relevant for organizations needing third-party audit and assurance.

Table 14.1: Frameworks for SOC

Each framework has unique strengths and applications, making it valuable for enhancing an SOC's security posture.

Compliance management

In today's highly regulated business environment, organizations face growing challenges in aligning their operations with compliance requirements. Compliance management is crucial to organizational governance, ensuring conformity with legal, regulatory, and industry standards.

Within the SOC framework, effective compliance management is pivotal in building trust with stakeholders, maintaining operational integrity, and safeguarding sensitive information.

Key components and best practices of compliance management are:

- Establishing clear policies and procedures that define expectations for compliance.

- Regularly assessing operations to identify and address compliance gaps. Conduct regular risk assessments to stay ahead of potential issues.

- Educating employees and stakeholders about their roles in maintaining compliance.

- Developing protocols for identifying, reporting, and addressing compliance breaches.

- Iteratively refining compliance practices to adapt to evolving regulations.

- Utilizing compliance management tools to automate monitoring and reporting.

- Basing compliance practices on recognized standards, such as the **International Standards Organization (ISO)**, **GDPR**, and **California Consumer Privacy Act (CCPA)**.

- Ensuring organizational leaders actively support compliance initiatives.

Compliance management is not without challenges. Let us look at some of them in detail:

- Constant changes in laws and standards require organizations to adapt quickly.

- Limited resources can hinder the development and implementation of effective compliance programs.

- Organizations with international operations must navigate diverse regulatory environments.

Organizations must navigate complex regulations, resource constraints, and evolving threats. Key solutions include fostering a culture of compliance, investing in training, and leveraging AI-driven tools for predictive risk analysis.

Here are some of the strategies to overcome these challenges:

- Embed compliance with the organizational culture to ensure buy-in at all levels.

- Provide ongoing training for employees to stay informed about regulatory requirements.

- Use flexible SOC frameworks to adapt to changing regulations seamlessly.

To understand the regulations and compliance, let us look at some specific examples:

- The healthcare domain is governed by the **Health Insurance Portability and Accountability Act (HIPAA)**. To comply with these regulations, the SOC2 framework can be followed. For example, organizations handling PHI must implement stringent access controls, encryption standards, and procedures for notifying breaches. SOC 2 + HITRUST provides a comprehensive framework to meet these requirements.

- The financial services domain is governed by the SOX and the PCI DSS. To comply with these regulations, SOC1 and SOC2 frameworks can be effectively exploited. For example, banks use SOC 1 to ensure financial reporting accuracy and SOC 2 to protect customer data. Compliance with PCI DSS is critical for secure payment processing.

- Technology SaaS domains are governed by the GDPR and the CCPA. The SOC2 framework can be effectively used to meet these regulatory compliances. For example, SaaS companies demonstrate compliance with GDPR and CCPA by implementing controls for data privacy, availability, and confidentiality.

Regulations

Regulatory compliance serves as the cornerstone of trust and accountability in today's complex business ecosystems. Organizations must not only demonstrate operational excellence but also align with a myriad of laws, regulations, and standards that govern their industries.

Regulatory compliance refers to an organization's adherence to laws, guidelines, and standards relevant to its operations. Non-compliance can lead to financial penalties, operational disruptions, and reputational harm. In the context of SOC, compliance is critical to ensuring trust and accountability in business practices.

Some major regulations influencing SOC are listed here:

- **GDPR**: It governs data privacy and protection in the **European Union (EU)**, influencing how organizations manage personal data globally. It primarily protects the personal data of EU citizens. SOC 2 frameworks address GDPR requirements by implementing controls for data encryption, access management, and breach notification. Adapting to GDPR's extraterritorial scope for global organizations is a significant challenge. To overcome this challenge, regular audits and updates to SOC controls can ensure ongoing compliance.

- **HIPAA**: It focuses on securing sensitive **personal healthcare information (PHI)** in the *United States*. SOC2 + HITRUST frameworks provide a structured approach to meet HIPAA's security and privacy rules. The major challenge in complying with HIPPA is balancing compliance with operational efficiency. This can be overcome by leveraging automation tools for monitoring and reporting.

- **SOX**: It ensures financial transparency and accountability, particularly for publicly traded companies. SOC 1 frameworks focus on internal controls over financial reporting. However, managing complex financial systems across multiple jurisdictions is a critical challenge. This can be mitigated by integrating SOC 1 with **enterprise resource planning (ERP)** systems for seamless compliance.

- **PCI DSS**: The PCI DSS is a set of security requirements designed to ensure the safe handling of cardholder information and protect against data breaches. Its primary focus is on securing card transactions, maintaining a secure network, protecting cardholder data, managing vulnerabilities, implementing robust access control measures, monitoring networks, and ensuring adherence to proper information security policies. Despite its comprehensive nature, organizations often face challenges in achieving and maintaining compliance, including the complexity of security requirements, high implementation costs, and the continuous evolution of threats.

To mitigate these challenges, organizations can adopt a proactive approach by regularly conducting risk assessments, investing in advanced security technologies, providing continuous employee training, and collaborating with specialized PCI compliance partners to ensure ongoing adherence to the standard.

- **CCPA**: The CCPA ensures that consumers have greater control over their personal information. It focuses on providing Californians with the right to know what personal data is being collected, the purposes for which it is used, who it is shared with, and the ability to access, delete, and opt-out of the sale of their data.

  Despite its commendable goals, organizations face challenges in complying with CCPA, such as identifying and tracking all personal data, managing consumer requests, and implementing necessary security measures. Mitigation strategies include adopting comprehensive data mapping, investing in technology solutions for automated data management, conducting regular employee training, and establishing clear processes for handling consumer rights requests to ensure ongoing compliance with CCPA's requirements.

- **Digital Personal Data Protection Act (DPDPA)**: The DPDPA of 2023 ensures the protection of digital personal data by recognizing individuals' rights to privacy and the necessity of processing personal data for lawful purposes in *India*. It focuses on establishing clear guidelines for data processing, consent management, data localization, and the rights and duties of data principals and fiduciaries.

  Organizations face challenges in complying with DPDPA, such as navigating complex regulatory requirements, ensuring data security, and managing cross-border data transfers. Mitigation strategies include implementing robust data protection policies, investing in advanced security technologies, conducting regular audits and risk assessments, and providing continuous training for employees to ensure compliance with the Act's provisions.

Regulations are an integral part of frameworks like SOC, shaping the way organizations approach compliance, risk management, and accountability. By aligning SOC practices with regulatory requirements, organizations can mitigate risks, enhance stakeholder confidence, and build a foundation for sustainable growth. As regulatory landscapes evolve, businesses must remain proactive and adaptive, ensuring their SOC frameworks continue to meet the highest standards of compliance.

Conclusion

The key components of frameworks in a SOC are foundational to ensuring a proactive, resilient, and efficient approach to security operations. Organizations can better navigate the complex landscape of cybersecurity threats by integrating governance, risk management, incident response, advanced technology, workforce development, and performance monitoring. This structured approach safeguards critical assets and enhances stakeholder confidence in the organization's ability to adapt and thrive in the face of evolving challenges.

Leading frameworks such as NIST CSF, MITRE ATT&CK, ISO/IEC 27001, CIS Controls, and others form the backbone of SOC operations. They offer structured approaches to threat detection, incident management, risk assessment, and compliance, enabling organizations to build resilient and adaptable security strategies. By adopting these frameworks, SOCs can enhance their operational maturity, proactively address emerging threats, and ensure alignment with global standards and best practices.

Compliance management is an indispensable element of organizational frameworks, including SOC. Organizations can mitigate risks, enhance efficiency, and foster trust by implementing robust compliance management practices. In the fast-evolving regulatory landscape, a proactive and well-structured compliance approach is essential for sustained success.

In the next chapter, we will examine the best practices for managing security operations in SOCs. The SOPs and TTPs will provide adequate measures for effectively managing SOCs.

Points to remember

Here are some key takeaways from this chapter:

- When establishing SOC, it is essential to keep in mind the significance of various leading frameworks, compliance management, and regulations.

- The leading frameworks covered in this chapter provide structured approaches for risk management, threat intelligence, and information security management, respectively.

- Compliance management involves adhering to industry standards like PCI DSS for payment card security and GDPR for data privacy, ensuring that SOC operations align with legal requirements and protect sensitive information.

- Additionally, regulations like the CCPA and DPDPA emphasize consumer rights and data protection, necessitating robust processes for data handling and privacy controls within the SOC.

- By integrating these frameworks and adhering to compliance and regulatory mandates, an SOC can effectively manage and mitigate cybersecurity risks, enhance operational efficiency, and maintain stakeholder trust.

Multiple choice questions

1. Which of the following frameworks is primarily focused on providing a detailed matrix of tactics and techniques used by adversaries?

    a. NIST CSF

    b. ISO/IEC 27001

    c. MITRE ATT&CK

    d. CIS Controls

2. Which of the following standards is focused on establishing an ISMS and is widely recognized for ensuring compliance and certification?

    a. PCI -DSS)

    b. ISO/IEC 27001

    c. GDPR

    d. CCPA

3. Which framework is focused on aligning IT strategy with business goals and includes governance and management practices?

    a. NIST CSF

    b. COBIT

    c. SANS Incident Response Framework

    d. Kill Chain Framework

Answers

1	c
2	b
3	b

Questions

1. Discuss the role of the NIST CSF in enhancing the security posture of an SOC.

2. Analyze the importance of compliance management in SOC operations and the impact of regulations such as GDPR and CCPA.

3. Evaluate the role of ISO/IEC 27001 in establishing an ISMS and its impact on SOC operations.

Key terms

Some key terms used in this chapter are:

- **ISMS**: Key international framework for information security management systems.

- **GDPR, HIPPA, CCPA, DPDPA**: Key data privacy regulations.

Join our Discord space

Join our Discord workspace for latest updates, offers, tech happenings around the world, new releases, and sessions with the authors:

https://discord.bpbonline.com

CHAPTER 15

Best Practices

Introduction

As cyber threats continue to evolve in complexity and sophistication, organizations must stay vigilant to protect their assets, data, and reputation. The backbone of an effective SOC lies in adhering to industry best practices that enhance threat detection, incident response, and overall security posture.

This chapter aims to provide a comprehensive guide to the best practices that can elevate your SOC's efficiency and effectiveness. From implementing advanced monitoring tools to fostering a culture of continuous improvement, we will explore key strategies and techniques that have been proven to bolster security operations. By adopting these best practices, your organization can proactively mitigate risks, respond swiftly to incidents, and maintain a resilient security framework.

Whether you are establishing a new SOC or seeking to refine an existing one, this chapter serves as a valuable resource for security professionals at all levels. These can be great resources to build, operate, and manage the SOC. Let us explore the essential best practices that will empower your SOC to stay ahead of the ever-evolving threat landscape and safeguard your organization's digital assets. The chapter covers some **standard operating procedures (SOP)** and TTP being followed worldwide to ensure a cyber-safe environment and associated tools.

Structure

In this chapter, we will discuss the following topics:

- Maintaining, reviewing, and improving SOC
- SOPs
- Tactics, techniques, and procedures

Objectives

By the end of this chapter, readers will gain insights in a structured framework for establishing and maintaining an effective SOC. This chapter aims to equip security professionals with proven strategies and methodologies that enhance threat detection, incident response, and overall security posture. By outlining key best practices, this chapter aims to enable SOC teams to proactively identify and mitigate risks, respond promptly to security incidents, and continually improve their operations.

Maintaining, reviewing and improving SOC

SOC is the nerve center for monitoring, analyzing, and responding to security incidents. However, a SOC is not a *set-it-and-forget-it* function. It must be continuously maintained, reviewed, and improved to keep pace with evolving threats, emerging technologies, and business needs.

Maintain

Ongoing maintenance of a SOC is crucial to ensuring its optimal functionality, performance, and adaptability to evolving security landscapes.

The key components of SOC maintenance are:

- **Technology upkeep**: Continuous technological upkeep ensures that security tools and systems remain up-to-date and effective against evolving cyber threats.

  SOCs can maintain optimal performance and resilience through the following practices:

  - **Regular updates**: Ensure that software and hardware, such as firewalls, IDS/IPS, and EDR tools, are updated regularly.

  - **Vulnerability management**: Patch systems to address known vulnerabilities promptly to prevent exploitation.

- **Staff training and development**: Ongoing staff training and development ensure that team members remain skilled in the latest security practices and technologies.

This continuous education enables the SOC to effectively address emerging threats and maintain high operational standards.

For effective implementation, ensure the following:

- o Equip SOC analysts with the latest certifications, such as **Certified SOC Analyst (CSA)** or **Certified Information Systems Security Professional (CISSP)**.

- o Conduct tabletop exercises and simulations to prepare staff for real-world security incidents.

- **Threat intelligence integration**: Integrating threat intelligence enhances the ability to predict, detect, and respond to emerging threats by leveraging real-time data and insights. This proactive approach ensures that the SOC remains agile and well-informed, reducing the risk of successful cyberattack. There is a need to integrate updated threat intelligence that continuously feeds to help analysts identify and mitigate emerging threats.

- **Documentation and runbooks**: Maintain updated incident response plans, SOPs, and escalation protocols to guide analysts during incidents.

For example, a retail organization maintains its SOC by implementing a monthly patch management cycle and holding quarterly training sessions for its analysts. This approach helps the team stay informed and prepared to handle new attack vectors.

Review

Regular reviews are essential for assessing the effectiveness of a SOC and identifying areas for improvement. Here are the objectives of SOC reviews:

- **Evaluate performance**: Measure the SOC's success in detecting, responding to, and mitigating incidents.

- **Identify gaps**: Highlight areas where processes, tools, or personnel may fall short.

- **Ensure alignment**: Confirm that the SOC's goals align with organizational objectives and current threat landscapes.

Key matrices as covered in *Chapter 9, People* and *Chapter 10, Processes,* are crucial to review the progress periodically and check the effectiveness of SOC.

Some methods for effective reviews are:

- **Internal audits**: Conduct audits to evaluate the SOC's adherence to established procedures and policies.

- **Red team/blue team exercises**: Simulate attacks to test the SOC's detection and response capabilities.

- **Incident post-mortems**: Analyze past incidents to identify lessons learned and areas for improvement.

For example, a financial services company conducted a quarterly SOC review and found a high false-positive rate in its threat detection tools. By fine-tuning alert thresholds and retraining the machine learning algorithms, the SOC reduced noise and improved efficiency.

Improve

Continuous improvement ensures that a SOC remains capable of tackling emerging challenges and delivering value to the organization. The strategies for continuous improvement include:

- **Leverage automation**: Adopt SOAR tools to automate repetitive tasks, such as alert triage and initial response. Use machine learning to improve threat detection and anomaly analysis.

- **Expand threat hunting**: Transition from reactive monitoring to proactive threat hunting to uncover hidden threats within the network. Train analysts in advanced threat-hunting techniques and tools.

- **Enhance collaboration**: Foster better communication between the SOC and other teams, such as IT, risk management, and executive leadership. Use collaboration platforms to improve information sharing.

- **Adopt Zero Trust principles**: Implement a Zero Trust architecture to minimize the SOC's exposure to insider threats and external breaches.

- **Invest in analytics and reporting**: Use advanced analytics to provide actionable insights for decision-makers. Develop comprehensive reports to communicate the SOC's value to stakeholders.

For example, a healthcare provider improved its SOC by implementing SOAR technology, reducing MTTD and MTTR by 30%. The SOC team also introduced proactive threat-hunting practices, uncovering a dormant ransomware attack that could have caused significant damage.

SOC teams often face several challenges. Let us look at them:

- **Resource constraints**: Limited budgets or understaffing can impact SOC performance.

- **Alert fatigue**: High volumes of false positives can overwhelm analysts and reduce their efficiency.

- **Evolving threats**: New and sophisticated attack vectors require continuous adaptation.

To overcome these challenges, there is a need to focus on the following:

- **Prioritize investments**: Focus on high-impact areas, such as automation and threat intelligence.

- **Streamline alerts**: Use AI and machine learning to reduce false positives.

- **Foster a learning culture**: Encourage continuous learning and adaptability to tackle evolving threats.

Standard operating procedures

Here are several SOP tailored for SOC. Each SOP serves as a guideline for specific tasks or responsibilities to ensure the SOC operates effectively and efficiently.

Incident detection and response SOP

This SOP serves as a cornerstone for ensuring timely identification, accurate categorization, and effective mitigation of security incidents. The steps involved are covered here:

- **Purpose**: To outline the steps for detecting, categorizing, and responding to security incidents.

- **Responsibility**: SOC Tier 1 Analysts, SOC Manager

- **Procedure**: Follow these steps:

  1. **Alert monitoring:**

     a. Monitor SIEM tools for alerts.

     b. Correlate alerts with threat intelligence to verify their validity.

  2. **Categorization:**

     a. **Categorize incidents based on severity**: Low, Medium, High, or Critical, with the following response timelines:

Severity	Description	Response time
Low	Minor anomalies, no immediate risk	Within 24 hours
Medium	Potential threat, limited impact	Within 4 hours
High	Confirmed threat, moderate impact	Within 1 hour
Critical	Severe breach, widespread impact	Immediate

Table 15.1: Alert severity levels

  3. **Response:**

     a. **For low and medium severity**: Notify appropriate teams for resolution.

     b. **For high and critical severity:**

        i.   Notify the IRT immediately.

        ii.   Follow the established incident response plan.

4. **Documentation**:

    a.   Record all incident details, including the timeline, steps taken, and resolution.

5. **Post-incident review**:

    a.   Conduct a RCA to prevent future occurrences.

SOC shift handover SOP

The SOC shift handover SOP establishes a structured framework to facilitate efficient and seamless knowledge transfer during shift changes. The steps involved are covered here:

- **Purpose**: To ensure continuity and efficiency between SOC shift teams.
- **Responsibility**: SOC analysts on shift and SOC manager.
- **Procedure**: Follow these steps:

    1. **Pre-handover tasks**:

        a.   Complete all ongoing tasks or provide detailed notes on pending actions.

        b.   Document critical incidents from the shift and their status.

    2. **Handover meeting**:

        a.   Conduct a verbal briefing with the incoming shift team.

        b.   Highlight critical alerts, incidents, and system health issues.

    3. **Handover documentation**:

        a.   Use a standardized template to record shift activities, incidents, and key metrics.

    4. **Post-handover check**:

        a.   The incoming team verifies the status of alerts, ongoing incidents, and monitoring tools.

SOC escalation SOP

The SOC escalation SOP provides a structured approach to streamline the escalation process, define clear roles and responsibilities, and outline actionable steps. The steps involved are as follows:

- **Purpose**: To establish a clear process for escalating security issues.
- **Responsibility:** SOC analysts and SOC manager.

- **Procedure**: Follow these steps:
  1. **Identification**:
     a. Determine if the issue exceeds the SOC's authority or capabilities.
  2. **Escalation criteria**:
     a. Escalate incidents based on predefined thresholds (e.g., critical severity alerts or prolonged outages).
     b. Escalation protocol:
        i. **Tier 1 to Tier 2**: High/critical incidents or incidents requiring advanced tools.
        ii. **Tier 2 to Tier 3**: Persistent threats, suspected APT, or legal implications.
        iii. **SOC manager**: Major breaches, data leaks, or incidents requiring executive notification.
        iv. **External entities**: Contact law enforcement or third-party vendors as per IRP.
  3. **Communication**:
     a. Notify the designated escalation point (e.g., incident response team, CISO).
     b. Provide comprehensive details, including logs, timelines, and initial analysis.
  4. **Follow-up**:
     a. Assist the escalation team as required.
     b. Document all communication and actions taken during escalation.
  5. **Closure**:
     a. Update SOC records with the outcome of the escalation.

Endpoint security monitoring SOP

This endpoint security monitoring SOP provides clear guidance for SOC analysts to proactively identify, assess, and mitigate risks related to endpoint devices. Follow these steps:

- **Purpose**: To guide SOC analysts in monitoring and protecting endpoint devices.
- **Responsibility:** SOC Analysts
- **Procedure**: Follow these steps:

1. **Tools setup**:

    a. Deploy and configure endpoint security tools (e.g., EDR solutions).

    b. Enable real-time monitoring for all endpoints.

2. **Monitoring**:

    a. Monitor alerts related to malware, unauthorized access, and suspicious behavior.

    b. Cross-reference alerts with threat intelligence and internal logs.

3. **Response**:

    a. Quarantine affected endpoints immediately for confirmed threats.

    b. Notify IT teams for remediation and recovery.

4. **Reporting**: Document endpoint incidents and generate monthly reports on endpoint security status.

Threat intelligence integration SOP

This threat intelligence integration SOP establishes a standardized framework for utilizing actionable intelligence to strengthen SOC capabilities. The steps involved are as follows:

- **Purpose**: To standardize the process of integrating threat intelligence into SOC operations.

- **Responsibility:** Threat intelligence analysts, SOC analysts, and SOC manager

- **Procedure**: Follow these steps:

    1. **Source Identification**:

        a. Subscribe to reputable threat intelligence feeds (e.g., ISACs, government advisories).

    2. **Data analysis**:

        a. Correlate threat intelligence with internal logs and alerts.

        b. Identify IOCs relevant to the organization.

    3. **Actionable intelligence**:

        a. Share validated threat intelligence with SOC analysts.

        b. Update detection tools (e.g., firewalls, IDS) with new IOCs.

    4. **Review**:

        a. Regularly assess the quality and relevance of threat intelligence sources.

Vulnerability management SOP

The vulnerability management SOP provides a structured methodology to guide the identification, assessment, and remediation of security weaknesses. The steps involved are as follows:

- **Purpose**: To ensure vulnerabilities are identified, assessed, and remediated effectively.
- **Responsibility**: SOC manager and compliance officer
- **Procedure**: Follow these steps:
    1. **Scanning**:
        a. Schedule weekly vulnerability scans using approved tools.
        b. Prioritize scans for critical systems and applications.
    2. **Assessment**:
        a. Assign risk scores to identified vulnerabilities (e.g., using CVSS).
        b. Classify vulnerabilities as critical, high, medium, or low.
    3. **Remediation**:
        a. Collaborate with IT teams to patch critical and high-priority vulnerabilities within agreed timelines.
        b. Develop mitigation strategies for vulnerabilities that cannot be immediately patched.
    4. **Validation**:
        a. Rescan systems post-remediation to confirm resolution.
    5. **Reporting**:
        a. Generate monthly vulnerability reports for leadership and stakeholders.

Log management and retention SOP

This log management and retention SOP establishes a standardized framework for systematic collection, secure retention, and thorough analysis of logs. The steps involved are as follows:

- **Purpose**: To standardize the collection, retention, and analysis of logs.
- **Responsibility:** Security engineers and SOC manager
- **Procedure**: Follow these steps:
    1. **Log collection**:
        a. Ensure all critical systems, applications, and devices are configured to send logs to a centralized SIEM.

2. **Retention policy**:

   a. Retain logs for a minimum of 6 months or as required by regulatory standards (e.g., PCI DSS mandates a 1-year retention).

3. **Analysis**:

   a. Analyze logs for anomalies, unauthorized activities, and indicators of compromise.

4. **Archiving**:

   a. Archive older logs securely for compliance and forensic purposes.

5. **Auditing**:

   a. Conduct periodic reviews of log configurations and retention policies.

Access control SOP

This access control SOP provides a structured approach to define and enforce access policies effectively. The steps involved are as follows:

- **Purpose**: To define the process for managing user access to systems and data.
- **Responsibility**: SOC manager
- **Procedure**:

  1. **User account management:**

     a. Outline the process for creating, modifying, and deleting user accounts.

     b. Define password policies.

  2. **Access review:**

     a. Establish a process for periodically reviewing user access privileges.

     b. Define procedures for revoking unnecessary access.

  3. **Privileged access management:**

     a. Define the process for managing and auditing privileged accounts.

     b. Define the usage procedures for those accounts.

     c. Document all changes.

Change management SOP

- **Purpose:** To ensure that changes to the IT environment are implemented in a controlled and secure manner.
- **Responsibilities:** Compliance manager, Security engineers, and SOC manager
- **Procedure:**

1. **Change request process:**

    a. Define the process for submitting and approving change requests.

    b. Specify the information required in a change request.

2. **Risk assessment:**

    a. Outline the process for assessing the security risks associated with a change.

3. **Implementation and testing:**

    a. Define procedures for implementing and testing changes.

    b. Specify rollback procedures.

4. **Documentation:**

    a. Define the documentation required for each change.

These SOPs provide a structured approach to managing various aspects of SOC operations. Tailoring these SOPs to your organization's specific requirements and regulatory obligations will enhance their effectiveness.

Tactics, techniques, and procedures

The TTP provides a structured approach to understanding and handling potential security incidents, as well as monitoring and detecting malicious activity within an organization's environment. In the upcoming subsections, we will be looking at various TTPs for SOC.

Tactic for threat detection and monitoring

The relevant techniques and procedures are as follows:

*   **Log analysis:**

    o   Collect logs from critical systems, firewalls, and endpoints using a SIEM tool.

    o   Correlate log data to identify anomalous patterns or IOCs.

*   **Real-time alerting:**

    o   Configure thresholds for alert generation based on behavioral patterns (e.g., excessive failed login attempts, unusual network traffic).

    o   Leverage automation to trigger alerts for immediate attention.

*   **Network traffic analysis:**

    o   Monitor network traffic for suspicious activities, such as data exfiltration attempts or communication with known malicious IPs.

    o   Use **deep packet inspection** (**DPI**) to gain insights into encrypted traffic if necessary.

- **Behavioral analytics:**
  - o Implement UEBA to detect deviations in normal user or system behavior.
  - o Utilize machine learning models to enhance anomaly detection.

Tactic, incident response and containment

Here are some relevant techniques and procedures:

- **Initial triage:**
  - o Prioritize and classify incidents based on severity levels: low, medium, high, critical.
  - o Validate incidents by comparing them against known IOCs and threat intelligence feeds.
- **Containment:**
  - o Isolate affected systems or endpoints to prevent the spread of malicious activity.
  - o Use firewall rules or network segmentation to contain threats at the network level.
- **Eradication:**
  - o Remove malicious files, malware, or compromised accounts from affected systems.
  - o Reset credentials and revoke access for compromised accounts.
- **Recovery:**
  - o Restore data from backups and reintegrate affected systems into production after thorough testing.
  - o Conduct post-incident reviews to update the Incident Response Plan.

Tactic for threat intelligence integration

Here are some relevant techniques and procedures are as follows:

- **Threat feed correlation:**
  - o Subscribe to external threat intelligence sources (e.g., ISACs, CERTs, or paid services).
  - o Correlate threat intelligence with internal data to detect known threats.
- **IOC updates:**
  - o Update detection tools, such as firewalls, IDS/IPS, and endpoint protection solutions, with newly discovered IOCs (e.g., malicious IPs, hashes, domains).

- **Threat actor profiling**:
  - o Analyze threat actors' behaviors and techniques using frameworks like MITRE ATT&CK.
  - o Build playbooks for handling specific threat actor activities.
- **Regular threat briefings**:
  - o Conduct regular briefings for SOC teams to discuss emerging threats and their implications.

Tactics for vulnerability management

Here are some relevant techniques and procedures:

- **Regular scanning:**
  - o Conduct vulnerability scans using tools like Nessus or Qualys on a weekly or monthly basis.
  - o Identify unpatched systems and prioritize remediation based on risk scores.
- **Patch management:**
  - o Collaborate with IT teams to apply patches for critical and high-severity vulnerabilities as per defined SLAs (e.g., within seven days for critical issues).
- **Mitigation strategies**:
  - o If patching is not feasible, implement compensating controls, such as virtual patching using firewalls or IDS/IPS.
- **Reporting and follow-up:**
  - o Create vulnerability management reports to track remediation progress and identify recurring weaknesses.

Tactics for proactive threat hunting

Here are some relevant techniques and procedures:

- **Hypothesis-driven hunts:**
  - o Formulate hypotheses about potential threats based on known attack patterns or threat intelligence.
  - o Use endpoint telemetry, log data, and network traffic for investigation.
- **Baseline analysis:**
  - o Establish a baseline of normal activity for critical systems and users.
  - o Investigate any deviations from this baseline to identify hidden threats.

- **Scripted queries**:
  - o Leverage SIEM or EDR tools to create and run custom queries to search for unusual activities (e.g., PowerShell executions, registry modifications).
- **Focused campaigns**:
  - o Target specific systems, such as high-value assets (e.g., domain controllers), for intensive scrutiny.

Tactics for post-incident analysis

Here are some relevant techniques and procedures:

- **RCA:**
  - o Determine the initial entry vector (e.g., phishing, exploitation of vulnerabilities).
  - o Identify any underlying weaknesses that led to the incident.
- **Documentation**:
  - o Create detailed incident reports, including timelines, actions taken, and lessons learned.
  - o Update the incident response plan with findings from the post-incident analysis.
- **Threat actor attribution**:
  - o Use available data to determine if the attack is linked to known threat actors or groups.
  - o Share findings with external intelligence-sharing platforms, if appropriate.
- **Internal feedback loop**:
  - o Conduct post-mortems to identify areas for improvement and reinforce employee awareness.

Tactics for SOC optimization and continuous improvement

Here are some relevant techniques and procedures:

- **Automation and SOAR integration**:
  - o Implement SOAR platforms to streamline workflows and reduce manual effort.
  - o Automate routine tasks like alert triage and report generation.
- **Metrics and KPIs:**
  - o Track KPIs such as MTTD, MTTR, and false-positive rates.

o   Use these metrics to identify inefficiencies and refine processes.

- **Red team/blue team exercises**:

  o   Conduct regular adversarial simulations to test the SOC's preparedness and response capabilities.

- **Training and skill development**:

  o   Encourage certifications such as CSA and **Global Information Assurance Certification (GIAC), Certified Incident Handler (GCIH)**.

  o   Provide training on emerging technologies, threats, and methodologies.

These TTPs offer a comprehensive foundation for operating and improving a SOC. By adopting these strategies, SOC teams can strengthen their defenses, enhance detection and response capabilities, and stay ahead of evolving threats.

Implementation of Zero Trust principles

The Zero Trust philosophy can provide practical insights and actionable steps for organizations looking to implement Zero Trust principles. Typical steps envisaged to implement Zero Trust systems include the following steps:

1. **Assess current security posture:** Conduct a thorough assessment of the organization's current security measures, identifying gaps and vulnerabilities. Evaluate existing access controls, authentication mechanisms, and network segmentation.

2. **Define security policies:** Develop clear security policies based on Zero Trust principles, including continuous verification and least privilege access. Establish guidelines for access control, data encryption, and network segmentation.

3. **Implement IAM:** Deploy IAM solutions to manage user identities and access permissions. Implement MFA to enhance security.

4. **Micro-segmentation:** Segment the network into smaller, isolated segments to limit the spread of threats. Use SDN to create dynamic and flexible network segments.

5. **Continuous monitoring and verification:** Implement continuous monitoring tools to track network activities and detect anomalies. Use SIEM systems to correlate and analyze security data in real-time.

6. **Automate security controls:** Integrate automated security controls to respond to incidents faster and more effectively. Deploy SOAR platforms to streamline security operations.

7. **Regular audits and updates:** Conduct regular audits to ensure compliance with security policies and regulatory requirements. Continuously update security measures to address emerging threats and vulnerabilities.

Conclusion

Maintaining, reviewing, and improving SOCs is an ongoing process that requires commitment, resources, and a proactive mindset. Organizations can strengthen their security posture and reduce risk by ensuring that the SOC remains aligned with organizational goals and adapt to new challenges. A well-maintained and continually improving SOC is a line of defense and a strategic enabler in today's digital landscape.

SOPs provide the necessary structure and consistency, ensuring all team members follow a unified approach, improving efficiency and reducing human error. TTPs offer a dynamic playbook that adapts to emerging threats, empowering SOC teams to stay ahead of adversaries through continuous learning and innovation.

In the next chapter, we will understand the impact of emerging technologies on SOC operations. Technologies such as AI and ML, blockchain, and quantum computing will significantly impact how SOCs manage their resources for effective security posture management.

Points to remember

Here are some key takeaways from this chapter:

- People must ensure the SOPs are followed in letter and spirit to ensure a structured approach to incidence response management.

- Continuous improvement must be embedded in every facet of security operations.

- SOPs and TTPs form the backbone of a resilient cybersecurity posture. By adhering to the best practices involving SOPs and TTPs, organizations can establish a solid foundation that mitigates risks and enhances security operations.

Multiple choice questions

1. **What is an essential practice for maintaining SOC infrastructure?**
   a. Ignoring hardware and software updates
   b. Regularly patching and updating systems
   c. Overlooking security incidents
   d. Minimizing resource allocation

2. **How can SOC teams improve their response to emerging threats?**
   a. By avoiding threat intelligence sharing
   b. By participating in information-sharing communities
   c. By reducing the frequency of security drills
   d. By ignoring new attack vectors

Answers

1	b
2	b

Questions

1. Evaluate the significance of regular training and certification for SOC staff. How can ongoing education and professional development contribute to the effectiveness of a SOC?

2. Analyze the challenges associated with maintaining a SOC infrastructure and propose solutions to address these challenges.

3. How can information-sharing communities enhance the effectiveness of a SOC? Provide examples of such communities and discuss the benefits and potential risks associated with information sharing.

Key terms

Some key terms used in this chapter are:

- **SOPs:** These are structures procedures for handling various activities in SOC.

- **TTPs:** These cover specific techniques and procedures to handle specific tactics.

Join our Discord space

Join our Discord workspace for latest updates, offers, tech happenings around the world, new releases, and sessions with the authors:

https://discord.bpbonline.com

Section 5
Changing Dynamics of SOC with Evolving Threats Fueled by Emerging Technologies

CHAPTER 16
Impact of Emerging Technologies

Introduction

The advent of emerging technologies is revolutionizing the landscape of SOCs. Traditionally, SOCs have played a crucial role in monitoring, detecting, and responding to cybersecurity threats, safeguarding organizations from potential breaches. However, with the rapid advancement of technologies such as **artificial intelligence (AI)**, **machine learning (ML)**, and big data analytics, the scope and efficiency of SOC operations are undergoing significant transformation. 5/6G wireless network, the **Internet of Things/ Internet of Everything (IoT/IoE)** will further complicate the cybersecurity domain as the attack surface will increase manifold and the diverse attack vectors will be difficult to mitigate. Quantum computing will add further complexity in cryptography and processing powers and significantly impact SOC operations.

These cutting-edge technologies also enable SOCs to process vast amounts of data at unprecedented speeds, identify patterns and anomalies that may indicate security threats, and automate routine tasks, allowing human analysts to focus on more complex and strategic aspects of cybersecurity. Additionally, integrating threat intelligence feeds and advanced analytics enhances the SOC's ability to predict and mitigate potential attacks before they can cause substantial harm.

Emerging technologies are significantly transforming SOC operations, enhancing detection, automation, and resilience. Here are some real-world examples:

- A global financial institution deployed AI-powered anomaly detection to identify unusual login attempts across employee accounts. By correlating behavioral analytics with external threat intelligence feeds, the SOC detected a coordinated phishing attack and automatically revoked compromised credentials, preventing account takeovers.

- A leading automotive manufacturer integrated Edge AI into its SOC to process security data locally, reducing latency and improving real-time threat response. This approach helped detect and mitigate cyber threats targeting IoT-enabled production lines.

- The Colonial Pipeline ransomware attack in 2021 highlighted the risks of IT/OT integration. In response, industrial SOCs implemented network segmentation and intrusion detection systems to protect critical infrastructure from similar cyber threats.

- A smart factory leveraged AI-driven predictive analytics to detect anomalies in industrial equipment. By identifying irregular patterns in sensor data, the SOC prevented cyber-physical attacks that could disrupt operations.

These advancements enable SOCs to transition from reactive security models to proactive, AI-enhanced defense strategies, ensuring resilience in evolving cyber landscapes. As we explore the impact of these emerging technologies on SOC operations, it becomes evident that they are enhancing cybersecurity professionals' capabilities and reshaping how organizations approach and manage their security strategies. The potential for these technologies to provide more robust, proactive, and adaptive security measures marks a new era for SOC operations, promising a more secure digital future. This chapter looks at emerging technologies impacting security operations and how they will shape the future.

Structure

In this chapter, we will discuss the following topics:

- Emerging technologies affecting SOC Operations
- Quantum computing and cryptography's impact on SOC
- Industry 4.0 and 5.0
- OT Security

Objectives

By the end of this chapter, readers will be able to understand the transformative impact of emerging technologies on SOC operations. By examining the integration and application of advanced technologies such as AI, ML, IoT/IoE, quantum computing, operational technology security, and automation, this chapter aims to provide a comprehensive understanding of how these innovations impact as well as enhance SOC capabilities.

Ultimately, this chapter seeks to offer valuable insights and practical guidance for cybersecurity professionals and organizations striving to leverage emerging technologies to fortify their security posture and effectively combat evolving cyber threats.

Emerging technologies affecting SOC operations

The SOC has always been reactive, constantly playing catch-up with the evolving threat landscape. However, the surge of emerging technologies is forcing a paradigm shift and demanding a proactive and adaptive approach. While offering immense potential, these technologies also introduce novel attack vectors and complexities that reshape the SOC's operational landscape.

The evolution of SOCs is being shaped by emerging technologies, such as AI/ML-driven detection, XDR platforms, and cloud-native SOC architectures. These advancements are transforming security operations by improving detection accuracy, reducing alert fatigue, and streamlining incident response.

AI/ML are revolutionizing SOC workflows by enabling real-time threat detection and automated response mechanisms. Traditional SOCs rely on rule-based detection, which often leads to false positives and reactive investigations. AI-driven SOCs, however, leverage behavioral analytics and anomaly detection to identify sophisticated threats that evade signature-based defenses. For example, AI-powered threat hunting can proactively detect lateral movement, privilege escalation, and data exfiltration by analyzing patterns across network traffic, endpoint activity, and user behavior. Additionally, ML models continuously refine detection algorithms, improving SOC efficiency by reducing manual triage efforts.

XDR platforms integrate security telemetry from endpoints, networks, email, and cloud environments, providing holistic visibility into cyber threats. Unlike traditional SIEM and SOAR solutions, XDR automates correlation across multiple data sources, enabling SOC analysts to identify attack chains more effectively. For instance, an XDR platform can link phishing attempts to credential theft and lateral movement, allowing SOC teams to contain threats before they escalate. Organizations adopting XDR benefit from faster incident resolution, improved threat intelligence integration, and reduced operational complexity.

With the rise of multi-cloud environments, SOCs are shifting towards cloud-native architectures that offer scalability, automation, and real-time monitoring. Cloud-native SOCs leverage serverless computing, containerized security applications, and API-driven integrations to enhance threat detection and response. For example, cloud-based SIEM solutions provide centralized log aggregation and AI-driven analytics, enabling SOC teams to detect anomalies across distributed infrastructures. Additionally, cloud-native SOCs integrate Zero Trust security models, ensuring continuous authentication and least-privilege access for users and applications.

The adoption of AI/ML, XDR, and cloud-native SOC architectures is driving significant improvements in SOC efficiency, detection accuracy, and response speed. These technologies enable SOC teams to:

- Reduce alert fatigue by automating triage and prioritization.
- Enhance threat detection through behavioral analytics and adversary mapping.
- Streamline incident response with automated containment playbooks.
- Improve security resilience by integrating MITRE ATT&CK frameworks into detection workflows.

SOCs have long been the backbone of an organization's defense against cybersecurity threats. With the ever-evolving landscape of cyber threats, SOCs must constantly adapt and innovate to stay ahead of malicious actors. The future of SOC operations is intrinsically linked to the advancement of emerging technologies. Let us explore the impacts of these emerging technologies on SOC.

AI and ML

AI and ML are the most transformative technologies impacting the SOC. Their ability to analyze massive datasets, identify patterns, and automate responses is revolutionizing security operations.

Artificial intelligence has emerged as a game-changer in the realm of cybersecurity. SOCs leverage AI to process vast amounts of data in real time, identify patterns, and detect anomalies that may indicate potential threats. AI-powered threat intelligence platforms can correlate disparate data sources to provide a holistic view of the threat landscape, enabling faster and more accurate assessment.

AI-driven tools can automate routine tasks such as log analysis and threat hunting, freeing up human analysts to focus on more complex and strategic activities. AI-driven SOAR platforms can automate routine security tasks, such as incident triage, containment, and remediation, freeing analysts to focus on more complex threats. Additionally, AI can enhance incident response by providing actionable insights and recommendations, reducing response times, and minimizing the impact of security breaches.

Machine learning, a subset of AI, improves threat detection capabilities within SOCs. ML algorithms can be trained on historical data to recognize patterns associated with known threats and predict future attack vectors. ML models can adapt to evolving threat landscapes and detect previously unknown threats by continuously learning from new data. ML algorithms can detect anomalies in network traffic and user behavior, flagging potential threats that traditional rule-based systems might miss.

Behavioral analytics, driven by ML, can establish baselines for normal activity and detect deviations that indicate malicious intent, such as insider threats or compromised accounts. This proactive approach to threat detection enables SOCs to stay ahead of cybercriminals and mitigate potential risks before they escalate.

The integration of AI and ML into SOC operations offers several benefits. Let us look at some of them:

- **Improved accuracy**: AI and ML technologies enhance the accuracy of threat detection by analyzing large datasets and identifying subtle patterns that may be missed by traditional methods. This reduces the likelihood of false positives and false negatives.

- **Faster response times**: AI-powered tools enable real-time monitoring and analysis, allowing SOCs to respond to security incidents more quickly. This rapid response minimizes the potential damage caused by cyberattack.

- **Scalability**: AI and ML technologies can scale to handle the increasing volume and complexity of data generated by modern networks. This scalability ensures that SOCs can efficiently manage large datasets and stay ahead of evolving threats.

- **Resource optimization**: By automating routine tasks, AI and ML free human analysts to focus on more complex and strategic activities. This optimizes resource use and enhances SOC operations' overall efficiency.

While integrating emerging technologies offers significant benefits, it also presents challenges that must be addressed. Let us look at some of these challenges:

- The black box nature of some AI algorithms can make it difficult to understand how they arrive at their conclusions, raising concerns about transparency and accountability.

- Integrating AI and ML technologies with existing SOC infrastructure can be complex and require significant modifications. SOCs need to ensure seamless integration to maximize the benefits of these technologies.

- Adversaries also leverage AI to develop sophisticated attack tools, such as deepfakes and polymorphic malware, creating an AI arms race.

- The need for extensive, high-quality data sets to train AI systems. Implementing AI and ML technologies can be resource-intensive and costly. Organizations must allocate sufficient budget and resources to support the adoption and maintenance of these advanced technologies.

- AI and ML models rely on high-quality data to function effectively. Poor data quality or biased data can lead to inaccurate predictions and analysis. Ensuring the integrity and diversity of training data is essential for accurate threat detection.

- One of the primary challenges of implementing AI and ML is the potential for false positives. AI algorithms may generate many false alerts, overwhelming analysts and leading to alert fatigue. Ensuring the accuracy and reliability of these technologies requires continuous monitoring, fine-tuning, and validation.

The future of SOC operations is intrinsically linked to the continued advancement of AI and ML technologies. As these technologies evolve, they will further enhance the capabilities of SOCs, enabling them to stay ahead of emerging threats. The following trends and developments are likely to shape the future of AI and ML in SOC operations:

- **AI-driven threat intelligence**: AI will play a central role in analyzing threat intelligence feeds from multiple sources, providing SOCs with a comprehensive view of the threat landscape. This enhanced threat intelligence will enable SOCs to make informed decisions and implement proactive security measures.

- **Advanced behavioral analytics**: ML algorithms will continue to evolve, enabling more sophisticated behavioral analytics. These advanced analytics will improve the SOC's ability to detect and respond to insider threats and APTs.

- **Human-AI collaboration**: The collaboration between human analysts and AI-powered tools will become increasingly important. AI will augment human capabilities, providing actionable insights and recommendations, while human analysts will provide the context and intuition that AI lacks.

- **AI-powered security orchestration**: The automation and orchestration of security tasks, powered by AI, will streamline SOC workflows and improve efficiency. AI-powered security orchestration platforms will enable seamless coordination of incident response efforts.

- **Ethical AI and bias mitigation**: As the adoption of AI and ML technologies grows, there will be a greater emphasis on ethical AI and bias mitigation. Ensuring fairness, transparency, and accountability in AI algorithms will be essential for building trust and confidence in these technologies.

AI and ML are fundamentally transforming SOC operations, enabling rapid threat detection, automated responses, and predictive analytics for cybersecurity teams. Microsoft Defender XDR leverages AI-powered threat intelligence to significantly reduce response times. In a 2024 case study, an enterprise SOC using Defender XDR identified and mitigated a ransomware attack 92% faster than traditional methods, cutting containment time from hours to minutes, drastically minimizing damage.

Another illustration of AI-driven security enhancement is Google Chronicle, which utilizes ML models to analyze enormous volumes of security telemetry in real time. A financial institution deployed Chronicle and observed a 68% reduction in false positives, freeing analysts from excessive alert fatigue and enabling them to focus on genuine high-risk threats.

Additionally, abnormal security has integrated **natural language processing** (**NLP**) into its email security solutions, enhancing phishing detection beyond conventional rule-based methods. An internal study found that AI-powered email filtering improved phishing identification accuracy by 85%, significantly reducing credential theft risks.

These cases demonstrate the transformative impact AI and ML have on SOC operations, moving from reactive defense strategies to predictive security frameworks. By automating routine tasks, refining anomaly detection, and improving incident response efficiency, AI-driven SOCs are redefining cybersecurity resilience.

Big data analytics

In today's digital age, the sheer volume of data generated by organizations is staggering. The rise of big data has transformed various industries, and cybersecurity is no exception. SOCs are at the forefront of defending against cyber threats, and the integration of big data analytics into SOC operations has brought about significant advancements.

Big data analytics involves the process of examining large and complex datasets to uncover hidden patterns, correlations, and insights. In SOC operations, big data analytics is crucial in enhancing threat detection, incident response, and overall security posture.

Big data analytics is relevant to SOC operations owing to its role, including the following:

- Big data analytics enables SOCs to analyze vast amounts of data from various sources, such as network traffic, logs, user behavior, and threat intelligence feeds. This comprehensive analysis helps identify anomalies and patterns indicating potential security threats.

- By leveraging big data analytics, SOCs can perform real-time monitoring of network activities. This capability allows for the immediate detection of suspicious activities and swift response to potential threats, minimizing the impact of security incidents.

- Big data analytics employs advanced machine learning algorithms to predict future attack vectors based on historical data and emerging threat trends. This proactive approach enables SOCs to anticipate and mitigate potential threats before they materialize.

- In the aftermath of a security incident, big data analytics facilitate forensic analysis by providing a detailed view of the events leading up to the breach. This helps SOCs understand the attack vectors, assess the damage, and implement measures to prevent future incidents.

The integration of big data analytics into SOC operations offers several benefits. Let us look at some of them in detail:

- **Improved accuracy**: Big data analytics enhances the accuracy of threat detection by analyzing large datasets and identifying subtle patterns that may be missed by traditional methods. This reduces the likelihood of false positives and false negatives.

- **Faster response times**: The ability to process and analyze data in real time enables SOCs to respond to security incidents more quickly. This rapid response minimizes the potential damage caused by cyberattack.

- **Actionable insights**: Big data analytics provide SOCs with actionable insights and recommendations, enabling them to prioritize and address the most critical threats. This improves the efficiency and effectiveness of their response efforts.

- **Scalability**: Big data analytics can scale to handle the increasing volume and complexity of data generated by modern organizations. This scalability ensures that SOCs can effectively manage large datasets and stay ahead of evolving threats.

Despite its numerous benefits, the adoption of big data analytics in SOC operations presents a few challenges. Let us look at them:

- The sheer volume and complexity of data generated by modern networks can be overwhelming. SOCs need advanced tools and substantial computational resources to process and analyze this data effectively.

- Integrating big data analytics tools with existing SOC infrastructure can be complex and require significant modifications. Ensuring seamless integration is essential for maximizing the benefits of big data analytics.

- The vast amount of data analyzed by big data analytics tools raises concerns about privacy and security. SOCs must implement robust data protection measures to safeguard sensitive information and comply with regulatory requirements.

- The adoption of big data analytics requires specialized skills and knowledge. SOC personnel need training and upskilling to utilize big data analytics tools and interpret the results effectively.

- Ensuring the quality and integrity of data analyzed by big data analytics tools is crucial for accurate threat detection. Poor data quality can lead to inaccurate analysis and false conclusions.

The future of SOC operations is closely tied to the continued advancement of big data analytics. As the volume and complexity of data continue to grow, SOCs must leverage advanced analytics to enhance their threat detection, response, and overall security management capabilities.

The following trends and developments are likely to shape the future of big data analytics in SOC operations:

- **AI and ML integration**: Integrating AI and ML with big data analytics will further enhance the accuracy and efficiency of threat detection and response. AI-driven analytics will enable SOCs to stay ahead of emerging threats and adapt to the evolving cyber landscape.

- **Automation and orchestration**: The automation and orchestration of security tasks, powered by big data analytics, will streamline SOC workflows and reduce the burden on human analysts. Automated responses to security incidents will improve response times and minimize the impact of attacks.

- **Advanced threat intelligence**: The use of big data analytics to analyze threat intelligence feeds from multiple sources will provide SOCs with a comprehensive view of the threat landscape. This enhanced threat intelligence will enable SOCs to make informed decisions and implement proactive security measures.

- **Collaboration and information sharing**: Big data analytics will facilitate greater collaboration and information sharing between SOCs and other stakeholders, such as industry peers and government agencies. This collaborative approach will strengthen collective defense efforts and improve overall cybersecurity.

Big data analytics is reshaping SOC operations by enabling security teams to process vast datasets, uncover hidden attack patterns, and strengthen forensic investigations. One example comes from a **global financial firm** that detected a banking Trojan campaign using advanced analytics. By correlating security logs, transaction behaviors, and external intelligence sources, the SOC identified subtle deviations in login attempts and fund transfers. Machine learning algorithms flagged these anomalies, leading to the discovery of a previously unknown malware variant, effectively preventing fraudulent transactions totaling **$15 million**.

Another case involves a **telecommunications provider** combating large-scale **DDoS attacks**. By analyzing real-time traffic patterns across its network, the SOC identified spikes indicative of botnet activity. Leveraging big data-driven behavioral modeling, the company implemented automated countermeasures that mitigated the attack in **seconds**, ensuring service continuity and preventing disruptions.

These examples highlight how SOCs harness big data analytics to shift from reactive security responses to predictive threat detection, improving response times, accuracy, and overall resilience against cyber threats. As cyber adversaries evolve, leveraging big data insights will be instrumental in maintaining robust security operations. Big data analytics has a profound impact on SOC operations, offering enhanced threat detection, real-time monitoring, predictive analytics, and actionable insights. As SOCs continue to integrate big data analytics into their operations, along with AI and ML, they will be better equipped to defend against evolving cyber threats and ensure the security and integrity of their organizations.

Blockchain

Blockchain technology, originally developed as the foundation for cryptocurrencies like Bitcoin, has emerged as a transformative force across various industries. Its decentralized and immutable nature offers unique advantages in securing data and ensuring transparency. Blockchain's inherent characteristics make it highly relevant to cybersecurity.

Blockchain eliminates the need for a central authority, reducing single points of failure and making it harder for cyber attackers to compromise the system. Once data is recorded on the blockchain, it cannot be altered or deleted. This ensures data integrity and prevents tampering. Blockchain allows transparent and verifiable transactions, making it easier to track and audit activities. Blockchain utilizes advanced cryptographic techniques to secure data, ensuring confidentiality and authenticity.

The integration of blockchain technology can significantly enhance SOC operations in various ways, as mentioned here:

- **Improved data integrity**: Blockchain's immutability ensures that logs and records are tamper-proof, enhancing the reliability of forensic investigations.

- **Enhanced threat intelligence sharing**: Blockchain can facilitate secure and transparent sharing of threat intelligence across organizations. SOCs are beginning to leverage blockchain-based platforms to share threat intelligence securely and anonymously with peers, improving collective defense against global campaigns like ransomware.

- **Decentralized identity management**: Blockchain-based identity management systems can provide a more secure and efficient way to manage user identities and access controls.

- **Automated incident response**: Smart contracts on blockchain can automate certain aspects of incident response, such as triggering predefined actions when specific conditions are met.

- **Supply chain security**: Blockchain can ensure the integrity and authenticity of hardware and software components within the supply chain, reducing the risk of supply chain attacks.

Blockchain and other decentralized technologies offer potential security benefits, but they also introduce new security considerations. Some of the challenges include the following:

- Smart contracts, which are self-executing contracts stored on a blockchain, can be vulnerable to bugs and exploits.

- Blockchain networks can face scalability issues, leading to slower transaction processing times and increased costs.

- Integrating blockchain with existing SOC tools and systems can be complex and require significant modifications.

- Compliance with regulatory requirements and legal frameworks can be challenging, especially in industries with strict data protection laws.

- Blockchain technology can be resource-intensive, requiring substantial computational power and energy consumption.

- The adoption of blockchain requires specialized skills and knowledge, necessitating investment in training and upskilling SOC personnel.

To address challenges associated with blockchain adoption, organizations can implement the following mitigation measures:

- Implement hybrid blockchain solutions that combine the benefits of both public and private blockchains to achieve scalability and privacy.

- Adopt and adhere to interoperability standards to ensure seamless integration with existing SOC tools and systems.

- Stay informed about regulatory developments and collaborate with legal experts to ensure compliance with relevant laws and regulations.

- Explore alternative consensus mechanisms, such as **proof of stake (PoS)**, to reduce the resource intensity of blockchain networks.

- Invest in training and education programs to equip SOC personnel with the necessary skills and knowledge to effectively utilize blockchain technology.

Blockchain technology is transforming SOC operations by enhancing threat intelligence sharing, automating incident response, and ensuring data integrity. A notable real-world application comes from **Interpol**, which utilizes blockchain to facilitate secure cyber threat intelligence exchange among law enforcement agencies. By leveraging a decentralized ledger, Interpol ensures threat indicators remain immutable and accessible only to authorized entities, minimizing the risk of tampering or unauthorized exposure.

Another use case is **Guardtime**, a cybersecurity firm that implemented blockchain-based integrity verification for SOC logs. In a major financial fraud investigation, Guardtime's blockchain framework validated forensic data, ensuring security logs remained untampered throughout the inquiry. This method strengthened the credibility of digital evidence, ultimately supporting legal proceedings.

Additionally, **smart contracts** are increasingly employed for automated incident response. A **European telecom provider** integrated blockchain-powered smart contracts into its security framework, enabling automated containment measures upon detecting network anomalies. This approach accelerated response times by 40%, effectively mitigating large-scale disruptions.

These examples illustrate how blockchain enhances SOC capabilities by ensuring secure, anonymous threat intelligence sharing, automating cybersecurity workflows, and preserving forensic integrity, ushering in a decentralized and resilient security landscape. Blockchain technology holds immense potential to revolutionize SOC operations by enhancing data integrity, enabling secure threat intelligence sharing, and automating incident response. While the adoption of blockchain presents several challenges, strategic planning and the implementation of mitigation measures can help organizations overcome these obstacles and fully leverage the benefits of blockchain. As the cybersecurity landscape continues to evolve, integrating blockchain into SOC operations will be essential for staying ahead of emerging threats and ensuring a robust security posture.

Cloud computing

Cloud computing has revolutionized how organizations manage their IT infrastructure, offering scalability, flexibility, and cost-efficiency. The widespread adoption of cloud computing and serverless architecture has transformed IT infrastructure, but it also presents new security challenges for the SOC. SOCs must adapt to this new environment as more businesses migrate to the cloud. Cloud computing introduces unique dynamics to cybersecurity, making it highly relevant to SOC operations.

Some key aspects impacting SOC are mentioned here:

- The ability to scale resources up or down based on demand allows organizations to handle varying workloads, making it easier to respond to cyber threats.

- Cloud services enable remote access to data and applications, which is essential for organizations with distributed workforces.

- Cloud platforms centralize data storage, simplifying data management but also creating attractive targets for cyber attackers.

- Cloud computing offers various service models, **infrastructure as a service (IaaS)**, **platform as a service (PaaS)**, **software as a service (SaaS)**, each with distinct security considerations and responsibilities.

The adoption of cloud computing has significant implications for SOC operations in many ways. Let us look at some of these in detail:

- Cloud providers offer advanced security tools and services that can enhance SOC capabilities. These tools leverage AI and ML to detect and respond to threats in real-time.

- SOCs need to maintain visibility and control over data residing in cloud environments. This requires integrating cloud security tools with existing SOC infrastructure to ensure comprehensive monitoring.

- Cloud platforms facilitate collaboration between SOC teams and cloud service providers, enabling faster and more coordinated incident response efforts.

- Cloud environments support automation and orchestration of security tasks, streamlining SOC workflows and improving efficiency.

Despite benefits, adopting cloud computing in SOC operations presents several challenges, such as:

- The distributed nature of cloud environments makes it difficult to gain comprehensive visibility into network traffic and user activity.

- Ensuring compliance with data protection regulations and maintaining data privacy in the cloud can be complex, especially for organizations operating in multiple jurisdictions.

- Understanding and managing the shared responsibility model between the organization and the cloud service provider is critical to ensure comprehensive security coverage. Managing access controls across multiple cloud platforms and services requires robust IAM solutions. Misconfigurations in cloud IAM policies can expose sensitive data to unauthorized access.

- Integrating cloud security tools with on-premises SOC infrastructure can be challenging and may require significant modifications.

- The ephemeral nature of serverless functions and containers creates challenges for traditional security monitoring tools. The proliferation of APIs in cloud environments creates new attack vectors that can be exploited by malicious actors.

- The adoption of cloud computing necessitates upskilling SOC personnel to effectively manage and secure cloud environments.

- Ensuring data resides in specific geographic locations to comply with regulatory requirements can be challenging in cloud environments.

To address the challenges associated with cloud computing adoption, organizations can implement the following mitigation measures:

- Emerging cloud technologies have accelerated the adoption of zero-trust models, where every access request is verified, reducing the attack surface. SOCs now prioritize IAM as a critical defense layer.

- Develop and implement a comprehensive cloud security strategy that includes policies, procedures, and controls to protect data and applications in the cloud.

- Foster strong partnerships with cloud service providers to ensure clarity on security responsibilities and leverage their expertise and resources.

- Implement continuous monitoring and auditing processes to maintain visibility and control over data and activities in the cloud.

- Invest in training and education programs to equip SOC personnel with the necessary skills and knowledge to effectively manage and secure cloud environments.

- Implement robust data encryption and access control measures to protect sensitive data in the cloud and ensure compliance with regulatory requirements.

Cloud computing has revolutionized SOC operations by enhancing scalability, real-time threat detection, and automated response capabilities. Capital One leveraged cloud-native security solutions to strengthen its SOC after migrating to AWS. By integrating AWS GuardDuty and Amazon Detective, the SOC improved anomaly detection, reducing false positives by 60% and accelerating incident investigation times by 40%.

Another case involves Netflix, which employs cloud-based security analytics to monitor billions of events daily. Using machine learning models within its cloud SOC, Netflix reduced alert fatigue by 70%, allowing analysts to focus on high-risk threats. The cloud infrastructure also enables seamless integration with SIEM and SOAR platforms, automating response workflows and minimizing manual intervention.

Additionally, a global healthcare provider adopted Microsoft Sentinel, a cloud-native SIEM, to enhance security monitoring across distributed environments. This transition improved threat correlation accuracy by 50%, enabling proactive defence against sophisticated cyber threats.

These examples highlight how cloud computing empowers SOCs with agility, automation, and predictive analytics, transforming cybersecurity operations into proactive, scalable defence mechanisms. Cloud computing is reshaping the cybersecurity landscape, offering new opportunities and challenges for SOC operations. By embracing cloud computing and addressing its associated challenges, SOCs can enhance their threat detection, response, and overall security management capabilities. A comprehensive approach to cloud security, coupled with collaboration and continuous monitoring, will enable SOCs to effectively protect their organizations in the dynamic cloud environment.

The integration of cloud computing into SOC operations holds immense potential for improving security posture and operational efficiency. However, organizations must carefully navigate the complexities and challenges associated with cloud adoption to fully realize these benefits. As the cybersecurity landscape continues to evolve, SOCs that successfully adapt to cloud computing will be better equipped to defend against emerging threats and ensure the security and integrity of their organizations.

Quantum computing and cryptography's impact on SOC

Quantum computing and advanced cryptography represent the frontier of technological innovation, promising to revolutionize numerous fields, including cybersecurity. Quantum computing, though still in its infancy as of March 2025, promises to revolutionize cryptography and, by extension, SOC operations. Its ability to perform complex calculations exponentially faster than classical computers could render current encryption standards like **Rivest-Shamir-Adleman (RSA)** and **Advanced Encryption Standard (AES)** obsolete.

Quantum computing leverages the principles of quantum mechanics to perform computations at unprecedented speeds. The key aspects of quantum computing that are significant for cybersecurity are as follows:

- **Enhanced computing power**: Quantum computers can solve complex problems much faster than classical computers, enabling more efficient data analysis and threat detection.

- **Breakthrough in cryptanalysis**: Quantum computing has the potential to break existing cryptographic algorithms, posing a significant threat to current encryption methods.

- **Development of quantum-resistant cryptography**: The advent of quantum computing necessitates the development of new cryptographic techniques that are resistant to quantum attacks.

The integration of quantum computing can transform SOC operations in various ways, such as:

- Quantum computers can analyze vast amounts of data in real-time, enabling SOCs to detect and respond to threats more quickly and accurately.

- Quantum computing can simulate complex cyber scenarios, helping SOCs predict potential attack vectors and develop robust defense strategies.

- Quantum computing drives the need for quantum-resistant cryptography, prompting SOCs to adopt new encryption methods to protect sensitive data.

- Quantum computing can enhance machine learning algorithms used in SOCs, improving threat detection and anomaly detection capabilities.

Despite its potential, the adoption of quantum computing in SOC operations presents several challenges. Let us look at some of them:

- Quantum computing requires specialized infrastructure and significant investment in hardware and facilities:

- Current cryptographic algorithms are vulnerable to quantum attacks, necessitating the development and standardization of quantum-resistant cryptographic techniques.

- The adoption of quantum computing requires specialized knowledge and skills, necessitating investment in training and upskilling SOC personnel.

- Ensuring compliance with regulatory requirements in quantum computing can be complex and challenging.

To address the challenges associated with quantum computing adoption, organizations can implement the following mitigation measures:

- Develop and adopt quantum-resistant cryptographic techniques to protect sensitive data from quantum attacks. SOCs will need to prepare for a post-quantum world by adopting quantum-resistant algorithms. This shift requires not just new tools but also retraining staff and rethinking data protection strategies.

- Partner with academic and research institutions to stay abreast of the latest developments in quantum computing and cryptography.

- Invest in training and education programs to equip SOC personnel with the necessary skills and knowledge to effectively utilize quantum computing technology.

- Work closely with regulatory bodies to ensure compliance with relevant laws and regulations in the context of quantum computing.

Quantum computing is poised to disrupt traditional cryptographic methods, forcing SOCs to adopt post-quantum security measures to safeguard sensitive data. A striking real-world example is the *U.S.* **National Security Agency (NSA)** accelerating its transition to quantum-resistant cryptography after simulations demonstrated that Shor's algorithm could break RSA-2048 encryption in a matter of hours, once large-scale quantum computers become viable. This urgency led to the NIST Post-Quantum Cryptography Standardization Project, which finalized quantum-safe algorithms like CRYSTALS-Kyber and SPHINCS+ for widespread adoption.

Another case involves IBM Quantum, which collaborated with financial institutions to assess quantum threats to banking encryption. Their research found that 60% of financial transactions rely on RSA-based encryption, making them vulnerable to quantum attacks. As a result, banks began integrating lattice-based cryptographic solutions to future-proof their security infrastructure.

Additionally, **Quantum Key Distribution (QKD)** is being deployed in SOCs to enhance secure communications. A European telecom provider implemented QKD across its network, reducing the risk of man-in-the-middle attacks by 95%, ensuring encrypted data remains secure even against quantum adversaries.

These examples highlight the urgency for SOCs to transition to post-quantum cryptography, ensuring resilience against emerging quantum threats while maintaining data integrity in an evolving cybersecurity landscape. While practical quantum computers are not yet widespread, SOCs must begin planning now, as retrofitting systems after a quantum breakthrough could leave organizations vulnerable.

Cryptography

Cryptography plays a crucial role in securing digital communications and protecting sensitive information. It is highly relevant for SOC operations as advanced cryptographic techniques ensure data confidentiality, integrity, and authenticity, safeguarding it from unauthorized access and tampering. Cryptography enables secure communication channels, protecting sensitive information exchanged between parties. Cryptographic methods are essential for verifying the identity of users and granting access to sensitive systems and data.

The adoption of advanced cryptographic techniques can enhance SOC operations in various ways, such as:

- Advanced cryptography ensures that sensitive data is protected from unauthorized access and tampering, enhancing overall security.

- Cryptographic methods provide robust authentication mechanisms, reducing the risk of unauthorized access and insider threats.

- Cryptography enables secure communication channels, ensuring that sensitive information exchanged between SOCs, and other entities is protected.

The adoption of advanced cryptographic techniques in SOC operations presents several challenges. Let us look at some of them:

- Implementing advanced cryptographic techniques can be complex and require significant expertise.

- Cryptographic methods can impact system performance, necessitating a balance between security and efficiency.

- Managing cryptographic keys securely and efficiently is a critical challenge in the adoption of advanced cryptography.

- Ensuring compliance with data protection regulations and cryptographic standards can be complex and challenging.

To address the challenges associated with the adoption of advanced cryptographic techniques, organizations can implement the following mitigation measures:

- Hire or train personnel with expertise in cryptography to effectively implement and manage advanced cryptographic techniques.

- Optimize cryptographic implementations to achieve a balance between security and system performance.

- Develop and implement robust key management practices to ensure the secure generation, storage, and distribution of cryptographic keys.

- Stay informed about regulatory developments and ensure compliance with relevant data protection regulations and cryptographic standards.

Quantum computing and advanced cryptography are poised to impact SOC operations, offering opportunities and challenges significantly. By embracing these emerging technologies and addressing their associated difficulties, SOCs can enhance their threat detection, response, and security management capabilities. A comprehensive approach to quantum computing and cryptography, collaboration, continuous monitoring, and investment in expertise will enable SOCs to protect their organizations in an evolving cybersecurity landscape effectively.

Integrating quantum computing and advanced cryptography into SOC operations holds immense potential for improving security posture and operational efficiency. However, organizations must carefully navigate the complexities and challenges of these technologies to fully realize their benefits. As the cybersecurity landscape continues to evolve, SOCs that successfully adapt to quantum computing and advanced cryptography will be better equipped to defend against emerging threats and ensure the security and integrity of their organizations.

Industry 4.0 and 5.0

Industry 4.0 and 5.0 represent significant shifts in the industrial landscape, characterized by the integration of advanced technologies such as the IoT, AI, robotics, and cyber-physical systems. The rollout of 5G networks and the proliferation of IoT devices have exponentially increased the number of endpoints SOCs must monitor. By March 2025, billions of devices, from smart thermostats to industrial sensors, will be connected, each creating a potential vulnerability.

The explosion of IoT devices and the increasing connectivity of **industrial control systems (ICS)** have expanded the attack surface to the physical world. These advancements have revolutionized manufacturing and other industrial sectors but also introduce new challenges and opportunities for SOCs.

The convergence of cyber and physical systems in Industry 4.0 and 5.0 has profound implications for cybersecurity, such as:

- **Increased attack surface**: The proliferation of connected devices and systems expands the attack surface, making it more difficult to secure the entire network.

- **Data explosion**: The massive amount of data generated by IoT devices and other connected systems require advanced analytics and security measures.

- **Interconnected supply chains**: The interconnectivity of supply chains introduces new vulnerabilities and necessitates collaborative security efforts.

- **Real-time monitoring and control**: The need for real-time monitoring and control of industrial processes requires robust and resilient security measures.

The integration of Industry 4.0 and 5.0 technologies significantly impacts SOC operations in several ways. Let us understand this in detail:

- Advanced analytics and AI-driven tools enable SOCs to detect and respond to threats in real time, improving overall security.

- The complexity of interconnected systems and devices requires SOCs to adopt more sophisticated security measures and monitoring techniques.

- SOCs must collaborate with other stakeholders, including **industrial control system (ICS)** operators, to ensure comprehensive security coverage.

- Ensuring the resilience of industrial systems against cyberattack becomes a critical priority for SOCs.

The adoption of Industry 4.0 and 5.0 technologies present several challenges for SOC operations, such as:

- Many IoT devices have limited security capabilities, making them vulnerable to attacks. The lack of standardized security protocols for IoT devices aggravates the problem.

- 5G's speed and low latency enable real-time threat detection across distributed networks and accelerate attack propagation.

- ICS environments often have legacy systems that are difficult to patch and secure. Integrating new technologies with legacy systems can be complex and require significant modifications.

- Attacks on ICS can have catastrophic consequences, disrupting critical infrastructure and causing physical harm.

- The adoption of advanced technologies necessitates upskilling SOC personnel to manage and secure industrial environments effectively.

- IoT devices generate massive amounts of data, overwhelming traditional security monitoring systems. Ensuring the security and privacy of the vast data generated by connected devices is a significant challenge.

- Securing data processed at the edge is a new and growing challenge.

- The interconnected nature of supply chains introduces new vulnerabilities that must be addressed.

To address these challenges associated with Industry 4.0 and 5.0 adoption, organizations can implement the following mitigation measures:

- Develop and implement a comprehensive security strategy that includes policies, procedures, and controls to protect industrial systems and data.

- Foster collaboration and information sharing between SOCs, ICS operators, and other stakeholders to ensure a holistic approach to security.

- Implement continuous monitoring and leverage threat intelligence to stay ahead of emerging threats.

- Invest in training and education programs to equip SOC personnel with the necessary skills and knowledge to effectively manage and secure industrial environments.

- Implement robust supply chain security measures to identify and mitigate vulnerabilities in interconnected supply chains.

Industry 4.0 and 5.0 are revolutionizing SOC operations by integrating smart automation, AI-driven security analytics, and collaborative human-machine frameworks to strengthen cybersecurity resilience. One notable example is Siemens, which implemented AI-powered anomaly detection across its **industrial control systems** (ICS). This deployment reduced cyberattack detection times by 60%, ensuring uninterrupted automated manufacturing processes and enhancing industrial security.

Similarly, Tesla incorporates real-time IoT security monitoring within its SOC to safeguard connected vehicle infrastructures. By analyzing telemetry data from millions of cars, Tesla's security operations identified firmware vulnerabilities and mitigated them, reducing potential exploits by 45%, a crucial step in protecting smart mobility ecosystems.

Industry 5.0 enhances SOC capabilities by emphasizing human-AI collaboration in threat detection. A European aerospace firm adopted AI-assisted threat hunting, where cybersecurity analysts worked alongside machine learning models to identify sophisticated cyber threats. This approach improved threat identification accuracy by 35%, demonstrating the powerful synergy between automation and human expertise.

These examples illustrate how Industry 4.0 and 5.0 are transforming SOCs into adaptive, intelligent security hubs that proactively defend against evolving cyber threats. As these technologies continue to advance, SOCs will evolve into even more resilient, high-speed defense infrastructures capable of responding to cyber risks with precision and agility. Industry 4.0 and 5.0 are transforming the industrial landscape, offering new opportunities and challenges for SOC operations. By embracing these advancements and addressing their associated difficulties, SOCs can enhance their threat detection, response, and overall security management capabilities. A comprehensive approach to security, collaboration, continuous monitoring, and investment in expertise will enable SOCs to protect their organizations in an evolving industrial environment effectively.

The integration of Industry 4.0 and 5.0 technologies into SOC operations holds immense potential for improving security posture and operational efficiency. However, organizations must carefully navigate the complexities and challenges of these technologies to fully realize their benefits. As the cybersecurity landscape continues to evolve, SOCs that successfully adapt to Industry 4.0 and 5.0 will be better equipped to defend against emerging threats and ensure the security and integrity of their organizations.

Operational technology security

Operational technology (OT) refers to the hardware and software systems used to monitor and control physical processes, devices, and infrastructure within industries such as manufacturing, energy, and transportation. With the convergence of IT and OT environments, ensuring the security of OT systems has become a critical priority.

The integration of OT systems with IT networks introduces new cybersecurity risks and challenges, such as:

- **Critical infrastructure protection**: OT systems are often part of critical infrastructure, making them prime targets for cyberattack that can have severe consequences for public safety and national security.

- **Interconnected environments**: The convergence of IT and OT environments increases the attack surface, requiring comprehensive security measures to protect both domains.

- **Legacy systems**: Many OT systems are built on legacy technologies that lack modern security features, making them vulnerable to cyber threats.

- **Real-time operations**: OT systems operate in real-time, necessitating quick and effective response to security incidents to prevent disruptions to critical processes.

The need to secure OT systems significantly impacts SOC operations in several ways. Let us look at this in detail:

- SOCs must extend their monitoring capabilities to include OT environments, ensuring comprehensive visibility and threat detection across both IT and OT domains.

- SOC personnel need specialized knowledge and skills to understand and manage OT security, including familiarity with **industrial control systems (ICS)** and protocols.

- SOCs must develop integrated incident response strategies that address both IT and OT security incidents, ensuring coordinated and efficient response efforts.

- SOCs need to collaborate closely with OT teams to ensure a holistic approach to security and to bridge the gap between IT and OT security practices.

The adoption of OT security measures presents several challenges for SOC operations such as:

- Achieving comprehensive visibility and monitoring of OT environments can be challenging due to the heterogeneity of systems and protocols used in OT.

- Integrating OT security tools with existing SOC infrastructure can be complex and may require significant modifications.

- Ensuring adequate resources, including personnel and budget, to address OT security needs can be challenging for SOCs.

- Compliance with industry-specific regulations and standards, such as **North American Electric Reliability Corporation Critical Infrastructure Protection (NERC CIP)** for the energy sector, adds complexity to OT security efforts.

To address these challenges associated with OT security, organizations can implement the following mitigation measures:

- Develop and implement a comprehensive security strategy that includes policies, procedures, and controls to protect OT systems and data.

- Provide cross-disciplinary training for SOC personnel and OT teams to ensure a mutual understanding of IT and OT security practices.

- Implement advanced threat detection tools and techniques, such as anomaly detection and behavioral analytics, to identify potential threats in OT environments.

- Foster collaboration and information sharing between SOCs, OT teams, and other stakeholders to ensure a coordinated approach to security.

- Conduct regular security audits and assessments of OT environments to identify vulnerabilities and ensure compliance with relevant regulations and standards.

The convergence of IT and OT environments presents new challenges and opportunities for SOC operations. By addressing the unique security needs of OT systems and adopting a holistic approach to cybersecurity, SOCs can enhance their threat detection, response, and overall security management capabilities. A comprehensive approach to OT security, coupled with collaboration, continuous monitoring, and investment in expertise, will enable SOCs to protect their organizations in an increasingly interconnected world effectively.

The integration of OT security into SOC operations is essential for protecting critical infrastructure and ensuring the resilience of industrial processes. As the cybersecurity landscape continues to evolve, SOCs that successfully address OT security challenges will be better equipped to defend against emerging threats and ensure the security and integrity of their organizations.

Conclusion

While emerging technologies empower SOCs, they also introduce complexities. Over-reliance on AI could lead to blind spots if models fail to adapt to novel threats. Quantum and blockchain adoption require significant investment, potentially widening the gap between well-funded enterprises and smaller organizations. Moreover, the use of AI in surveillance or profiling raises ethical questions about privacy and bias, issues SOCs must navigate as they balance security with societal impact.

Emerging technologies are reshaping the SOC, demanding a proactive and adaptive approach to security. By embracing AI, cloud security best practices, IoT security measures, and exploring the potential of blockchain, SOCs can enhance their ability to detect, respond to, and prevent cyber threats. However, it is crucial to address the challenges associated with these technologies, including the skills gap, the need for robust data governance, and the evolving tactics of adversaries. The future of the SOC lies in its ability to leverage emerging technologies to create a more resilient and secure digital world.

SOCs will become more distributed in the coming years, leveraging edge computing and cloud-native architectures to protect increasingly decentralized organizations. The winners in this space will be those who harness emerging technologies not as a panacea but as tools to amplify human ingenuity, the earnest heart of cybersecurity.

In the next chapter, we will discuss cyber-resilient systems. It is important to leverage emerging technologies to improve any organization's security posture management. At the same time, handling the complex threat landscape requires proactive measures to make information systems more cyber-resilient.

Points to remember

Here are some key takeaways from this chapter:

- Emerging technologies bring in potential benefits, including improved threat detection, faster response times, and more efficient resource allocation, as well as addressing the challenges and considerations associated with implementing these technologies.

- For SOCs, these emerging technologies offer both opportunities and challenges, necessitating a re-evaluation of current practices and strategies.

- The adoption of emerging technologies necessitates investment in training and upskilling SOC personnel to effectively utilize these tools and maximize their potential.

Multiple choice questions

1. **Which of the following technologies is primarily used to automate routine tasks in SOC operations, freeing up human analysts for more complex activities?**

   a. Blockchain

   b. AI

   c. Quantum computing

   d. Big data analytics

2. **Automation in SOC operations primarily helps with:**

   a. Increasing the manual workload

   b. Handling larger volumes of data and alerts

   c. Reducing the need for threat intelligence

   d. Slowing down the response times

3. **What is the primary function of quantum computing in enhancing SOC operations?**

   a. Automating routine tasks

   b. Breaking existing cryptographic algorithms

   c. Simulating complex cyber scenarios

   d. Reducing energy consumption

Answers

1	b
2	b
3	c

Questions

1. Discuss the role of AI and ML in enhancing threat detection and response in SOC operations. What are the potential benefits and challenges of implementing these technologies?

2. Analyze the role of blockchain technology in enhancing SOC operations. What are the benefits and challenges of integrating blockchain into SOCs?

3. Explain the significance of the IoT and the IoE in the context of SOC operations.

4. How do these technologies impact the capabilities of SOCs?

Key terms

Some key terms used in this chapter are:

- **AI and ML, big data analytics**: Emerging technologies significantly impacting SOC operations.

- **Quantum computing**: Evolving technology poses a significant threat and savior for cryptography.

Join our Discord space

Join our Discord workspace for latest updates, offers, tech happenings around the world, new releases, and sessions with the authors:

https://discord.bpbonline.com

CHAPTER 17
Cyber Resilient Systems

Introduction

In today's rapidly evolving threat landscape, SOCs face unprecedented challenges. Sophisticated threat actors, APTs, and increasingly complex IT environments demand more than traditional security measures. Cyber resilience, the ability to prepare for, respond to, and recover from cyber threats while maintaining business continuity, has become foundational to effective security operations. This chapter explores how modern SOCs implement cyber resilient systems to withstand, adapt to, and rapidly recover from disruptions.

Traditional security approaches focused primarily on prevention through perimeter defenses. While prevention remains critical, the cybersecurity community has recognized that breaches are inevitable. Modern SOCs now embrace a holistic approach, integrating prevention with detection, response, and recovery capabilities to maintain essential functions even during security incidents.

A leading financial institution faced an unprecedented cyberattack on a routine Monday morning. What initially appeared as failed login attempts escalated into a multi-vector intrusion, combining AI-driven credential stuffing with a zero-day exploit targeting its payment processing system. As unauthorized transactions began appearing, panic spread among business leaders fearing reputational damage and financial loss. However, its cyber resilient SOC swiftly countered the attack using SOAR-powered automated containment, AI-driven threat intelligence, and self-healing system architectures. The compromised module was automatically rolled back, fraudulent transactions were blocked, and predefined incident response playbooks ensured operational continuity. Within minutes, the threat was neutralized, without disruption to customers or financial services. This incident underscores the necessity of cyber resilience in SOC operations, proving that security is not just about defence but about ensuring uninterrupted functionality even under attack.

Cyber resilience extends beyond conventional information security by adopting principles from business continuity, disaster recovery, and operational resilience. This evolution represents a significant paradigm shift from a binary secure or compromised perspective to a continuum of operational capabilities that can adapt under adverse conditions.

Structure

In this chapter, we will discuss the following topics:

- Significance of cyber resilience
- Components of cyber resilience
- Lifecycle of cyber resilience
- Building self-healing systems

Objectives

By the end of this chapter, readers will gain insight into designing cyber-resilient systems, peppered with real-world examples that bring the stakes to life. Ranging from the chaos of ransomware lockdowns to nation-state espionage, these stories illustrate why resilience is the SOC's new superpower.

Significance of cyber resilience

Cyber resilience is an organization's ability to anticipate, withstand, recover from, and adapt to adverse cyber events. For an SOC, this means shifting from a fortress mentality, where every attack must be blocked, to a more fluid approach that assumes breaches will happen and prepares accordingly.

Consider the 2017 WannaCry ransomware attack. This global outbreak exploited a vulnerability in Microsoft Windows, infecting over 200,000 systems across 150 countries in hours. Hospitals in the *UK's* **National Health Service (NHS)** were hit hard; ambulances were rerouted, surgeries canceled, and patient records locked behind a $300 Bitcoin ransom demand. The organizations that bounced back quickly did not have the tallest walls; they had resilient systems—redundant backups, rapid patching pipelines, and SOCs ready to pivot from detection to containment.

For SOCs, cyber resilience is a mission. Analysts must evolve from ticket-closers to strategic defenders, wielding tools like AI-driven anomaly detection and threat-hunting platforms. Leaders must champion resilience metrics, MTTD and MTTR over outdated breach-free scorecards. And collaboration with IT, DevOps, and even C-suite execs is non-negotiable, resilience spans silos.

Cyber resilience in action

In this subsection, we will be looking at some real-life examples of cyber resilience in action:

- **The Maersk meltdown**: The value of resilience can be better understood through real-life examples like the 2017 NotPetya attack on Maersk, the global shipping giant. What started as a targeted strike on *Ukraine* spiraled into a $300 million disaster for Maersk when NotPetya's self-replicating malware tore through its unpatched Windows systems. Ports froze, ships sat idle, and 45,000 PCs turned to digital ash. The SOC's initial response was chaos, disconnected networks left teams scrambling via WhatsApp.

  However, here is where resilience sparkled. Maersk's IT crew found a single uninfected domain controller in *Ghana* (thanks to a timely power outage) and used it to rebuild their Active Directory from scratch. Within 10 days, they restored operations, not because they stopped the attack, but because they adapted under fire. The SOC learned hard lessons: patch management became gospel, and offline backups went from *nice-to-have* to non-negotiable.

- **The Equifax incident, a resilience wake-up call**: The 2017 Equifax breach is a stark reminder of the consequences of insufficient resilience planning. When attackers exploited a known vulnerability in Apache Struts, they accessed sensitive information affecting 147 million consumers. The company's response was hampered by inadequate visibility, limited segmentation, and challenges in coordinating incident response across the enterprise.

  The incident, which ultimately cost Equifax over $1.7 billion in remediation and settlements, highlighted the critical importance of resilience planning. Organizations across industries took note, accelerating investments in detection capabilities, response processes, and recovery systems.

- **The SolarWinds response, adaptation in action**: When news of the SolarWinds supply chain compromise broke in December 2020, organizations worldwide faced a sobering reality: A trusted software update mechanism had been weaponized to deliver malicious code to thousands of customers. Western manufacturing's SOC had implemented a resilience strategy that included network segmentation, privileged access monitoring, and regular threat hunting. While they could not have anticipated this specific attack, their resilience-focused architecture limited the potential impact.

The company's response demonstrated the value of designing systems to withstand partial compromise. By isolating critical manufacturing systems and implementing the least-privilege access controls, they contained potential damage and maintained production capabilities throughout the incident.

- **KPIs, the retail success story in resilience**: After suffering a payment card breach in 2018, *Northeast Retail Corporation* implemented a comprehensive resilience measurement program. The company developed a balanced scorecard approach monitoring technical metrics like MTTD and MTTR, operational metrics like the percentage of systems with verified backups and recovery testing success rates, and strategic metrics like time to implement critical security patches and security debt reduction.

  Over three years, Northeast Retail reduced its MTTD from 24 days to 4 hours and its MTTR from 72 hours to eight hours. Perhaps most importantly, when it faced an attempted ransomware attack in 2021, it detected and contained it before encryption could begin.

- **Zero Trust transformation, a government agency case study**: After suffering repeated compromises through stolen credentials, a federal government agency embarked on an ambitious Zero Trust transformation in 2020. The agency implemented continuous authentication and authorization for all users, device health verification before granting system access, fine-grained access controls to applications and data, encryption of all data in transit and at rest, and comprehensive logging and monitoring.

  Two years into the transformation, the agency reported a 74% reduction in successful phishing attacks and a 60% decrease in the time required to detect unauthorized access attempts, making the systems more resilient.

- **Designing for failure, the Netflix approach**: *Netflix's Chaos Monkey*, a tool that deliberately terminates random instances in production, exemplifies the design for failure philosophy that underpins cyber resilience. By intentionally introducing failures during normal operations, Netflix ensures their systems can withstand disruptions without affecting the customer experience.

- **War game approach, financial services innovation**: A consortium of financial institutions in *Singapore* developed an innovative approach to measuring and improving cyber resilience: industry-wide war games. Twice yearly, the institutions conduct comprehensive simulations involving multiple attack vectors across the financial ecosystem. These exercises test communication protocols between organizations, identify dependencies and single points of failure, validate industry-wide response procedures, and build relationships between security teams.

Following each exercise, participants implement improvements based on lessons learned, creating a continuous improvement cycle that has demonstrably enhanced the sector's overall resilience.

SOCs can adopt similar principles by adopting the following measures:

- Regularly testing failover and recovery procedures.
- Conducting tabletop exercises simulating loss of critical systems.
- Designing detection systems with redundancy and graceful degradation.
- Implementing alternative processing capabilities for core functions.

Components of cyber resilience

Building resilience is a mindset ingrained into every layer of an SOC's operations. Truly resilient SOC systems operate on four fundamental principles:

- **Anticipation**: A resilient system starts with knowing what is coming. SOCs must leverage threat intelligence to predict attacks before they land. Proactive SOCs do not wait for the alarm; they hunt for weak spots. Take the 2020 SolarWinds supply chain attack, a masterclass in stealth by *Russian* hackers. They slipped malicious code into a routine software update, compromising thousands of organizations, including *U.S.* government agencies.

  The SOCs that fared best were not blindsided because they would have been tracking nation-state tactics via threat feeds and anomaly detection. By simulating supply chain attacks in their own environments, they would already have hardened their defenses. Tools like MITRE ATT&CK mappings and red team exercises can turn vague intel into actionable blueprints.

- **Withstanding**: Resilience demands systems that do not collapse when one piece fails. Withstanding entails implementing controls that limit the impact of security incidents through defense-in-depth strategies and security by design. Think of the 2021 colonial pipeline ransomware attack. A single breach shut down 45% of the *U.S. East Coast's* fuel supply, spiking gas prices and sparking panic buying. The attackers did not even hit the **operational technology** (**OT**) systems, just the billing infrastructure. However, poor segmentation and lack of redundancy meant the whole pipeline was grounded to a halt. A resilient SOC would have ensured critical functions had failover mechanisms, keeping fuel flowing even as IT burned. Segmentation in such a scenario is a lifesaver. SOCs should enforce micro-segmentation and maintain hot backups because downtime is the enemy of resilience.

- **Recovery**: Recovery is not just about restoring files; it is about learning to fight better next time. It entails rapidly restoring systems and data to maintain business operations with minimal downtime and data loss. In 2021, the Kaseya ransomware attack hit over 1,500 businesses via a compromised IT management tool. The resilient ones did not just pay the ransom or wipe their systems; they rebuilt with stronger encryption, updated playbooks, and tighter vendor controls. Their SOCs turned a nightmare into a springboard. SOCs should treat every incident as a chance to refine their stack and train their people.

- **Adaptation**: Learning from incidents to improve defenses, processes, and response capabilities in an iterative cycle. Speed is everything when containment is the goal. The 2013 target breach is a classic cautionary tale. Hackers stole 40 million credit card numbers over weeks, all because a **Heating, Ventilation, and Air Conditioning (HVAC)** vendor's credentials opened the door. Target's SOC had the alerts, FireEye flagged the malware early, but no one acted until it was too late.

  A resilient system pairs detection tools with a hair-trigger response team, cutting the window of damage from weeks to hours. Invest in automation. SOC can adapt using SOAR platforms to slash response times, turning a potential catastrophe into a blip.

A resilient SOC implements multiple overlapping defensive mechanisms to protect critical assets. This approach ensures that if one control fails, others remain in place to mitigate damage. The key components of this approach include the following:

- Network segmentation and micro-segmentation
- Privileged access management
- Endpoint protection and detection
- Data-centric security controls
- Cloud security architecture
- Zero Trust implementation

Rather than assuming perfect protection, resilient systems are designed with the expectation that components will fail. This assumed breach mentality drives several design characteristics:

- Redundancy in critical systems and data
- Isolation mechanisms that contain compromise
- Graceful degradation capabilities that maintain core functions
- Automated recovery processes that minimize human intervention

Technical components of resilient SOC systems

The technical components while implementing resilient SOC system include:

- At the heart of a resilient SOC lies its robust detection and response infrastructure. This includes the following:
  - SIEM platforms with high availability configurations.
  - XDR systems that provide visibility across domains.
  - UEBA to identify anomalous activity.
  - SOAR platforms that streamline incident handling.

These systems must themselves be resilient, with redundant components, geographic distribution, and protection against tampering. A typical SOAR workflow for creating cyber resilient systems is covered in the following table:

Step	Action	Tools involved	Outcome
Threat detection and ingestion	Gather alerts from email security, threat intelligence, SIEM	Proofpoint, Microsoft Defender, Splunk	Suspicious email or domain identified
Alert triage and analysis	Correlate phishing indicators, extract metadata	MITRE ATT&CK mapping, sandbox analysis	Risk level determined
Automated containment	Quarantine email, block links, isolate endpoint if confirmed malicious	EDR (CrowdStrike, Defender ATP), Firewall rules	Phishing impact mitigated
Threat hunting and impact assessment	Identify related phishing attempts, analyze affected users	SIEM (Splunk, QRadar), DNS logs	Broader attack visibility gained
Automated remediation	Block malicious domains, notify affected users, update response playbook	Firewall, threat intelligence updates	Future phishing defenses strengthened
Post-incident review	Generate reports, refine workflows, update intelligence	SOAR metrics tracking, KPI evaluation	Continuous improvement enabled

Table 17.1: Typical SOAR workflow

- Resilient SOCs leverage threat intelligence to maintain situational awareness and proactively adapt defenses. This requires the following:
  - Multiple intelligence sources providing strategic, tactical, and operational insights
  - Automated intelligence processing and correlation
  - Feedback loops between intelligence and detection systems
  - Threat-hunting capabilities informed by intelligence

- Data protection with backup and recovery systems forms a critical component of cyber resilience. Modern SOCs implement the following:
  - Immutable backups resistant to ransomware attacks
  - Air-gapped storage solutions
  - Tiered recovery systems based on criticality

- o Regular testing of restoration processes
- o Backup verification and validation procedures

- Identity remains central to security operations. Resilient systems must implement the following:
  - o Risk-based authentication that adapts security requirements to context
  - o Multiple authentication factors and methods
  - o Continuous authentication rather than point-in-time validation
  - o Identity governance with regular entitlement reviews
  - o Break-glass procedures for emergency access

Challenges and future directions

While making resilient systems, it is important to understand the challenges. Key challenges and mitigating directions are listed here:

- **Balancing security and usability**: One persistent challenge in building resilient systems is balancing security requirements with operational needs. Overly restrictive controls can drive users toward workarounds that ultimately reduce security. Progressive SOCs implement the following:
  - o User experience design in security solutions
  - o Security champions programs that embed security awareness
  - o Frictionless security where possible, with friction applied strategically
  - o Regular feedback collection from business units

- **Cloud and distributed architecture considerations**: As organizations adopt cloud services and distributed architectures, resilience strategies must evolve to address:
  - o Shared responsibility models with cloud providers
  - o Multi-cloud resilience strategies
  - o Container and microservices security
  - o DevSecOps integration
  - o API security and resilience

- **Emerging technologies and approaches**: Looking forward, several factors promise to enhance SOC resilience, such as:
  - o AI-augmented detection and response
  - o Security mesh architecture
  - o Digital twins for security testing

o   Self-healing systems and infrastructure

o   Quantum-resistant cryptography

- **The human factor in building resilient teams**: Technical systems are only as resilient as the people who operate them. The organization needs to implement several changes, such as:

  o   Cross-training team members across different specialties

  o   Establishing clear shift rotations during extended incidents

  o   Creating a reserve team of trained staff from other IT functions

  o   Implementing wellness programs and mandatory rest periods

- **Quantum computing is the next resilience challenge**: As quantum computing advances, organizations face a new resilience challenge: preparing for the potential compromise of current cryptographic systems. Forward-thinking SOCs must ensure the following:

  o   Inventorying systems that rely on vulnerable cryptographic algorithms.

  o   Implementing crypto agility to enable rapid algorithm transitions.

  o   Participating in post-quantum cryptography standards development.

  o   Developing migration roadmaps for critical systems.

  o   Ensuring quantum readiness checklist including:

    - Identify cryptographic dependencies in existing SOC systems.

    - Adopt crypto-agile frameworks supporting hybrid encryption.

    - Integrate post-quantum algorithms into security architecture.

    - Evaluate security solutions for NIST-approved PQC support.

    - Test resilience against quantum-based decryption attacks.

    - Update SOC playbooks to include PQC migration strategies.

The quantum revolution brings immense possibilities but also security challenges. Early adoption of post-quantum security measures is crucial for ensuring cyber resilience. If organizations plan for issues in advance, they will survive the cyber onslaught.

Lifecycle of cyber resilience

While understanding the theory behind cyber resilience is essential, organizations often struggle with the practical aspects of implementation. Building cyber-resilient systems that can withstand, adapt to, and recover from security incidents is paramount in today's dynamic threat landscape. We will focus on actionable steps, technical configurations, and organizational processes that security teams can implement today.

Foundation with risk-based architecture

Establishing a robust foundation with risk-based architecture is pivotal in accelerating cyber resilience within the SOC lifecycle. Organizations can ensure a proactive and resilient defense strategy by prioritizing and addressing the most critical threats.

Key steps include the following:

- Cyber resilience begins with knowing what you are protecting. Without a clear asset inventory, organizations risk exposure to unpatched systems, shadow IT, and misconfigured services. Automated asset discovery tools such as Rumble, Armis, and native cloud provider services (AWS Config, Azure Defender) provide continuous visibility, ensuring SOC teams can track every endpoint, network device, and cloud resource in real time. Once assets are identified, **Attack Surface Management** (ASM) ensures continuous monitoring of exposed services and unauthorized infrastructure across on-prem and cloud environments. Solutions like Expanse, Censys ASM, and Randori Recon detect externally accessible systems, misconfigurations, and potential entry points. Cloud-native ASM tools such as AWS GuardDuty and Microsoft Defender for Cloud further strengthen security posture. By integrating automated asset discovery with ASM, SOCs enhance cyber resilience by eliminating blind spots, reducing attack surfaces, and ensuring proactive security enforcement.

- Develop a tiered classification system that prioritizes protection based on business impact. For example:

  o **Tier 1 (Crown jewels)**: Systems that would cause severe business impact if compromised.

  o **Tier 2 (Critical)**: Systems that would significantly disrupt operations.

  o **Tier 3 (Important)**: Systems that support business functions but have workarounds.

  o **Tier 4 (Standard)**: General business systems with limited impact if disrupted.

  A typical classification framework can be as follows:

Asset type	Protection requirements	RTO	RPO
Tier 1	Full redundancy, air-gapped backups, enhanced monitoring	< 4 hours	< 15 minutes
Tier 2	HA configuration, daily backups, standard monitoring	< 8 hours	< 24 hours
Tier 3	Regular backups, standard monitoring	< 24 hours	< 48 hours
Tier 4	Weekly backups, basic monitoring	< 72 hours	< 1 week

Table 17.2: Asset classification framework

- Map dependencies between systems to understand cascade effects. Document these relationships in a CMDB or purpose-built tool like Lucidchart with appropriate tagging.

Technical implementation defense in depth

Effective network segmentation contains attacks and prevents lateral movement. Ensure the following measures for defense in depth strategy:

- Implement zero-trust micro-segmentation using tools like Illumio, Guardicore, or VMware NSX. Configure policies that ensure the following conditions:

  o Restrict east-west traffic between servers.

  o Limit communication to required services only.

  o Enforce authentication for all network connections Create security zones based on data sensitivity and function.

  o Deploy network traffic analysis tools at segment boundaries to detect unusual movements. Configure baselining and alerting for deviation from normal patterns.

- **Endpoint hardening**: Resilient endpoints resist and contain compromise. Implement the following measures to ensure endpoints are secure:

- Implement application allowlisting rather than signature-based blocking. Use Windows AppLocker, macOS Gatekeeper, or third-party tools like CarbonBlack or CrowdStrike. A sample policy can be as follows:

```
allow_publishers: [Microsoft, Adobe, Trusted_Internal_
Certificate]
allow_paths: [C:\Program Files\*, C:\Windows\*]
allow_hashes: [specific_trusted_binaries]
default: deny
```

- Deploy exploit prevention technologies that mitigate common attack vectors, such as **Address Space Layout Randomization** (ASLR), **Data Execution Prevention** (DEP), control-flow integrity protection, and memory protection features.

- Configure local firewalls with default-deny outbound policies.

Resilient authentication systems

Identity is the new perimeter and must be hardened accordingly. Ensure the following measures for effective authentication mechanisms:

- Implement multi-factor authentication with fallback methods such as:

  o **Primary**: Push notification to mobile app

- o **Secondary**: **Time-based one-time password (TOTP)**
- o **Tertiary**: Hardware security keys
- o **Emergency**: Pre-generated recovery codes stored in a secure location
- Deploy password less authentication where possible using technologies such as:
- o Windows Hello for Business
- o FIDO2 security keys
- o Certificate-based authentication
- Create tiered admin accounts with separate credentials and access pathways, such as:
- o **Tier 0**: Domain controllers, identity systems
- o **Tier 1**: Server administration
- o **Tier 2**: Workstation management
- o **User**: Standard user account

Resilient data management

Data resilience ensures business continuity despite system compromise. Ensure the following measures to implement effective data management policies:

- Implement the 3-2-1-1-0 backup strategy:

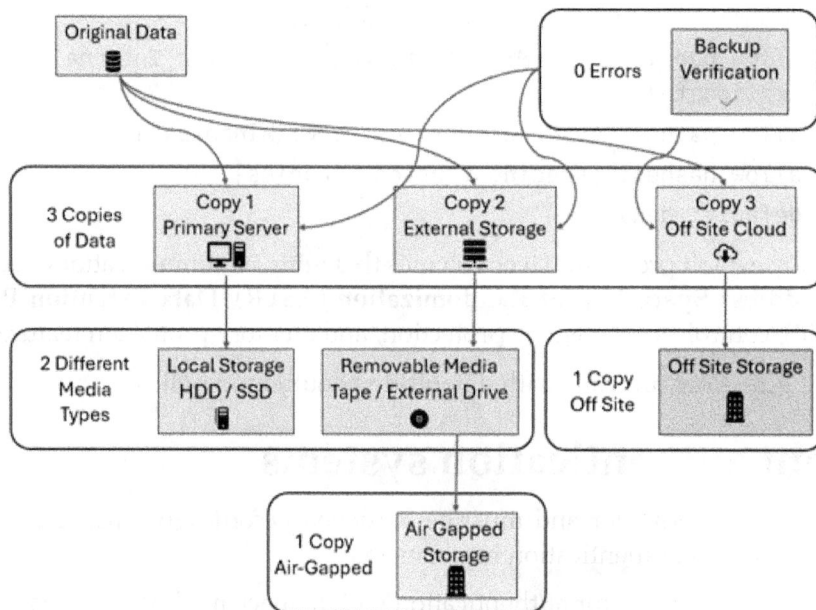

Figure 17.1: *3-2-1-1-0 backup strategy*

- Configure immutable backup storage using technologies such as:

    o   AWS S3 Object Lock with compliance mode

    o   Azure Blob Storage with immutable storage

    o   Veeam's immutable repositories with Linux hardening

    o   **Write Once Read Many (WORM)** storage systems

- Implement data access governance with tools such as Varonis or Microsoft Purview:

    o   Integrate **data loss prevention (DLP)**, real-time classification, and content inspection into security workflows.

    o   Scan for sensitive data that exists outside proper repositories.

    o   Apply automatic classification and protection.

    o   Monitor and alert on unusual access patterns.

    o   Implement least-privilege access controls.

SOC infrastructure resilience

The SOC's infrastructure must be resilient. For this, we implement distributed detection systems, such as:

- Deploy distributed log collection with multiple aggregation points.

- Implement multiple detection methods that operate independently, including **network-based detection (NDR)**, EDR, **cloud-based detection (CDR)**, UEBA, and Threat hunting.

- Create out-of-band detection mechanisms that operate on separate infrastructure:

    o   Passive network sensors with independent reporting channels.

    o   Host-based integrity verification with separate communication paths.

    o   Cloud API monitoring through segregated systems.

- Conduct quarterly scenario-based exercises addressing different threats, such as ransomware infection, business email compromise, data exfiltration, insider threat, and supply chain compromise.

- Document, address lessons learned, and validate restoration capabilities before they are needed.

- Implement destructive testing in controlled environments.

The journey toward resilience is continuous, requiring ongoing investment, leadership commitment, and adaptation to evolving threats and business requirements. The most successful organizations approach resilience as a strategic capability rather than a technical project, integrating it into their culture, processes, and systems.

Building self-healing systems

Self-healing systems are designed to identify and remediate issues autonomously. They leverage advanced technologies such as AI, ML, and automation to ensure continuous operation and rapid recovery. By integrating self-healing capabilities, organizations can enhance their SOC's efficiency, reduce downtime, and improve overall cyber resilience.

Self-healing systems are designed to detect deviations from normal operations and take automated corrective actions without human intervention. Their effectiveness is measured through key metrics and KPIs, such as **Auto-Remediation Success Rate (ARSR)**, which tracks the percentage of incidents resolved without manual intervention, and **mean self-recovery time (MSRT)**, evaluating the system's ability to restore operations autonomously within an optimal timeframe. Additionally, **Incident Detection-to-Remediation Speed (IDRS)**, **False Positive Reduction Rate (FPRR)**, and **System Adaptability Index (SAI)** ensure self-healing systems evolve and improve over time, reinforcing operational resilience against sophisticated cyber threats.

In cybersecurity, these systems combine elements of:

- **Continuous monitoring** to establish baselines and detect anomalies.
- **Predetermined response actions** that trigger based on specific conditions.
- **Automated recovery mechanisms** that restore systems to known good states.
- **Feedback loops** that improve detection and response over time.

Unlike traditional security automation, which typically focuses on specific tasks within a larger human-driven process, self-healing systems close the entire loop from detection through recovery. An effective self-healing system operates in a continuous cycle, as shown in the following figure:

Figure 17.2: Self-healing system lifecycle

The self-healing system lifecycle includes these stages:

- **Monitor**: Collect telemetry from systems, applications, and network devices.
- **Detect**: Identify deviations from normal behavior or known indicators of compromise.
- **Decide**: Determine appropriate response actions based on the nature and severity of the issue.

- **Act**: Implement recovery actions to restore normal operations.

- **Learn**: Update baselines, detection rules, and response playbooks based on outcomes.

Each phase builds upon robust foundational capabilities and leverages a combination of predetermined rules and adaptive learning. Let us learn through some case studies, how self-healing systems improve SOC functioning.

Case study: A regional bank began with a targeted implementation focusing on its web application infrastructure. They configured their web application firewalls to perform the following:

- Detect unusual request patterns indicative of attacks.

- Automatically implement temporary IP blocks for suspicious sources.

- Scale up resources during legitimate traffic spikes.

- Run hourly configuration verification to detect unauthorized changes.

This limited implementation reduced their security team's alert volume by 47% while improving their average response time to potential web attacks from 45 minutes to under 5 minutes.

Case study: In the early hours of a Saturday morning in 2023, a significant e-commerce platform detected unusual activity in its payment processing infrastructure. Rather than triggering alerts that would wake the on-call engineer, the platform's self-healing capabilities were able to:

- Identified the affected microservice instances

- Quarantined them from the production environment

- Spun up new instances from verified images

- Rerouted traffic to the healthy instances

- Preserved the compromised instances for forensic analysis

By the time the security team arrived Monday morning, the platform had already contained the incident, preserved evidence, and restored normal operations, all autonomously.

Case study: An e-commerce company expanded its self-healing capabilities by implementing the following:

- A CI/CD pipeline that automatically deploys containerized applications.

- Behavioral analysis of application metrics to detect anomalies.

- Automated container replacement when suspicious behavior is detected.

- Canary deployment testing before full restoration.

Their system now automatically remediates 82% of application-level incidents without human intervention, with an average recovery time of four minutes.

Conclusion

In an era where cyberattacks are not a question of if but when, the concept of cyber resilience has emerged as a cornerstone for modern SOCs. Unlike traditional cybersecurity, which focuses on preventing breaches, cyber resilience is about surviving them, ensuring systems can withstand, adapt, and recover from attacks with minimal disruption.

Cyber resilient systems represent the future of effective security operations. By integrating technical controls with operational processes and organizational culture, SOCs can build the capability to withstand, adapt to, and recover from the full spectrum of cyber threats. The journey toward resilience is continuous, requiring ongoing investment, leadership commitment, and adaptation to evolving threats and business requirements. In an environment where compromise is inevitable, the ability to maintain critical functions despite adversity differentiates mature security operations centers.

As of 2025, the threat landscape is only getting uglier. AI-powered phishing, quantum decryption threats, and IoT vulnerabilities are rewriting the rules. SOCs that cling to prevention-only mindsets will crumble; those that embrace resilience will thrive. The WannaCrys and NotPetyas of tomorrow would not wait for perfection, they will test your ability to bend, not break. So, build systems that fight through the storm. Your SOC is not just a shield, it is the backbone of a business that refuses to die.

In the next chapter, we will understand the future of SOCs. It will explore the impacts of emerging technologies, the rapidly evolving threat landscape, and how SOCs can stay ahead of the curve to ensure that information systems remain secure and resilient.

Points to remember

Here are some key takeaways from this chapter:

- Cyber resilience is no longer just a security imperative; it is a business differentiator.

- Organizations that can maintain critical functions despite cyber disruptions gain customer trust, regulatory favor, and operational advantages over less resilient competitors.

- Utilize AI, ML, orchestration and automation platforms, and cloud services to build effective self-healing systems that adapt to evolving threats.

Multiple choice questions

1. **What is the primary goal of cyber resilience in SOC?**

    a. To prevent all cyber attacks

    b. To ensure continuous operation and rapid recovery from cyber incidents

  c. To increase the complexity of security systems

  d. To replace human analysts with AI

2. **MITRE ATT&CK mappings can help in?**

  a. Withstanding

  b. Anticipation

  c. Recovery

  d. Adaptation

3. **What technology is commonly used in self-healing systems to enhance threat detection and automated response?**

  a. Blockchain

  b. Virtual reality

  c. AI and ML

  d. Quantum computing

Answers

1	b
2	b
3	c

Questions

1. Explain the concept of cyber resilience and its importance in the context of modern cybersecurity.

2. How does cyber resilience differ from traditional cybersecurity approaches?

3. Explain the fundamental principles of resilient SOC operations.

4. Describe the process of implementing self-healing systems in an SOC.

Key terms

Some key terms used in this chapter are:

- **Cyber resilience**: Holistic approach that encompasses preparation, detection, response, and recovery to ensure continuous operation and swift recovery from cyber threats.

- **Self-healing systems**: Key enabler in handling rapidly evolving cyber threats.

Join our Discord space

Join our Discord workspace for latest updates, offers, tech happenings around the world, new releases, and sessions with the authors:

https://discord.bpbonline.com

CHAPTER 18
Future Directions

Introduction

The SOC is no longer just a room full of screens blinking with alerts, it is the nerve center of an organization's cyber defense, a living entity that must evolve as fast as the threats it faces. In 2023, the average data breach cost hit $4.45 million, according to *IBM*, and by early 2025, we have seen ransomware groups like LockBit 4.0 deploy AI-driven attacks that adapt in real time. Threat actors are not standing still, and neither can SOCs. This chapter peers into the future, exploring how SOCs must transform to stay ahead in a world where continual improvement is not optional; it is survival.

On September 15, 2024, a global financial services firm detected unusual memory modifications across thousands of servers. Their SOC analysts, augmented by AI-based detection systems, identified a novel attack technique exploiting a previously unknown vulnerability in a widely used hypervisor. Within minutes, their automated defense systems contained the threat, and the coordinated response team pushed out mitigations to protect critical infrastructure.

This scenario, unthinkable just a few years ago, represents the new reality of security operations. Today's SOCs bear little resemblance to their predecessors, and the pace of change shows no signs of slowing. As threat actors deploy increasingly sophisticated techniques, security teams face unprecedented challenges in detection, analysis, and response capabilities.

This chapter explores the future directions of SOCs, examining emerging threats, evolving adversary techniques, current challenges, and the technologies that will define tomorrow's security operations. By understanding these trajectories, security leaders can better prepare their organizations for the ever-shifting security landscape that lies ahead.

Structure

In this chapter, we will discuss the following topics:

- Emerging threat scenario
- Advanced techniques by threat actors
- Challenges in the present scenario
- SOC in future

Objectives

By the end of this chapter, security practitioners will have a comprehensive understanding of emerging threat landscapes and advanced adversary techniques and insight into the limitations and challenges facing contemporary SOC models. The objective is to provide a practical vision of how SOCs will evolve to meet future security demands and actionable guidance for organizations planning their security operations roadmap.

We aim to map the future roadmap for SOCs, highlighting emerging threats, advanced adversarial techniques, current challenges, and the innovations that will define tomorrow's cyber defenses. By the end of the chapter, readers should understand why the SOC of the future will not just detect and respond, it will predict, adapt, and out-maneuver.

Emerging threat scenario

Picture this: a manufacturing firm in *Ohio* discovers its robotic assembly line has been hijacked. The ransomware is not just locking files; it is reprogramming machines to sabotage products, all orchestrated by a generative AI bot that learned the company's systems faster than any human could. This is not science fiction; it represents the bleeding edge of today's threat landscape. The attack surface organizations must defend continues to expand exponentially.

Several key trends are reshaping the threat landscape. Some of these trends are:

- **Weaponized AI**: Adversaries use ML to craft polymorphic malware that changes its signature hourly, evading traditional detection. As organizations increasingly rely on machine learning systems for business-critical functions, these systems themselves become high-value targets due to:

  o Model poisoning attacks that subtly corrupt training data.

o   Adversarial inputs are designed to manipulate model outputs.

o   Model theft through extraction attacks.

o   Privacy violations through inference attacks.

- **Supply chain attacks**: The 2020 SolarWinds breach was a wake-up call; now, attackers target smaller vendors to infiltrate giants, with 70% of breaches in 2024 linked to third parties (per Verizon's DBIR). Modern organizations rely on deeply integrated digital supply chains, creating new attack vectors that bypass traditional perimeter defenses. Key aspects of such attacks include:

o   Software dependencies with hidden vulnerabilities.

o   Hardware components with embedded security flaws.

o   Cloud service interdependence creates cascading failure risks.

o   API ecosystems with complex access control requirements.

The 2023 CloudFlare attack demonstrated this risk dramatically when a vulnerability in a widely used logging library allowed attackers to pivot through interdependent services across thousands of organizations in less than 48 hours.

- **IoT and edge exploitation**: With 5G and billions of connected devices, attackers exploit smart thermostats or factory sensors as entry points, amplifying attack surfaces. By 2026, analysts project over 64 billion IoT devices will be deployed globally, where computing power is distributed across thousands of interconnected devices. These environments introduce unprecedented security challenges, such as:

o   Limited visibility into device security posture.

o   Constrained update and patching mechanisms.

o   Blurred boundaries between enterprise and consumer technology.

o   Distributed vulnerability across heterogeneous systems.

- **Critical infrastructure convergence**: The rapid convergence of OT and **information technology (IT)** is creating new vulnerabilities that lie at the intersection of physical and digital systems, such as:

o   Industrial control systems with internet connectivity.

o   Smart city infrastructure with cascading dependency risks.

o   Healthcare devices with a direct impact on human safety.

o   Energy grid systems with the potential for widespread disruption.

The 2024 incident, which affected multiple water treatment facilities in the southwestern *United States,* demonstrated how attackers are increasingly targeting these convergence points, exploiting IT vulnerabilities to impact physical infrastructure.

These trends are summarised in the following table:

Threat category	Targeted sectors	Notable incidents	Key defense measures
Weaponized AI	Cybersecurity, elections, financial systems	AI-driven misinformation campaigns, FraudGPT enabling large-scale phishing	Robust AI governance, deepfake detection tools, adversarial AI countermeasures
Supply chain attacks	Software, hardware, cloud infrastructure	Malicious backdoor in SolarWinds software, Stuxnet disrupting industrial controls	Rigorous vendor assessment, secure development practices, real-time monitoring
IoT and edge exploitation	Smart cities, healthcare, industrial automation	Mirai botnet hijacking connected devices, Point-of-Sale system vulnerabilities exploited	Zero Trust implementation, micro-segmentation, regular firmware updates
Critical infrastructure breaches	Energy, water, transportation	Ransomware attack crippling Colonial Pipeline, cyber threats targeting operational technology	Network segmentation, strong authentication, continuous threat surveillance

Table 18.1: Emerging threats

Advanced techniques by threat actors

Threat actors are borrowing from sci-fi playbooks, deploying techniques that outpace yesterday's defenses. Advanced methods exploited by the threat actors include:

- **AI-powered and augmented attacks**: In 2024, a phishing campaign targeting a European bank used AI to mimic the CEO's writing style, pulling details from public X posts and LinkedIn. Over 60% of recipients clicked. Artificial intelligence has democratized advanced attack capabilities. Other AI and ML-enabled possibilities are listed here:

  - **Polymorphic malware evolution**: Modern malware uses machine learning to continuously modify its code, behavior, and communication patterns to evade signature-based detection. The BlackMamba malware family discovered in early 2024 demonstrated the ability to customize its evasion techniques based on the specific security tools detected in the target environment.

  - **Intelligent target reconnaissance**: Threat actors leverage AI to analyze massive datasets of potential targets, automatically identifying high-value systems and individuals. This enables highly personalized social engineering at scale, as seen in the 2023 campaign targeting defense contractors that automatically generated convincing spear-phishing emails based on victims' public professional histories.

- o **Behavior-based evasion**: Advanced malware now monitors its environment and modifies its behavior to appear legitimate. The ShadowSpider campaign observed in late 2023 demonstrated malware that could mimic legitimate user behavior patterns, timing its activities to blend with normal operations and evade behavioral analytics.

- o **Deepfake deception**: Audio deepfakes tricked finance staff at a *UAE* firm into wiring $35 million to attackers in 2023, a tactic now scaling with cheap tools.

- **Quantum threats**: While quantum computing is not mainstream yet, nation-states are harvesting encrypted data today to decrypt later, a *store-now, crack-later* strategy.

- **Weaponizing legitimate tools**: Sophisticated attackers increasingly avoid introducing malware by weaponizing legitimate tools. Some of the measures employed by threat actors are listed here:

- o **Fileless persistence mechanisms**: Modern attacks establish persistence entirely in memory or through legitimate system mechanisms, leaving minimal forensic evidence. The CosmicBison threat group demonstrated this capability by maintaining access to financial institutions through manipulated scheduled tasks and registry modifications that survived multiple system reboots.

- o **Cloud resource hijacking**: Rather than deploying attack infrastructure, adversaries compromise legitimate cloud resources and repurpose them for attack operations. The 2024 CloudHarvest campaign demonstrated this approach by hijacking serverless functions across multiple cloud platforms to create a distributed command and control network.

- o **Supply chain code injection**: Instead of directly attacking targets, adversaries compromise development pipelines and inject malicious code into legitimate software updates. The widely publicized DepRaider campaign in 2023 compromised multiple open-source Python packages by targeting the continuous integration systems of project maintainers.

- **Advanced evasion techniques**: Threat actors employ sophisticated measures to avoid detection:

- o **Multi-stage execution chains**: Attacks distribute malicious logic across multiple seemingly benign components that only reveal their true purpose when executed in sequence. The FragmentedThreat campaign observed in government networks used legitimate administrative scripts that, when executed in a specific order, assembled and executed malicious payloads.

- o **Cross-platform kill chains**: Advanced adversaries distribute attack components across different systems and platforms, making it difficult to detect the complete attack lifecycle. The OceanLotus group demonstrated this technique by using compromised endpoint systems solely for initial access, Linux servers for command and control, and cloud storage for data exfiltration.

- **Intermittent execution**: Rather than operating continuously, sophisticated malware executes intermittently with long dormant periods, complicating detection efforts that rely on continuous monitoring. The PatienceHarvester implant discovered in critical infrastructure organizations would activate only once every 30-45 days, making the correlation of security events extremely difficult.

These methods exploit human trust and technological gaps, forcing SOCs to rethink detection and response. Sophisticated threat actors continue to evolve their TTPs, presenting significant challenges for traditional detection and response approaches.

Challenges in the present scenario

Contemporary SOCs face significant limitations in addressing these evolving threats. Today's SOCs face a perfect storm of constraints, some of which are covered here:

- **Operational challenges**: Current SOC models struggle with fundamental operational constraints such as:

  - o **Alert fatigue and false positives**: Despite advances in detection technology, SOCs continue to struggle with high volumes of alerts and false positives. A 2024 industry survey revealed that the average enterprise SOC processes over 11,000 alerts per day, with analysts spending approximately 25% of their time on false positives.

  - o **Staffing and skill gaps**: The global cybersecurity talent shortage continues to worsen, with an estimated 3.5 million unfilled positions worldwide as of 2024. SOCs struggle to recruit and retain qualified personnel, especially those with specialized skills in cloud security, OT protection, and threat hunting.

  - o **Legacy systems**: Many organizations still run older operating system versions or unpatched IoT devices, creating vulnerabilities that no SOC can fully shield.

  - o **Budget constraints**: Small firms allocate just 5-10% of IT budgets to security, per a 2025 Ponemon study, leaving SOCs underfunded against sophisticated foes.

  - o **Tool proliferation and integration challenges**: The average enterprise SOC now manages over 75 distinct security tools, creating significant integration challenges and leaving visibility gaps between disparate systems. This complexity increases response times and creates potential blind spots that adversaries can exploit.

- **Technical limitations**: Beyond operational challenges, SOCs face significant technical constraints, such as:

  - **Detection speed versus. sophisticated threats**: The time advantage increasingly favors attackers. While the average dwell time for attackers has decreased to approximately 21 days in 2024, sophisticated threat actors can achieve their objectives much faster. The 2023 QuantumBreak ransomware campaign averaged just 72 hours from initial compromise to complete encryption of target environments.

  - **Cloud and container visibility gaps**: Traditional security monitoring approaches struggle with ephemeral cloud resources and containerized applications. A 2024 study found that 64% of organizations have limited or no visibility into container security events, and 71% cannot effectively monitor serverless function execution.

  - **Supply chain trust verification**: Organizations lack effective mechanisms to verify the integrity of their digital supply chains. The SolarWinds incident demonstrated that compromises can remain undetected for months, even in environments with sophisticated security monitoring. Implementing **Software Bill Of Material (SBOM)** and continuous **Software Composition Analysis (SCA)** ensures better transparency and security in software development. SBOM provides a detailed inventory of software components, helping track dependencies and assess risks. Continuous SCA scans dependencies for vulnerabilities, ensuring compliance and proactive threat mitigation. By integrating these into CI/CD pipelines and SOC workflows, organizations can enhance supply chain security and automate remediation of risks.

- **Strategic challenges**: At a strategic level, SOCs face fundamental questions about their operating model, such as:

  - **Reactive versus proactive posture**: Most SOCs remain primarily reactive, detecting and responding to attacks after they occur rather than proactively hunting for threats or addressing root vulnerabilities. This approach leaves organizations perpetually on the defensive.

  - **Technology versus process focus**: Many organizations over-invest in security technologies while under-investing in the processes and people needed to leverage those tools effectively. A 2024 industry analysis found that organizations typically utilize less than 40% of their security tools' capabilities.

  - **Business alignment**: SOCs often struggle to align security operations with business priorities, leading to protection models that do not reflect actual business risks or resilience requirements. This misalignment can result in both over-protection of low-value assets and under-protection of critical systems.

SOC in the future

The next generation of SOCs will evolve dramatically to address cyber challenges, incorporating modern technologies, methodologies, and organizational models. The SOC of the future will be a hybrid of human ingenuity and cutting-edge tech, driven by continual improvement. Different aspects shaping the SOC in the future are covered here.

AI-driven security operations

As cybersecurity threats grow in scale and complexity, traditional SOCs must evolve to incorporate AI and ML for enhanced detection, automation, and response. By leveraging AI-driven automation, SOCs can reduce alert fatigue, improve threat intelligence correlation, and optimize incident response strategies. Modern SOCs can integrate random forest for anomaly classification and Transformer-based models for real-time threat detection. Azure Sentinel ML rules automate threat correlation by analyzing attack patterns. Tools like Splunk Phantom and Cortex XSOAR streamline response workflows, while MITRE ATT&CK mapping refines detection precision. Implementation involves embedding AI models in SIEM pipelines, automating playbook-triggered responses, and continuously refining detection accuracy through adaptive learning. Some of the ways AI and ML will transform SOC operations are as follows:

- **Autonomous detection and response**: Autonomous detection and response powered by AI and machine learning is transforming SOC operations by enabling real-time threat mitigation without human intervention. Advanced machine learning systems will autonomously detect, verify, and respond to routine threats. SOAR platforms integrate AI-driven threat detection with automated response workflows, reducing the burden on security analysts. For instance, in response to a detected endpoint compromise, AI models can trigger predefined SOAR playbooks that isolate the affected device, revoke compromised credentials, and initiate forensic analysis, all without manual oversight. Google's BeyondCorp framework exemplifies this approach by autonomously handling over 90% of routine security events, ensuring continuous protection. As AI-driven SOCs evolve, automated threat containment will become a standard feature, accelerating response times and minimizing security risks in dynamic threat environments.

- **Predictive security analytics**: Rather than detecting attacks in progress, AI systems will identify precursors and predict potential attacks before they occur. JPMorgan Chase's AI-based security platform reportedly prevented over 85,000 potential attacks in 2023 by identifying attack preparations in their earliest stages.

- **Natural language interfaces**: Security analysts will interact with security tools through natural language interfaces that translate questions into complex queries across multiple data sources. Microsoft's Security Copilot represents an early version of this capability, allowing analysts to investigate incidents through conversational interactions.

- **Continuous security validation**: AI systems will continuously test and validate security controls against simulated attacks, automatically identifying and addressing gaps before attackers can exploit them. The *U.S.* Department of Defense's autonomous security testing platform successfully detected 74% of deliberately introduced vulnerabilities without human guidance. Continuous security validation powered by AI ensures proactive threat mitigation by systematically testing security controls against simulated attacks. AI-driven platforms autonomously identify vulnerabilities, reducing the window of opportunity for attackers. **Breach and Attack Simulation** (**BAS**) tools like AttackIQ, SafeBreach, and MITRE Caldera play a pivotal role in this approach, allowing organizations to simulate real-world attack scenarios, assess defense efficacy, and refine security posture continuously. These tools enable SOCs to validate configurations, detect misconfigurations, and enhance automated response mechanisms, ensuring resilience against emerging cyber threats without waiting for actual breaches to occur.

- **Predictive threat intelligence**: Predictive threat intelligence will transform SOCs by shifting security operations from reactive responses to proactive threat anticipation. By leveraging big data analytics and behavioral modeling, SOCs can forecast cyber threats before they materialize, much like meteorologists predict storms by 2030. Standardized threat intelligence formats such as STIX and TAXII as covered in *Chapter 8, Threat Intelligence and Hunting*, facilitate seamless data sharing and automation. Platforms like MISP and recorded future further enhance threat intelligence ingestion by aggregating real-time indicators from diverse sources, including dark web forums and social media. These tools empower SOCs to detect emerging attack trends and neutralize threats before they escalate. In 2025, a *U.S.* retailer's SOC used predictive models to spot a supply chain attack brewing on X chatter and dark web forums, neutralizing it before launch.

There is need for clear roadmap covering a structured, actionable approach to embedding AI/ML capabilities into SOC environments, ensuring alignment with compliance frameworks, optimizing alert triage, and enhancing proactive threat mitigation. By leveraging AI-driven analytics, automation tools, and real-time anomaly detection, SOCs can transition from reactive postures to predictive security operations, strengthening their ability to combat evolving cyber threats. Phase wise AI-driven SOC transformation with actionable steps are covered in the following *Table 18.2*.

Integrating AI into SOC operations demands a strong emphasis on security and ethical AI practices to mitigate risks associated with automation and decision-making. Secure AI implementation starts with robust data governance, ensuring AI models are trained on validated, threat-relevant datasets while adhering to compliance standards like ISO/IEC 27001 and NIST frameworks. Transparency in AI-driven decisions is critical, SOCs must implement **explainable AI** (**XAI**) principles to prevent algorithmic biases and ensure accountability. Additionally, continuous model validation and adversarial testing safeguard AI systems against manipulation or evasion by sophisticated threat actors. By embedding security-first AI practices, SOCs can enhance threat detection accuracy while maintaining resilience against adversarial AI threats, regulatory scrutiny, and ethical concerns in automated security operations. These secure AI practices must be structured as shown in following table 18.3. This ensures SOCs remain secure, ethical, and efficient while preventing risks associated with AI bias, data leaks, and model degradation.

ML-driven SOC transformation: The following table outlines actionable steps at each phase of the strategic roadmap to future-proof SOC operations and maximize resilience against evolving cyber threats by integrating AI/ML into SOC workflows:

Phase	Key initiatives	Actionable steps	Impact on SOC
Foundation and readiness	Build a strong AI/ML baseline	Conduct a SOC maturity assessment to identify AI integration points. Establish a data strategy with centralized logging and structured event correlation. Train SOC analysts on AI fundamentals, adversarial ML, and model interpretation.	Strengthens SOC's ability to integrate AI with compliance frameworks like NIST SP 800-53 and MITRE ATT&CK. Ensures high-quality security data for AI-driven decision-making.
Prototyping and experimentation	Test AI use cases for security operations	Identify priority areas for AI adoption (e.g., anomaly detection, phishing analysis). Develop baseline ML models for alert classification, fraud detection, and behavioral analytics. Conduct validation using historical attack data; incorporate human-in-the-loop feedback.	Enables early-stage AI experimentation without disrupting SOC workflows. Enhances AI accuracy through iterative learning and expert validation.
Operationalization and automation	Deploy AI Across SOC Workflows	Integrate AI-powered models into SIEM and SOAR platforms (Splunk Phantom, Cortex XSOAR). Strengthen threat intelligence mapping by correlating CTI feeds with AI-driven insights. Introduce reinforcement learning for automated alert triage and dynamic incident response.	Elevates SOC efficiency by automating low-level tasks and enhancing correlation capabilities. Ensures proactive threat mitigation and optimized resource allocation.

Phase	Key initiatives	Actionable steps	Impact on SOC
Continuous learning and governance	Monitor AI performance and ethics	Establish KPIs (precision, recall, FPR) for AI models. Develop ethical AI guidelines with explainability features and bias detection. Explore next-gen AI applications like XDR, deception-based defense, and autonomous SOC operations.	Maintains AI integrity and ensures compliance with regulatory standards. Future-proofs SOC operations with cutting-edge AI advancements.

Table 18.2: *AI and ML driven SOC transformation in phases*

While implementing this AI driven SOC, secure AI practices, as covered in the following table, must be considered:

Key area	Real-world challenge	AI-powered solution	Actionable steps	Impact on SOC security
AI model security	Attackers manipulate AI with adversarial data poisoning to evade detection.	AI-driven anomaly detection with adversarial defense mechanisms.	• Deploy AI explainability tools to validate model integrity. • Apply adversarial learning techniques to harden models against manipulation.	• Reduces false negatives and enhances AI robustness. • Ensures resilience against evolving threats.
Ethical and responsible AI use	AI models exhibit bias, leading to unfair threat scoring & detection inaccuracies.	Bias-aware AI models with fairness audits.	• Perform periodic AI bias evaluations. • Utilize interpretability tools like SHAP & LIME. • Train models on diverse datasets.	• Ensures AI-driven alerts are fair, explainable, and trustworthy. • Improves SOC analyst confidence in AI decision-making.

Key area	Real-world challenge	AI-powered solution	Actionable steps	Impact on SOC security
Secure data handling and privacy	AI models process vast logs, increasing risk of data leaks and unauthorized access.	AI-enhanced encryption and data governance frameworks.	• Implement **role-based access controls** (**RBAC**) for AI workflows. • Apply cryptographic integrity checks for sensitive logs. • Ensure AI models adhere to GDPR and NIST guidelines.	• Protects sensitive security logs. • Prevents attackers from manipulating AI-based threat analysis.
Continuous learning and AI governance	AI models degrade over time due to lack of retraining, increasing false positives.	AI lifecycle monitoring with reinforcement learning optimization.	• Establish KPIs for AI model accuracy (precision-recall monitoring). • Implement AI ethics frameworks with compliance integration. • Conduct continuous retraining for adapting to new threat patterns.	• Maintains AI performance over time. • Reduces false alarms and operational inefficiencies.
AI and human integration in SOC automation	AI-based auto-response blocks legitimate users due to rigid rules.	Human-in-the-loop AI-assisted security automation.	• Use analyst-assisted decision-making for high-risk alerts. • Implement multi-layer AI-driven playbooks that allow human overrides. • Introduce predictive AI models for preemptive threat mitigation.	• Prevents critical security automation errors. • Enhances SOC efficiency while preserving analyst expertise.

Table 18.3: Secure AI practices in AI-driven SOC implementation

Distributed security architecture

The centralized SOC model will evolve towards distributed security operations, such as:

- **Edge detection and response**: Security monitoring and response capabilities will shift toward network edges, enabling faster detection and containment of threats. Cloudflare's edge security platform demonstrates this approach, with distributed nodes providing both monitoring and automated response capabilities across global infrastructure.

- **Mesh security models**: Rather than centralized security choke points, organizations will implement security mesh architectures that distribute and coordinate security functions across the environment. Gartner estimates that by 2025, organizations with security mesh architectures will reduce the financial impact of security incidents by an average of 90%.

- **Embedded security operations**: Security capabilities will be embedded directly into development and operational processes rather than bolted on afterward. Netflix's approach of embedding security engineers directly in development teams has reduced security defects by over 70% compared to traditional security review processes.

- **Zero Trust architecture**: The *trust no one* mantra will dominate. Zero Trust architecture is becoming the foundation of modern cybersecurity, eliminating implicit trust and enforcing continuous authentication across all users, devices, and applications. Future SOCs will enforce micro-segmentation and continuous authentication, even for internal users. Zero Trust adoption spiked after a 2024 insider breach at a tech firm cost $20 million, and it is expected to be ubiquitous by the decade's end. By 2030, identity-based segmentation will be a standard security practice, ensuring that even internal users undergo rigorous authentication before accessing sensitive resources. This shift will redefine SOC operations, making security more adaptive and resilient against evolving threats. This approach minimizes attack surfaces and prevents lateral movement within environments. Key components and tools in implementing zero-trust architecture are as follows:

Component	Description	Example tools
Identity-based segmentation	Access is granted based on identity verification rather than network trust.	Okta, Microsoft Entra ID, Ping Identity
Micro-segmentation	Limits access between workloads and applications to prevent lateral movement.	Zscaler, VMware NSX, Cisco Secure Workload
Continuous authentication	Users and devices are continuously verified, reducing reliance on static credentials.	BeyondCorp, Duo Security, CyberArk

Component	Description	Example tools
Threat detection and response	AI-driven analytics monitor and respond to anomalies in real time.	CrowdStrike Falcon, Microsoft Defender XDR, Palo Alto Cortex XDR

Table 18.4: Key components of Zero Trust architecture

Integrated risk and resilience

Future SOCs will focus on resilience alongside traditional security. The key resilience aspects shaping the SOCs in future are:

- **Business continuity integration**: Security operations will merge with business continuity functions to ensure organizational resilience against both security and operational disruptions. Financial institutions like *Goldman Sachs* have already integrated their security and operational resilience teams under unified leadership.

- **Cyber resilience integration**: Future SOCs will bake resilience into their DNA, ensuring operations endure attacks. Think Maersk's NotPetya recovery, but faster—automated failover systems and air-gapped backups will keep critical functions humming.

- **Automated recovery capabilities**: Next-generation security platforms will incorporate automated recovery mechanisms that restore systems to known good states following compromise. Google's BeyondProd security model demonstrates this approach, automatically rebuilding compromised container environments from verified images.

- **Risk-adaptive protection**: Security controls will automatically adjust based on real-time risk assessments, applying stricter protections to higher-risk users, data, and transactions. The *U.S.* Department of Homeland Security's **Continuous Diagnostics and Mitigation** (**CDM**) program incorporates this approach, dynamically adjusting security requirements based on ongoing risk assessments.

- **Quantum-ready defenses**: As quantum computing nears, SOCs will deploy post-quantum cryptography. In 2026, NIST's finalized algorithms will roll out, and forward-thinking SOCs will encrypt data today to thwart tomorrow's quantum decryption. Quantum-ready defences are crucial as the threat of quantum decryption looms. SOCs must adopt a crypto-agility framework, ensuring flexibility in transitioning to **post-quantum cryptographic** (**PQC**) algorithms once they are standardized. By embracing **crypto-agility**, organizations can future-proof their security infrastructure and seamlessly transition to **NIST's PQC standards**, ensuring long-term data protection against quantum threats.

Human-machine teaming

The dynamic between security analysts and technology is poised for a fundamental transformation. As advanced automation, artificial intelligence, and adaptive security frameworks become integral to cybersecurity operations, analysts will shift from reactive incident response to strategic oversight, threat hunting, and AI-driven decision augmentation. This evolution necessitates a deep integration of analytical expertise with intelligent automation, redefining traditional workflows and enhancing operational efficiency.

To examine this transition in detail, we must assess the impact of machine learning-driven threat detection, automated response orchestration, and predictive analytics on security operations. The synergy between human expertise and AI-enabled tools will not only optimize SOC efficiency but also establish a resilient, scalable framework for proactive security defense. Human-machine teaming in SOC must ensure the following:

- **AI-augmented analysis**: Rather than replacing analysts, AI systems will augment human capabilities by handling routine tasks and surfacing insights that merit human attention. By 2027, SOCs will use *AI co-pilots* to triage alerts, reducing false positives by 80% and suggesting responses based on past incidents. Imagine an analyst facing a ransomware spike: the AI flags it, isolates affected systems, and proposes a containment plan, all in seconds. Analysts at Mastercard's fusion center reportedly handle 8x more security events with the help of AI-based analysis tools.

- **Immersive security interfaces**: Analysts will interact with security data through immersive interfaces that visualize complex attack patterns in intuitive ways. The Idaho National Laboratory's CAVE visualization environment allows analysts to literally walk through network traffic patterns to identify anomalies.

- **Expertise amplification**: AI systems will capture and amplify the expertise of senior analysts, allowing junior team members to benefit from their insights and decision-making patterns. IBM's Watson for cybersecurity incorporates this approach, learning from expert analysts to improve its recommendations over time.

- **XAI and auditability**: These are crucial for building trust in AI-driven SOCs. As cybersecurity automation increases, analysts and auditors need transparent models that justify decisions. Without interpretability, AI models like transformer-based anomaly detection or random forest classifiers may flag threats without clear reasoning. Tools like LIME, SHAP, and IBM AI Explainability 360 help visualize AI decisions, ensuring security alerts are understandable. Azure Sentinel ML rules can integrate these explainability techniques to make threat assessments auditable. To enforce accountability, SOCs should log AI-driven alerts in platforms like Splunk, Elastic SIEM, or Cortex XSOAR, creating verifiable records for compliance checks. Continuous validation through attack simulations ensures AI models remain reliable. Regulatory frameworks like NIST SP 800-53 and ISO/IEC 27001 also mandate traceability in automated security decisions, reinforcing ethical AI practices. Integrating XAI in SOC workflows strengthens analyst confidence and regulatory trust, making cybersecurity operations more resilient.

Collaborative defense models

Security operations will increasingly extend beyond organizational boundaries. The key aspects shaping this evolution in SOC include:

- **Collaborative ecosystems**: SOCs will not fight alone. Organizations within critical industries will form deeper collaborative defense communities with real-time threat sharing and coordinated response capabilities. The **Financial Services Information Sharing and Analysis Center (FS-ISAC)** already demonstrates this model, with member institutions sharing threat intelligence and coordinating responses to industry-wide threats. By 2030, industry-specific threat-sharing hubs, like ISACs, will evolve into real-time, AI-driven networks. A bank SOC in London could instantly warn a retailer SOC in Tokyo about a new exploit, cutting response times from days to minutes. Similarly, CISA **Automated Indicator Sharing (AIS)** allows organizations to exchange cyber threat indicators in real time, enhancing detection capabilities. Platforms like ThreatConnect and MISP provide structured intelligence sharing, ensuring security teams can correlate threats effectively. By leveraging IBM X-Force Exchange, SOCs gain AI-driven insights to strengthen response mechanisms.

- **Supply chain security ecosystems**: Organizations will form security ecosystems with key suppliers and partners, implementing coordinated monitoring and response across supply chains. Microsoft's supply chain security program exemplifies this approach, with continuous monitoring and automated alerting across its global supplier network.

- **Federated threat hunting**: Security teams across organizations will conduct coordinated hunting operations to identify threats affecting multiple entities. The *U.S.* Cyber Command's hunt forward operations with international partners demonstrate this collaborative model on a national scale.

- **SOC playbooks**: Inter-org SOC playbooks ensure standardized procedures across organizations, enhancing coordination during large-scale cyber incidents. Federated incident response playbooks define workflows for handling threats that affect multiple entities, while MITRE ATT&CK-based guides refine detection strategies. Threat intelligence enrichment playbooks automate the collection of security indicators, improving analysis speed. Multi-org crisis management playbooks are widely used in financial institutions and critical infrastructure sectors, enabling joint response efforts to contain cyber threats efficiently.

Co-managed SOC models

Co-managed SOCs are gaining traction as a hybrid security model that allows organizations to balance internal oversight with external expertise. This approach enables businesses to maintain control over key security functions while leveraging **managed security service providers** (**MSSPs**) for specialized threat intelligence, automation, and response capabilities. Some co-managed SOC implementations include:

- **Secureworks Co-Managed SOC**: Secureworks partners with organizations to provide advanced threat monitoring and intelligence while allowing internal security teams to retain operational control. This setup ensures round-the-clock protection without requiring extensive in-house resources.

- **IBM Security Services**: IBM's co-managed SOC solution blends AI-driven analytics with human expertise, helping enterprises scale security operations while focusing on business objectives.

- **CrowdStrike Falcon Complete**: While primarily a managed SOC service, CrowdStrike offers collaboration with internal teams, enabling businesses to participate in detection and response efforts alongside their dedicated security experts.

By adopting a co-managed SOC approach, organizations benefit from enhanced scalability, cost efficiency, and improved security posture. This model ensures that businesses can access external expertise while retaining strategic control over their cybersecurity framework, making it a practical solution for evolving threat landscapes.

SOC-as-a-service models

Cloud-native SOC-as-a-service is reshaping cybersecurity by providing scalable, AI-powered security operations without the limitations of traditional on-premises SOCs. Organizations can enhance threat detection, automate incident response, and gain real-time insights while reducing infrastructure complexity and costs. Some of the examples of cloud-native SOC-as-a-service in action include:

- **CrowdStrike Falcon Complete**: A managed SOC solution that integrates AI-driven EDR with proactive threat hunting, offering continuous monitoring and rapid incident resolution without requiring an internal SOC team.

- **Microsoft Defender XDR**: This cloud-native security platform combines SIEM, XDR, and automated response across hybrid and multi-cloud environments, streamlining security workflows with AI-powered analytics.

- **Google Chronicle**: A security analytics platform designed for large-scale threat detection, enabling SOCs to process vast amounts of security data in real-time, improving investigation speed and accuracy.

Embracing cloud-native SOC-as-a-Service allows businesses to bolster their cybersecurity posture, improve detection precision, and optimize response efficiency while maintaining operational flexibility. These solutions exemplify the evolution of SOCs, where automation, AI, and cloud scalability drive the next generation of cyber defense.

Conclusion

The SOC's future is not about perfection; it is about evolution. As threat actors wield AI, deepfakes, and quantum tools, SOCs must counter with predictive intelligence, augmented analysts, and resilient designs. The journey starts now: every unpatched system, untrained employee, or ignored alert is a crack in tomorrow's defenses. Continual improvement is not a buzzword but the lifeline that will carry SOCs into the next decade.

Driven by the need to counter increasingly sophisticated threats and protect expanding digital footprints, security operations will become more distributed, automated, and integrated with business processes. The transformation will not happen overnight, nor will it be purely technological. Organizations must evolve their processes, skills, and organizational structures alongside their security technologies to realize the full potential of next-generation security operations.

The most successful security teams will embrace this evolution, viewing it not as disrupting existing practices but as an opportunity to fundamentally reimagine how security operations can better protect their organizations in an increasingly complex threat landscape.

Points to remember

Here are some key takeaways from this chapter:

- Threats are smarter, faster, and broader, AI and IoT are game changers. Today's SOC struggles with fatigue, skills, and legacy tech.

- Tomorrow's SOC predicts, adapts, and collaborates, powered by AI and Zero Trust. Resilience is not optional; it is the future.

Multiple choice questions

1. **Which of the following is considered a key trend in the future evolution of SOCs?**

   a. Increased reliance on manual processes

   b. Wider adoption of AI&ML

   c. Complete elimination of threat intelligence platforms

   d. Reduced focus on cloud security

2. **What is a major future challenge that SOCs are likely to face?**

   a. Decline in cybersecurity job opportunities

   b. Over-reliance on outdated software

   c. An increasing volume and complexity of cyberattacks

   d. Decreasing investments in cybersecurity technologies

3. **What is a key advantage of adopting cloud-based SOC solutions for the future?**

   a. Limited scalability

   b. Increased hardware dependency

   c. Improved flexibility and scalability for global organizations

   d. Restricted access to real-time threat data

Answers

1	b
2	c
3	c

Questions

1. Discuss the role of AI and ML in shaping the future of SOCs.

2. Highlight the potential benefits and limitations of these technologies in enhancing SOC capabilities.

3. Analyze the key challenges SOCs are likely to face in the future, such as the growing complexity of cyber threats and the cybersecurity talent gap.

4. Propose strategies to address these challenges.

5. How does investing in human resources contribute to the long-term success of SOCs amidst rapidly evolving cybersecurity threats?

Key terms

Some key terms used in this chapter are:

- **Weaponized AI**: A key threat for SOCs of the future.

- **Human machine teaming**: An important element in future SOC implementations.

Join our Discord space

Join our Discord workspace for latest updates, offers, tech happenings around the world, new releases, and sessions with the authors:

https://discord.bpbonline.com

Index

D